Crescent Moon over Carolina

Crescent Moon over Carolina

William Moultrie and American Liberty

C. L. Bragg

The University of South Carolina Press

© 2013 University of South Carolina

Published by the University of South Carolina Press
Columbia, South Carolina 29208
www.sc.edu/uscpress

Manufactured in the United States of America

Frontispiece: William Moultrie, from a painting by Alonzo Chappel, 1828–1887.
From the Society of the Cincinnati, Washington, D.C. Reproduced with permission.

22 21 20 19 18 17 16 15 14 13   10 9 8 7 6 5 4 3 2 1

Library of Congress Cataloging-in-Publication Data
Bragg, C. L., 1957–
Crescent moon over Carolina : William Moultrie and American liberty / C. L. Bragg.
pages cm
Includes bibliographical references and index.
ISBN 978-1-61117-269-0 (hardbound : alk. paper)   1. Moultrie, William, 1730–
1805.   2. South Carolina—History—Revolution, 1775–1783—Biography.   3. United
States—History—Revolution, 1775–1783—Biography.   4. Generals—United States—
Biography.   5. Governors—South Carolina—Biography.   I. Title.
E207.M85B73 2013
355.0092—dc23
[B]
2013013547

. . . posterity will be astonished when they read that on the twenty-eight of June an inexperienced handfull of men under your Command repulsed with loss and Disgrace a powerfull Fleet and Army of Veteran Troops headed by officers of the first Rank and reputation.

JOHN HANCOCK
President of the Continental Congress, in a letter to
Col. William Moultrie dated July 22, 1776

Contents

Part III

Illustrations

Preface

"Were there nothing else in the life and career of William Moultrie," wrote William Gilmore Simms in *Washington and the Generals of the American Revolution* (1848), "his gallant defence of the Palmetto fortress of Carolina, in the opening of the Revolution, against the combined land and sea forces of Great Britain, led by Sir Peter Parker, would render him honourably dear to all succeeding time." Simms was right. The name of William Moultrie will be forever remembered for his part in the defense of an unfinished log fort on Sullivan's Island at the entrance to Charleston Harbor. Every fort that has since occupied the site has borne his name. Inexplicably no author has attempted a full-length biography of Moultrie. Only short sketches that concentrate by and large on his military career have appeared in works and compilations over the past two centuries.[1]

Moultrie's success on June 28, 1776, had far-reaching consequences. The British had already occupied Boston and would soon occupy New York and Philadelphia. Though discouragement followed discouragement, Moultrie and his South Carolinians proved that inexperienced American soldiers could stand firm and prevail against British might. His celebrated victory aside, Moultrie was much more than the iconic defender of Charleston. He was a son, brother, husband, father, legislator, soldier, rebel, prisoner of war, governor, debtor, presidential host, Federalist—then a Republican, and finally a memoirist. Examining Moultrie's life, particularly the layers of his personality, presented challenges not faced by biographers of more famous Americans whose life histories were recorded soon after our nation's founding or who left behind reams of personal correspondence. Daniel Halévy aptly stated in *Péguy and Les Cahiers de la Quinzaine*, "Fortunate are novelists who know all about their characters! Biographers know very little, and must never forget it."[2]

Some facets of Moultrie's persona were easily discernible—his military and political careers, for example. Other characteristics have been lost to time, if they were ever recorded at all: his likes and dislikes, his emotions, his personal frustrations. Unlike many of his contemporaries who traveled widely and left behind large bodies of private communications, with few exceptions Moultrie remained in the vicinity of Charleston for most of his life. The close proximity of his family members accounts for a dearth of personal letters that would otherwise shed light on his innermost thoughts. Instead Moultrie's personality comes to us through a few words of his contemporaries. He was known to them as a generous and hospitable man of integrity and impartiality. A friend described him as "cheerful, manly, sincere. . . . Unassuming and unostentatious, he was an easy, affable and agreeable companion."[3]

The history of South Carolina as a royal colony (1719–76) is fascinating and complicated. The first half of Moultrie's life is, in essence, the history of the Carolina lowcountry during this era. The opening chapters of this book consider his life in the milieu of the lowcountry planter aristocracy and within the framework of events that transpired during the last decades of South Carolina's colonial era. This period includes the Cherokee War, the evolution of the colonial and provincial legislatures, and the developing Revolutionary crisis in the colony. In many instances only a few of the exact details of Moultrie's involvement are known, but it is certain that he was present as an active participant. This is especially true concerning his tenure as a representative in the Commons House of Assembly and the Provincial Congress of South Carolina.

Against the backdrop of the Revolutionary War, Moultrie played a pivotal role in securing the liberty of his home state and, in a broader sense, the independence of the United States. Contrasting the sketchy details of his life during the colonial era, Moultrie's well-established military record is addressed in the middle part of this work. I was greatly aided in my task as his biographer by the fact that Moultrie, who considered the preservation of history to be his duty, published his *Memoirs of the American Revolution* in 1802. His memoirs became an important primary source that were often quoted in other works and are still regarded as one of the best personal accounts of the Revolutionary War.

Far less dramatic than his defense of the fort on Sullivan's Island but equally worthy of consideration is Moultrie's military service from 1776 until 1783. He was very active during this period. He defended Port Royal and made a tactical retreat in the face of a superior foe that culminated in the first siege of Charlestown in 1779. His controversial inaction at Stono Ferry later that same year is covered, as is the disastrous second siege of Charlestown that occurred in May 1780. The subsequent surrender of Charlestown resulted in the loss of the most important American southern city and the capture of the entire southern Continental Army by the British, yet it was perhaps as a prisoner of war that Moultrie rendered his most sublime service as an American general.

The latter chapters of this book address the immediate postwar years, the founding of the Society of the Cincinnati in South Carolina, and Moultrie's business pursuits, encompassing his two terms as governor and his role as one of South Carolina's most influential elder statesmen of the closing decades of the 1700s. During this interval he contributed to the establishment of his state government, and though he was only an infrequent actor on the national stage, Moultrie counted among his friends, associates, and correspondents many of our nation's ardent patriots and founding fathers. His devotion and untiring service to his state and country entitle him to a place among them.

Acknowledgments

To South Carolina's historians of the past and present, whose collective works enabled me to place William Moultrie in the context of his day, I am indebted beyond measure. I am also grateful for the encouragement of the Society of the Cincinnati of the State of South Carolina, particularly Henry B. Fishburne Jr. of Charleston, S.C., who suggested this project, and George L. Brailsford of Mount Pleasant, S.C. As always, my friend and medical colleague Dr. Patrick B. Fenlon of Thomasville, Georgia, provided invaluable editorial guidance, as did Elizabeth Frengel, manager of reader services at the Society of the Cincinnati Library in Washington, D.C. I am also particularly obliged to Alexander Moore, acquisitions editor at the University of South Carolina Press in Columbia, and Bill Adams, managing editor at the press, who shepherded me through the publication process with wisdom and compassion.

Aside from doing research in the field, perhaps the most enjoyable part of working on a book project is making new friends and acquaintances. Many of them freely shared their knowledge and expertise, and all of them have my sincere appreciation for their research and editorial assistance, helpful advice, and generous support: Charles B. Baxley of Lugoff, S.C.; Douglas W. Bostick, executive director of the South Carolina Battleground Preservation Trust in Charleston; Ruth Bowler, photo and digital imaging coordinator at the Walters Art Museum in Baltimore, Md.; Julian V. Brandt III of Charleston; Amy Elizabeth Burton at the Office of Senate Curator, U.S. Senate, Washington, D.C.; Bonnie B. Coles, senior search examiner at the Library of Congress in Washington, D.C.; Wade H. Dorsey, reference archivist at the South Carolina Department of Archives and History in Columbia; Graham Duncan, manuscript librarian at the South Caroliniana Library, University of South Carolina in Columbia; Mary Jo Fairchild, reference archivist at the South Carolina Historical Society in Charleston; Henry G. Fulmer, curator of manuscripts at the South Caroliniana Library; Fritz Hamer, chief curator of history at the South Carolina State Museum in Columbia; Dr. C. Leon Harris of Mount Pleasant, S.C.; Carol Jones, librarian at the Charleston Library Society in Charleston; Harriott Cheves Leland, archivist at the Huguenot Society of South Carolina in Charleston; Dr. Thomas C.

Johnson of Isle of Palms, S.C.; Col. William C. Kennerty, U.S. Army (ret.), of Charleston; Patrick M. Kerwin and Bruce R. Kirby, manuscript reference librarians at the Library of Congress in Washington, D.C.; Dr. Charles H. Lesser, senior archivist at the South Carolina Department of Archives and History; R. Douglas MacIntyre of Charleston; Angela B. McGuire at the Thomas County Public Library in Thomasville; David Neilan of Bethel Park, Pennsylvania; Dr. Richard D. Porcher of Mount Pleasant; Daniel Ravenel Jr. of Charleston; Katherine A. Saunders, associate director of preservation at the Historic Charleston Foundation in Charleston; David M. Sullivan of Rutland, Massachusetts, the administrator of the Company of Military Historians; Walter and Helen Taylor of Columbia; Dr. Olga Tsapina, Norris Foundation Curator of American Historical Manuscripts at the Huntington Library in San Marino, Cal.; and Jack D. Warren Jr., executive director of the Society of the Cincinnati in Washington, D.C.

The staffs of the following institutions deserve recognition for their friendly assistance in the countless ways that help make a researcher's visit more productive: the Charleston County Library; the Coleman Karesh Law Library at the University of South Carolina in Columbia; the Gibbes Museum of Art in Charleston; the South Caroliniana Library at the University of South Carolina; the Robert Manning Strozier Library at Florida State University in Tallahassee; the South Carolina Department of Archives and History in Columbia; the Special Collections Department of the Marlene and Nathan Addlestone Library at the College of Charleston; the Thomas Cooper Library at the University of South Carolina; the Thomas University Library in Thomasville, Ga.; and the Thomasville Genealogical, History and Fine Arts Library.

Finally a special thank you goes to my wife, Kim, and my three sons, Chris, Taylor, and Thomas. For five years they tolerated my absences, preoccupations, and my tenacious monopolization of the family computer. *Crescent Moon over Carolina* is dedicated to them.

This book was sponsored in part by the Major General William Moultrie Statue Committee of Charleston, S.C.

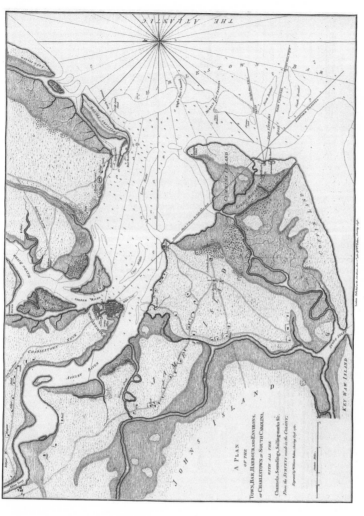

A Plan of the Town, Bar, Harbour and Environs, of Charlestown in South Carolina. London: William Faden, 1780. Courtesy of R. Douglas MacIntyre, Charleston, S.C., and the South Caroliniana Library, University of South Carolina, Columbia, S.C. The islands designated on the map as Cummins Island and Light House Island together form Morris Island.

Prologue

Charleston, the second largest city in South Carolina, is a thriving seaport on the Atlantic coast of the southeastern United States. The city is located on a peninsula formed by the meeting of the Ashley River from the northwest and the Cooper River from the northeast. The mouths of these two rivers widen into a capacious harbor that is bounded on the north by the mainland and on the south by James Island. The harbor opens to the Atlantic between two coastal sea islands: Sullivan's Island to the northeast, and Morris Island to the southwest. Prior to navigational improvements made to the harbor in the late 1800s, the Charleston Bar, a long submerged sandbar penetrated by a few narrow channels, ran from north to south just outside the harbor from Sullivan's Island to a point beyond the lighthouse on the southern tip of Morris Island. The main approach into the harbor that was navigable by deep-draft vessels, the Ship Channel, crossed the bar some distance to the south, but once inside the bar, the channel turned northward to pass near Sullivan's Island.

Sullivan's Island has a prominent role in this narrative. The island is named for Capt. Florence O'Sullivan, a late seventeenth-century Irish emigrant and deputy of the Lords Proprietors who was stationed on the island in 1674. Armed with a single cannon, O'Sullivan kept watch for approaching ships and signaled the town when he spotted masts on the horizon. Sullivan's Island is about four miles long and about a half mile wide at its broadest point as it curves along the mainland from northeast to southwest toward Charleston, approximately four miles away as the crow flies. The northeast tip of Sullivan's Island is separated by a narrow inlet from the next island in the barrier chain to the northeast, which was formerly called Long Island but is now known as Isle of Palms. The southwest third of Sullivan's Island forms a cove between Sullivan's Island and the north side of the harbor mainland, and about a mile or so across the cove on the mainland is Haddrell's Point.

William Moultrie spent the majority of his life in Charleston or on nearby lowcountry plantations. Charlestown, as it was known before 1783, was the economic, social, and political epicenter of colonial South Carolina. Surpassed in size only by Boston, Philadelphia, New York, and Newport, Charlestown was unquestionably the wealthiest of them all, a city filled with gorgeous architecture where commerce flourished, artisans of all kinds prospered, and any desired goods and services could be obtained. Commodities were brought into Charlestown from the interior, and bustling docks, shipyards, and mercantile establishments made Charlestown a regional center for shipping to England, the colony's principal trading partner. Following English tastes in every imaginable way, the lowcountry elite—the planters, merchants, and lawyers—overindulged in entertainment, dress, food, and drink and enjoyed music, theater, and dance with great enthusiasm. Drinking, gaming and betting on the horses, hunting, and fishing were pursued with vigor.[1]

Charlestown was known in the other colonies for the unashamed pursuit of wealth and pleasure, but lowcountry society had another side. A rudimentary education was available at public and private schools, and the townspeople were generally literate, demonstrated by the public's voracious appetite for newspapers. Charlestown's population was diverse long before diversity became fashionable or politically correct. The city's inhabitants were evenly divided black and white, and the white residents were composed of a mix of English, Scotch, Irish, French Huguenot, German, Dutch, and Creole. Nowhere in the colonies was religious tolerance and harmony more prevalent as in Charlestown. The Church of England predominated in the lowcountry, but excepting Roman Catholicism, non-Anglican congregations flourished, evidenced by the several denominations represented among Charlestown's old churches. This was the Charlestown of William Moultrie.[2]

Part I

I.

The Second Son

William Moultrie, the second son of Dr. John Moultrie and his wife, Lucretia Cooper, was born on November 23, 1730. The month-old infant received the sacrament of holy baptism into the Anglican Church on Christmas Eve.[1]

The Moultrie family of Scotland is from the lowland estates of Seafield, Markinch, and Roscobie, an area in southeastern Scotland northward across the Firth of Forth from Edinburgh. The family is documented in old Scottish manuscripts as far back as 1252, when Adam de Moultere swore fealty to King Edward I of England at Berwick-on-Tweed. Moultrie ancestors variably appear in the records spelled as *Moutray, Mowtray, Moultrere, Multrare,* and *Moultray.* Progenitor John Multrare received a land grant as a royal favorite of the court of Mary, Queen of Scots, in 1547, and he subsequently took the Catholic side against the Protestants at the beginning of Queen Mary's rein. As a result Multrare ran afoul of Calvinist authorities (without lasting consequence, it seems) when the Protestants returned to power during the Scottish Reformation in 1560. Roscobie, situated between Loch Leven and Dunfermline, was the seat of the Moultrie family after 1631. The family retained the property through the generations until it was finally sold in 1800.[2]

Dr. John Moultrie was born in 1702 in Culross, Scotland, in the Shire of Fife. Where he received his medical training is unknown, for it appears that he did not attend or graduate from the University of Edinburgh in the country of his birth. Moultrie served with distinction as a surgeon in the Royal Navy, and after several years of military service, he settled in Goose Creek near Charlestown around 1728. He practiced medicine in Charlestown until his death in 1771. At a time when the practice of medicine was more art than science, Moultrie was distinguished as a physician of great skill, particularly in obstetrics, but he also served as port physician and president of the local medical society, the Faculty of Physic. The ladies of Charlestown considered his demise in 1771 to be a public calamity, some of them going so far as to "bedew his grave with tears." An unusual increase in the number of maternal deaths during childbirth was noted in the year following his death.[3]

The name of John Moultrie is listed among the founding members and presidents of the St. Andrew's Society of Charlestown; he was a member of the Charlestown Library Society, the third subscription library founded in the colonies; and he served as junior warden of the Grand Masonic Lodge. A pillar of the church, throughout the years he served terms as vestryman and churchwarden at St. Philip's Church and St. Michael's Church. After acquiring an 893-acre plantation in the parish of St. James Goose Creek, Moultrie represented the parish in the Twenty-Third Royal Assembly from 1760 until 1761.[4]

Little is known about William Moultrie's mother. Lucretia Cooper, daughter of Dr. Barnard Cooper of Goose Creek, was also born in 1702. She and John were married in 1728 in Charlestown. Theirs was a warm and loving marriage that spanned nearly two decades. At her death in 1747, the *South Carolina Gazette* noted her to be "a Gentlewoman possessed of every Quality that could render her an Ornament to her Sex." In that era a man, especially one with children to be raised, often remarried within a year. John married Elizabeth Mathewes, a wealthy widow, in 1748.[5]

John Moultrie had five sons that survived to adulthood, four by his first wife and one by his second. William Moultrie's older brother John Moultrie Jr. was born in 1729. He first studied medicine under his father and subsequently earned his medical doctorate at the University of Edinburgh in 1749, becoming the second native-born physician on the continent and the first from South Carolina. His highly acclaimed thesis, written in Ciceronian Latin and subsequently translated into French and German, was an excellent description of yellow fever. The treatise endured for more than a century as an authority on the often fatal mosquito-borne illness that was so prevalent in the lowcountry. John's first marriage, in 1753, was to a wealthy young widow named Dorothy Morton, and their union established him with the lowcountry elite, removing the necessity for the pursuit of a medical career, although he certainly practiced medicine in Charlestown during the early 1750s.[6]

John Moultrie Jr. became a widower in 1757. In 1762 he eloped with Eleanor Austin, the daughter of a prosperous merchant and Royal Navy captain who strongly disapproved of the couple's marriage. John's friendship with East Florida governor Col. James Grant, forged during the Cherokee campaign, led to his 1764 selection by Grant to the Royal Council of East Florida. His political rise and the family's move to St. Augustine fostered an eventual reconciliation between John and Eleanor's father. As president of the Royal Council in 1771, he became acting governor of the province when Grant departed East Florida for England, and he was soon afterward appointed to the office of lieutenant governor. A zealous Loyalist to the end, John Moultrie Jr. remained in the office of lieutenant governor during the Revolutionary War and afterward moved his family to England when Britain ceded Florida to Spain in 1784. He died in London in 1798.[7]

William Moultrie had two younger brothers, James and Thomas, and a younger half-brother, Alexander. James Moultrie was born in 1734 and was elected to the colony's Commons House of Assembly in 1762, the same year that he was admitted to London's Inner Temple to study law. In 1764 James served as attorney general of the province of South Carolina. Like oldest brother John, he moved to St. Augustine, where he accepted an appointment as chief justice of East Florida, serving until his death in 1765.[8]

Thomas Moultrie, born in 1740, became a lieutenant in the Second South Carolina Regiment in 1775 and was present with his brother William for the defense of Fort Sullivan on June 28, 1776. By the time of the British siege of Charlestown in 1780, Thomas had risen to the rank of captain. He perished defending his home city from the British in 1780. Alexander Moultrie was born about 1750. He was the only child of John Sr. and his second wife, Elizabeth Mathewes. The first four Moultrie sons loved their stepmother dearly, and despite the differences in their ages, they were very close to "Sandy," as Alexander was called. Alexander was admitted to the study of law at the Middle Temple of London in 1768, and he joined the South Carolina bar in 1772. He was elected to the Second Provisional Congress of South Carolina in 1776 and became South Carolina's first attorney general under the new constitution adopted later that year. During the war Alexander Moultrie commanded the Musketeers, a Charlestown militia company. His postwar political career became almost inseparably entwined with that of his older half-brother William, and not in a positive sense.[9]

Since no record of William Moultrie exists from the time of his baptism in 1730 until his marriage in 1749, the manner of his education is not precisely known. He was brought up in a relatively sophisticated southern society that highly valued literacy. The first public library in America was founded in the southern seaport in 1698. The Charlestown Library Society, a private institution founded in 1748, contained more than five thousand books when it was engulfed by fire in 1778. Newspapers kept the populace informed on matters of politics, theology, history, art, and science. Many wealthy citizens possessed extensive book collections.[10]

The children of the affluent often received their earliest lessons from private tutors. Perhaps William attended one of the several schools that were operated in the vicinity of Charlestown. Subjects taught by tutors and schools alike included some mix of the classical languages, grammar, mathematics, science, and drawing. Students seeking to advance their education on this continent sought instruction at institutions in the northern provinces, often attending lectures at Princeton, Brown University, or the University of Pennsylvania. On the other hand, William's older brother John received his medical training in Edinburgh and younger brothers James and Alexander studied in London, so it is possible that William studied abroad. As the province grew more prosperous, it became fashionable for the wealthy to send their children to England for their education.[11]

Whether at home or abroad, William Moultrie received a solid education. His adult letters are well written and demonstrate familiarity with classical literature. That he was a habitual keeper of journals and demonstrated a high degree of skill with quill and ink also argue well for this possibility. The most compelling evidence against an education obtained abroad is perhaps the lack of evidence itself. Moultrie played a prominent role in the history of his state and nation, and if he had studied abroad like many of his contemporaries, the fact would be generally known.

However nebulous his scholastic background, Moultrie was a staunch supporter of education in Charlestown, becoming a member of the South Carolina Society in 1757 and the St. Andrew's Club in 1758. The South Carolina Society, organized in 1737 by French Huguenots, was the oldest of several charitable associations dedicated to the promotion of education of children of both sexes in the colony by paying the salaries of schoolmasters and schoolmistresses. Founded in 1729, Charlestown's St. Andrew's Club was the first St. Andrew's society formed in the colonies. It existed to fulfill both social and charitable purposes. Like his father Moultrie also joined the Charlestown Library Society.[12]

In a sense Moultrie made his money the old-fashioned way—he married it. He and Damaris Elizabeth de St. Julien were united in holy matrimony on December 10, 1749. Neither the bride's physical attributes—dark or fair, short or tall—nor the details of their courtship are known, but from external appearances theirs was a happy union. William and Damaris had two children. A daughter named Lucretia was born on October 13, 1750. She died at the age of thirteen. A son, William Jr., was born on August 7, 1752. William Jr. would serve alongside his father in the Continental Army.[13]

Damaris Moultrie, six years William's senior, was the great-granddaughter of Huguenot emigrants from France and the fifth child of Pierre de St. Julien and Sarah Godin. She came from a Huguenot heritage rich in both history and land. The family plantation, Pooshee, began as a land grant of one thousand acres, and St. Julien holdings eventually grew to include eighty-eight hundred acres and five Charlestown lots. A French Huguenot Protestant Church existed in

Charlestown, but for sundry reasons many Huguenot families affiliated with St. Philip's Church. The recording in the St. Philip's register of her parents' marriage, Damaris's baptism in 1728, and her own wedding make a strong case for the Anglican affiliation of the prosperous and politically influential St. Julien family.[14]

The Moultrie–de Julien union secured William's wealth and social standing in the Carolina lowcountry society, for now he was a man of property. Under English common law, a married woman had the status of *feme covert,* without individual legal rights distinct from those of her husband, particularly where money and property were concerned. The husband controlled everything. In 1752, for the sum of three thousand pounds "current money of the Province of South Carolina," William obtained from his brother-in-law Benjamin de St. Julien an estate of 1,020 acres called North Hampton.* The plantation was about thirty-five miles due north of Charlestown, located in St. John's parish in Berkeley County, some two miles west of Black Oak Church and along one of the routes the British would take on their way to and from Camden.[15]

It was at North Hampton's plantation house, a square 1716 structure with a basement and first story of massive brick walls, that Moultrie and Damaris made their home. Five years later he extended his holdings when he acquired, as part of the settlement of Benjamin's estate, the adjoining plantation named Indian Fields. Eventually Moultrie added acreage on the Congaree River and several lots in Charlestown. He had advanced his position as the second son of a physician to become a planter, husband, and father. The birth of children and property transactions with his extended family foster a presumption of Moultrie's domestic felicity.[16]

Once a planter, Moultrie began to accumulate wealth through the cultivation of rice and indigo. Aside from produce grown for home and local use, the agricultural focus of the Carolina lowcountry plantations was the cultivation of rice, which was the primary staple commodity of the province. Rice grew luxuriantly in the deep, mucky inland cypress swamps, but the process necessitated a huge labor force of black slaves. Despite being labor intensive, growing rice generated enormous profits. Indigo, the second great staple of the province, was introduced from the West Indies during the 1740s by Miss Eliza Lucas, the mother of Moultrie's close friend Charles Cotesworth Pinckney. Parliament subsidized the indigo industry by paying the indigo farmers a bounty, helping to make the growth and production of indigo quite lucrative.[17]

The years of Moultrie's early life and young adulthood were ones of unprecedented prosperity in South Carolina. The lowcountry had the most developed society in perhaps the wealthiest colony in the British Empire. Rice and indigo

---

*The estate is referred to as "Northampton Plantation" in the indenture between Benjamin de St. Julien and William Moultrie dated August 18, 1752, but in his personal correspondence Moultrie called it North Hampton.

North Hampton, home of William Moultrie and his family. Built in 1715, the house was rectangular in shape and constructed of large English-style brick laid in English bond. A two-story porch sheltered the basement and main floor. The fireplaces of the interior chimneys opened into both the front and rear rooms, and the chimney stacks extended through the ridge of the roof. The windows were arched and the front windows had keystones. The upper story of wood was added when the house was rebuilt after the house burned about 1850. The plantation was covered by Lake Moultrie in 1940 as part of the Santee Cooper Hydroelectric and Navigation Project. The floor plan of North Hampton was drawn by Thomas T. Waterman in 1940. From the Library of Congress Historic American Buildings Survey.

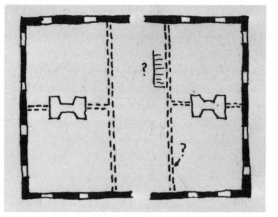

brought great fortunes to the planter class, but wealth and affluence extended to merchants, physicians, and lawyers as well. William and Damaris Moultrie undoubtedly had the means to participate in the open-house hospitality that characterized the lifestyle of the gentry: elegant parties and balls, a home crowded with guests. Enjoyment of life was of paramount importance, and the luxuries of the day were within reach, primarily because of the colony's monopolistic trading relationship with the mother country. The lowcountry Carolinians were excessively fond of British manners and tried to emulate them in every way possible—clothes, architecture, furniture, carriages. In the years immediately following the Revolutionary War, this addiction to English culture would nearly be the lowcountry's undoing.[18]

Horse racing was exceedingly popular in colonial South Carolina. To further emulate the English, many planters imported studs and mares and bred their own lines. A race course called the New Market Course was laid out about a mile from town on the Charlestown Neck in 1754 and was first used in 1760. Moultrie was quite fond of the sport and was known to trade in expensive horses from England and Virginia. One of his horses, an English import named Old Starling, was considered by good judges of horseflesh to be the most handsome horse in America. The February races were central to Charlestown's social life. Moultrie belonged to the Carolina Jockey Club, whose annual ball was the highlight of the social season. As interest in racing increased, contests were held in nearby Jacksonborough, Ferguson Ferry, Beaufort, and at Childsberry (later Strawberry), St. John's Parish, near the Moultrie home.[19]

Horse racing was banned at the onset of the Revolutionary War. South Carolinians were willing to fight and die for the cause of liberty, yet they did not take kindly to this prohibition and disregarded the racing ban until the war effectively stopped the sport for want of horses. After the war and the resumption of the sport, Moultrie did not indulge in the expensive and time-consuming pastime, except perhaps as a spectator or mentor to his son William Moultrie Jr., who helped to establish the South Carolina Jockey Club and build the Washington Racecourse.[20]

Household management in South Carolina was based on the English model, but it was in modification of the model by the institution of slavery that the colony differed most with the mother country. It took far more slaves to run a plantation than was necessary to operate an English manor. In addition to the innumerable field hands, plantations required a butler, coachmen, cooks, maids, seamstresses, carpenters, blacksmiths, coopers, tailors, and shoemakers, all thoroughly organized into a complete system. The exact number of slaves owned by Moultrie at any given time is unknown, although during the war he numbered them at about two hundred.[21]

Moultrie's character and disposition made him a relatively kind and benevolent master, perhaps to a fault. He was later criticized (it will be shown) by his superior officers for being too easy and goodhearted to maintain proper discipline. These qualities endeared him to his subordinates, and this aspect of Moultrie's personality likely extended to his servants, for he embraced the paternal ideology that emerged during the last quarter of the eighteenth century, when slaveholders began to view their slaves as inferior humans rather than purely chattel. Paternalism combined "fairness and firmness, a balance of affection and discipline. This familial treatment would produce the masters' preferred form of subordination among slaves, willing obedience. Masters were responsible not only for churching their slaves but for practicing Christianity in their treatment. Paternalism would render slaves more manageable, slave labor more efficient, and slave unrest less common."[22]

Moultrie's own writing, thought to have been penned around 1800, reflected this paternalistic philosophy when he wrote of great moderation and indulgence lately afforded the lowcountry slaves. "I am very much pleased," he said, "to see the treatment of the slaves in the country is altered so much, for their ease and happyness [sic]," by conduct that favored tenderness and humanity. He loathed the harsh treatment of decades past where slaves were summarily lashed for not completing a task "when it was perhaps impossible for them to do it." Good treatment of slaves contributed to their longevity and profitability, and he boasted that he could prove this with records of slave births and deaths that he had kept for thirty years.[23]

2.

A Military Apprenticeship

The colonial government of South Carolina, modeled on the English system, consisted of executive, legislative, and judicial branches, with considerable overlap of the executive branch and the other branches. The executive branch consisted of the governor, the lieutenant governor, and the advisory twelve-member Royal Council, all appointed by the king. Concurrent with his executive responsibilities, the governor also exercised legislative, judicial, ecclesiastical, military, and diplomatic powers. The legislative branch was composed of the Royal Council and the Commons House of Assembly. The members of the Royal Council, in addition to their executive advisory duties, conceived themselves to be the provincial equivalent of the English House of Lords. The judicial system of the province was based on English common law. Justices and officers of the higher and lower courts were appointed by the king or the governor. That judiciary and council appointments were often made irrespective of qualifications was a source of vexation to South Carolinians.[1]

The Commons House of Assembly was popularly elected from the parishes. It generally followed the procedures and customs of the British House of Commons to enact public and private statutory legislation. The Commons House controlled public finances, typically providing a yearly subsidy to the governor's salary, and was therefore able to apply enough financial pressure to encroach upon the power of the governor and, by default, the Royal Council. The South Carolina elite took representation very seriously. The Commons House, like its English counterpart, was the protector of the people. A representative had to be free to act without obligation to others, public-spirited, and mindful of duty, a man of property with a stake in the stability and prosperity of society. It was into this milieu that William Moultrie entered the world of politics and government.[2]

Moultrie began his legislative career in 1752 when he won a special election in St. John's Berkeley Parish for a seat in the Commons House during the Twentieth Royal Assembly. Twenty-one years old, he replaced his brother-in-law Peter (Pierre) de St. Julien, who declined to serve, most likely on account of illness (he died later that year). Voters of St. John's Berkeley, the parish of Prince Frederick, and the parish of St. Helena subsequently returned him to office for every Royal Assembly until 1773, excepting the twenty-third (1757–60). Concurrent with his legislative service, Moultrie held the office of justice of the peace for Berkeley County during 1756, 1767, and 1769 and served as commissioner to issue paper currency in 1760.[3]

On Tuesday morning, March 10, 1752, having received notice that Moultrie had been duly elected as a member of the Commons House of Assembly to represent St. John's Berkeley, the House issued an order for him to appear before the assembly. Moultrie complied by attending the opening of the session on the following Monday. He was called inside, where the Speaker of the House ceremoniously informed him of his election and asked if he was willing to qualify himself as a member of the House, to which Moultrie replied in the affirmative. The House ordered Dr. Thomas Glen and Thomas Lynch Sr. to accompany Moultrie to the office of Gov. James Glen, who administered the oath of allegiance and supremacy and the oath of abjuration. Moultrie also signed a declaration against transubstantiation.* Having fulfilled all requirements, Moultrie took his seat in the Commons House of Assembly.[4]

During Moultrie's freshman term, the Commons House dealt with the pressing financial crisis that resulted from the devastation wrought by a hurricane that struck Charlestown on September 15, 1752. Moultrie and the other House members also considered matters of Indian diplomacy concerning the Creek, Cherokee, and Shawnee tribes, intercolonial affairs, taxes and monetary policy, the construction of harbor fortifications, and the impending outbreak of the French and Indian War. Over the course of Moultrie's successive terms in the Commons House, these matters occupied the assembly on a more or less chronic basis.[5]

Disputes between the Commons House, the governor, and the Royal Council resulted in a slow but steady gain in the power and autonomy of the Commons House. Not every matter considered by the lower legislative body, however, required political wrangling between the branches of government. One example that all parties seemed to agree on is the September 23, 1755, directive of the Commons House ordering the installation of Benjamin Franklin's new device, the lightning rod, on the powder magazine in Charlestown and at Fort Johnson on nearby James Island.[6]

---

*The oath of abjuration was a repudiation of the right of any member of the House of Stuart to the English monarchy. The declaration against transubstantiation effectively disqualified Roman Catholics from holding public office.

The journals of the Commons House of Assembly during Moultrie's tenure reveal that he was generally present and engaged in the business of the legislature. During times of absence, he applied in writing to be excused, as was customary, and when present he received his share of committee assignments for the review of various and sundry petitions received by the Commons House from parishes throughout the province. On many occasions he was sent by the Commons House to deliver messages and reports to the provincial governor and the Royal Council. He also served on a committee that inspected the condition of the arms in the public armory.[7]

The Moultries were faithful Anglicans, attending services at Biggin Church, the parish church of St. John's Berkeley. Moultrie served as a vestryman, along with fellow communicant Henry Laurens. His election to the vestry was not necessarily indicative of his piety, but it was a sign that his character and judgment were highly esteemed. After the church burned to the ground in 1755, Moultrie lobbied the assembly for the construction of a new church, introducing a bill to that effect in the Commons House in February 1756. The bill passed after the obligatory three readings, and he was appointed to be one of five commissioners to raise subscriptions, rebuild the church, and sell pews.[8]

South Carolina governors and acting governors during Moultrie's tenure in the Commons House of Assembly included the abovementioned James Glen (1743–56), William Henry Lyttelton (1756–60), William Bull II (1760–61, 1764–66, 1768, and 1773–75), Thomas Boone (1761–64), Lord Charles Greville Montague (1766–73), and Lord William Campbell (1775–76). Moultrie got along well with Governor Lyttelton and developed a warm friendship of sorts with Lord Montague. William Bull, a native South Carolinian, became one of the most beloved men of the province, even during and after the Revolutionary War, despite his loyalty to the Crown. Bull and Moultrie knew each other quite well. Moultrie had significant political differences with Lord William Campbell that would play out at the end of Campbell's tenure.[9]

Periods of political infighting notwithstanding, the colonial inhabitants of South Carolina lived in the midst of danger and potential enemies: Spaniards to the south, Indians northwest along the frontier, and black slaves who outnumbered the whites. For the most part, British military forces were absent, so the organization of the men of the province into militias was an imperative. By law all white males between the age of sixteen and sixty years old were enrolled in the militia of their parish. Planters, professional men, and the members of the Royal Council or the Commons House were generally exempt except in times of crisis. The militia formed the basis of Moultrie's introduction to military life. Exactly when he began militia duty is unknown, but in 1759 he was appointed aide-de-camp to Gov. William Henry Lyttelton and was a member of an expeditionary force that Lyttelton later led against the Cherokees.[10]

By the mid-1700s the territory of the Cherokee Indians of the southern Appalachia extended to cover a large portion of the South Carolina backcountry. The Cherokee had been English allies during the French and Indian War, and the tribe had allowed, even encouraged, frontier outposts. As time passed, however, broken promises and French interference increased discontent on the part of the Cherokees. Open hostilities finally erupted in 1758 when a party of Cherokee warriors, homeward bound after aiding the British against the French at Fort Duquesne, were killed by Virginia colonists in a dispute that resulted from a misunderstanding over the ownership of some horses. Cherokee war parties raided several white settlements, murdering and scalping white people in retaliation. This rapid escalation of violence set into motion the first of three campaigns prosecuted over a two-year period that came to be known as the Cherokee War.[11]

The first of the three campaigns was led by Lyttelton, who set off on an ill-advised expedition to relieve the imperiled frontier settlements and humble the Cherokees. Having rebuffed peace overtures made by a delegation of fifty-five Cherokee who had journeyed to Charlestown, and ignoring good advice from Lt. Gov. William Bull, Lyttelton set out from Charlestown on October 26, 1759. Accompanying his column was a body of volunteers that included his not quite twenty-nine-year-old aide-de-camp, Moultrie. The two men must have enjoyed cordial relations—Lyttelton lodged at Moultrie's North Hampton plantation on the second night out. By the time the governor rendezvoused with his militia at the Congarees, a point on the Congaree River near present-day Columbia, his force consisted of about fourteen hundred men.[12]

Lyttelton's army was poorly armed and undisciplined. The campaign, while notable for an absence of bloodshed, was plagued by miserably wet and cold weather, fatigue, hunger, and outbreaks of measles and smallpox. Hundreds of disgruntled militiamen deserted the ranks, giving young Moultrie his first taste of the militiamen's unreliability. In the end Lyttelton forced a treaty on the Cherokee tribes, whose chiefs he treated scornfully. Claiming victory (albeit an inglorious one), he returned to Charlestown on January 8, 1760, where he was greeted by joyful demonstrations meant to honor a conquering hero. Very little was accomplished by the campaign beyond arousing the Cherokee's anger and resentment, however, and Lyttelton's "victory" virtually assured that peace would be short-lived.[13]

Moultrie was scarcely settled at home from the Lyttelton campaign when a bloody incident in the northwest corner of South Carolina reignited violence on the frontier. In February 1760 at Fort Prince George on the east bank of the Keowee River opposite the Cherokee Lower Town of Keowee (north of present-day Clemson, South Carolina), a Cherokee war party attacked and killed fourteen white soldiers, precipitating the retaliatory massacre of twenty-six hostage Cherokee chiefs. Enraged Cherokee warriors recommenced their attacks on backcountry settlements with a vengeance, mercilessly killing men, women, and children. Lyttelton appealed to Gen. Jeffery Amherst, commander-in-chief of British forces in North America, informing him of the emergency, and Amherst reacted by immediately dispatching British troops to South Carolina. On April 1, 1760, Col. Archibald Montgomery, commanding twelve companies of British regulars, sailed into Charlestown Harbor.[14]

Montgomery's twelve-hundred-man army marched from Monck's Corner on April 23 to join a small contingent of the provincial militia at the Congarees. Among the provincials were the Gentlemen Volunteers, a company captained by Thomas Middleton. John Moultrie Jr. was the company's lieutenant, and his brother William was likely along, but this has not been confirmed. The campaign, which lasted the better part of the summer, began auspiciously for the British, who burned a number of Cherokee Lower Towns and crop fields, killing warriors and taking women and children captive along the way.[15]

Advancing deeper into Indian territory in late June, Montgomery allowed his force to be lured into an ambush in a narrow, rugged valley on the Little Tennessee River (near present-day Franklin, North Carolina) a few miles south of the Middle Town of Etchoe, called Etchoe Pass or "the Narrows." The Cherokee warriors enjoyed the advantage of rifle-barreled guns and fought in standard Indian style, while the musket-armed whites fired by platoons. Twenty of Montgomery's men were killed, and seventy were wounded. At the end of the ferocious and bloody encounter, the British and provincial troops retained possession of the battleground, but the army was pretty much used up by the declared "victory." A retreat was called and safely accomplished, and the exhausted soldiers reached Charlestown within a few weeks. Montgomery and most of his troops subsequently sailed for New York.[16]

Montgomery's abortive campaign only worsened the Indian crisis. Emboldened by the British retreat, Cherokee warriors took the field intent on avenging the deaths of their friends and relatives and the desolation wrought by the British on their homes and crops. William Bull—acting as governor in the absence of Lyttelton, who had unceremoniously departed for Jamaica—applied a second time to General Amherst for military support. In response Amherst dispatched twelve companies of British regulars under the command of Lt. Col. James Grant, who had been Montgomery's second in command.[17]

The Scotsman Grant arrived in Charlestown in early 1761. From his experiences in North America, he had developed a general contempt for provincial militia, whom he blamed for his failure and capture at the Battle of Fort Duquesne in western Pennsylvania during September 1758.And he had been particularly critical of the behavior of some South Carolinians during the previous campaign. That Grant had impugned their courage made him unpopular with the South Carolinians, who were determined to redeem their honor.[18]

The coat-of-arms of William Bull II affixed to his monument at Ashley Hall plantation near Charleston. Note the crescent on the shield. Author's collection.

As a consequence of the Cherokee rampages that continued through the latter part of 1760, and stung by criticism that the province had done little for its own defense, the Commons House of Assembly passed an act on August 20, 1760, raising a new regiment of foot soldiers, the South Carolina Provincial Regiment. Lieutenant Governor Bull commissioned the officers: Thomas Middleton rose to regimental command with the rank of colonel, Henry Laurens received a lieutenant colonel's commission, and Moultrie's older brother John was promoted to the rank of major. William Moultrie received command of a company with the rank of captain, and Francis Marion became his lieutenant. Isaac Huger and Andrew Pickens were also company-grade officers in the regiment. Grant saw great promise in the Provincial Regiment that he largely attributed to the high quality of the regiment's officers, and in this he was prescient. Moultrie, Marion, Huger, and Pickens all became general officers in the war that would came in the next decade.[19]

Though not by any means professional soldiers, the Provincial Regiment strove to look the part by wearing a regimental uniform that consisted of collarless coatees of blue with scarlet lapels, cuffs, and linings. Waistcoats and breeches

South-Carolina, *By the Honourable William Bull Esq.[r] Lie[ut]*
Gov[r] and Commander in Chief in & over the...

To Thomas Middleton Esq.[r]

Whereas in the present situation of affairs, it is thought necessary for the immediate protection of the several Inhabitants of this province raise a Regiment of Foot, to consist of one thousand men, besides Officers into which the three provincial Companies, called the Buffs, are to be Incorporated, as part of the said Regiment; And I reposing especial Trust and Confidence in the Loyalty, Courage and Good Conduct of You the said Thomas Middleton, have commissioned, constituted and appointed, and these presents do commission, constitute and appoint you the said Thomas Middleton to be Colonel of the said Regiment: which said Regiment you are to Lead, Train, Muster and exercise, according to Military Duty And you are to follow and observe all such orders and Instructions as you shall receive from time to time, receive from me or the Commander in chief for the time being; according to the Rules and discipline of War, and in pursuance of the Trust hereby reposed in You, And all Inferior Officers and Soldiers belonging to the said Regiment, are hereby strictly required & commanded to obey You as Colonel of the same.

This Commission to continue during Pleasure.

By his Honor's Command   *Given under my Hand and Seal at Cha[rles...]*
W[m] Murray Dep[y] Sec[ry]   *this sixteenth day of September Anno Domini 1760 and in the Thirty fourth year of His Maj[es...] Reign.*

            W[m] Bull

A sketch of Lt. Gov. William Bull's coat-of-arms is located in the upper left corner of Thomas Middleton's appointment to the rank of colonel of the Provincial Regiment. The heraldic crescent may have inspired the crescent hat insignia of the Provincial Regiment of 1760, then the crescent hat insignia of the First and Second South Carolina Regiments, and finally the crescent that appeared on South Carolina's provincial flag during the Revolutionary War. Courtesy of the South Carolina Department of Archives and History; Columbia, S.C.

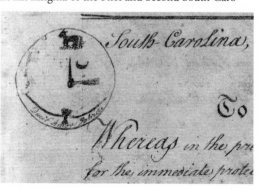

were blue, stockings or leggings were brown, and belts and crossbelts were buff. A black light-infantry cap was fashioned by removing most of the brim of a felt hat, except for the front portion, which was turned up vertically. To this false front was fastened a silver crescent believed to have originated from Lieutenant Governor Bull's seal or heraldic crest. As symbols of their rank, the officers carried small swords and often wore silver gorgets suspended from their necks. Silver aiguillettes adorned their right shoulders, over which crimson sashes were worn diagonally across their trunks.[20]

By the time Colonel Grant returned to South Carolina, the Provincial Regiment was in winter camp at the Congarees. Grant devised a plan that utilized the settlement of Ninety-Six as his forward base of operations and accordingly, on March 27, 1761, ordered Maj. John Moultrie to march two hundred provincials from the Congarees to Ninety-Six to guard a supply depot established there. Grant recognized that Moultrie had no professional military background, but he readily acknowledged his military aptitude, enthusiasm, and reliability. The two men became close friends and political allies.[21]

Major Moultrie was, in turn, less sanguine of the recruits, writing that they were as "rough and riotous fellows to manage, as ever got together; add to these some young gentlemen [the junior officers] that require a good deal of looking after." The major observed that in keeping in character with military campaigns of that era, "there are some . . . among us, whom though not very delicate I will call camp ladys [sic]." He found that the ladies also required military instruction and discipline, for they resembled noisy, riotous, and troublesome cattle.[22]

Captain William Moultrie did not accompany his brother to Ninety-Six. Instead he sat as a member of a regimental court-martial that convened at the Congaree encampment on April 6, 1761, to try the cases of seven men who had been arrested for desertion. The prisoners all admitted to being guilty of the charges and cast themselves on the mercy of the court. One man who had returned to camp voluntarily was acquitted. Three of the convicted men were sentenced to receive two hundred, four hundred, or eight hundred lashes on their bare backs, and three men were sentenced to be executed by hanging. Colonel Grant approved the verdicts and the punishments handed down by the court. He mercifully commuted the sentences and pardoned the men, except for one poor soul who was hung as an example.[23]

Grant marched his force of regulars and provincials from the Congarees on a northwestward course to Ninety-Six and then to Fort Prince George, departing on May 3 and arriving on May 27. After rebuffing a peace overture offered by a Cherokee chief named Attakullakulla (known to whites as Little Carpenter), Grant launched his invasion into Indian territory on June 7 by marching his two-mile-long column of more than twenty-five hundred regulars, provincials, and Indian allies against the Cherokee Lower Towns. Flanking parties were alert to prevent surprise, and every man was expected to fight. The column moved quickly to get as deep as possible into Indian territory before the Indians could mount any opposition. Prior to departure Moultrie was given command of a company of light infantry consisting of seventy picked men who were deployed as skirmishers to cover the column's rear and baggage train during the march.[24]

It was in the vicinity of Etchoe just after daybreak on July 10, near Montgomery's ambush of the year before, that an estimated six hundred warriors simultaneously attacked the army's line of march from both flanks and supply train in the rear. Grant quickly deployed his force to meet the threat. According to legend Francis Marion led a contingent of provincials up a gloomy defile to drive the Indians from the heights on the right, taking heavy casualties, while the rest of the army forged through the pass. It was a sharp engagement, but the regulars and provincials finally broke the Cherokee, who retreated in disarray. Details are wanting, but it is known that Moultrie and his company acquitted themselves admirably in the action, as did the entire Provincial Regiment. Afterward Grant was uncharacteristically complimentary of their performance, saying that they "executed their orders which they received very properly and behaved with great coolness."[25]

After the battle the army summarily reduced Etchoe to ashes. Thus opened a thirty-day campaign through the territory of the Middle Cherokee settlements. Every village and plantation encountered was put to the torch, more than fourteen hundred acres of orchards and crops destroyed, and countless cattle slaughtered. Women, children, and old men were left without any means of subsistence, and upward of five thousand Cherokee fled into the mountains. This scorched earth tactic was enacted on the grounds that a lasting treaty could be obtained only after the Cherokee people had been fully chastised and humbled. Virtually unopposed, the regulars moved rapidly, but the Provincial Regiment followed more slowly in their wake with provisions, the wounded, baggage, and cattle. The grueling pace, sickness, short rations, and desertion eventually wore down the army to the point that Grant was forced to terminate the campaign. The exhausted soldiers returned to Fort Prince George on July 9.[26]

On August 29 a delegation of Cherokee chieftains led by Little Carpenter came to Grant's camp to sue for peace. Grant was unable to reach a suitable agreement with the Indians, so he furnished the delegation with a guard to escort them to Charlestown to confer with Lieutenant Governor Bull over the terms of the treaty. Col. Henry Laurens and Capt. William Moultrie were given charge of the escort. Laurens, Moultrie, and the Cherokees struck out from Keowee on September 2 and headed southward bound for Charlestown. The Commons House and Royal Council were meeting at Shem Town at Ashley Ferry because of an outbreak of yellow fever that was raging in Charlestown, so it was there that Laurens and Moultrie brought the delegation. Negotiations between Bull and the chieftains went well, and the subsequent treaty restored peace to the frontier.[27]

When Laurens and Moultrie returned to Fort Prince George after the peace talks, they found their comrades in a pathetic state, having been greatly reduced in numbers by desertion during the summer and fall. In late October Grant dispatched those who remained back to the Congarees, and when the regiment finally returned to Charlestown in November, fewer than a hundred men were present. The dilapidated condition of the regiment notwithstanding, in comparison to Lyttelton's and Montgomery's campaigns, the Grant campaign was a success.[28]

The three campaigns against the Cherokee Indians provided a military apprenticeship for young South Carolinians such as William Moultrie, Francis Marion, Isaac Huger, Christopher Gadsden, and Andrew Pickens, and later events would prove that they profited from their lessons. In the meantime during the period of relative calm that followed, Moultrie returned home and took his seat in the Commons House of Assembly representing the parish of Prince Frederick. From the time of the Cherokee War until the end of the colonial period, the record of his militia service is relatively quiet, but the experience he gained against the Indians did not dampen his martial ardor in the least. By 1773 he was a major of the provincial regiment of horse, and he was promoted to the rank of colonel in 1774.[29]

3.

A Shadow Government

For a number of years, the South Carolina Commons House of Assembly had passed annual tax and appropriations bills, and one example was an act to defray the expense of the late expedition against the Cherokee Indians passed on July 31, 1760. The inhabitants of South Carolina, through their elected representatives, were taxing themselves—taxation *with* representation. In addition to levying taxes on the inhabitants of the province, this legislation authorized the issue of provincial currency to pay for the prosecution of the war. William Moultrie was one of several commissioners appointed for "stamping, signing and making public orders." These public orders were bills of credit issued by the province as legal tender—in other words paper currency to be used by the province for reimbursement of costs incurred while making war.[1]

The economic policies of Great Britain decisively favored the industry, commerce, and shipping of the mother country to the subordination of the welfare of her colonies. Moreover Parliament began to levy taxes so that the colonies would bear a portion of the cost of the French and Indian War. In doing this Parliament arguably undermined the rights and privileges of American colonists, who as loyal English subjects held fast to a precept that was central to the English conception of political liberty as articulated by the seventeenth-century English philosopher John Locke: that taxation and the consent of the taxed were inseparably connected. Trade restrictions and taxes imposed by Parliament significantly increased provincial discontent, particularly in New England. The escalating tension over home-rule autonomy and the authority of a distant legislative body to impose its will on its colonial citizens thus began a decade before the "shot heard 'round the world" was fired on the town green at Lexington, Massachusetts.[2]

Parliament passed the Stamp Act in March 1765, requiring that all legal and commercial documents bear a tax stamp: newspapers, pamphlets, and playing cards, literally every piece of paper the colonists used. While not the first act passed by Parliament for the sake of raising revenue and restricting colonial trade, it was the first law that truly galvanized the colonies into widespread and organized resistance. The actual cost of the Stamp Act was quite small and the British rationale for taxing the provinces not completely unreasonable, but the colonists vehemently resented being taxed without consent or redress—taxation *without* representation.

News of the Stamp Act produced immediate and negative consequences in Charlestown that mirrored the reaction of the northern colonies. Anyone suspected of supporting the act was threatened with demonstrations, rioting, and mob violence. The Commons House passed a series of forceful denunciations of the Stamp Act and sent delegates to the Stamp Act Congress held in New York during October 1765. The Stamp Act Congress subsequently adopted a fourteen-point Declaration of Rights and Grievances that asserted the rights of the colonists as Englishmen. In Charlestown when the Commons House approved and adopted the resolutions of the Stamp Act Congress, William Moultrie, representing the parish of St. Helena, voted in support of the measures.[3]

Parliament repealed the Stamp Act in March 1766, an action that was celebrated with bonfires, bell ringing, and the candlelight illumination of nearly every house in Charlestown. Coincident with the repeal of the Stamp Act, Parliament proclaimed through the Declaratory Act its "full power and authority to make laws and statutes of sufficient force and validity to bind the colonies and people of America . . . in all cases whatsoever." The Declaratory Act attracted little notice among the populace, but the Townshend Acts, proposed by Charles Townshend and passed by Parliament in June 1767, certainly did. The Townshend Acts imposed duties on common imports such as lead, paper, paint, glass, and tea. In addition to raising revenues, asserting British imperial authority in America, and tightening customs enforcement, the Townshend duties were meant to undermine the power of the provincial assemblies by funding the salaries of governors and other civil officials. This deprived the legislatures of any financial leverage that existed heretofore.[4]

Like the Stamp Act, the Townshend Acts aroused the outrage of the colonists, who responded with civil unrest. At the official level, the Commons House of Assembly instructed its London agent to work for repeal of the acts. But in November 1768, the Commons House received a letter written by Samuel Adams that was being circulated by the House of Representatives of Massachusetts. The substance of what became known as the Massachusetts Circular Letter was that taxation of the colonies by Parliament without representation was unconstitutional and a violation of colonial rights. The Commons House approved the

Massachusetts Circular Letter and ordered it to be published alongside South Carolina's resolutions of support.[5]

Of the fifty-five members that constituted the Commons House, only twenty-six were present at the time of adoption of the resolution. The vote of approval of the Massachusetts Circular Letter was unanimous, earning the legislators the sobriquet the "Unanimous Twenty-Six." Moultrie was numbered among those twenty-six, who won for themselves a measure of popular fame—glasses were raised in their honor in all of the colonies. An infuriated Governor Lord Charles Greville Montague dissolved the Commons House. Nevertheless each of the Unanimous Twenty-six was successful in his bid for reelection to the forthcoming assembly.[6]

By repeatedly exercising his power of prorogation (postponement without dissolution), Governor Montague refused to allow the Commons House to reconvene until June 26, 1769. Once back in session, the assembly grappled with demands made by Maj. Gen. Thomas Gage, who commanded British forces in North America. Gage required quarters for British troops to be garrisoned in Charlestown. Just a few years earlier, the redcoat soldiers had been hailed as the colony's defenders against the heathen savages, but now their presence was an unwelcome source of fear and apprehension. The Commons House appointed Moultrie to a committee formed to consider compliance with Gage's demands. The committee's decision not to provide for the troops was based on its consensus opinion that the troops were not present in South Carolina to garrison the frontier and that the expense of providing for a military force had been defrayed by the large revenues generated by the Townshend Acts.[7]

During the intervals that Lord Montague's prorogations prevented the Commons House from showing solidarity with the other provinces in defiance of British colonial taxation, opposition in South Carolina was carried out using extralegal means. Nonimportation agreements had been in effect in Boston since October 1767, and several of the northern provinces had followed suit. Most of the members of the Commons House signed nonimportation agreements, and in July 1769 when a committee of thirty-nine planters, merchants, and artisans met to establish and enforce a nonimportation association, Moultrie was among the representative planters. At times he chaired the committee's meetings.[8]

The nonimportation association prohibited importation of any but the most necessary goods and mandated cancellation of all pending orders from England. And though nonimportation ultimately failed, complaints from English merchants were a factor in Parliament's decision to repeal all of the Townshend Acts except for the tea duty in April 1770. But the rallying of public opinion behind nonimportation had important implications beyond the repeal of the Townshend Acts. Mob rule evident in South Carolina during the Stamp Act crisis had been replaced by small group meetings that increased in size as time passed until they resembled New England town meetings. As Parliament and the king became increasingly deaf to the complaints voiced by the colonists, the colonists found the means of self-government beyond the framework of royal authority, sowing the seeds of independence.[9]

The nonimportation committee formed in Charlestown in 1769, of which Moultrie was a member, was the first extralegal body to form anywhere in the years prior to the Revolutionary War. The importance of this precedent cannot be underestimated. The royal government could interfere with the provincial government almost at will but exercised no authority whatsoever over the extralegal committees that began to function as a shadow government. This Committee of Thirty-Nine was superseded in 1773 by a General Committee of which Moultrie was not a member. The General Committee continued to function as an emerging pre-Revolutionary government of South Carolina.[10]

Despite growing contentions between the representatives of the Crown and the Commons House of Assembly, Moultrie found himself in the direct service of the royal governor in 1772. Delineation of the boundary between South Carolina and North Carolina had been a matter of dispute between the two provinces since 1730. Surveys in 1735, 1737, and 1764 were to run the boundary line northwest from a coastal point thirty miles south of the mouth of the Cape Fear River until it intersected the thirty-fifth parallel. Unfortunately the 1764 surveyors erred in locating the thirty-fifth parallel before continuing the line due west to the Charlestown-Salisbury road near Waxhaw Creek. This inaccuracy placed more than six hundred square miles of South Carolina land on the wrong side of the boundary.[11]

A third survey was planned for 1772 to extend the line up the Catawba River to its fords, then due west again until it reached Tryon Mountain, deviating from the original intended line so as to encompass the entirety of the Catawba Indian reservation within the boundary of South Carolina and thereby to compensate for the 1764 error. Political jurisdiction of land for future settlement was at stake, so both provinces had a vested interest in seeing that the survey was accomplished to its own best advantage. The royal governors of the two colonies appointed commissioners to attend to the mission, and Moultrie was one of the two commissioners appointed by Lord Montague to represent South Carolina.[12]

Dissension between the Commons House of Assembly and the governor notwithstanding, Moultrie and Montague must have been on good terms. Montague had twice appointed him justice of the peace and knew of Moultrie's backwoods experience from the campaigns against the Cherokee, and at some point the two men developed a warm friendship. Montague knew that Moultrie was one of the Unanimous Twenty-six and a proponent of nonimportation, but the governor may have hoped for a chance to bring him into the Tory camp. It would not be the last time Lord Montague would attempt to use their friendship to influence Moultrie's politics.[13]

The forty-one-year-old Moultrie departed North Hampton on May 16, 1772, for a journey of more than three weeks' duration. He took with him two slaves named Tobias and Dick, one five-gallon keg each of wine and rum, and for his bed only two blankets and a bearskin—tents were left behind. According to the journal he kept during the trip, on the first day he crossed the Santee River and covered thirty-five miles. He rendezvoused the next morning with indigo planter and Indian fighter Col. William Thomson, the other commissioner appointed by Montague, at Thomson's Belleville plantation in the parish of St. Matthew (later the Orangeburgh District) on the Congaree River.[14]

Thomson, born in 1727, served as a major of rangers during the Cherokee War and was also known to Moultrie from the Commons House of Assembly. The depth of their acquaintance at this point is unclear, but their paths became inseparably entwined in the future. The following day Moultrie and Thomson's party arrived at Camden, where it was joined by surveyors James Cook and Ephraim Mitchell. On May 20, after two days of hard travel, the group reached the termination point of the previous survey on the Salisbury road in the Waxhaws. There they were joined by the North Carolina delegation.[15]

The North Carolina contingent consisted of commissioners Col. John Rutherford and Col. William Dry and surveyors Col. Thomas Rutherford (John Rutherford's brother) and Capt. Thomas Polk. They were better equipped than their South Carolina counterparts, having brought chain carriers and trailblazers, probably slaves, and hauling their tents and gear in a wagon. Moultrie recorded that when the two parties met, "after the usual compliments and a glass or two of wine, we proceeded immediately to business."[16]

Having amicably agreed on procedural matters, the next morning the combined team of surveyors and commissioners embarked on thirteen continuous days of trailblazing and surveying, pausing only on Sunday, May 24, to visit Charlotte Town (Charlotte) in North Carolina. Along the way Moultrie made daily journal entries recording observations of the topography and the mileage traveled. He observed white settlements on the Catawba River that nearly encroached on Indian land, and he noted fine range for cattle. With future settlement in mind, Moultrie described certain terrain as very good and other lands as the worst he had ever seen. On the eighth day, the group camped two miles from Kings Mountain. A nearby wagon road ran to Charlestown some 180 miles distant by Moultrie's reckoning.[17]

The North and South Carolinians finished their work of surveying and marking sixty-two miles of boundary on June 2, 1772, when they reached the Cherokee Line at a point about six or seven miles below Tryon Mountain. Two days later the plats were completed and jointly signed by the surveyors and commissioners. In his journal Moultrie logged nearly 250 miles. The Commons House of Assembly paid him a generous seventeen hundred pounds for his work as a boundary commissioner. More important, he obtained some 9,500 acres of land in Craven County in the northern region of backcountry South Carolina and 5,100 acres across the border in Tryon County, North Carolina.[18]

4.

A Martial Spirit

On December 16, 1773, two hundred members of the Sons of Liberty dressed as Mohawk Indians dumped East India Company tea from three ships into Boston Harbor in an incident that later became known as the Boston Tea Party. In retaliation an outraged Parliament passed four new acts in 1774 to punish Massachusetts and to serve notice to the other twelve colonies that failure to comply with British policies would bring severe consequences. The Intolerable Acts (also called the Coercive Acts) was the collective name given by the colonists to the four punitive measures passed in 1774. The Intolerable Acts garnered considerable sympathy for the citizens of Massachusetts. Americans of all classes and occupations, whatever their misgivings over the expanding rift between Britain and her colonies, recognized the common threat to their liberty in these four acts. South Carolinians understood that if the port of Charlestown were to suffer the same ill fortune as Boston, the economy of South Carolina would be devastated.[1]

One of the best of the personal accounts of the Revolutionary War is William Moultrie's *Memoirs of the American Revolution*, a collection of extracts, orders, letters, journals, and commentary published in 1802. His memoirs open with an examination of Boston's response to the Intolerable Acts. On May 13, 1774, a Boston town meeting sent an appeal to the other colonies to cease importation from Great Britain and the West Indies until repeal of the Intolerable Acts was accomplished. When a copy of the deliberations of the Boston meeting reached Charlestown, the General Committee reacted by calling its own town meeting held at the Corner (Dillon's Tavern), a popular establishment at the corner of Broad and Church Streets. The committee decided to summon parish delegates to meet in Charlestown on July 6, 1774.[2]

The parish delegates, Moultrie included, met in the cellar under the Royal Exchange and Custom House, where they warmly debated the reinstitution of nonimportation. After several days they were unable to reach a consensus, and the matter was dropped. Historically nonimportation had been difficult to enforce and had ultimately failed in 1770 due to noncompliance. Nonetheless after considerable political wrangling between Charlestown's mechanics and merchants, the parish representatives chose five delegates to attend the First Continental Congress that was scheduled to convene to convene in Philadelphia on September 5. The chosen delegates were Thomas Lynch Sr., Christopher Gadsden, and John Rutledge, all veterans of the Stamp Act Congress, along with John's younger brother, Edward Rutledge, and Henry Middleton. In a controversial move, the Commons House of Assembly appropriated funds to cover the expenses of the delegates but authorized them only to agree to such *legal* measures that were likely to move Parliament to repeal the objectionable acts and redress American grievances.[3]

Before adjourning, the parish delegates appointed a Committee of Ninety-Nine composed of sixty-nine planters, fifteen mechanics, and fifteen merchants. This committee was empowered to correspond with the committees in the other colonies and for a time became the de facto government of South Carolina. Moultrie was one of the planters appointed to this important governing committee.[4]

Delegates from twelve of the thirteen colonies convened the First Continental Congress in Philadelphia on September 5. Only Georgia was unrepresented. By the time of adjournment on October 26, 1774, the Continental Congress had composed a Declaration of Rights and Grievances addressed to George III; adopted nonimportation, nonexportation, and nonconsumption agreements; and planned a second congress for May 1775. After considering the actions of the First Continental Congress, the Committee of Ninety-Nine called for a Provincial Congress of South Carolina, to consist of representatives from every parish and district. The first Provincial Congress met on January 11, 1775.[5]

The Committee of Ninety-Nine determined the apportionment of the representatives, and it is not surprising that they disproportionately favored the lowcountry. Most of the members previously elected to the Commons House of Assembly were reelected to the Provincial Congress, and likewise Moultrie was elected to represent the parish of St. Helena. "This is the manner in which the Representation of this Country was established at the Revolution," Moultrie wrote in his memoirs. "I am well acquainted with the circumstance, because I was there when it was agreed upon." The parish of St. Helena also returned him to the Second Congress on November 1, 1775. He served on various committees such as the Ways and Means Committee and the Committee for the State of the Colony. As a senior militia officer, he was an obvious choice to serve on the committee formed to frame rules and regulations for South Carolina's military force.[6]

The Provincial Congress of South Carolina met at the Exchange on January 11 and then promptly reconvened in the chamber of the Commons House of Assembly in the State House. After several days of deliberation, the assembled delegates ratified the actions of the Continental Congress. As a matter of formality, the Provincial Congress sent a message to Lt. Gov. William Bull on January 17, 1775, requesting that he seat the Commons House of Assembly for the conduct of public business. Bull was governing in the place of Lord Montague, who had departed the colony in 1773, and he adamantly refused to recognize formally the Provisional Congress. His refusal to convene the Commons House signaled the beginning of the end of royal authority in South Carolina.[7]

On the day of the exchange of messages between the Provincial Congress and Lieutenant Governor Bull, the representatives in the Provincial Congress recommended that the people of South Carolina diligently train themselves in the use of arms and that their officers muster them for training once a fortnight. Without alluding to his direct role, Moultrie noted the enthusiasm that pervaded the lowcountry. "Agreeable to a recommendation of the Provincial Congress, the militia were forming themselves into volunteer companies; drums beating, fifes playing; squads of men exercising on the outskirts of town; a military spirit pervaded the whole country; and Charlestown had the appearance of a garrison town; every thing wore the face of war; though not one of us had the least idea of its approach."[8]

Outward appearances to the contrary, South Carolina was not politically homogenous, and many lowcountry inhabitants were by no means ready to take measures that might permanently sever ties with the England. Moultrie was a moderate. He was not like the agitator Christopher Gadsden or the royalist turned ardent revolutionary William Henry Drayton. He did not make fiery speeches or publish incendiary pamphlets. Instead he worked in the Commons House of Assembly, on extralegal committees, and in the Provincial Congress to counter what he understood to be egregious abuse of power at the hands of Parliament. But when the tocsin of war finally sounded, Moultrie stood ready to unsheathe his sword in defense of his home.[9]

The distressing news of the Battles of Lexington and Concord fought between British regulars and Massachusetts militiamen on April 19, 1775, demonstrated the British Ministry's resolve to quell colonial grievances by force of arms rather than by peaceable means. This, combined with rumors of a black insurrection instigated by the royal government, gave the inhabitants of Charlestown good reason to be alarmed. A war seemed to be inevitable. Their foe would be the country that had planted them in America, a country with which they shared consanguinity, a common language and culture, a religion, and a legal system. Great Britain was one of the most powerful nations on the earth, and her armies and navies, with their able generals and experienced admirals, appeared to be invincible. "This great nation we dared to oppose," Moultrie said, remarking on the apparent hopelessness of the American situation, "without money; without arms; without ammunition; no generals; no armies; no admirals; and no fleets; this was our situation when the contest began."[10]

A war on the North American continent that pitted poorly organized colonists against such a powerful adversary would by virtue of these circumstances be fought defensively. Comprehending this, the Provincial Congress organized South Carolina into twelve militia districts. In each district the militiamen were organized into a regiment of infantry. Because of the diversity of political opinion in the districts, particularly in the backcountry districts, the Provincial Congress worried that the compulsory militia would be unreliable. Volunteer regiments were needed, and to that end the Congress passed a resolution on June 6, 1775, authorizing two infantry regiments of 750 men each for use on the coast and a regiment of 450 mounted rangers for use in the backcountry.[11]

The field grade and company grade officers of the First and Second Provincial Regiments of Foot, chosen by congressional ballot on June 9, were mostly rich, propertied gentlemen who were willing to risk their substantial fortunes for the sake of principle. Experience gained against the Cherokees was a factor that was weighed in the balance. The Provincial Congress gave Christopher Gadsden the colonelcy of the First Regiment and selected Moultrie to lead the Second Regiment. Moultrie's future brother-in-law, Isaac Motte, became his lieutenant colonel, and Alexander McIntosh was elected major. Francis Marion began as a company captain, but he was promoted to major in February 1776. Moultrie's younger brother Thomas was elected first lieutenant, and the colonel's son, William Jr., was appointed second lieutenant.[12]

The uniform coats and caps of the First and Second Regiments were reminiscent of the uniforms worn by the Provincial Regiment of 1760. Colonel Moultrie ordered every officer to "provide himself with a blue cloth coatee, faced and cuffed with scarlet cloth, and lined with scarlet . . . also, a cap and black feather." On the front of the cap was a silver or white metal crescent. The crescent of the First Regiment was engraved with the Latin motto "Ultima Ratio," which means "Force as the last resort," and the crescent of the Second Regiment was engraved with the motto "Liberty or Death" (or perhaps just "Liberty").[13]

On June 14 the Provincial Congress created a civil body to carry out the business of the colony when Congress was in recess. This thirteen-man Council of Safety was vested with great power, its authority extending to command of the army. Civilian control of the military was established as a precedent, and for this reason no military officer in the service of the colony could occupy a seat upon the council. Despite the enormity of the measures that had been instituted to govern South Carolina beyond the bounds of royal authority, some members of the Council of Safety saw their position as a forlorn hope. They were hesitant to issue money, give orders to the military, or issue commissions for concern that these acts would appear to independent or, at worst, treasonous. Rather than a proper commission issued under seal, Moultrie thus received a paper certificate dated June 17, 1775, and worded, "In Pursuance of the Resolutions of the Provincial Congress, We do *Certify* [emphasis added], that William Moultrie, Esq. is Colonel of the Second Regiment of Foot in the Provincial Service."[14]

Gadsden was attending the Second Continental Congress when the regiments were organized, and he remained there until February 1776. In the interim Moultrie commanded both regiments. Moultrie and his staff began recruiting as soon as they were appointed, and he was pleased to report to the Council of Safety on July 17, 1775, that after only one month, 470 men from around Charlestown had enlisted. Moultrie considered this a good indication of how zealous the people were in the cause. In August he sent officers of the First and Second Regiments to Virginia, North Carolina, and the South Carolina backcountry seeking recruits. When they came down, the new enlistees were sent to the barracks in Charlestown for training.[15]

Moultrie left South Carolina for New York City during the last week of July. He does not mention this episode in his memoirs, but writing to Gadsden in Philadelphia, he confessed that he was "forced to seek for health in this happier climate." Neither did he specify to Gadsden the nature of his complaints, but it is known that Moultrie suffered from gout and malaria, a relapsing mosquito-borne disease that was endemic to the lowcountry. Whatever the cause, Moultrie was not gone from Charlestown for very long. He took advantage in his correspondence with Gadsden to pass along a request from Lt. Isaac Huger for thirty-five epaulettes and fifes and drums for the First Regiment.[16]

As the commanding officer of a freshly recruited regiment, Moultrie faced a challenge—despite their appearance in their new blue, red, and white uniforms, these were not parade-ground soldiers. The officers were reliable, but the enlisted men were another matter—some were forced to enlist as a punishment for crime or vagrancy. It was hoped that recruiting in the backcountry would bring in hardy young farmers looking for an opportunity to better their social standing. Instead many of the rank-and-file soldiers came from the lower rungs of the social ladder, and companies were filled with vagabonds, thieves, unemployed sailors, and British deserters. Courts-martial were common, and harsh discipline was often required to maintain order. Maintaining order was made all the more difficult by familiarity and fraternization between the officers and men, and Moultrie would develop a reputation for fraternization.[17]

Many of the new recruits were strangers, and their allegiance was unproven. A Secret Committee composed of five gentlemen appointed to procure arms and ammunition, admonished Moultrie that great care should be taken to secure the regiments' stores. The committee recommended that only sentries known to be friends of liberty should be given duty guarding the ammunition. Moultrie commented in his memoirs that such was the suspicion of some men—tactfully referring to certain members of the committee—that the fidelity of the soldiers who were to fight their battles was in doubt.[18]

By mid-September seven hundred recruits had enlisted, though recruiting had been hindered by a shortage of cash to pay enlistment bounties. The long and grueling march from Virginia, North Carolina, and the South Carolina backcountry had taken its toll on the men brought in from these regions; a number of them had contracted a fever, and the hospitals were soon full. And there had been problems in town with drunkenness, insubordination to officers, and a host of other offenses committed by men who were unaccustomed to military authority. Moultrie arranged for them to be moved across the Cooper River to Mount Pleasant, where barracks would be constructed. Conditions were more healthful there, and Moultrie and his officers could keep a tighter rein on the troops, unlike in Charlestown, where liquor was easily obtained.[19]

5.

The Dawn of Revolution

The last royal governor of South Carolina arrived in Charlestown on June 17, 1775, on board the *Scorpion,* bearing instructions to restore the colony to royal hegemony. A Scotsman by birth, Lord William Campbell had close ties to the port city. He had served the Royal Navy, commanding a ship stationed in Charlestown Harbor in 1763, and had married Miss Sarah Izard, a daughter from a prominent Charlestown family. Campbell received a chilly, even sullen reception from the town's populace when he landed.[1]

Three days passed before Campbell received a visit from a delegation of the Provincial Congress that included William Moultrie as a member. The delegation presented an address to the new governor that set forth the sentiments that had for so long been the disposition of many South Carolinians. Whereas the actions of the British government and the British army had compelled His Majesty's loyal American subjects to organize and arm themselves, the people still hoped for a speedy reconciliation with their mother country. Any reconciliation, however, would have to have constitutional principles as its foundation.[2]

Like his immediate predecessor, William Bull, Lord Campbell also refused to recognize the Provincial Congress. But unlike Bull, Campbell was arrogantly dismissive of colonial grievances and warned of the fatal consequences of the provincials' actions. Campbell turned out to be a wolf in sheep's clothing, and his tenure in Charlestown was destined to be brief. A storm of popular indignation arose when it came to light that the governor had been acting surreptitiously to provoke backcountry Loyalists against the revolutionary government and to incite the Indians to "lift the hatchet for the king." Were that not enough, suspicions that Campbell had requested British reinforcements turned out to be true.[3]

The mood in Charlestown descended into a general state of anxiety, and the royal sloops *Tamar* and *Cherokee* lying in Rebellion Road, the channel between Fort Johnson and Sullivan's Island, only heightened the sense of trouble and uneasiness. Just the loosening of their sails was enough to cause an alarm to be spread immediately through town that attack was imminent. Moreover the warehouse district of Charlestown, located on the Cooper River waterfront, stored enough tar, pitch, and turpentine to turn Charlestown into ashes if ignited by bombardment. Compounding this fear of an attack on the town was the widespread expectation that British reinforcements might sail into the harbor on any day.[4]

Positive action was required. On September 14, 1775, the Council of Safety ordered Moultrie to dispatch 150 men to capture Fort Johnson on the east end of James Island. Erected in 1708 of bricks and sand on a promontory known as Windmill Hill, an enlargement of this fragile fort had begun during the French and Indian War but had never reached completion. Fort Johnson now existed in a perpetual state of disrepair. Its strength, however, was in its twenty-one guns: seven twenty-six-pounders, twelve eighteen-pounders, one twelve-pounder, and one nine-pounder. The fort commanded the narrow southern channel used by ships to approach Charlestown from the sea and was the only harbor stronghold still in the possession of the British. Moultrie's orders from the council emphasized the importance of maintaining the utmost secrecy.[5]

Moultrie in turn directed Lt. Col. Isaac Motte to take overall command of the expedition. Motte was one of the most experienced military men in the colony, having held a British army commission in His Majesty's Sixtieth Royal American Regiment while serving in Canada during the French and Indian War. The force under his command consisted of Capt. Charles Cotesworth Pinckney's and Capt. Barnard Elliott's grenadier companies, supported by Capt. Francis Marion's light infantry. Fifty men of the James Island militia joined with the provincial troops for the mission.[6]

Motte's contingent proceeded quietly under the cover of darkness at midnight on September 15. Embarking from Gadsden's Wharf on the Cooper River around midnight, the assault force landed on a mud flat about a quarter mile from the fort. The light of dawn threatened to compromise the element of surprise, but the South Carolinians, who expected stiff resistance, resolutely waded ashore in waist-deep water. The raid turned out to be both uncontested and anticlimactic. Anticipating the attack, the British had dismounted the fort's guns from their carriages and absconded with most of its store of gunpowder when they abandoned the fort a few hours before the Americans landed.[7]

The capture of Fort Johnson had consequences beyond the American occupation of a British stronghold. The very day Moultrie's men seized Fort Johnson, Lord Campbell dissolved the Commons House of Assembly and fled to safety aboard the *Tamar*, vowing never to return to Charlestown until he could uphold the king's authority and protect His Majesty's loyal subjects. Royal government in the province of South Carolina totally ceased, and the fate of South Carolina was completely in the hands of the Patriot government.[8]

The *Tamar* and *Cherokee* moved in to attack Fort Johnson the following morning but when the tide and prevailing winds prevented them from making more than a demonstration, they returned to their anchorage in Rebellion Road. The possibility of another attempt on the fort by the ships prompted Moultrie to strengthen the garrison at Fort Johnson with an additional 250 men. Capt. Thomas Heyward Jr.'s company of Charlestown Artillery, using gin and tackle, had three cannons remounted almost immediately. Directing Motte to defend the fort against any British landing party, Moultrie also cautioned his friend to withdraw his men to safety beyond the range of cannon should the *Tamar* open a bombardment. He put the officers of the two South Carolina regiments on high alert and sent gunpowder, ordnance stores, and public records to Dorchester for safekeeping.[9]

Several accounts of the seizure of Fort Johnson suggest that a new banner was raised within days of the fort's capture. Moultrie's memoirs, written nearly twenty-five years after the fact, probably form the basis of these anecdotes:

> A little time after we were in possession of Fort Johnson, it was thought necessary to have a flag for the purpose of signals: (as there was no national or state flag at that time) I was desired by the Council of Safety to have one made, upon which, as the state troops were clothed in blue, and the fort was garrisoned by the first and second regiments, who wore a silver crescent on the front of their caps; I had a large blue flag made with a crescent in the dexter corner, to be in uniform with the troops: This was the first American flag which was displayed in South Carolina: On its being first hoisted, it gave some uneasiness to our timid friends, who were looking forward to a reconciliation: They said it had the appearance of a declaration of war.[10]

Over the next month, workmen floated two thousand palmetto logs across the harbor to refortify the tabby walls of Fort Johnson, and they constructed a new battery just west of the fort. The strength of the fort's garrison was augmented by at least five hundred men who camped in tents on James Island, both for the sake of their health and to shield them from the temptation of liquor that was so readily available in town. Moultrie's soldiers made a handsome appearance. They were well armed, well accoutered, and well clothed. Drill instilled discipline as they learned the evolutions of infantry and artillery. In time they began to look and feel like soldiers.[11]

Not everyone was pleased with the progress at Fort Johnson. Writing privately to Christopher Gadsden on October 3, 1775, Thomas Ferguson, a member of the Council of Safety, implored him to come home: "Our little army really wants you; Col. Moultrie is a very good man, but very indolent and easy, so that things go on very slow. We have had the Fort in possession about twenty days, and he was desired to put it in good order as soon as possible, and spare no expense, but there is very little done."[12]

The camp on James Island was more than just a training camp, however. A report circulated that the *Tamar* and *Cherokee* intended to pass the fort and attack the town. In November the Council instructed Moultrie to oppose the passage of these ships by any military means necessary. He clearly understood that this order was the first authorization actually to fire upon the British. To carry out his orders, the Council of Safety kept Moultrie's force well supplied with powder and ammunition, most of it confiscated from the king's stockpiles.[13]

As the Carolinians worked to fortify their town against an incursion from the harbor, Moultrie took charge of repairing and enlarging the city's old batteries—Broughton's, Lyttelton's, Grenville's, and Craven's—and building new ones at several wharves along the Cooper riverfront and on a commanding piece of ground to the west of Fort Johnson. Lookout posts were erected on the sea islands. Residents of Charlestown who were able to bear arms were asked not to leave, and those who were absent were asked to return. Several militia companies were activated, while others were held in reserve. Charlestown began to take on the appearance of an armed fortress.[14]

In the Provincial Congress, new schemes for Charlestown's defense were proposed and debated. A case in point was a plan to prevent enemy vessels from entering the harbor by sinking thirty-one schooners in the two main channels that passed through the Charlestown Bar, a shallow but obstructive sandbar that ran north-south for several miles just outside of the harbor. Another suggestion made was to abandon the town and build a defensive line across the Charlestown Neck. Moultrie referred to this idea as curious and ridiculous, and he would have known—he was one of four commissioners appointed to explore the proposal. During the debate of the commissioner's report in Congress, "a gentlemen very shrewdly observed, that we may as well build a wall round a Cuckoo to keep him in, as to suppose these lines would prevent the enemy from going into the country."[15]

What Moultrie does not say in his memoirs about the fortification of Charlestown is as revealing as what he does. It had been decided to defend the town to the last extremity, yet there was an absence of defenses on the land side. Apprehension about an attack from the sea had almost become an obsession, yet there was little if any anxiety at all over the possibility of an overland assault from the rear. Nor were any measures taken to defend against one. The immediate consequences of this inactivity would be minimal, but there were dire consequences later on.[16]

As arrangements for harbor defense were underway on land, the Carolinians were hardly inactive on the water. The Provincial Congress launched a small navy, and Moultrie played a role by furnishing soldiers for service as marines. In November 1775 two pilot boats were taken into service, armed, and manned for a ten-day cruise out through Stono Inlet and along the coast to the north of the bar. So positioned, they could warn vessels away from the harbor lest they be captured by the *Tamar* or *Cherokee*. Congress ordered Moultrie to provide nine privates and a sergeant for duty aboard each of the two pilot boats. This was considered hazardous duty, and during the time that they were employed in this service the soldiers received double pay. With the port blocked by the British men-of-war, many sailors had been discharged from their vessels and had had no alternative but to enlist in the army to keep from starving. Moultrie detailed many of the shore-bound sailors to man these boats and armed schooners. These pilot boats maintained their watch well into 1776, and Moultrie shifted men from boat to boat as needed.[17]

Moultrie detached a captain and thirty-five privates to act as marines on board the *Defence,* a schooner that was fitted out with two nine-pounders, six six-pounders, and two four-pound guns and sent to guard the mouth of Wappoo Creek. These marines saw action on November 11 when the *Defence* engaged the *Cherokee* and the *Tamar* while covering the sinking of hulks to obstruct the mouth of Hog Island Channel.[18]

The purpose of the mission, a more reasonable alternative to the ill-conceived plan to sink ships on the bar, was to block British ships from gaining access to the Cooper River via the secondary Hog Island Channel and to force them to pass under the guns of Charlestown's batteries if they attempted to sail upriver. Shots were exchanged between the *Defence* and her British adversaries, though little damage was done. Moultrie declared this skirmish to be the commencement of hostilities (in terms of the actual shooting war) in South Carolina. Fort Johnson managed three shots from her twenty-six-pounders at the *Tamar* during the engagement but ceased fire for lack of range. It was said that during this affair the *Defence* flew an indigo-colored provincial flag from her masts.[19]

At different times Moultrie also detached forty to fifty privates from the regiments to serve as guards aboard the *Prosper,* a merchant ship impressed into the service of the colony, armed with twenty guns of various calibers and fitted out as a frigate of war. The mission of the *Prosper* was to guard the harbor and prevent ships from entering or leaving, to gather intelligence, to support Fort Johnson, and if possible, to capture or sink the *Tamar* and *Cherokee* in Rebellion Road. William Henry Drayton eventually became captain of the *Prosper.* Moultrie was seldom inclined to make disparaging remarks about others, however about

Drayton he commented that though the man was a "gentleman of great abilities, he was no sailor and did not know any one rope in the ship from another."[20]

Thus far little mention has been made of Moultrie's personal life other than broad generalizations based on what is known about the life of lowcountry planters in the middle of the eighteenth century. The historical record is mostly silent concerning Moultrie's wife, Damaris Elizabeth, with one exception. The *South Carolina and American General Gazette* reported her death on Friday, November 24, 1775. She was forty-seven years old. No details of her demise were given in the *Gazette,* although the obituary noted that she was esteemed and respected by all who knew her and that her death was an irreparable loss to her relations and acquaintances. Her cause of death was most likely an illness, but whether it was acute or chronic is unknown. Nor is it known whether she died in town or at North Hampton, as no record or evidence of her grave has been located. In keeping with his practice of avoiding comments of a personal nature in his memoirs, her bereaved husband does not mention the tragic event.[21]

Providing security for the harbor brought Moultrie into a delicate situation on December 15, 1775, when two small boats attempting to reach the *Cherokee* via Hog Island Channel were intercepted by the provincial guard at Gadsden's Wharf. Lady Campbell, the former Sarah Izard of Charlestown, had joined her husband on the *Cherokee.* The captured boats were carrying two of Lord Campbell's domestic servants, three black people, unspecified property of the inhabitants of Charlestown, provisions, and letters. The Council ordered Moultrie to restore to Lady Campbell all items of apparel belonging to her or her children and to dispose of the other articles for the use of the troops in any way he deemed proper.[22]

Fort Johnson was secure, the ad hoc navy had commenced maritime operations in the harbor, and the batteries in Charlestown were ready to defend the city if British ships came within range. The Council of Safety determined that the next step would be to place artillery on Haddrell's Point and Sullivan's Island to threaten the British ships in Rebellion Road. The Royal Navy would be forced either to change their station or to leave the harbor outright. As an added benefit, a battery on Haddrell's Point would also give the provincials command of the cove at the back of Sullivan's Island and would allow free passage between the island and Haddrell's Point. This plan had been considered before and abandoned as being too dangerous for fear of provoking attack from the ships in the harbor, which now numbered three with the arrival of the *Scorpion* on November 29. But when Sullivan's Island became haven for runaway slaves and a staging point for British sallies along the coast of Christ Church Parish, the Council decided that the gains were worth the risks.[23]

The plan came to naught, at least at first. A secret 150-man expedition sent by Colonel Moultrie to Sullivan's Island to capture escaped slaves, Loyalists, and

British sailors camping on the island was forced to turn back when a frustrated Maj. Charles Cotesworth Pinckney was unable to find a suitable ford to cross to the island from Haddrell's Point. Accordingly Moultrie received new instructions on December 17 to erect a fascine battery for four cannons at Haddrell's Point. Moultrie assigned his young friend Pinckney to the task, which he accomplished with the help of twelve junior officers and two hundred privates, together with a number of mechanics and laborers. The Council ordered Col. Benjamin Huger of the Regiment of Artillery to take enough artillerists to work his four eighteen-pound brass field pieces, and Moultrie ordered Capt. Barnard Beekman of the artillery to provide the ammunition for the cannon.[24]

Moultrie assembled his force at Gadsden's Wharf on the bitterly cold evening of December 19. The moon showed only a sliver of a waning crescent, so the darkness of the night helped to cover their movement. Slowed by a contrary tide, the artillerists and supporting light infantrymen from the First Regiment crossed the Cooper River and landed in Shem Creek near Mount Pleasant at sunrise the next morning. Moultrie and Dr. David Oliphant followed with a contingent of gentlemen volunteers, the First's grenadiers. The ordnance and baggage train brought up the rear. Despite the unpleasant conditions, the detachment was in high spirits over the prospect of surprising the British sloops that had threatened their city for months. Work began in earnest at sunset on December 21.[25]

"Everyone fell to work," Moultrie later wrote, recounting the expedition, "and by day-light [on December 23] we were ourselves well covered [from the ship's armament], and in a few hours more, laid our platforms, and some guns mounted, and shortly after, opened our embrasures." Under the very noses of the British, the Carolinians had constructed earthworks twenty-four feet thick strengthened by fascines (rough bundles of sticks or branches tied together), and mounted two of their eighteen-pounders. Moultrie ordered the artillerists to open fire at about a mile's distance, and a few shots from the "Bull Dogs," as the soldiers called them, caused the *Tamar* and the *Cherokee* (the *Scorpion* had departed a few weeks before) immediately to move their stations and fall back opposite Sullivan's Island a mile or more offshore. The hard night's work left the South Carolinians weary but jubilant.[26]

Part II

6.

Open Rebellion

The entrance to Charlestown Harbor is guarded on its northern shore by Sullivan's Island, which extends northeasterly about four miles. The northern end of Sullivan's Island is separated from Long Island (now Isle of Palms) by a narrow inlet that at the time of the Revolutionary War was said be fordable. Long Island extends some six miles farther up the coast to the northeast, where it is in turn separated from Dewees Island by a broader inlet.[1]

Moultrie described Sullivan's Island at the time of the Revolution as being quite a wilderness covered with live oak, myrtle, and palmetto trees. The deep, loose sand was ill-suited for the movement of troops and artillery, and a thick, deep swamp occupied what would be the most strategically advantageous point. Accessibility from the sea was subject to the vagary of the tides, and the island was not easily reached from the landward side on account of immense tracts of green salt marshes that lay between the islands and the mainland. Sullivan's Island was a natural fortress.[2]

The British withdrawal from Rebellion Road gave control of the cove between Haddrell's Point and Sullivan's Island to the South Carolinians. Better still, on January 6, 1776, the Council of Safety learned that the British ships had left the harbor altogether. When the British sloops headed southward for Savannah, Georgia, they carried the last royal governor of South Carolina with them. A collective sigh of relief was in order, but there was no time for complacency. Two days after the British sails disappeared over the horizon, a committee from the Council of Safety visited the southern tip of Sullivan's Island, and after an inspection tour, they recommended fortification of the site.[3]

The Council ordered Lt. Col. Owen Roberts of the Provincial Regiment of Artillery to erect a temporary battery to defend the position while more permanent structures were built. The fort would be constructed not of tabby but of palmetto logs. The Council contracted with Cornelius Dewees for the delivery of the indigenous logs to Sullivan's Island—as many as he could as fast as he could, until he received orders stating otherwise. By the Council's specification, the logs were to be at least ten inches in diameter, a third of them to measure eighteen feet in length, and the other two-thirds to be twenty feet long. Over the months that followed, thousands of palmetto logs were rafted to Sullivan's Island from the mainland by black work gangs.[4]

On January 10 the Council of Safety ordered Moultrie to detach one hundred men, with proper officers, from each of the colony's two infantry regiments to take post on Sullivan's Island to cover the men at work erecting the fort. To expedite the movement, Moultrie sent from the garrison at Fort Johnson two companies who were ferried across the harbor aboard Captain Simon Tufts's schooner, *Defence*. A few days later, Tufts likewise transported artillerists and two field pieces of the Charlestown Artillery from Fort Johnson to Sullivan's Island.[5]

The decision to transfer these forces to Sullivan's Island was prescient. On January 11 two British warships, the twenty-eight-gun *Syren* and the eighteen-gun *Raven*, materialized off the bar, along with a single-masted sloop. When a ten-oared barge manned by a lieutenant and fourteen armed men rowed into the harbor to gather intelligence, the men in Fort Johnson opened fire. The barge, in turn, exchanged a few shots with an armed pilot boat in the harbor. The arrival of these British frigates warranted immediate action. The Council expedited the transfer of troops from Fort Johnson and ordered Captain Tufts to anchor the *Defence* near Sullivan's Island.[6]

Moultrie and Tufts were directed to open fire on any British vessel that came within range. The reappearance of British warships offshore, combined with a threat made by the lieutenant commanding the barge to return to "make the Commander of the Fort smart for his Insolence" and to "batter the Fort & Town about their Ears," threw Charlestown's inhabitants back into the turmoil that had subsided only days before when the *Tamar* and *Cherokee* departed. Moreover the whereabouts of the *Tamar* and *Cherokee* were unknown, and the expectation of their return to Charlestown was a source of great trepidation.[7]

British threats aside, Moultrie believed Charlestown was capable of repelling an attack from the sea. Fort Johnson and all of the town's batteries were finished and ready for action. His greatest fear was that the distraction of an engagement with the British warships might allow "enemies which we had among us" to engage in acts of arson and fire the town. When the Council of Safety requested his plan for the town's defense, he gave explicit instructions and put them into effect. He posted the regiment of Charlestown militia at the State House and various corners in town, along with sufficient numbers of black men equipped with fire engines, fire hooks, ropes, and axes to extinguish any fires rapidly. If a fire broke out at night, men from the guardhouse were to climb into the steeple of St. Michael's Church and point out the direction using a lantern mounted on a pole. Moultrie assigned other militia companies to occupy various wharfs, bastions, and batteries, and he strengthened key positions with detachments of provincial soldiers.[8]

While Moultrie deployed his troops in Charlestown, the Council reinforced Haddrell's Point with several companies of militia. Acting on orders from the council, Lt. Col. William Thomson also sent sixty-six riflemen and eight officers over to Sullivan's Island on January 13. Thomson, the redoubtable Scotch Irish Indian fighter given the sobriquet "Old Danger" by his men, was a reliable officer in whom Moultrie placed great trust. Twenty-eight prisoners who had declared themselves willing to assist with the construction of the works on Sullivan's Island accompanied Thomson's rangers.[9]

During the next week, teams hauled four twelve-pounders from the lines on Charlestown Neck and sent them to the battery at Haddrell's Point. This allowed larger eighteen-pounders that were at Haddrell's Point to be shifted to the battery on Sullivan's Island. By January 20 workmen had fully mounted five guns, and crews labored to strengthen the defensive position. The next day the Council of Safety sent more armament to Sullivan's Island—three large twenty-six-pounders collected from batteries around Charlestown. The Council charged Capt. Edward Blake with providing proper boats and men to transport cannons and stores from town to Sullivan's Island. Moving large guns was arduous and often dangerous work that did not always go quite according to plan. A flatboat laden with cannons bound for Sullivan's Island ran aground on the spit in Hog Island Channel. Fortunately the stranded vessel was refloated before the guns were lost.[10]

South Carolina's most radical delegate to the Continental Congress, Christopher Gadsden, arrived from Philadelphia on the night of February 8. Gadsden had been recalled from Philadelphia to resume his military duties in the face of the ongoing emergency, and he lost no time immersing himself in the business of the Provincial Congress. In addition to a copy of Thomas Paine's pamphlet *Common Sense,* Gadsden brought a recommendation from the Continental Congress based on credible intelligence of an impending British expedition to attack places in Virginia, North Carolina, and Charlestown. Charlestown, advised the Continental Congress, should "by all possible means, prepare to make a vigorous defence and opposition."[11]

Citing the absolute necessity of maintaining a considerable force for the colony's defense in a time of imminent danger, the Provincial Congress acted on February 22, 1776, to bring the First and Second Regiments and the Regiment of Rangers up to full strength. The Congress also authorized an additional regiment of expert riflemen as the Fifth Regiment and approved the addition of three new artillery companies for the defense of Beaufort, Georgetown, and Charlestown. Five days later a motion was made and passed in favor of a Sixth Regiment to consist primarily of riflemen. Thomas Sumter was duly elected this regiment's commanding officer at the rank of lieutenant colonel.[12]

So that there might be warning of approaching ships, the Council of Safety approved new signals for use at the lighthouse on Morris Island, on Sullivan's Island, and at Fort Johnson. These new signals supplanted the firing of signal guns specified in the militia law: six discharges fired two at a time at three-minute intervals. Instead signal flags would be used, and only in the case of foggy weather would the guns be fired. On January 26, 1776, the Council ordered Moultrie to develop these new signals and the next day sent him "two whole pieces and 23 yards of new blue cloth." The historical record does not categorically indicate that the blue signal flags were to adhere to Moultrie's flag design that had become the colony's banner, but circumstantial evidence is strong. In March, Colonel Gadsden ordered the men of his regiment to raise and lower the new provincial flag once for every man-of-war that appeared offshore.[13]

Among the several roles that Moultrie played as one of the senior military officers in Charlestown was that of acting provost marshal. As provost Moultrie bore responsibility for the safekeeping and security of detained or paroled Loyalists and suspected enemies of the revolutionary government. This duty could extend to their immediate families.

One example is the case of Sarah Stuart, the wife of British superintendent of Indian affairs John Stuart, a notorious and fiery Loyalist who was suspected of stirring up the Catawba and Cherokee tribes against the provincials. Stuart was arrested in June 1775, but he escaped and fled to West Florida. In February 1776 Mrs. Stuart and her daughter were placed under house arrest in the Stuarts' Charlestown home on Tradd Street. As a courtesy to the lady, Moultrie sent two officers to inform her of her arrest before he posted a guard to prevent her from leaving, and measures were taken to avert any disturbance of the family's property. Sarah Stuart was able to receive visitors only with Moultrie's permission, and visitors were received only if accompanied by an officer appointed by Moultrie. She could travel with the colonel's express permission, but only with an officer as her escort. Despite these precautions, Mrs. Stuart and her daughter somehow slipped away to Florida, where she joined her husband.[14]

Without actual constitutional authority, the Continental Congress had assumed and exercised some of the powers of a sovereign nation—raising an army, for example. In truth no organized national government existed, nor was there any established constitutional government in the colonies. The colonies had defied, even overthrown the royal and proprietary governments, or as in the case of

South Carolina, the royal government had abandoned the colony, but actual representative government had not yet been formally instituted. Instead, as in South Carolina, the provincial assemblies governed the various colonies by extra-legal committees and councils. Even though the need for separate and independent governments for the colonies was apparent, a prevailing sentiment existed, particularly among moderates in South Carolina, that the formation of a new government would be a temporary measure adopted until reconciliation with Great Britain was accomplished.[15]

Under a proposed constitution, the Provincial Congress would reconvene as a General Assembly that would elect from its ranks a thirteen-member Legislative Council. These two legislative bodies would then elect a president and vice president. The vice president would preside over the Privy Council, the president's advisory board composed of three members from the General Assembly and from the Legislative Council. The conservatives opposed this new government on the grounds that it truly lacked full and free representation as called for by the Continental Congress.[16]

The debates over a new constitution and government ended on March 21, 1776, when the Provisional Congress received a packet from Savannah that contained a copy of an act of Parliament of December 21, 1775. Great Britain had declared the colonies to be in open rebellion. Furthermore the act authorized the capture of American shipping and legalized all seizures of persons and property that had occurred before the passing of the act. The moderates were galvanized into decisive action, and the new constitution was adopted on March 26, 1776. Thus in South Carolina was established the first independent legally defined government in America. John Rutledge was elected president, and Henry Laurens was elected vice president.[17]

How often Moultrie was present during the debates that preceded the establishment of the new government is unknown, but he retained his seat in the General Assembly representing the parish of St. Helena. On March 28 he was elected to the Legislative Council to fill the vacancy left by the election of Laurens to the vice presidency, demonstrating his peers' appreciation of his numerous abilities. His military duties prevented him from taking his seat until September 1776. Half-brother Alexander Moultrie became the attorney general. When the General Assembly adjourned on April 11, the Council of Safety and General Committee were abolished, and the president and Privy Council were left to carry out government functions in their place.[18]

Gadsden, the ranking provincial colonel, assumed command of the troops defending Charlestown Harbor on February 13. He made his headquarters at Fort Johnson, the position generally considered to be the key to the defense of the harbor and the town. The Council of Safety gave Gadsden responsibility for the western battery on James Island and the construction of the batteries on Sullivan's Island and Haddrell's Point as well as oversight of the bastions and batteries in Charlestown. All of these duties had thus far been performed by Moultrie, who had presided over the capture of Fort Johnson and the occupation of Haddrell's Point, provided marines for the province's fledgling navy, and assigned troop dispositions for the defense of Charlestown and Sullivan's Island.[19]

Instead of being relegated to a secondary role, on March 2—just two weeks into Gadsden's resumption of authority—Moultrie received orders giving him command of Sullivan's Island. According to Moultrie this spot was now considered the key to the harbor rather than Fort Johnson. And with intelligence received that the British at New York were preparing for an expedition against Charlestown, a decision had been made not to limit the Sullivan's Island defenses to batteries but to construct a fort large enough for a thousand men.[20]

It is more likely that Gadsden, with his fiery persona and radical politics, was given command over that which was mostly finished in order to free Moultrie to concentrate on the fortification of Sullivan's Island. In the end there is no evidence to suggest that Gadsden and Moultrie operated in a way other than cooperatively. The Provincial Congress named both men to a committee formed to delineate the duties of a muster-master general that would be appointed for the colony's naval and land forces. If Moultrie perceived any affront at the hands of either Gadsden or the Council, he would soon be vindicated.[21]

7.

"I never was uneasy"

To grasp the magnitude of the tactical events that reached their climax on June 28, 1776, it is useful to review the overall strategic situation on the North American continent. The first year of the Revolutionary War was by and large inconclusive. Little of note had happened militarily in the South during 1775 other than the taking of Fort Johnson in Charlestown Harbor. There were the minor exchanges between South Carolina's little navy and the British ships in the harbor, skirmishes in the backcountry between Patriots and Loyalists at Ninety-Six and the Great Cane Brake, and the few shots from Sullivan's Island that drove the British from Rebellion Road. The seat of the emerging national government was in Philadelphia. Gen. George Washington's nascent Continental Army had the British bottled up in Boston, and it appeared that the northern colonies would be the epicenter of the conflict.

The British strategy formulated during the early part of 1776 was to isolate and conquer New England. This plan would be accomplished by a campaign that would commence by the summertime. In the meantime royal governors in exile Josiah Martin of North Carolina and Lord William Campbell of South Carolina convinced the British government that southern Loyalists would rise en masse and destroy the rebels if they were assisted by British regulars. Restoration of royal government in the southern colonies would have profound consequences for the entire continent. And if this scheme failed, the British could at minimum establish a coastal base from which to launch raids into the interior. North Carolina was the proposed campaign's primary objective, but Charlestown, the region's center of commerce, was a favored discretionary target.[1]

Fifteen hundred seasoned redcoats,* consisting of light infantry and High-landers under the command of Bunker Hill veteran Maj. Gen. Sir Henry Clinton sailed south from Boston on January 20, 1776. Clinton proceeded to Cape Fear on the coast of North Carolina, where he intended to aid a Loyalist uprising. This plan was wrecked when Patriot militia routed Scottish loyalists at Moore's Creek Bridge near Wilmington on February 27, 1776. Rather than mounting a campaign in North Carolina, Clinton remained at Cape Fear to await the arrival of a naval squadron from Cork, Ireland, commanded by Cdre. Sir Peter Parker. Parker's transports carried Maj. Gen. Charles Earl Cornwallis with seven British army regiments and two companies of Royal Artillery—about twenty-five hundred men altogether.[2]

After enduring a grueling, three-month ocean voyage during which his ships encountered days of violent storms and high seas, Parker and his weather-beaten squadron finally arrived at Cape Fear on May 3. Parker was aware of the slowly progressing construction of a fort on Sullivan's Island in Charlestown Harbor. The uncompleted fort was vulnerable to attack, and if the British could take it, they could control the harbor, capture Charlestown, and establish a base for future operations inland. Clinton was wary; taking Charlestown would be exceedingly difficult with the relatively small number of troops at his disposal. Nor was he confident that establishing a Loyalist government in Charlestown would contribute much to the reestablishment of order. He cautiously agreed to press ahead, but without a moral certainty of rapid success, he would proceed no farther than Sullivan's Island. Early on the morning of May 31, the combined seaborne force left North Carolina waters and sailed southward toward Charlestown.[3]

Presuming that there would be action on two fronts, the Continental Congress created a Southern Department consisting of Virginia, the two Carolinas, and Georgia. The department would be led by a major general, an assignment that was given to Maj. Gen. Charles Lee. An eccentric former career British officer who preferred the company of his pack of dogs over men, the acerbic Lee was acknowledged to be the most experienced soldier on the American side. Congress gave overall command of the American forces to George Washington from Virginia. Lee resented being passed over for command in favor of Washington, but he served brilliantly under Washington prior to being ordered south.

Lee started south from New York to Charlestown on March 7. Along the way he garnered 500 Continental troops from Virginia and 1,400 from North Carolina. Lee's Continentals augmented the 1,950 South Carolina regulars, 700

---

* The term *redcoat* is used in this narrative to refer to British soldiers in a general sense with the understanding that later in the war British forces engaged in the southern campaigns also comprised Hessian soldiers, who wore blue or green coats.

Charlestown militia, and 1,972 country militia mustering to defend Charlestown and the forts and batteries ringing the harbor. While Lee was en route, Brig. Gen. John Armstrong from Pennsylvania appeared in Charlestown bearing an appointment to the command of Continental forces in South Carolina, subordinate to Charles Lee. There were, of course, no Continental forces in South Carolina at the time, but he was received cordially by President Rutledge and Colonel Moultrie.[4]

Until General Lee arrived on the scene, Armstrong temporarily served as Rutledge's military adviser. Moultrie liked Armstrong and described the Pennsylvanian as a good and brave officer. If he had a fault, it was that he was unfamiliar with the employment of forts and heavy batteries in the art of coastal defense. Still, Armstrong's (and eventually Lee's) presence was a comforting indication of Continental support, given that word had filtered to Charlestown that South Carolina would likely be called upon by the British expeditionary force. The exact destination of the British flotilla was unclear, but the reports stimulated intensified efforts to fortify Charlestown in case of a British attack.[5]

By the end of March, President Rutledge and the Privy Council had assumed the duties of the Council of Safety, thus functioning as the de facto government when the General Assembly was not in session. On April 26 Rutledge ordered Moultrie to send a party up the coast as far as Santee Creek (Sampit River) to observe two British men-of-war that had anchored offshore of a barrier island named Raccoon Key. It was crucial to determine if the British ships were acting independently or if they were the vanguard of a larger fleet. And Moultrie's men were to prevent the British from stealing livestock from Bull's Island. Moultrie sent Capt. Peter Horry with a detachment to complete the mission. It was not as large a force as Moultrie would have liked, but he was hampered by a shortage of suitable boats to carry out the assignment.[6]

Moultrie did not share the general opinion of Charlestown's defensibility. Conventional wisdom held, particularly among the local sailors, that despite the many batteries of heavy cannon around the harbor—at least a hundred pieces of ordnance by Moultrie's estimation—"two frigates would be sufficient force to knock the town about our ears." But when the British finally appeared, they brought much more than two frigates. On the afternoon of May 31, 1776, couriers from Christ Church Parish reached Rutledge with the news that a large British fleet had been seen off Dewees Island, just twenty miles north of the harbor. By the next day, upward of fifty vessels anchored just outside of the bar, giving the appearance of a veritable forest of masts and sails. Cdre. Sir Peter Parker and Maj. Gen. Sir Henry Clinton had come, accompanied by South Carolina's royal governor, Lord William Campbell, who was impatient to reassert royal authority. Charlestown was now clearly the object of this joint army-navy expedition.[7]

Moultrie informed Rutledge on June 3 that a British schooner and a tender had been sounding the depths at Breach Inlet and all along Long Island, seeking the best point to attack the advance guard at the northeastern point of Sullivan's Island. He had no doubt that this position, just across Breach Inlet from Long Island, would bear the brunt of an assault. Moultrie's report was accurate; the British had indeed spent several days marking channels by placing buoys. Moultrie also informed Rutledge that the fort on Sullivan's Island was fully enclosed. On this he exaggerated; the rear and eastern sides of the fort were only a few feet high. Moultrie bemoaned his need for more men but acknowledged that troops could not be spared from town and that he would make do with those he had. His actual troop strength on the island at that time is uncertain, but he was confidant that he had enough to give four or five hundred British troops a great deal of trouble if they tried to dislodge him.[8]

Major General Lee and Brig. Gen. Robert Howe reached Haddrell's Point on June 4 and proceeded onward to Charlestown after reviewing the fort on Sullivan's Island. The panic and disorder in Charlestown, coupled with volunteer troops led by newly commissioned officers, was a source of great irritation to Lee, who was accustomed to strict military discipline, and he was inclined to find fault in everything he saw. Moultrie's officers also had a difficult time at first reconciling Lee's rough manners with his reputation for military prowess, but Moultrie agreed with those who considered his coming as being equal to a reinforcement of a thousand men.[9]

One thing Lee accomplished was to help the Carolinians overcome their awe of British military superiority, on one occasion telling a cheering crowd of soldiers that he had served under Clinton and knew him to be a "dam'd fool." Lee boasted that if Clinton did not attack soon, he would send him a challenge. Despite all of the bluster, Moultrie observed Lee rigorously working to make Charlestown secure, personally directing the work from horseback or in a small boat, laboring from sunrise to sunset, seemingly everywhere at once. Lee energized the population of Charlestown, and excepting a few disaffected Tories and men of property, all classes of society pitched in together.[10]

Defensive measures implemented during the previous nine months had been carried out in response to a threat posed by a small number of British warships (two or three) on station in the harbor. The appearance of fifty British ships off the bar was another matter altogether. The town was thrown into a perfect frenzy—"all was hurry and confusion," in Moultrie's words. But Lee took charge and began to bring order out of chaos. He placed the troops in Charlestown under the command of General Howe. Rutledge called in the militia. The army collected supplies and horses. Gentlemen sent their families into the countryside by carriage or boat for their protection. Officials moved the town's printing presses and public records to places of safety.[11]

Construction crews erected defensive works everywhere. They raised traverses across principal streets and built two-faced, angle-shaped outworks called flèches anywhere troops could land. Scavengers removed lead from the windows of churches and dwelling houses for casting into musket balls. Laborers leveled stores and warehouses on the wharves to provide fields of fire for muskets and cannon along the earthworks on East Bay Street. "You would scarcely know the environs of the town again," wrote Charles Cotesworth Pinckney to his mother; "so many lines, bastions, redans, and military mince-pies have been made all around it, that the appearance of it is quite metamorphosed. All the houses on the wharves are pulled down, so that the town looks from the water much handsomer than it ever did."[12]

Lee was well versed in the science of military engineering, and his immediate dislike of the South Carolinians' position on Sullivan's Island bordered on disgust. In his view the fort was imperfect and ill planned, a veritable slaughter pen that would not hold for half an hour. He predicted that the garrison would be inevitably and needlessly sacrificed, and it was beyond his comprehension just why the island had been occupied and fortified in the first place. These arguments could not persuade Rutledge and Moultrie. The South Carolinians remembered how much trouble had been taken to dislodge a small enemy force from the island the previous December. Moreover a British foothold on Sullivan's Island would serve as a staging area for more extensive operations.[13]

Lee finally committed to the defense of Sullivan's Island against his better judgment. To his credit he applied his usual zeal (and brusqueness) to correct the island's defensive flaw—an unfinished fort that was vulnerable to attack from three directions: from the sea, from Long Island via Breach Inlet, and from the rear should the enemy gained a foothold on the mainland. And Lee was driven to distraction by the fact that the men on Sullivan's Island lacked an escape route if retreat from the island under fire became necessary.[14]

The construction and strengthening of Sullivan's Island never progressed to Lee's satisfaction. Convinced by British deserters of an impending and simultaneous attack on Charlestown and Haddrell's Point, Lee finally called for a meeting with Rutledge and the Privy Council on June 22, where he urged the spiking of the cannon, the demolition of the powder magazine, and the abandonment of the island. Rutledge and the Privy Council, however, had the final say over the deployment of provincial forces, and they were encouraged by Moultrie's confident reports that the island and fort could be defended. There would be no withdrawal. Rutledge laconically advised Moultrie that "General Lee wishes you to evacuate the fort. You will not do so without an order from me. I would sooner cut off my right hand than write one."[15]

Were they just stubborn, or rather, being unschooled in the art of military fortification, were Moultrie and Rutledge blind to their position's weaknesses? If

Moultrie truly found himself on the horns of a dilemma, he provided no insight in his memoirs. On one hand he possessed "the countenance and support of the Governor, and he knew the courage and endurance of the men he commanded," but on the other hand, "he could not fail to recognize the scantiness of his means of defence, and he was acting against the advice and almost the command of his superior officer, a trained and experienced soldier." From the outside looking in, it appears that he kept to the business at hand with a cool confidence in a successful outcome.[16]

Lee advanced the work of fortifying Charlestown, but as far as Sullivan's Island was concerned, retreat remained uppermost on his mind. Soon after he arrived, he ordered the construction of a narrow bridge of boats for use as an escape route across the cove. Moultrie and his field officers first assured Lee that the bridge could be built, and Lee sent flats, ropes, and anchors to be used for that purpose. But within a few days, he was angered to learn that Capt. Ferdinand J. S. De Brahm, a French engineer in the service of South Carolina, had declared that building such a bridge was impracticable. The mile-long distance to the mainland was too far for the number of available small craft to be used as pontoons. Moultrie and De Brahm shared the opinion that troops could be transported by boat if retreat became necessary. This notion of extracting troops on Sullivan's Island by boat across the cove to Haddrell's Point in the face of a British attack only fueled Lee's restlessness.[17]

Instead of a bridge of boats, a floating bridge was fashioned by assembling a catwalk of ropes and planks fastened to empty hogsheads that were anchored in place with grapnels, with two planks laid side by side from barrel to barrel. An improvised bridge was completed, but when Lt. Col. Thomas Clark attempted to march a detachment of two hundred North Carolinians from Haddrell's Point across, the bridge sank so low—underwater by some reports—that Clark's men were obliged to return immediately to shore. By this time the bridge was a virtual obsession for Lee, and he entreated Moultrie again and again to complete construction of another bridge with all haste. Lee never seemed to grasp that even if time allowed the construction of a proper bridge, such a structure would be vulnerable to enemy fire. He redoubled his efforts to have a second bridge erected between Sullivan's Island and the mainland, insisting on its completion as late as six o'clock in the morning on June 28.[18]

As the month of June drew to a close, Lee accepted the inevitability of defending Sullivan's Island. Now his abiding apprehension over the bridge shifted from its use as an avenue for retreat to a route for reinforcement. Moultrie, on the other hand, maintained an air of unconcerned assurance in his ability to defend the fort, and he perhaps regarded Lee's anxieties as an annoying distraction. Moultrie later recalled, "I never was uneasy on not having a retreat because

I never imagined that the enemy could force me to the necessity; I always considered myself as able to defend the post against the enemy."[19]

By June 7 the majority of the British squadron's lighter frigates and troop transports had crossed the bar and anchored in Five Fathom Hole, a broad anchorage off Morris Island that was safely beyond the range of the guns on Sullivan's Island. The main ship channel from Five Fathom Hole into the harbor ran very near the southern shore of Sullivan's Island, and a when a British truce boat sailing that course approached the island from the fleet, an alert sentry disobeyed orders and fired upon it, forcing the boat to turn back. Another guard on the shore waving a white cloth on the end of a musket could not convince the British messenger that the shot had been fired in error. Supposing that the British vessel was serving only the ceremonial interests of protocol, an apologetic Moultrie notified Rutledge of the unlucky accident.[20]

Rutledge was as embarrassed as Moultrie that the truce boat had been fired upon, but he was rightly suspicious of British motives. Though the primary purpose of the truce boat had been to deliver a proclamation from General Clinton, its course had been deliberately plotted to allow observers to gather intelligence on the condition of the fort. The president asked Moultrie to send a truce flag and a discreet officer bearing a letter to explain the mistake to the commander of the British fleet and to give assurance that future messengers would be properly received. But at the same time, Rutledge cautioned Moultrie be vigilant to prevent the British from discovering, "under the appearance of a [truce] flag," what they ought not to know.[21]

Moultrie sent Capt. Francis Huger to Sir Peter Parker's flagship, the *Bristol,* the next day. Huger was cordially received aboard, and his explanation and letter of apology were accepted by Parker, who made the deprecatory comment that the letter came "from a Person who stiles Himself Colonel Moultrey." Huger received a copy of Clinton's proclamation to deliver to Moultrie on Sullivan's Island. Aside from a desire to convince Clinton by their adherence to protocol that they were gentlemen in command of a young and inexperienced but professional army, had Moultrie or Rutledge known the substance of the British message, they would have been less apt to bother with an explanation and apology over a breach of etiquette. In his proclamation Clinton urged a deluded people to return to their sovereign. He offered them pardon if they submitted, but he likewise warned of the miseries of a civil war that would result from their refusal. Clinton's proclamation was summarily ignored.[22]

On June 7 Moultrie detected the presence of an advance scouting party in boats headed north seeking a place on Long Island to put troops ashore. Lee commended Moultrie's alertness and encouraged an attack while the Americans held a numerical advantage, but he left this at Moultrie's discretion. Lee thought an assault could be launched from the mainland, but having recently arrived and misapprehending the topography of the area, he did not understand that any force marching from that direction would have to traverse miles of marshland.[23]

Any advance against the British on Long Island would have to be made from Sullivan's Island. When Lee realized that the terrain was favorable for riflemen, he encouraged Moultrie to send Thomson's Regiment of Rangers and Sumter's Sixth Regiment of riflemen plus three companies of militia on a reconnaissance in force to dislodge the enemy. Ever concerned about retreat, Lee reminded Moultrie to secure Breach Inlet between Sullivan's Island and Long Island, and he strongly advocated the movement of two field pieces to the advance guard to cover a withdrawal if one became necessary.[24]

Lee also notified Moultrie that he was reinforcing Thomson with additional riflemen, but he seemed to have little confidence in the attack that he was to commence at daybreak on June 10. The plan became confused when his dispatches did not reach Sullivan's Island until that very afternoon, far too late for Moultrie to proceed on the proposed timetable. Without foreknowledge of Lee's intent, Moultrie sent Thomson's force to the advance guard. There the men would remain with their boats, hidden until nightfall when they could cross Breach Inlet to scout the British position until daylight.[25]

On June 9, while Moultrie and Lee procrastinated, the British landed five hundred regulars at the north end of Long Island. By this time the whole British fleet had crossed the bar and anchored in Five Fathom Hole. Lee was unwilling to provoke the British fleet and canceled the mission on the night of June 10. Thus an opportunity for a bold stroke against the British landing party passed. If anything the British ships in the harbor and Clinton's force on Long Island only heightened Lee's desire to see the bridge from Haddrell's Point to Sullivan's Island completed. Moultrie, on the other hand, was relieved that Lee had countermanded his orders for the expedition. British sentries on Long Island had prevented his scouts from determining the precise location of the enemy camps, greatly reducing the likelyhood of success.[26]

8.

The Eve of Destruction

Fort Sullivan on Sullivan's Island was built in the conventional shape of a square with a bastion at each corner. A distance of 550 feet separated the bastions, and when finished the fort would be large enough to accommodate a thousand men. The fort's construction was ongoing before Moultrie took command on March 1, 1776, but when he arrived at the site, "it was little more than an outline. Its shape was described upon the sand, and the palmetto rafts lay around it, waiting to be moulded into form." The name of the engineer responsible for the fort's initial design is not known for certain, but it may have been Captain De Brahm, who was present with Moultrie on Sullivan's Island. He would have been familiar with the precepts set forth by John Muller, the eighteenth century's foremost military engineer. Charles Lee also had considerable input when he arrived on the scene. Regardless of who laid out the fort, Moultrie was responsible for completing its construction.[1]

The fort's primary construction material was not the traditional masonry of the Carolina coast but instead the porous and spongy but straight logs of the *Sabal palmetto,* commonly known as the Cabbage Palmetto. This salt- and cold-tolerant tree native to the southern Atlantic coast may attain heights of fifty to sixty feet and trunk diameters up to two feet. Workmen used palmetto logs to build the fort because they were the most readily available material at hand, a circumstance that would prove to be most fortuitous. Black crews rafted thousands of the logs from the mainland to the construction site in fulfillment of the Council of Safety's contract with Cornelius Dewees made in January.[2]

After hauling the logs ashore on Sullivan's Island, the workmen incorporated them into walls that were sixteen feet thick, constructed of two horizontal parallel rows of logs laid atop one another. Carpenters transversely joined and bolted these parallel rows of palmetto logs at intervals with dovetailed timbers of yellow pine. Laborers, slaves most likely, and later on details of enlisted men filled the space between the parallel rows of logs with sand.[3]

Behind the wall a twenty-five-foot-wide platform of pine planks on which the cannon were mounted provided enough space to allow a recoiled piece to be sponged out after firing. The platform was supported by brick pillars and protected by battlemented parapets—walls that rose ten feet higher than the platforms. The height of the parapets from the ground was twenty feet. Gun embrasures opened through the battlements. Merlons, the solid part of the battlements, extended ten feet above the platforms and were constructed like the walls of the fort: sixteen feet thick, revetted (faced) with palmetto logs stacked and notched at the angles, strengthened with pine supports, and filled with sand. Below the platform were rooms, possibly used as officers' quarters. Chimneys from below the platform extended through the merlons or perhaps through the platforms[4] (see figures, page 61 and 62).

A 1974 archaeological excavation at the site of Fort Sullivan revealed details that are not found in contemporaneous accounts. Positioning the fort to command the harbor's northern channel required that the fort be sited fairly close to the water's edge on a morass or marshy area. The foundation timbers for the walls were laid only two feet above sea level and were probably protected from the high tides by a line of barrier dunes. This protection may not have been complete, for it was said that the inside of the fort was so marshy that the garrison could not fall into formation if the tide was high. Also the use of square-hewn timbers interlocked with mortised-and-tenoned joints show that this was no mere field fortification hurriedly erected to meet the exigency of a pending attack. The archaeological evidence is consistent with a plan formulated by a trained engineer rather than a crude structure hastily erected by rank amateurs.[5]

The slope of the log walls of the fort would allow it to be easily scaled by attacking infantry. Writing in 1777, Baron Johann De Kalb noted that the fort was built without the usual ditch surrounding it. De Kalb opined, albeit retrospectively, that the valor of the troops, all good marksmen, combined with sufficient artillery rendered a ditch unnecessary. De Kalb was either mistaken or present at the site before the ditch was very far advanced, because there was certainly was a five-foot-wide wet ditch or moat around part of the fort, probably at the rear. General Lee sent orders on June 24 for it to be deepened and widened.[6]

Five months from the time the Council of Safety recommended fortification of the site (the previous January), the fort was far from finished. When Lee took command on June 8, only the south (front) and west (right side) curtains were complete; the north (rear) and east (left side) curtains had been raised only to a height of a few feet, and the fort was not fully enclosed. During the next three

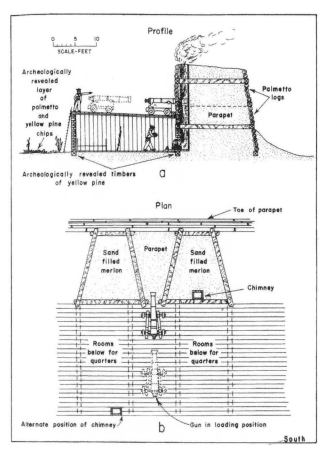

Reconstructive Views Based on Historical Archaeology, drawn by Stanley A. South and found in the upper right corner of figure 1 of South, *Palmetto Parapets: Exploratory Archaeology at Ft. Moultrie, South Carolina, 38CH50,* Anthropological Studies 1 (Columbia: South Carolina Institute of Archaeology and Anthropology, 1974). Courtesy of the South Carolina Institute of Archaeology and Anthropology, Columbia, S.C.

weeks, progress accelerated, no doubt motivated by exhortation on the part of the commanding general. "Courage alone will not suffice in war," Lee told the men at Fort Sullivan. "True soldiers and magnanimous citizens must brandish the pick-axe and spade, as well as the sword, in defence of their country; one or two days labour, at this critical juncture, may not only save many worthy families from ruin, but many worthy individuals from loss of limbs and life."[7]

The mechanics and black workmen sent to Sullivan's Island to assist Moultrie were so numerous in the fort that for a time only guards were stationed in the finished portions. The rest of the men camped behind the works in tents or huts

Fort Moultrie—1776: A Reconstructive View of the Southeast Bastion, drawn by Michael Hartley and found in the lower right corner of Figure 1 of Stanley South, *Palmetto Parapets: Exploratory Archaeology at Ft. Moultrie, South Carolina, 38CH50,* Anthropological Studies 1 (Columbia: South Carolina Institute of Archaeology and Anthropology, 1974). Courtesy of the South Carolina Institute of Archaeology and Anthropology, Columbia, S.C.

covered with palmetto fronds. In keeping with General Lee's entreaties, they all, even the soldiers, worked hard to finish the fort before any action took place. Such a notion would have easily passed muster in a European army, but in colonial South Carolina, manual labor was considered beneath the dignity of most white men. But they all had a stake; they were preparing to defend their homes and families. Once the British fleet crossed the bar, Moultrie ordered the tents to be struck and the shelters razed. From that time onward, the men slept inside the fort, where they felt relatively safe from British bombardment.[8]

By June 28 the southeast bastion had been added to end of the south (front) curtain and the southwest bastion connected the south (front) and west (right) curtains. The northeast and northwest bastion and the north (rear) and east (left) curtains were logged up to a height of only about seven feet, but progress was being made. The platform extended along the inside of the south (front) and west (right) curtains and both southern bastions. Hastily erected side works called cavaliers extended the line of defense laterally from the front corners of each rear bastion to protect the men and guns.[9]

To defend against an escalade of the unfinished walls, thick upright planks were fastened along the outside wall to extend the height by ten or fifteen feet. Narrow platforms called banquettes were built for men to stand and fire their muskets through loopholes bored through the planks. The magazine was located in the northeast bastion, the one place thought to be safest from a naval bombardment. A flagstaff that had once been a ship's mast was raised above the southeast bastion, and the soldiers hoisted a blue banner bearing a white crescent in the dexter corner. Emblazoned on the crescent was the word *Liberty*.[10]

A canal that ran from the cove to a point near the entrance of the fort at the north curtain (rear) allowed the nearby landing of supplies and building materials from Charlestown. The fort's gate through the rear curtain was unfinished at the time of Lee's arrival and remained so. In the meantime the opening was barricaded with pieces of timber eight to ten inches square that were so heavy that three or four men were required to move each piece. Taking Moultrie aside one day while inspecting the work, Lee came straight to the point when he asked if Moultrie thought he could maintain the post. Lee received a matter-of-fact "Yes, I think I can," and that was all he said of the matter.[11]

On another occasion Moultrie walked the platform with Capt. Clement Lempriere, distinguished commander of South Carolina's armed sloop *Commerce*. The sea captain asked for Moultrie's thoughts concerning the British fleet visible in the harbor, and the colonel replied with quiet determination that "we should beat them." Lempriere took a contrarian view when he expressed an opinion, one that he shared with all of the local sailors, that the British men-of-war would come alongside the fort and "knock it down in a half hour." Not to be dissuaded, Moultrie replied that the South Carolinians would then "lay behind the ruins and prevent their men from landing."[12]

If the British tried to batter the fort, Moultrie and his South Carolinians would answer in kind. The total armament at Fort Sullivan consisted of thirty-one guns. The southeast bastion mounted a total of five guns: three eighteen- and two nine-pounders. Six French twenty-six-pounders and three English eighteen-pounders faced directly to the front. The southwest bastion was home to three French twenty-six-pounders and two nine-pounders. Six twelve- and nine-pounders were spaced along the west curtain. Three twelve-pounders were mounted on each cavalier. Only twenty-five cannon could be brought to bear on an attack from the front facing south, and of these the four nine-pounders mounted on the two inner sides of the front bastions would be of limited use.

Ironically the fort's nine French guns had been captured by the British during
the French and Indian War in 1758 and sent to South Carolina as a gift from
George II.[13]

Because the palmetto fort was situated on a northwesterly bend of Sullivan's
Island, Lee was understandably concerned that it was weak on the right flank. A
vessel that passed the fort and took position to the west or in the cove between
Sullivan's Island and Haddrell's Point could bring enfilading fire to bear upon the
fort's exposed platforms and heavy guns. Moultrie recognized the vulnerability
as well, and he proposed a solution to the commanding general on June 11: "If
our armed schooner was posted near our Bridge, she would prevent Tenders from
coming to cut it away, and effectively secure our retreat. We can lay her so as to
be out of the way of damage from large ships."[14]

Moultrie sent Capt. Simon Tufts and his schooner *Defence* into the cove on
June 16 with orders to destroy any enemy that came in reach of his guns. In a way
that neither Lee nor Moultrie could appreciate at the time, Moultrie's foresight
would have unexpected but important consequences. To protect the fort further
from an attack from that quarter, Lee ordered the erection of flèches and screens
on the platforms of the unfinished walls to shield the gunners. He also ordered
the construction of a six-foot-high traverse of breastworks across the back of the
fort to be made of sand reinforced with fascines and old timber. Banquettes were
to be raised behind the traverse so that the men could fire their muskets over the
breastworks if the enemy managed to storm the unfinished rear parapet and gain
a foothold in the rear of the fort. Contrary to Lee's orders, the flèches and screens
were never begun, nor was the traverse executed to his satisfaction.[15]

Clinton had taken steps to bolster his situation at the southern end of Long
Island by concentrating his troops and by pushing his artillery, a total of about
ten pieces of ordnance, to forward positions on an oyster bank off the mainland just north of Sullivan's Island and on nearby Green Island to the northeast.
He also anchored an armed schooner and a few floating batteries offshore. The
Americans reacted by withdrawing from their somewhat exposed position at the
advance guard and relocating to a new position about five hundred yards back
from Breach Inlet. There on an extended front, Captain De Brahm put up extensive breastworks of palmetto logs on a brick foundation behind the sand hills and
myrtle bushes about a mile distant from the British. Older fortifications at the
site were razed to offer a clear field of fire sloping down to Breach Inlet between
the two barrier islands. The new works were beyond the range of British artillery
but close enough to the beach and inlet to oppose a landing.[16]

The American advance guard at Breach Inlet was protected by an abatis in
front, on the left flank by a morass, and on the right flank by a battery consisting

of an eighteen-pound siege gun, a six-pound brass field piece, and another field piece of unspecified size sent to the point by General Lee. This battery commanded the inlet and could open fire at seven to eight hundred yards before the enemy could attempt a crossing. Moultrie manned these works with a capable but hodgepodge collection of some 780 men under Colonel Thomson's command: 300 riflemen of Thomson's Third Regiment of Rangers, 200 North Carolina Continentals under Lt. Col. Thomas Clark, 200 South Carolinian militiamen under Col. Daniel Horry, Capt. John Allston's elite Raccoon Company of Riflemen, some 50 other militiamen including a detachment of artillerists, and a company of about 30 Catawba Indians.[17]

If the British did manage to force a crossing from Long Island, Thomson's contingent orders were to retire to the fort. His riflemen would be able to harass the British flank under good cover behind the barren dunes from a distance not more than fifty yards away as the redcoats marched the three miles along the hard beach toward Fort Sullivan. Once Thomson's men were inside the fort, the defenders would number more than a thousand. Given the available manpower to mount a defense, even in a worst-case scenario, Moultrie was sure that the odds favored his success, as he explained in his memoirs: "I therefore felt myself perfectly easy because I never calculated upon Sir Henry Clinton's numbers to be more than 3,000 men."[18]

In addition to the advance guard, construction began on two other posts outside the fort. Breastworks erected a quarter mile east of the fort at Sullivan's Island's narrowest point were termed the quarter guard. Midway between the fort and the northwest point of Sullivan's Island was the site of the rear guard, also known as the advance flèche, erected to repel an enemy attacking from the cove. Neither of these two works reached anything close to a state of completion by the end of June, but they were nonetheless manned by small detachments each commanded by a lieutenant.[19]

Twelve hundred men and ten thousand pounds of gunpowder were on Sullivan's Island when Lee took command. The South Carolinians clearly were not going to abandon the post. To make the island more secure, Lee worked to strengthen Haddrell's Point. On June 11 he ordered Moultrie to detach five hundred men to join General Armstrong on the mainland to extend the American line from Haddrell's Point leftward toward Long Island. This would prevent the British from erecting works to cut off a retreat from Sullivan's Island. Moultrie quickly complied by sending men from both Sumter's and Thomson's regiments and three companies of militia. At 8:30 P.M. Moultrie informed Lee that he had received word from Col. Horry at Haddrell's Point that the enemy was close to coming ashore at Bennett's Landing, a place about six miles from Horry's position. The threat seemed real at the time—Horry sent the detachment in the direction of the supposed British landing, where "poping shotts" had been heard. Nothing came of the affair, and by midnight the troops were back at their assigned post.[20]

The shuffling of troops increased Armstrong's force to upward of fifteen hundred men. Lee's purpose in doing this was threefold. First, Armstrong required sufficient strength to oppose the British in the unlikely event that they crossed the two miles of mucky marshland from Long Island to the mainland "for the purpose of seizing Haddrell's Point, and advancing against the town from that quarter." Second, Armstrong's presence in reserve at Haddrell's Point would allow reinforcement of Moultrie, provided of course that there was adequate means for a body of troops to cross the cove between Haddrell's Point and Sullivan's Island. Third, Moultrie's reassurances aside, Lee constantly fretted over the defensibility of Sullivan's Island. Therefore any men he could order off the island were men that would be saved from capture or death when the British launched a land and naval assault. Likewise for gunpowder. About the same time he transferred the troops across the cove to Haddrell's Point, Lee also removed more than half of Moultrie's supply of powder.[21]

Lee notified Moultrie on June 15 that from that time forward Brigadier General Armstrong was to be his commanding officer. Armstrong shared Lee's concerns about the bridge, but he and Moultrie enjoyed good relations, and Moultrie obediently kept the brigadier informed of British activity on Long Island. Moultrie reported to Armstrong that Lieutenant Colonel Thomson had been watching the redcoats on Long Island and that the British were landing troops as fast as their flatboats and rowboats could carry them to shore. Clinton's second wave, about seventeen hundred strong, obviously planned to stay awhile—Thomson perceptively observed that every six men carried a tent with which to set up an encampment. The British buildup prompted Thomson, using Moultrie as intermediary, to ask Armstrong to return his detached manpower to Sullivan's Island. Armstrong agreed to send Thomson reinforcements if Moultrie would send boats over to get them.[22]

With Armstrong nominally in command, Lee still micromanaged affairs on Sullivan's Island, on June 25 sending Continental engineer Baron Massenbourg there to finish the bridge. Massenbourg was frightened out of his wits at the precarious situation of the troops on the island and told Lee as much. Lee also sent over a carpenter, a man who had run off at least once before, and admonished Moultrie, "it is your fault if he escapes again: keep a guard over him," adding an emphatic postscript: "Finish the bridge."[23]

Not surprisingly the proximity of the British on Long Island to the Americans at Thomson's advance guard just across Breach Inlet led to skirmishes. The engagements boosted the morale of the Americans, although one on June 21 earned them orders from Lee that muskets were not to be fired at targets outside of 150 yards and that no artillery should be fired at a range greater than 400 yards. To conserve ammunition and maintain discipline, Lee advised Moultrie and Thomson to make an example of the first man who disregarded the orders. The troops at Breach Inlet were itching to fight, however, and were hard to restrain.[24]

Moultrie's men were in high spirits and ever vigilant despite the increasing danger, but across the cove discipline was a different matter as Armstrong coped with the independent nature of the militia. A detachment from Colonel Horry's regiment refused to move from Haddrell's Point to Sullivan's Island until a safe passage between the two could be secured. Boats were scarce, Lee's bridge was still inoperable, and cooperation between Armstrong's and Moultrie's men had been poor; orders to stake out a pathway and lay down planks through the marsh on the Sullivan's Island side of the bridge had not been followed. Lee was furious that a part of Horry's regiment had "most magnanimously refused to ease Thomson's regiment of their heavy duty," sarcastically declaring to Moultrie that "we shall live I hope to thank them."[25]

On the evening of Thursday, January 27, 1776, Lee sent boats into the harbor to intercept small British vessels and gather intelligence. He asked Moultrie to prevent his sentinels from challenging or firing on the outbound boats to avoid alerting the enemy. Lee could not restrain himself on this occasion from expressing his everlasting hope that the bridge would be finished enough to permit Moultrie's reinforcement. As night fell over Charlestown, neither the city's inhabitants nor General Lee, nor Colonel Moultrie, nor the soldiers posted at Fort Sullivan could know that by next day's end the confrontation that all had faced with dreadful anticipation would be concluded. An improvised army of inexperienced officers, raw recruits, and uncertain militia on Sullivan's Island would test their mettle against the military and naval might of Great Britain, whose experienced officers, soldiers, and sailors patiently waited aboard their ships and across the Breach Inlet on Long Island.[26]

On June 28, 1776, Moultrie commanded a garrison of only 435 men inside the palmetto fort: infantrymen of the Second South Carolina Regiment numbering 413 and a detachment of 22 artillerists from the Fourth South Carolina Regiment. Out of these, 36 men were sick and unfit for duty, surprisingly low considering the local prevalence of malaria and yellow fever, not to mention the intense June heat and humidity that was hardly lessened by the coastal sea breeze. Moultrie had the assistance of able subordinates: future brother-in-law Lt. Col. Isaac Motte, Maj. Francis Marion, and regimental adjutant Andrew Dellient. Present among the companies' lieutenants were Moultrie's half-brother Thomas;

his son, William Jr.; Motte's younger brother, Charles (another future brother-in-law); and Marion's nephew Gabriel Marion. The ranks of the other junior officers were riddled with the scions of prominent lowcountry families.[27]

Moultrie was determined to stay at Fort Sullivan over Lee's strident objections. And by failing to complete the bridge, he appeared to walk a fine line between disobedience and unenthusiastic compliance. That there developed no personal enmity between the two men is surprising. Lee was renowned for his brusque personality, sarcastic wit, and profane language. He was a martinet—rigid, harshly critical, and dictatorial—who was accustomed to having his orders obeyed by professional European soldiers. Moultrie's personality and leadership style were the polar opposite. He was affable, disinclined to excitement, and steadfast, if not a little stubborn. Dissimilarities aside, they took a liking to each other, and Lee would certainly develop feelings of warm friendship after June 28.[28]

Cognizant of his own defects yet generous to his abrasive superior officer, in the end Moultrie offered no explanations or excuses for his conduct. When he assembled his papers for inclusion in his *Memoirs of the American Revolution,* he did not fail to include correspondence from Lee in which the commanding general upbraided him for being too easy in command and too relaxed in discipline. To Lee, Moultrie's good nature and laid-back temperament were not virtues under their present circumstances. On June 22 he lectured Moultrie on the art of command and reminded him of the enormity of his responsibility: "Soldiers running at random wherever their folly directs, is an absolute abomination not to be tolerated; for heaven's sake, sir, you are in a most important post; a post where you have the opportunity of acquiring great honor."[29]

Lee had personally observed specific instances of lax military discipline at the fort and at Thomson's post on the northern end of Sullivan's Island, and he held Moultrie responsible. He disapproved of Moultrie's fondness for fraternizing with his officers and men, many of whom he had known for a long time. He exhorted Moultrie to be more aggressive and to exert himself. By exerting himself, Lee explained, "I mean, when you issue any orders, suffer them not to be trifled with. . . . Let your orders be as few as possible but let them be punctually obeyed. I would not recommend teasing your men and officers with superfluous duties or labor; but I expect that you enforce the execution of whatever is necessary for the honor and safety of your garrison."[30]

Lee could also be complimentary. On one occasion he told Moultrie that he could not wish the post on Sullivan's Island to be in better hands. Another time, trying to cajole Moultrie out of inactivity, he praised his judgment, spirit, and zeal. Applying peer pressure, Lee also pointed out that while Moultrie was known by his friends to possess sufficient courage, these same friends were apprehensive that misfortune attributed to negligence or inertness might tarnish the reputation of such a respectable gentleman. Despite Lee's well-intentioned mentorship, the seemingly dilatory colonel's failure to act in compliance with his orders nearly led to Moultrie's removal from command on the evening of June 27. His patience sorely tried, Lee intended to replace Moultrie with Col. Francis Nash of the North Carolina Continentals on the morning of June 28.[31]

9.

Never Did Men Fight
More Bravely

Arising early on the Friday morning of June 28, 1776, Moultrie rode northeast in the direction of the advance guard at Breach Inlet to consult with "Danger" Thomson. The breeze on his face put him on edge, for it told him that the wind was right for an attack. The previous afternoon the Royal Navy had hoisted topsails, fired a signal gun, and seemed to be getting under way in his direction, but thankfully, a squall came up and shifted the wind away from the fort. Now he wanted to confer with Thomson while he still had a chance. If the British ships were going to rouse themselves again today, Thomson would be facing the British infantry, who would try to cross Breach Inlet from Long Island.[1]

The middle-aged and heavyset colonel, clad in his uniform of scarlet-trimmed blue coat, white breeches, and cap trimmed with a black feather, knew that the day would be overbearingly hot and humid. An attack of gout only compounded his misery. If today was like most days, he would contend with an incessant barrage of orders from the waspish, nagging, and nitpicking General Lee, who would undoubtedly direct him, as he had done repeatedly, to finish the bridge and fort before the British attacked. Moultrie had already received one such message earlier that morning. He may have pondered, as his horse plodded for three miles along the sandy path through clumps of myrtle, palmettos, and scrubby live oaks, just how he would manage the coming fight. Or perhaps this quiet morning ride was an opportunity to reflect on life and how it had changed so drastically during the last year. He had attained military command—that much was true—but he had also lost his beloved wife, dead now seven months. At least his work organizing the defenses of Charlestown and erecting the fort on Sullivan's Island had been a welcome distraction from his grief.[2]

Moultrie approached Thomson's post about mid-morning. The path he traveled emerged from brush-covered dunes into a clearing from where his attention was immediately drawn to a number of British boats in motion on Long Island, looking as if they were preparing to descend on Thomson's advance guard. As he and Thomson discussed how best to counter this threat, lookouts pointed in the direction of Five Fathom Hole. What Moultrie saw gave him a start. The British men-of-war had loosened their topsails again, a clear sign that they were getting under way.[3]

Wheeling his horse around, he galloped the three miles back to his fort, not knowing that he was riding toward his defining moment in history, his destiny. When he reached the fort, he shouted orders for the drummers to beat the long roll, sending 435 officers and men to their posts. As a signal to Fort Johnson, Haddrell's Point, and the other batteries around the harbor that the British were on the move, the crescent banner was lowered and raised once for every man-of-war that had been spotted. Powder was issued from the magazine. Colonel Moultrie, Lt. Col. Isaac Motte, and Maj. Francis Marion shouted last-minute instructions and encouragement. The men of the Second South Carolina Regiment, assisted by artillerists from the Fourth South Carolina Regiment, had barely manned their guns when the British warships brazenly sailed up as if their victory was a foregone conclusion.[4]

After sailing from Cape Fear, the British fleet anchored off the Charlestown Bar on June 4. Small boats sortied out to sound the bar and mark the channels with buoys to guide the fleet's entrance into the harbor. Over the next three days, all of the frigates and most of the transports crossed the bar and anchored in Five Fathom Hole, off Morris Island and a few miles south of the fort on Sullivan's Island. Cdre. Sir Peter Parker's flagship, the fifty-gun *Bristol,* traversed the bar with difficulty on June 10. Because of her deep draft, she could not negotiate the channel until her heavy guns and stores were offloaded to smaller ships. Once lightened, she passed over the bar, and her guns were hurriedly remounted in their embrasures.[5]

General Clinton and Commodore Parker originally planned to reduce the fort on Sullivan's Island with a sudden and rapid stroke consisting of an amphibious assault on the north end of the island that would be launched simultaneously with a naval bombardment of the fort—a coup de main. When Clinton reconnoitered the islands in a small sloop, he was disappointed to find that the violent surf that pounded the shore of Sullivan's Island made a landing in the face of the enemy too hazardous. Alternatively Long Island would be considerably easier to occupy. Clinton and General Cornwallis agreed that army cooperation with the movements of the fleet against Sullivan's Island could be best managed if the army established a base there.[6]

Hence Clinton landed at the north end of Long Island with five hundred redcoats on June 9. It took the balance of a week or so for a total of nearly three thousand British soldiers, marines, and sailors to slog ashore, and it was only then that Clinton discovered that reports of the channel between Long Island and Sullivan's Island being passable on foot at low tide were false. To his unspeakable mortification, the British general found that Breach Inlet, said to be only eighteen inches deep at low tide, was in fact seven feet deep. Clinton had fifteen lightly armed flatboats, enough to put six or seven hundred men across the inlet at a time, but Thomson's North and South Carolinians with their breastworks and cannon rendered a landing on Sullivan's Island impossible without great sacrifice.[7]

Having been "enticed by delusive information," Clinton notified Parker that he could not attack across Breach Inlet as planned; the army could offer no more than a diversion in support of Parker's naval attack on the fort. Clinton proposed, as an alternative, to transport troops from Long Island by boat and land within a few miles of Haddrell's Point to attack the rebel battery and capture Mount Pleasant. Parker agreed in principle to send frigates in support to "enfilade the communication between the main and Sullivan's Island," but this plan was never positively developed. If Clinton's intelligence regarding the depth of Breach Inlet was faulty, then his knowledge of Haddrell's Point was doubly so, for General Armstrong waited at Haddrell's Point with more than fifteen hundred men.[8]

Clinton's proposals aside, Parker still considered the reduction of Fort Sullivan to be a primarily a naval operation. Once a naval bombardment silenced the batteries in the fort, Parker planned to land seamen and marines under the guns to storm the embrasures. A Union flag would be hoisted at the fort as a signal for Clinton to bring over troops to help the sailors and marines retain possession of the fort in case of a counterattack. That Clinton's force was in no position to assist beyond creating a diversion at Breach Inlet would be a matter of long discussion afterward, but for now Parker meant to continue the Royal Navy's long record of success against land fortifications. Parker's strength increased when the fifty-gun *Experiment* anchored off the bar on June 25 and crossed over a day later. As with the *Bristol,* British seamen had to offload its cannon before the *Experiment* could enter the anchorage.[9]

The winds were fair from the southwest on the morning of June 28. At 9:30 A.M. Parker signaled to Clinton that he would commence the attack, and at 10:30 A.M. a gun on board the *Bristol* fired the signal to weigh anchor. The men-of-war sailed up the channel toward Sullivan's Island, arriving abreast of the fort about forty-five minutes later, and let go their anchors. Ropes called springs tied from the ships' sterns to their bow anchors enabled the crews to maintain directional control once anchored, so that the gunners could bring their ordnance to bear on a target without having to depend on steering under sail.[10]

The first line of ships, anchored 350 to 400 yards from the fort, consisted of the *Bristol* and the *Experiment* in the center with their fifty guns each, flanked on the left and right respectively by the twenty-eight-gun frigates *Active* and *Solebay.* The bomb ketch *Thunder* with eight guns, protected by the armed transport *Friendship*'s twenty-two guns, anchored to the east and behind the line about a mile and a half from the fort. In the meantime the twenty-gun corvette *Sphynx,* accompanied by the twenty-eight-gun frigates *Acteon* and *Syren,* formed a second parallel line behind the first, filling the intervals between the ships of the first line.[11]

General Lee was also up early on Friday morning, as was his custom. One of the first things on his mind that day was the still-uncompleted bridge from Sullivan's Island to the mainland, and at six o'clock he sent a dispatch to Colonel Moultrie regarding the matter. Lee had spoken to Col. Francis Nash from North Carolina the night before and instructed Nash to report this morning for written orders to relieve Moultrie on Sullivan's Island. Before Nash could find Lee, the commanding general received word that the British fleet was in motion. Observing the ships making their approach toward Sullivan's Island, Lee set out from Charlestown toward the island in a small boat, sending word to John Rutledge that if he did not find matters to his liking he intended to supersede Moultrie personally. But the same fateful wind that pushed Parker into position now hampered Lee's progress by sweeping his craft toward Haddrell's Point, temporarily saving Moultrie's command.[12]

At 11:30 A.M. the *Thunder* opened the ball by lobbing a thirteen-inch explosive mortar shell in a high trajectory toward the fort. The projectile landed on the magazine in the northeast bastion. The battle might have come to a dramatic conclusion then and there, but the shell was a dud. It failed to explode and did inconsiderable damage. Thus began what has been rightly called one of the fiercest cannonades in the annals of eighteenth-century warfare. As soon as the frigates came in range of the fort's guns, Moultrie opened fire with the guns nearest them in the southwest bastion.[13]

Capt. Peter Horry described the tense and interminable moments leading to exchanges of iron between the fort and the ships, emphasizing that the Carolinians were not "standing all this while with finger in mouth, idly gaping like children at a raree show. No, by the Living! But fast as they neared us, we kept still our thunder close bearing upon them, like infernal pointers at a dead set,

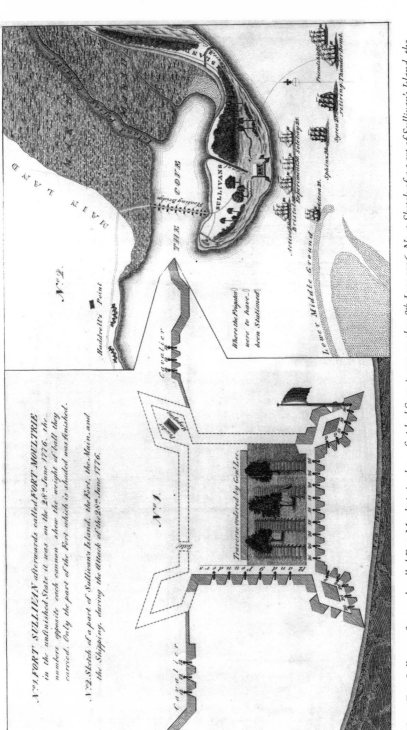

No. 1. *Fort Sullivan afterwards called Fort Moultrie in the unfinished State it was on the 28th June 1776. No. 2 Sketch of a part of Sullivan's Island, the Fort, the Main, and the Shipping, during the Attack of the 28th June 1776.* Published in John Drayton, *Memoirs of the American Revolution*, vol. 2 (Charleston: A. E. Miller, 1821), after page 290. The Robert Charles Lawrence Fergusson Collection, the Society of the Cincinnati; Washington, D.C. Reproduced with permission.

and as soon as they were come within point blank shot, we clapped our matches and gave them a tornado of round and double headed bullets, which made many a poor Englishman's head ache."[14]

The *Active* came into range first and was struck by four or five shells, but once anchored she poured in a broadside. "Nor were they long in our debt," Horry said, using apocalyptic imagery, "they opened all their batteries and broke loose upon us with a roar as if heaven and earth had been coming together." The sudden incoming fusillade naturally rattled Moultrie and his young soldiers, who had never before witnessed such an awful scene, but after a few rounds they managed to collect their wits. Declared Horry: "with heads bound up, and stripped to the buff, we plied our bull-dogs like heroes."[15]

The other British men-of-war came on line and unleashed a furious storm of ball and grape. The blue flag flying from the southeast bastion made a convenient aiming point, but many shots passed harmlessly overhead. Others fell short, plowing into the turf and sand with a dull thud. Quite a number of the enemy missiles, however, were right on target. But apart from the repeated concussions of balls impacting the fort's walls and merlons, little actual damage was done. The shots that actually struck the front of the fort buried themselves in the three-layered, sixteen-foot-thick walls—the two parallel rows of palmetto logs with sand filled in between. The spongy palmetto logs did not shatter or splinter when struck by the heavy projectiles but absorbed the shots, protecting the garrison from injury.[16]

Even with the protection offered by the palmetto logs and sand, the American works were not unscathed by the barrage. The British ships were unable to breach the front-facing south curtain with their cannonade, but from their offshore position they had the angle to enfilade the southwest curtain, striking the guns on that platform so often that they had to be abandoned. Neither were the walls of the cavaliers projecting from the left of the northwest bastion high enough to protect the men who manned the three twelve-inch guns emplaced there—this position was also vacated. Outside the fort, the British gunnery had a shredding effect. By the time it was all over, not a tree or hut on the island had entirely escaped damage from enemy shot.[17]

Only twelve to fifteen of the fort's guns could be brought to bear on the British attackers, and most of the gunners were not trained artillerists. Even so they gave His Majesty's navy a warm reception. Moultrie had them take slow and careful aim through the clouds of smoke, and he methodically directed most of their cannonade at their two largest and most dangerous adversaries, the *Bristol* and the *Experiment*. Before long the spring of the *Bristol*'s cable was shot away, causing her stern to swing around toward the fort, giving the fort's pointers an irresistible target. They raked the stern of the *Bristol* with an accurate fire that twice swept the quarterdeck clear of everyone save Sir Peter, who, Moultrie wryly noted, "was not at all obliged to us for our particular attention." The commodore was wounded in the thigh and knee, and he suffered the indignity of having the hind part of his breeches shot away, laying bare his backsides.[18]

About an hour after the bombardment began, the *Sphynx, Acteon,* and *Syren* received a signal to sail in a westerly direction past the fort and take a new position in the cove on the fort's right flank. Their mission, in part, was to screen the main attacking force from fireships or other rebel vessels. Once on station the three frigates could then enfilade the fort and cut off a retreat across the cove if the rebels were driven from their works and tried to escape to the mainland. Had this movement been successful, General Lee's worst fears would have been realized. Moultrie's position in the fort would become untenable, and surrender would be inevitable since retreat was impossible.[19]

Fortune smiled on the Americans when the three ships attempted to pass clear of the ships engaged with the fort. The captains of the frigates had no one on board who was thoroughly familiar with the channel, only dragooned black pilots who may not have been local men. The inexperienced pilots guided the vessels too far out toward the Middle Ground, a sandbar that projected outward from James Island. The *Acteon* and the *Sphynx* ran afoul of each other as all three ships became stranded in the shallows of the Lower Middle Ground southwest of the main line. Inexplicably Parker had not a single officer with him that possessed intimate knowledge of the harbor despite the fact that the Charlestown waters were well known to many officers of the Royal Navy. The *Syren* and *Sphynx* got off of the shoal later in the afternoon, the *Sphynx* with the loss of her bowsprit, and both ships eventually rejoined the action in support of the main line, but the *Acteon* remained stuck fast.[20]

During the afternoon another British ship was forced to drop out of the fight. At a distance of a mile and a half, the *Thunder* was beyond her effective range, and many of her shells fell short or burst in midair. The *Thunder's* engineer added more powder to her mortars, but the concussive recoil of the overcharged guns was too much for the structural integrity of bomb ketch's reinforced decking. After firing about sixty shells, the mortar beds shattered, and the *Thunder's* captain was forced to call for cease-fire. Moultrie explained why the *Thunder* did so little damage, stating (incorrectly) that most of her shells fell within the fort, "but we had a morass in the middle, that swallowed them up instantly, and those that fell in the sand in and about the fort, were immediately buried, so that very few of them bursted amongst us." For all her effort, the *Thunder* succeeded in wounding one man slightly and killing three ducks, two geese, and a turkey.[21]

With upward of 270 guns, the British had many times the firepower of the Americans, although the difference was lessened by the fact that the British could only bring half of their guns, either port or starboard, to bear on their target. Nevertheless this is an enormous disparity, especially taken in light of the fact that the British were amply supplied with powder and ammunition whereas Moultrie and his artillerists were not. For Moultrie the supply of gunpowder and ammunition was his only source of distress. Lee, it may be recalled, had previously depleted more than half of the fort's powder supply by having it transferred across the cove to Haddrell's Point, and so Moultrie began the battle with only forty-six hundred pounds of powder. In his memoirs he equated this supply as being not more than twenty-eight rounds for the use of twenty-six of his guns and twenty rounds per man for musketry (not accounting for the fact that he actually had only twelve to fifteen of his guns in play during the battle).[22]

Some two hours into the fight, General Lee sent word from Haddrell's Point that if the powder in the fort was expended, Moultrie should spike the cannon and evacuate. To Moultrie this was unthinkable. Not only was he having unprecedented success against the Royal Navy, but to retreat would be tantamount to forsaking Thomson and his men at the advance guard. Moultrie is said to have become rather annoyed by Lee's last effort to have the Carolinians withdraw and earnestly requested in his reply, "Only give me a further supply of ammunition and I will save the Fort and destroy the Fleet." Meanwhile, to conserve powder and forestall an obligation to comply with Lee's instructions to withdraw if the powder ran out, Moultrie ordered that the cannons be discharged at intervals of ten minutes for each gun and then only when a clear target was sighted through the smoke. Every shot must count.[23]

About 3 p.m. Moultrie received a report that British troops had landed between the advance guard and the fort. Gunpowder was now running critically short, compelling Moultrie to cease firing almost completely. If the report of a British landing was true, the remaining powder would be needed for musketry and grapeshot to defend the fort against the impending infantry assault. Fortunately the report was false, but the relative silence of the fort's guns led the British to believe for a time that the fort had been abandoned. "It seems extraordinary that a detachment of land forces were not in readiness on board of the transports, or boats, to profit of such an occasion," Moultrie later said.[24]

The situation appeared to be so dire at one point that Lt. John Spencer of the artillery climbed up on the platform ready to spike the cannon, but Moultrie stopped him and ordered him to carry off the spikes. To remedy the powder shortage, Moultrie sent Marion and a small party from the fort to see Captain Tufts on the *Defence.* The armed schooner was anchored behind the fort in Stop Gap Creek, the cove's navigable channel. Marion returned with three hundred pounds of powder. Lee's aide-de-camp, Maj. Francis Otway Byrd, who had passed over from Haddrell's Point to Sullivan's Island in a small canoe bearing the general's instructions to spike guns and retreat when the powder ran out, reported to Lee that matters were going astonishingly well inside the fort. Responding to the positive news, Lee sent word of the powder shortage to Rutledge and dispatched

Col. John Peter Gabriel Muhlenberg with seven hundred Virginia Continentals to reinforce Thomson.[25]

On receipt of Lee's message regarding the fort's want of powder, Rutledge sent Moultrie only five hundred pounds, parsimony based on the premise that Sullivan's Island could be better supplied from Haddrell's Point. This supply reached Sullivan's Island about 5 P.M. Rutledge included a laconic note of encouragement written on a small slip of paper that read "Honor and Victory, my good sir, to you, and our worthy countrymen with you. . . . P. S. Do not make too free with your cannon. Cool and do mischief." No doubt Moultrie appreciated the president's heartening words, but he would have rather had more powder. "There cannot be a doubt," reflected Moultrie, "but that if we had had as much powder as we could have expended in the time, that the men-of-war must have struck their colors, or they would certainly have been sunk, because they could not retreat, as the wind and tide were against them."[26]

According to various calculations, Moultrie's men expended 4,766 pounds of an available supply of 5,400 pounds, firing their eighteen- and twenty-four-pounders about 960 times and striking the British hulls about 70 times. The British, on the other hand, consumed 34,000 pounds of powder firing approximately 12,000 shots at the fort. Moultrie estimated that on the day after the battle some 1,200 projectiles of every size and caliber were picked up in and around the fort.[27]

While Moultrie awaited more powder, his garrison took advantage of the lull for refreshment and midday rations, with the officers enjoying the respite to smoke their pipes. "It being a very hot day, we were served along the plat-form with grog [probably a weak alcoholic beverage made with water or beer and rum] in fire-buckets, which we partook of very heartily," remembered Moultrie, who continued: "I never had a more agreeable draught than that which I took out of one of those buckets at the time; it may be very easily conceived what heat and thirst a man must feel in this climate, to be upon a plat-form on the 28th June, amidst 20 or 30 heavy pieces of cannon, in one continual blaze and roar; and clouds of smoke curling over his head for hours together, it was a very honorable situation, but a very unpleasant one."[28]

For the British the smoke of the cannon fire from the ships and the fort made it difficult to evaluate the results of their broadsides. At one point the men in the ships' masts believed that the Carolinians were quitting the fort when they observed a number of men run from the platforms, but what they actually saw was Lt. Gabriel Marion and eight or ten men running to unbar the heavy gate for the entry of General Lee. Later, observing the activity in the fort through his spyglass, Parker believed he saw large parties driven from the fort several times only to be replaced by reinforcements from the main. At about 3:30 P.M. Parker watched one of these supposed reinforcements from Mount Pleasant hang a man, a deserter he thought, on a tree at the back of the fort. The commodore was mistaken. As a matter of fact, some of Moultrie's men had removed their scarlet-faced blue coats when the action began, the day being so miserably hot, and they threw these coats on top of the merlons. A shot from the men-of-war carried one of the coats into a small tree behind the platform in plain view of the British.[29]

Lee made his way to the palmetto fort at about 4 P.M. with a mind to encourage the defenders with his presence, braving enemy fire to navigate the passage from Haddrell's Point to Sullivan's Island. Moultrie and several of his officers were smoking their pipes and giving orders when Lee arrived on the scene nearly an hour later. Out of deference to his rank and desiring to present a more military appearance, they put away their pipes. Mounting the platform, Lee exhibited coolness and self-possession as he walked about issuing orders. He lavished praise upon the South Carolinians, stating that though he had seen many bombardments and cannonades, none in the past were equal to what he had witnessed this day, and that veterans could not have behaved better. The Carolinians in turn assured him that they would never abandon their posts but with their lives. Lee, the man who again and again had predicted catastrophe, took time to aim two or three cannon at the British before saying, to Moultrie's immense satisfaction, "Colonel, I see you are doing very well here, you have no occasion for me, I will go up to town again." In all Lee's visit lasted only about a quarter of an hour.[30]

10.

America's First Absolute Victory

While the palmetto fort on Sullivan's Island absorbed a withering British naval bombardment, Colonel Thomson and his men waited at the northeast end of Sullivan's Island for General Clinton's long-anticipated attack. He was not disappointed. British cannon and mortars opened a covering fire on Thomson's redoubt while Clinton moved his army from camp to where the redcoat vanguard loaded into flat-bottom boats for an amphibious assault on the mainland or on Sullivan's Island, whichever circumstances directed. So when the grounding of the *Acteon, Syren,* and *Sphynx* ruined his plan for landing his troops on the mainland, Clinton began to undertake a crossing of Breach Inlet. The schooner *Lady William,* together with an armed sloop sailed to provide close artillery support for Clinton's amphibious landing by passing down the narrow channel of Hamlin Creek between Long Island and the mainland to flank and enfilade the advance guard. Behind in single file was the flotilla of loaded flatboats boats.[1]

The British attack, whether diversionary or a real effort to mount an assault on the fort from the rear, began to falter almost immediately. The incoming tide that brought the Parker's ships to Sullivan's Island threatened to swamp the British forward artillery position on the oyster bank, compelling his artillerists to limber up and withdraw. As soon as the *Lady William* and her accompanying sloop came into range of the Americans, they ran aground and became sitting ducks. Thomson's sharpshooters and cannons raked the ships and boars with rifle fire, ball, and grapeshot, forcing them to disperse and retire up Hamlin Creek.[2]

Two or three crossing attempts demonstrated that without close artillery support, an attacking force would be decimated while trying to establish a beachhead on Sullivan's shore. Clinton canceled the operation. The two sides kept up a desultory fire for the rest of the day and into the evening until the Americans were all but completely out of gunpowder. The result was that the British troops on Long Island were reduced to the role of mere bystanders of the battle that raged at the fort.[3]

Nearly seven miles away in Charlestown, the tension was palpable as thousands of spectators looked on anxiously from their vantage points on the waterfront or second story windows. For many of them, their fathers, brothers, and husbands were inside the fort, and their "hearts must have been pierced at every broad-side." The spirits of the people were restored by what turned out to be one of the most dramatic scenes of the war: "After some time our flag was shot away; their hopes were then gone, and they gave up all for lost! supposing that we had struck our flag, and had given up the fort." Maj. Barnard Elliott described the incident in a letter to his wife, Susannah, telling her that when his old grenadier, Sgt. William Jasper, saw that the shot had carried away the flagstaff, he called out to Colonel Moultrie, "Col., don't let us fight without our flag." When Moultrie asked what could be done, Jasper volunteered to retrieve it.[4]

Jumping from one of the embrasures, Jasper hurried the length of the fort through the thickest fire to where the flag had fallen outside the fort. He cut the flag from its broken staff, climbed over the wall back into the fort, tied the flag to a sponge-staff, and then replanted it on the rampart of the southeast bastion. "Our flag once more waving in the air, revived the drooping spirits of our friends; and they continued looking on, till night had closed the scene, and hid us from their view," wrote Moultrie, concluding his narrative of the day's battle. As darkness fell on Charlestown, the view of the battle took on the appearance of a heavy thunderstorm with its continual flashes of lightning and peals of thunder.[5]

The British in the harbor and the Americans inside the fort continued battering each other until about seven o'clock in the evening. After dusk when the ammunition again ran low, Moultrie once again ordered his men to slow their firing. Clouds of smoke in the still night air obscured the light of an almost full moon, but he and his men inside the fort could hear the shots very distinctly strike the ships. By half-past nine the harbor was altogether quiet. The day's contest had been settled with iron and blood. At length the British ships quietly slipped their cables and unceremoniously rode the last of the ebb tide to their former anchorage in Five Fathom Hole. When the firing finally ceased, the people of Charlestown were once more in unhappy suspense, with the fate of the fort uncertain. To everyone's relief a dispatch boat sent by Moultrie arrived with the news that the British ships had retired and that the South Carolinians were victorious.[6]

The disparity between the casualties suffered by each side during the battle was a remarkable testament to the design and construction of the fort. Despite ten hours of continuous bombardment, only twelve men inside the fort were killed. This included ten men of the Second Regiment, one gunner of the Fourth Regiment, and a mulatto boy. Moultrie personally knew each and every casualty and noted that most of the men that were killed or wounded were struck by shots that passed through the embrasures. Three fatalities among the privates of the Second Regiment occurred at once when the men were engaged in hand-spiking a loaded eighteen-pounder up to its embrasure in the southeast bastion. A lucky British cannonball passed through the opening and cut all three men down instantly. Twenty-five Americans were wounded, five so grievously that they subsequently died of their injuries, raising the fort's final death toll to seventeen.[7]

British admiral Horatio Nelson later stated "a ship's a fool to fight a fort," and something along those lines might have crossed Cdre. Sir Peter Parker's mind before the day was over. By Parker's count the British suffered 205 sailors and marines killed and wounded. About half occurred on the *Bristol* alone, including her captain, who was mortally wounded. Though American gunnery cleared the quarterdeck twice, Commodore Parker refused to go below deck and was slightly injured—the seat of his breeches was shot away, exposing his bare posterior, and he was pierced near the kneecap by a flying splinter. The *Bristol* was so riddled that her seaworthiness was in question. Had the wind that day not been light or the harbor calm, she might well have gone down.[8]

The carnage on the *Experiment* was almost as bad as on the *Bristol*. So great was the slaughter on board these two ships that Parker was warned that if the fire from the fort continued, the two ships and their arms would be utterly destroyed. Their abandonment was being contemplated when the fire from the fort slackened for lack of gunpowder. During the battle royal governor Lord William Campbell, who had joined Parker aboard the *Bristol*, was given command of guns on the lower deck. While directing the fire from this safer location, he received a wound in his side. Campbell's condition was not thought to be serious at the time. The wound, likely a deep splinter, festered, however, and would not heal. Campbell subsequently died in England in 1778, the last casualty of the battle.[9]

Early on the morning of June 29, Colonel Moultrie observed that the frigate *Acteon* was still fast ashore on the Lower Middle Ground about a mile distant. He ordered a few shots fired at her from the fort's French twenty-six-pounders, and the *Acteon's* captain promptly and gallantly returned the favor before setting his ship afire. The captain and his crew then abandoned ship, leaving her guns loaded and colors flying. Lt. Jacob Milligan, a naval officer of the *Prosper* who commanded a party of sailors on Sullivan's Island, organized a daring salvage mission and rowed out to the *Acteon*, boarding her before she was completely ablaze. Milligan fired four of the ship's cannon in the direction of the *Bristol* and then departed, his men making off with the *Acteon's* bell and as much of her sails and stores that could be carried in their three small boats.[10]

Flames soon engulfed the hulk, and as his crews put their backs into the oars, Milligan hoisted the captured British ensign upside down. The jubilant scavengers had scarcely left the *Acteon* when the fire reached the ship's magazine. Moultrie found a peculiar irony in the ensuing detonation, reporting that "from the explosion issued a grand pillar of smoke, which soon expanded itself at the top, and to appearance, formed the figure of a palmetto tree." He sent the *Acteon*'s bell to North Hampton, where it was used to summon the plantation's slaves to their morning's work.[11]

Colonel Moultrie thanked his men for their gallant and soldierly behavior during the engagement of the previous day, stating that it would always be an honor to the man that could say that he was on Sullivan's Island and fought against the British fleet. Newspaper accounts laced his praise with hyperbole when quoting him spiritedly cheering his officers and soldiers: "My gallant companions, you see the advantage of courage and fortitude; you have fought and conquered, and the brave fellows who fell in the cannonade yesterday, are now in heaven, riding in their chariots like the devil."[12]

From Charlestown, General Lee penned a short congratulatory note to Moultrie apologizing for not making a personal appearance at the fort but promising to do Moultrie justice in his letters to Congress. Lee likewise notified Moultrie that he had requisitioned more gunpowder for the fort and that he was having a generous supply of rum sent to the victorious garrison of Sullivan's Island. President Rutledge also sent Moultrie a letter on the morning of June 29, commending the "heroic behavior of yesterday" and pledging to send more powder in case the British attacked again. Rutledge was incredulous that the fort had exhausted its supply of powder and he went on to convey in excruciating detail the importance of firing slowly to conserve ammunition. Considering that during the battle the fort's cannon were nearly silenced for want of powder, Moultrie must have been perplexed over the contents of the president's rambling and condescending message.[13]

Lee finally revisited the fort on the afternoon of June 30, reviewing and giving his personal approbation to the troops that had been called out in formation for the occasion. Susannah Elliott, wife of Maj. Barnard Elliott of the artillery who had formerly captained the Second Regiment's company of grenadiers, took advantage of the occasion to present a pair of elegantly embroidered silk colors to the Second Regiment, one flag of blue and the other one red. The blue flag bore the marking of the Second Regiment along with a motto, "Vita Potior Libertas" (Liberty Rather than Life), with the year 1775.[14]

Colonel Moultrie and Lieutenant Colonel Motte received the colors on behalf of the regiment from Mrs. Elliott, who then addressed the regiment. "Your gallant behavior in defense of liberty and your country, entitles you to the highest

honors; accept these two standards, as a reward, justly due to your regiment."
Mrs. Elliott continued, "I make not the least doubt, under heaven's protection,
you will stand by them, as long, as they can wave in the air of Liberty." Moultrie
returned his thanks with a promise that the banners would be honorably carried
and never tarnished by the Second Regiment.[15]

Christopher Gadsden, writing from Fort Johnson on the first of July, applauded the drubbing given to the British on June 28. Gadsden also forwarded
information that he had gleaned from five deserters who had reached Fort Johnson from the British fleet. These men, two from the *Bristol* and three from the
Acteon, were all American seamen who had been forcibly impressed into His
Majesty's service when their ships had been stopped at sea. The sailors reported
to Gadsden that in the unlikely event of a second British attempt to take the
palmetto fort, Parker would surely bring his ships as close as possible in order to
rake the fort with musketry from the ships' tops.[16]

What Moultrie could not have known during the battle is that one of his first
shots at the *Bristol* killed a man in the rigging, causing Parker to order all of his
men out of the tops and depriving the British of a vantage point from which to
attempt to pick off Americans in the fort. But at four hundred yards, the Brown
Bess musket was terribly inaccurate, and it is doubtful that their fire would have
had much effect. The deserters also testified that the common men of the fleet
spoke loudly in praise of Moultrie's garrison. This was perhaps the greatest compliment they would receive.[17]

Moultrie received a dispatch from General Lee on July 1. Col. Isaac Huger's
regiment of riflemen had offered to work on completion of the fort, although
Lee thought a corps of blacks would have been better. President Rutledge and
Vice President Laurens disagreed and overruled him. Ever the micromanager,
Lee enjoined Moultrie to encourage Baron Massenbourg to press the carpenters
to finish the gate and to build the redoubt that he had previously ordered to
be constructed on the beach to prevent a landing. About British casualties Lee
drolly stated, "Inclosed I send you a list of the murders your garrison have to
answer for, but I hope it will sit light on your consciences." Despite his attempt
at levity, Lee counseled Moultrie to remain vigilant, "for it is almost proverbial in
war, that we are never in so great danger as when success makes us confident."[18]

President Rutledge and coterie of citizens visited the fort on July 4 to offer
their congratulations. Rutledge, who had insisted over Lee's objections that the
fort be defended, thanked the men for their gallant conduct and gave special
recognition to the bravery of Sergeant Jasper by presenting him with Rutledge's
own personal sword. Charlestown merchant and Patriot William Logan sent a
hogshead of old Antigua rum along with his compliments to Colonel Moultrie
and the garrison on Sullivan's Island. Logan's gift was thankfully received, as rum
was quite scarce in town at the time.[19]

After the first flush of victory passed, Moultrie still had an unfinished fort to occupy his attention. Likewise for Lee, who worried about a shortage of building materials. A week after the battle, Lee suggested to Moultrie that while they waited for supplies to be delivered, the black workmen could be usefully employed filling up the merlons and constructing a palisade (a wall made of vertical wooden stakes or timber beams) to protect the vulnerable low parts of the uncompleted embrasures and angles. Lee also inquired about the progress on the gate and of course the bridge. He and Moultrie were on quite favorable terms, and the usually irascible Lee sent Moultrie a friendly note on July 7 requesting that the colonel visit him in town as soon as he was able. Lee added his hope that Moultrie would soon obtain relief from his gout.[20]

The British spent the first part of July licking their wounds while anchored off Morris Island in Five Fathom Hole, several miles distant from the fort. Ships required repair and resupply, the wounded needed care, and Parker's decimated officer corps and command structure had to be reconstituted. For the dead it was burial at sea. Their mission a catastrophic failure, the British transports began to cross the bar to retrieve Clinton and Cornwallis's redcoats from Long Island on July 12. Conveyance of the army back to New York began on July 21, but it was not until August 2 that the last British ship sailed away, leaving the South Carolina coast clear for the first time in two months. The Americans were able to inflict two last indignities before the British departed. A party of 320 Patriots attacked and dispersed a detachment of Royal Marines at the lighthouse on Morris Island on July 11, and an American ten-gun row-galley captured the transport *Glasgow Packet* on July 21.[21]

While the battle raged in Charlestown on June 28, another historic event took place in faraway Philadelphia. Benjamin Franklin, John Adams, and Thomas Jefferson laid a draft of the Declaration of Independence before the Continental Congress. At the very moment that the Declaration was being read, Sir Peter Parker was pouring broadsides into Moultrie's palmetto fort on Sullivan's Island. Congress adopted the Declaration of Independence on July 4, the same day that John Rutledge addressed the garrison of the fort that soon would be referred to as Fort Moultrie. On August 2, the day the last of the British ships sailed from the harbor, a messenger delivered a copy of the Declaration of Independence to Charlestown. Now there were two reasons to celebrate. Independence was formally declared by the civil government on August 5, a day marked by a parade of Continental and provincial troops near the Liberty Tree, beneath which the Declaration was proudly read by Maj. Barnard Elliott.[22]

The British never expected a contemptible ragtag army to prevail against their formidable military might, but the South Carolinians did exactly that. When the battle was over, Moultrie and his resolute but now experienced band held the fort while the vanquished British men-of-war slipped their cables and dropped with the tide out of reach of American guns. It was Moultrie's gallant leadership in battle, backed by the accurate gunnery and intrepid determination of his officers and men, that was the key to battle on June 28, 1776, but luck and British blundering were also major contributing factors. Clinton could not force a crossing of Breach Inlet. The channel was too deep, and if Clinton had managed to mount an amphibious assault against Thomson's fortified position, the redcoats would almost certainly have met with disaster. Nor did the British bring their warships close enough to shore for the use of grapeshot and musketry against the fort's defenders. On the other hand, if the British ships had come closer, as was their usual strategy against coastal fortifications, the awful devastation wrought by the rebel gunners could have been much worse.

Finally, the absence of skilled pilots prevented the Royal Navy from completing the one maneuver that could have rendered Moultrie's position indefensible and fulfilled Charles Lee's prophesy that the fort would become a slaughter pen. Moultrie later admitted that if the *Acteon, Sphynx,* and *Syren* had indeed flanked and enfiladed the fort, he and his men would have been driven us from their guns. And if chance had reversed any single one of these British misadventures, the outcome of the battle might have been quite different. As it turned out, Col. William Moultrie was the right man at the right place at the right time. He was brave, but he was also very lucky.[23]

Moultrie knew that Lee had nearly relieved him of command of the fort just before the battle, but he noted sardonically that afterward Lee made him his "bosom friend." Basking in the reflected glory of victory, Lee received his share of well-deserved accolades for his contributions to the safety of Charlestown and the successful defense of Sullivan's Island. And as promised he was truly magnanimous in his praise of Moultrie when he wrote to George Washington a few days after the battle that Moultrie deserved the highest honors. Lee was also generous in his recognition of William Thomson, and he commended the valor of the soldiers under Moultrie's and Thomson's commands, who he described as "the Officers being all Boys, and the men raw recruits."[24]

In his report to the Continental Congress, Lee praised Moultrie in the strongest of terms. The president of the Continental Congress, John Hancock, in turn forwarded to Moultrie a copy of a formal Congressional resolution of thanks. Hancock personally expressed gratitude for Moultrie's spirited exertions on behalf of liberty and his country, adding that "posterity will be astonished when they read that on the twenty-eight of June an inexperienced handfull [*sic*] of men under your Command repulsed with loss and Disgrace a powerfull [*sic*] Fleet and Army of Veteran Troops headed by officers of the first Rank and reputation." In his reply to Hancock, Moultrie generously credited his success entirely to the bravery of his officers and men.[25]

Besides the obvious consequences of victory, Henry Laurens had another reason for satisfaction. British general James Grant, who had campaigned in South Carolina against the Cherokees, remarked in the House of Commons in 1775 that having served in America and knowing the Americans well, he was certain that they would not fight. Americans, according to Grant, who ridiculed their religion, manners, and ways of living, would never dare to face an English army, nor did they possess any of the qualifications necessary to make good soldiers. Describing the events of June 28 with relish to his son John, Laurens averred that "there was every appearance to give General James Grant the flat Lie. It was the fortune of his old friend Will. Moultrie to speak first & he Monopolized the Glory of the Day."[26]

Alexander Garden likened the stand of Moultrie and his South Carolinians on Sullivan's Island to Leonidas and the Spartans at Thermopylae. Hyperbole aside, the battle now known as the Battle of Fort Moultrie was the first absolute American victory and certainly ranks with the three most decisive American victories of the Revolutionary War, the other two being Saratoga and Kings Mountain. Unbeknownst to the participants, the battle had broad-reaching ramifications. If the dawn light of June 29, 1776, had revealed the British colors flying from the southeast bastion of the palmetto fort, the entire outcome of the war and the course of the United States might have been entirely different.[27]

The American victory at Sullivan's Island also had an effect beyond keeping the British out of Charlestown. South Carolinians, particularly the wealthy elite who held out hope for reconciliation, were galvanized to the idea of independence by the armed invasion, bloodshed, and victory. Reluctant rebels were been converted to firebrands. And the state now had a new symbol—the palmetto tree—an emblem that would endure as the central element of the state seal and ultimately, the state flag.[28]

II.

South Carolina's Senior Brigadier

The British departure from Charlestown ushered in a period of tranquillity in South Carolina. Georgia did not enjoy the same quietude. Loyalists from Georgia and the Carolinas had found a safe haven in East Florida. Raiding parties of British regulars, Tories, and Indians made predatory incursions from there into southern Georgia, spreading terror throughout the region, kidnapping or killing frontier settlers, stealing cattle, and seizing slaves. Though sparsely settled and militarily vulnerable, Georgia was South Carolina's buffer to the Creeks on the western frontier and the British in East Florida who lusted for Georgia's vast stores of livestock, rice, and other foodstuffs. Buoyed by the victory of June 28, General Lee allowed himself to be convinced against his better judgment and good counsel that a weakly garrisoned St. Augustine could be captured by a force of sufficient strength.[1]

Lee concocted an ill-advised scheme to lead a detachment of troops on a secret mission to take St. Augustine. He sought volunteers from the ranks of the North Carolina and Virginia Continentals by promising them glory and plunder as reward for their service, with little risk of dange. President Rutledge and his Privy Council categorically opposed the use of South Carolina troops in Georgia for fear that the British would return, and they objected in particular to Lee's offering up booty rather than liberty as the purpose of the expedition. Despite all objections Lee rode south on August 8 with the Virginian and North Carolinian troops on what would be the first of three East Florida expeditions. When Rutledge finally consented to commit men to the operation, Moultrie set out on August 11 to join Lee in Savannah with a detachment of 240 South Carolinians and two field pieces. Once united, Lee's force totaled upward of fifteen hundred men.[2]

Moultrie took his South Carolinians south to the coastal town of Beaufort before turning inland toward Purrysburg, about fifteen miles upstream from Savannah on the South Carolina side of the river. When Moultrie reached Savannah, Lee suggested that he take command of the expedition against St. Augustine, provided of course that that he had no objection to moving against his brother John Moultrie, who was East Florida's royal lieutenant governor. Moultrie assured Lee that his brother did not present an obstacle, but to carry out the mission he required eight hundred well-equipped men and ample provisions. Moultrie understood the rigors of campaign in the wilderness, and he had firsthand knowledge of what could happen to an army trekking through Indian country. He agreed to accept the mission only if his conditions were met.[3]

Lee sent to Augusta, Georgia for supplies, and he prepared for the march, but before he could get under way, he received orders from the Continental Congress summoning him northward to Philadelphia. When Lee departed during the first week in September, he took with him the North Carolinians and Virginians, crippling the plan to capture St. Augustine. The main body of the expedition reached only as far as Sunbury, forty miles from Savannah on the Ogeechee River. Summertime in the Ogeechee swamps exacted a heavy toll in terms of morbidity and mortality, higher than would have a bloody campaign. Burials were a daily occurrence, and most of the officers became dangerously ill. By the time the South Carolina troops were recalled to Charlestown, they had been spared battle, but disease and death had thinned their ranks.[4]

Moultrie and his South Carolina troops had not long returned from Georgia when they were formally brought into the Continental establishment. The tug-of-war between the Continental Congress and South Carolina for control of its provincial regiments illustrates the difficulty that the Continental Congress had in obtaining cooperation from the states whose assemblies desired to maintain autonomy. Congress had attempted to incorporate South Carolina's army on November 4, 1775, when it authorized three battalions* of infantry to be maintained at Continental expense and entitled South Carolina officers and men to receive the same pay as the Continental Army. South Carolina paid little heed. Then on March 25, 1776, the Continental Congress further *permitted* South Carolina to raise two additional battalions.[5]

Ahead of Congress, South Carolina had already raised Gadsden's, Moultrie's, and Thomson's regiments in June 1775. They added Benjamin Huger's artillery regiment in November 1775 and created two rifle regiments in February 1776. The Council of Safety thanked Congress for its interest in the security of the

---

* The Continental Congress authorized battalions, and the South Carolina government raised regiments. In the foregoing discussion, the terms *battalion* and *regiment* are used synonymously.

province, but the prevailing circumstances (the threat posed by the British expedition to the Carolinas) and the heavy expenses already incurred by the colony's defensive preparations warranted keeping the regiments under provincial control rather than under the Continental establishment. This is why Gen. John Armstrong had no real Continental troops to command when he reached Charlestown in June 1776. In fact Gen. Charles Lee had to *assume* command of the provincial forces when he arrived in Charlestown, and only by John Rutledge's indulgence, even though Congress had, or thought it had, brought South Carolina's forces under its governance.[6]

The Continental Congress passed another in a series of resolutions on September 16, 1776, requiring South Carolina to furnish a quota of six battalions to serve for the duration of the war. In the same session, Congress appointed Col. Gadsden and Col. Moultrie the rank of brigadier general. In Charlestown on September 20, the South Carolina General Assembly tacitly conceded that it was now inconvenient for troops serving together to be governed by different laws, and thus consented to the Congressional resolutions. The six South Carolina provincial regiments finally joined the Continental Army. In his resignation from the Second Regiment, General Moultrie wished all health and happiness to the officers and men, secure in the hope that they would always support the good name they had bravely acquired, adding that though he had resigned, he "still has a Command over them and will look upon them with a partial eye."[7]

In September 1776 Brig. Gen. Robert Howe was the ranking officer in South Carolina. The scion of prominent North Carolina planter family, Howe had shown promise as the colonel of the Second North Carolina Regiment before coming south with Lee. He also had familial ties to the South Carolina lowcountry that went back to the days of proprietary rule, though he was not particularly popular in Charlestown. Aside from his reputation as a notorious womanizer, in many ways—age, education, militia service, and legislative experience—Howe's life paralleled the life of Moultrie, and the two men seem to have enjoyed cordial relations.[8]

Howe had observed Lee's preparations for Charlestown's defense during the previous June and sent Rutledge comprehensive recommendations for improving those defensive works in town and around the harbor that had been hastily thrown up ahead of the British attack. Howe fully understood that Charlestown's geography was a tremendous liability. Though situated at a confluence of rivers that commanded inland navigation, and possessing a harbor that could admit almost any number of ships, Charlestown was almost completely surrounded by water. Despite the heroics of June 28, Howe understood that Charlestown would sooner or later present a plum target for the British. The South Carolina General

Assembly favorably received Howe's recommendations, agreeing to almost every point, but little was actually accomplished at the time for lack of funding. The General Assembly, however, named Moultrie, Charles Cotesworth Pinckney, and others to a committee appointed to acquire land at Haddrell's Point for construction of barracks and fortifications.[9]

A signal event in the struggle for American independence occurred in June 1777 when a weary and bedraggled Marquis de Lafayette made landfall near Georgetown, South Carolina, after a perilous seven-week journey across the Atlantic. Charlestown cordially welcomed Lafayette and feted him for eight days before he set off for Philadelphia, where he would offer his services to the Continental Army. "My own reception has been most agreeable," Lafayette wrote to his wife not long after his arrival. "I have just passed five hours at a large dinner given in compliment to me by an individual of this town. Generals Howe and Moultrie, and several officers of my suite were present," he noted, adding, "We drank each other's health and endeavoured to talk English, which I am beginning to speak a little."[10]

During the time that Lafayette was in Charlestown, Moultrie and Christopher Gadsden gave him a tour of Charlestown's fortifications. Lafayette was so enthralled with the valiant defense of the fort on Sullivan's Island that he presented Moultrie with clothing, arms, and accouterments for one hundred men. The marquis left Charlestown for Philadelphia on June 26, but if he had he procrastinated but a few days longer he would have been on hand to help celebrate the first anniversary of Moultrie's victory.[11]

Known thenceforth as Palmetto Day (and later Carolina Day), the commemoration of the victory on Sullivan's Island was observed by the ringing of church bells, the firing of artillery, and a military parade complete with a *feu de joie* (a running firing of muskets in salute) returned by ships in the harbor. Feasts were given around the city, culminating in an evening of illuminated entertainment. A speech befitting the occasion was given at St. Michael's Church, the first of a tradition that would continue into the present century. Glasses were raised in honor of General Moultrie, Sergeant Jasper, and the ten men who gave their lives defending the fort. The officers of the Second Regiment dined together, and a number of ladies provided the soldiers with a genteel dinner that the officers supplemented with a quantity of claret and beer. Francis Marion admonished the men to behave with sobriety and decency in the presence of the ladies, and he advised them to look their best out of respect for General Moultrie, who would view them on parade.[12]

An unpleasant episode between Moultrie and Lt. Col. Owen Roberts, commanding officer of the Fourth South Carolina Regiment (Artillery), marred Lafayette's visit. When the marquis toured Fort Johnson on June 21 with Generals

Howe and Moultrie, the American generals were embarrassed to find that Colonel Roberts was absent from duty. Moultrie issued an order three days later directing that Roberts or one of his field officers were to be on duty inside the fort at all times, with the admonition that Moultrie expected this order to be strictly followed. Roberts in turn complained that Moultrie's order was not only unprecedented but ungentlemanly. Angered by Roberts's perceived insubordination, Moultrie had him arrested and charged with quitting his post and being frequently in town without leave of the commander-in-chief or his brigade commander, Howe and Moultrie respectively.[13]

A general court-martial convened on July 14, 1777, and found that Roberts had violated the strictest and literal sense of Moultrie's order, but that post commanders had customarily been allowed to leave their forts without petitioning their superior officers. In the court's opinion, Roberts had always exercised this privilege with discretion and moderation. He was acquitted on the absence charge, and the insubordination charge was dismissed. The incident is extraordinary in that Moultrie was anything but a martinet and was generally too lenient, not at all given to pettiness. Roberts was an ardent Patriot and longtime comrade of Moultrie dating back to the Cherokee War. The underlying cause of their quarrel is unknown, but the matter was settled. Roberts returned to his command, and all evidence indicates that he and Moultrie fully cooperated from that time forward.[14]

President Rutledge and the Privy Council were justifiably concerned that South Carolina's trade would suffer from the presence of four British warships cruising just outside of the harbor. To help counter the Royal Navy, Rutledge asked Howe to provide Continental soldiers for marine service on board the thirty-two-gun Continental frigate *Randolph* anchored in Charlestown Harbor. Howe was about to return to Georgia, and he would leave Moultrie in command at Charlestown, but before he departed for Savannah, he ordered Moultrie to summon a council of war to consider Rutledge's request. Moultrie called the field officers of South Carolina's Continental regiments to meet at his quarters on the afternoon of December 13, 1777.[15]

When the council of war convened, Moultrie presented Howe's proposal to use Continental troops as marines in accordance with President Rutledge's wishes. The members of the council decided that while there was no impropriety in sending a detachment aboard the *Randolph,* there were insufficient numbers of troops on hand to defend the state from attack. Moultrie concurred with the council's decision to deny Rutledge's request. And when Howe asked the council to reconsider on the grounds that the military would be censured for failure to comply, Moultrie and the members of the council stood their ground, declaring that "they cannot alter their former opinion, and they would be unworthy of the commission they hold if they could be induced by the dread of censure . . . to give any opinion contrary to their honor and conscience."[16]

In a move that would have dreadful consequences, Rutledge finally persuaded Moultrie to relent and release soldiers for marine duty. Rutledge argued that ships were expected any day, bringing military stores and other much-needed articles to Charlestown. Unless the British warships were driven from the coast, these supply ships could not enter the harbor to land their cargoes. It was also possible that the *Randolph* might take a prize or two from among the English ships bound to the West Indies. Moultrie relented and detached 150 soldiers for shipboard service.[17]

The blockade of maritime traffic by British men-of-war posed a more immediate concern than the mere disruption of trade and commerce. The British were sending boats into town under the cover of darkness to obtain provisions from Charlestown's many Tories and to gather intelligence. Moultrie blamed these interlopers for setting a fire that broke out in a kitchen or outbuilding on Union Street near Queen Street about four o'clock on the morning of January 15, 1778.[18]

Although small at first, winds whipped the fire into an inferno that raged with a fury that defied all efforts to quench the flames. Before long the conflagration spread to neighboring houses. Sparks carried the fire to Broad, Elliot, and Tradd Streets, then Church Street, Bedon's Alley, and East Bay Street. Burning more or less out of control until six o'clock in the evening, the fire engulfed 252 of approximately 1,434 wooden dwellings along with their kitchens and back buildings. The six to seven thousand volumes owned by the Charlestown Library Society were almost totally lost, and considerable quantities of rice, indigo, and tobacco were incinerated in the warehouses along the bay. Elkanah Watson noted in his memoirs that the flames reduced to indigence many who had retired to their beds in affluence.[19]

Moultrie was quite affected by the sad spectacle. The town's inhabitants ran through the streets in search of shelter for themselves and their children against a night so bitterly cold that water thrown upon the houses to extinguish the flames ran down and hung in icicles. Goods and property were piled in the streets; the people were careworn, shivering, and distressed. The soldiers and officers from the regiments on duty in town were extraordinary in their efforts to extinguish the blaze and assist the townspeople. Moultrie conveyed the thanks of the grateful citizens of Charlestown to the army in his general orders.[20]

On January 27, 1778, the *Randolph* and five ships of the South Carolina navy sailed from Charlestown Harbor to capture military stores on Tobago, the most southeastern island of the West Indies in the Caribbean Sea. Along the way they sought to oppose blockaders, challenge privateers, and take prizes whenever possible. The 150 marines detached from the state's Continental regiments were dispersed among them. After about ten weeks at sea and nearing their destination, the squadron sighted the British sixty-four-gun double-decked frigate *Yarmouth*. Despite being severely outgunned, the *Randolph* engaged the enemy, firing broadsides at a "most infernal rate," and drew so near the *Yarmouth* that the sailors in the riggings were able to throw their hand grenades upon each others' decks.[21]

By all accounts the *Randolph* was winning the fight through a combination of audacity and superior gunnery until an errant spark or perhaps a British cannonball found the ship's magazine. The American frigate suddenly disintegrated in a great ball of fire that showered the *Yarmouth* with flaming debris. Except for four rescued seamen, every other soul on board perished, including the promising young captain Nicholas Biddle and fifty marines detached from the First Regiment. Even though the *Randolph* was left in pieces at the bottom of the sea, the incident served notice to the British that the South Carolinians were prepared and willing to defend their coast aggressively.[22]

Among the *Randolph*'s escorts, one ship in particular played a critical role in the short but ferocious and costly sea battle, the *General Moultrie*, a three-masted twenty-gun privateer built in Beaufort in late 1777 and outfitted for sea duty just before the cruise. Documentation is scant, but Moultrie may have had a financial stake in his namesake privateer. And ironically the destruction of the *Randolph* may have been the fault of Capt. Philip Sullivan, who was at the helm of the *General Moultrie* during the engagement with the *Yarmouth*. According to a member of the *General Moultrie*'s crew, when Biddle realized the *Yarmouth* was a ship of the line, he signaled his squadron to make sail to escape. All of the American ships complied except the *General Moultrie*, and this inaction forced Biddle to engage at close quarters a much larger and more heavily armed vessel.[23]

Apart from the failure of the British to establish a foothold in the South, the events that transpired in the Southern Department from mid-1776 until the end of 1777 had predominately minor regional and local implications. In the northern theater, however, the course of the war had taken dramatic turns. The Continental Army had suffered a string of defeats punctuated by an occasional victory. Washington's army was ousted from New York and forced to retreat through New Jersey to Pennsylvania, but it rallied to defeat a Hessian force in an audacious surprise attack at Trenton, New Jersey, on December 26, 1776. Washington was again victorious at Princeton on January 3, 1777, yet he suffered defeats at Brandywine and Germantown on September 11 and October 4.

The British occupied Philadelphia, the American capital, on September 26, 1777; however Maj. Gen. Horatio Gates's victory at Saratoga, New York, on

October 17 convinced France to enter the war on the side of the Americans. By December 1777 Washington's tattered and worn-out army was in winter quarters about twenty-five miles northwest of Philadelphia at Valley Forge, beaten but not defeated. On the political front, the Continental Congress adopted the Articles of Confederation, the first constitution of the United States of America, on November 17, 1777.

12.

Crisis in Georgia

The terms of the South Carolina Constitution of March 26, 1776, were instituted as temporary measures until the unhappy differences between Great Britain and America were settled. The framing of the constitution was necessary at this time to complete the transition from royal to extralegal government to provincial government. Subsequent events rendered the document obsolete after just a few months, the most important of these events being the thirteen colonies' adoption of the Declaration of Independence.

Touted as a full and free representation of the people, South Carolina's first General Assembly was actually self-constituted from the Provincial Congress rather than being formed through an electoral process. A formal election was later held in the fall of 1776, during which the parishes of St. Philip and St. Michael returned Moultrie to the legislature. In December the General Assembly reconvened to prepare a permanent constitution, and by the spring of 1777, a draft document ready for consideration.[1]

Governmental structure under the terms of the proposed constitution was very similar to that of the government in force with a few notable exceptions. The former General Assembly would become the House of Representatives. The Legislative Council would be replaced by a popularly elected Senate, making it more representative of the state as a whole rather than the lowcountry.* The governor could not serve consecutive terms and would be denied the power of veto. As was the case with South Carolina's previous governments, the new constitution

---

* In common parlance, a meeting of the House of Representatives and Senate was referred to as a General Assembly.

favored the elite, giving the lowcountry aristocracy disproportionate representation in the House of Representatives.[2]

President Rutledge opposed the new constitution. Without a presidential veto and with an elected Senate, the new government would be too democratic, and the lowcountry gentry would be deprived of a measure of their power. Moreover Rutledge did not wish to close the door on reconciliation with England. He vetoed the bill to enact the new constitution on March 5, 1778, and on the expectation that the General Assembly would not back down, he tendered his resignation. Rawlins Lowndes was elected president in Rutledge's place, and Christopher Gadsden was elected vice president. The General Assembly formally adopted the constitution on March 19, 1777, but it did not to go into effect until November 1778.[3]

Moultrie's attendance at these sessions is presumed but cannot be verified. Sometime during the fall of 1777, he had an accident from which he sustained a fractured femur, a serious injury even by present-day standards. The injury occurred while Moultrie was on furlough and resulted from a fall from a horse. Fortunately his recovery was uneventful, and he was fit for duty by the middle of December.[4]

Any quietude General Moultrie had lately enjoyed was interrupted in early April 1778 when he received a letter from South Carolina's president, Rawlins Lowndes, warning of Tory agitation in the backcountry. Lowndes had only half of the story. While Patriot leaders attended their state legislatures, British Loyalists in Georgia and South Carolina took advantage of their absence to rise up and organize. Moultrie soon received a second letter from an exceedingly anxious General Howe in Savannah that painted a more complete picture. Five or six hundred Scopholites* had crossed the Savannah River from South Carolina into Georgia below Augusta on April 4, pillaging and committing other depredations along their way. Furthermore enemy movements at St. Augustine, their operations on the St. Johns River, and circumstances at Pensacola corroborated evidence that the Scopholites and a band of disaffected Georgia Tories meant to join forces with the East Floridians. Howe wanted Moultrie to immediately bring two hundred South Carolina troops to Georgia's aid, for that state was completely unprepared to come to her own defense.[5]

Moultrie reported to Howe on April 10 that the South Carolina militia had overtaken, killed, and captured a few of the Scopholites, but he had reservations about marching men into Georgia. For one thing he doubted the ability of the

---

* *Scopholites* were Tory insurgents named for their leader Colonel Joseph Coffel (sometimes spelled Scophol). In his memoirs Moultrie uncharacteristically described the man as an illiterate, stupid, noisy blockhead.

British in St. Augustine to mount any meaningful incursions into Georgia, adding that "their numbers are so few . . . they had better stay at home and take care
of their own castle." Besides that, the lowcountry inhabitants lived in fear of
invasion or an attack in the interior of the state. They wanted their own troops
kept close to home. Putting his reservations aside, Moultrie organized 150 men
from Thomson's regiment and 50 from Sumter's to march at a moment's notice.[6]

Moultrie had to put away any doubts about sending South Carolina troops
to Georgia when he received Howe's dispatch of April 14. Howe wanted 250
South Carolina infantrymen and 30 artillerists with two field pieces to march
immediately to Purrysburg. This time Moultrie would not take the field against
the Loyalists in East Florida but instead would play a logistical role, a part that
would bring him more aggravation than glory. Howe also wanted Moultrie to
furnish every military requisite but not to delay the march while preparations
for supply were being completed. Matters in Georgia were far worse than Howe
had anticipated; he described the state as "deplorably weak" and in need of every
support South Carolina could give it.[7]

Acceding to Howe's wishes, Moultrie sent President Lowndes a list of items
needed by the Continental Army, including sixty tents and three hundred haver-
sacks. Lowndes equivocated and procrastinated. He told Moultrie that he would
provide what he could—as much as he could spare—but the supply of tents,
iron, lead, and cartridge paper would be limited. As for money he could not
ascertain the quantity or species without further inquiry, cautioning that he was
in no condition to supply cash in any considerable amount.[8]

Without funding of its own, the Continental Army was dependent on the
state to provide money for the paymaster and the deputy quartermaster general,
at the very least in the form of a loan. Consequently Moultrie emphasized two
key points to Lowndes. First, without help in the form of supplies, both Georgia
and South Carolina risked dangerous consequences; second, General Howe was
pressing Moultrie to expedite the departure of the South Carolina troops, so it
was important for Lowndes to act with celerity.[9]

Moultrie did in fact order detachments from the First, Third, and Sixth Regiments plus artillery to march on April 19 and 20, all under the command of
Col. Charles Cotesworth Pinckney of the First Regiment. He did not succeed in
securing funds from South Carolina's treasury to support the Continental troops.
In a dispatch to Howe, Moultrie complained about Lowndes's reluctance to advance money and supplies for Continental use, claiming that if Howe had given
more particulars about the numbers and posture of the enemy, perhaps Lowndes
might have been more easily swayed. Instead Lowndes defiantly refused to release
funds because the state auditors had not examined the Continental accounts for
past disbursements.[10]

Lowndes not only demanded strict accounting for prior expenditures, but he treated deputy quartermaster general Francis Huger in a peremptory manner when Huger sent his books to the president for inspection. Moultrie on the other hand was of a mind that the existing emergency necessitated cutting through red tape. In his view a Continental officer, Huger in this case, should not be answerable to civil authorities who were not competent to judge if his accounts were right or not. Besides, the Continental accounts were sent for review to the Board of War and to the quartermaster general, Maj. Gen. Thomas Mifflin, who forwarded them to Congress for approval.[11]

Moultrie tried to persuade Lowndes to untangle the bureaucratic snarl by suggesting that the dispute over the release of funds was a product of Lowndes's misunderstanding the intent of the Continental Congress. Lowndes, however, remained steadfast on the grounds that a congressional resolve of February 9, 1778, recommended that state executives give attention to the conduct and behavior of all Continental officers in the execution of their responsibilities and that the state executives were empowered to suspend military officers for misbehavior or neglect of duty. Lowndes assumed this power and applied it to Huger. All the while that Moultrie and Lowndes were trying to settle their differences, General Howe could not move for lack of troops and supplies, and he was counting on Moultrie's diligence to resolve matters and prevent further delay.[12]

Exasperated by Lowndes, Moultrie finally appealed to a higher power. Writing on April 20 to president of the Continental Congress Henry Laurens, he related in detail the obstacles thrown in the way by Lowndes. Moultrie explained that he disagreed with Lowndes's actions, but he wished to avoid further difficulty with the executive authority. Moultrie asked Laurens to have Congress rectify the problem. But Lowndes had also written to Laurens giving his side of the argument, and Moultrie was disappointed to learn from Laurens not only that Congress upheld Lowndes's actions, but that the president's actions were generally applauded. "We are much in the dark with regard to the resolution of Congress," Moultrie later told Laurens. "We may be guilty of errors and neglect of duty without the least intention of either," he said, explaining that the problem between Lowndes and Huger was because Huger had no idea that Congress had given the president such power over him.[13]

While Moultrie worked his way through the red tape that bound his supply line to General Howe, he received word that the British in East Florida were mobilizing to invade Georgia. Brig. Gen. Augustine Prévost was rumored to be trekking from St. Augustine to the Altamaha River with as many as eleven hundred men, leaving only three hundred behind to garrison the town. Prévost's force was augmented by three hundred backcountry South Carolina Loyalists encamped on the St. Marys River, and seven hundred more Loyalists were expected to join him. There were also reports that hostile Creek Indians were moving to join the offensive.[14]

The South Carolina troops sent to Georgia were en route to rendezvous with Howe in Savannah by April 23. In Charlestown, Moultrie readied the remainder of Thomson's and Sumter's regiments in case they were needed. In addition he sent ten thousand pounds of gunpowder, cannon shot, cartridge papers, and other provisions by galley to Savannah. Once men and materiel began to flow from Charlestown to Savannah, a lag in communications between Moultrie's and Howe's headquarters gave rise to another round of aggravations. On April 26 he received an express from Capt. John F. Grimké, Howe's aide-de-camp, conveying Howe's need for the remainder of South Carolina's Continental troops, the men from Thomson's and Sumter's regiments. They should bypass Savannah and proceed immediately to Fort Howe on the north bank of the Altamaha by the shortest route. Moultrie replied on May 1 that the reinforcements were on the way but that they had left too long ago to order them directly to the Altamaha as Howe had requested.[15]

Howe and his army marched from Savannah to Fort Howe, arriving there by May 9. The force would ultimately total upward of 2,500 men and would be composed of Pinckney's 600 South Carolina Continentals joined by 800 South Carolina militiamen under Col. Andrew Williamson. The South Carolinians were increased by the addition of Col. Samuel Elbert's 500 Georgia Continentals and 550 Georgia militia led by Georgia's Patriot governor, John Houstoun.[16]

The timing of the late spring–early summer campaign imposed terrible hardships on the officers and soldiers. The temperature was stultifying. Disease ravaged the men, desertion was rampant, and the misery of the troops was compounded by a shortage of camp equipment such as kettles, canteens, and tents. The failure of the South Carolina galley to deliver ammunition and provisions from Charlestown threatened to cripple the entire operation. Meanwhile, the enemy was posted in strength on the St. Marys River and was fortifying positions on both sides of the St. Johns River. All the same Howe would stand a fair chance of dislodging the enemy if he could logistically sustain the operation.[17]

Charles Cotesworth Pinckney laid the blame for inadequate supply squarely on Moultrie's shoulders: "I cannot help lamenting to you, (and I owe it to candor and friendship) that you have been much too parsimonious in your fitting us out for this expedition." Pinckney was unaware of the troubles Moultrie had been having with Lowndes and that Moultrie was sending onward everything he could get his hands on. Furthermore Pinckney was of the opinion that the state considered no expense too great to attract recruits, but once the men were enlisted into the ranks, not enough was done to preserve their health. "What can be more cruel than crowding eight, ten, and twelve men into one tent, or to oblige those who cannot get in, to sleep in the heavy dews," Pinckney asked, adding that one camp kettle to ten to fifteen men or one canteen per six to eight men was patently insufficient in the hot climate.[18]

Moultrie was stung by his friend's words, and he defended his actions, stating emphatically, "I am also sorry to find ammunition and provisions were so long in getting to hand; it must be due to mismanagement. . . . you charge me with parsimony in fitting you out for the expedition, and say I have only allowed a tent for eight, ten or twelve men, which I believe must be a mistake; I gave orders for 120 tents which I thought sufficient for 600 men, especially as quarter and regular guards and out posts, always build bowers in summer, for their shelter in these southern climates, which is done almost as soon as pitching a tent; I also sent a camp kettle for every five men." Moultrie's view, based on his past experience in Cherokee country, was that the men would fare better and be more healthy on the march if they were not crowded into tents or encumbered by excess baggage.[19]

On June 22 Moultrie relayed credible reports to Howe indicating that twelve hundred men and a number of Indians had set out from St. Augustine with two field pieces. Supported by two galleys on the St. Johns River armed with twenty-four-pounders and other heavy cannon, the British were marching north to dispute the American approach to St. Augustine. On the American side, the South Carolina and Georgia militias were lagging days and miles behind, and Moultrie advised Howe to halt and wait for them to catch up. Counseling Howe to keep his little army together instead of moving about as detachments, he warned Howe to be alert for a surprise attack, even if the enemy were far away. To emphasize the enemy's mobility, Moultrie harkened back to the Cherokee campaign, when Col. Archibald Montgomery's force of Highlanders marched forty-eight miles in twenty-four hours from Twelve-Mile River to Sugartown and back.[20]

Moultrie had also gleaned information concerning St. Augustine's readiness for an assault, and he outlined several possible approaches to the city. Sharing Howe's exasperation over the tardiness of the militia, he suggested that if all Howe's forces were united, and if they were well provisioned, they might actually have an easy conquest of St. Augustine. But he also feared that the season was too far advanced: "If your men should fall sick fast, as you approach the enemy, I think it would be much the best to retreat in time, before you get too near, as it will be very difficult to come off; dragging a number of sick after you, you must expect the Indians and light troops to harass your rear."[21]

By mid-July none of Moultrie's preconditions for success had been met, and the campaign ground to a halt. Howe's Continentals reached Fort Tonyn south of the St. Mary's River in East Florida, but the militia was late, and when they arrived their commanders would not cooperate with Howe whatsoever. Antagonism among the three elements of his army denied Howe the unification of command that was so vital to a successful operation. Lack of provisions and shelter dispirited the men, and malaria and other diseases put fully half of the Carolinians in their graves or in the hospital. The divided heterogeneous commands, the season of the year with its attendant sickness, and the inadequacies of supply rendered retreat practically impossible if the Loyalists had put up any resistance. Had not the East Floridians retreated south of the St. Johns River, the expedition would have been a total failure. In the end Howe characterized this expedition into East Florida as one of the most unfortunate accidents of his life.[22]

Moultrie had been against the expedition from the beginning, but when he observed the campaign from a distance, he came to a different conclusion. The peace of South Carolina and Georgia did, it seem, appear to depend on the reduction of St. Augustine, and certainly not during the summertime. Moultrie bypassed Howe and proposed an alternate plan of invading East Florida to Laurens.[23]

Moultrie proposed to begin well in advance of the actual campaign, gathering a number of batteaus, pack saddles, and necessary provisions with the batteaus. Setting off no earlier than November when the weather was moderate and not very cold, he would convey most of the troops, artillery, and baggage by galley convoy to the St. Johns River and have cattle driven overland in the company of a strong guard of cavalry and light troops. He would then gather his force within thirty miles of St. Augustine, halt and prepare for a short march. The men would be fit, fresh, and ready for immediate action. Moultrie was confident that with a force of three thousand men, a small train of artillery, and some siege guns, success would be guaranteed. It was a good plan, but he would never put it into action. After Howe's last disastrous excursion, there would be no more American offenses against East Florida.[24]

Maj. Gen. William Moultrie, oil on canvas after Rembrandt Peale (1778–1860). The badge of the Society of the Cincinnati is attached to Moultrie's left lapel. Courtesy of the Society of the Cincinnati of the State of South Carolina, Charleston, S.C.

The Second South Carolina Regiment, 1775–1780, by Darby Erd. Company of Military Historians, *Military Uniforms in America,* Plate No. 450. Courtesy of Darby Erd, West Columbia, S.C.

The Battle of Fort Moultrie, by John Blake White (1781–1859), oil on canvas. U. S. Senate collection. The group of officers in the right foreground consists of (left to right) Col. William Moultrie, Maj. Francis Marion, Lt. Col. Isaac Motte, Maj. Gen. Charles Lee, and Lt. Col. William Thomson. Sergeant William Jasper has just restored the flag to its rightful place above the southeast bastion.

A View of the Attack Made by the British Fleet Under the Command of Sir Peter Parker against Fort Moultrie on Sullivans Island June 28, 1776, and a distant View of the Transports in Five Fathom hole, by Nicholas Pocock, 1783. Courtesy of the South Caroliniana Library, University of South Carolina, Columbia, S.C.

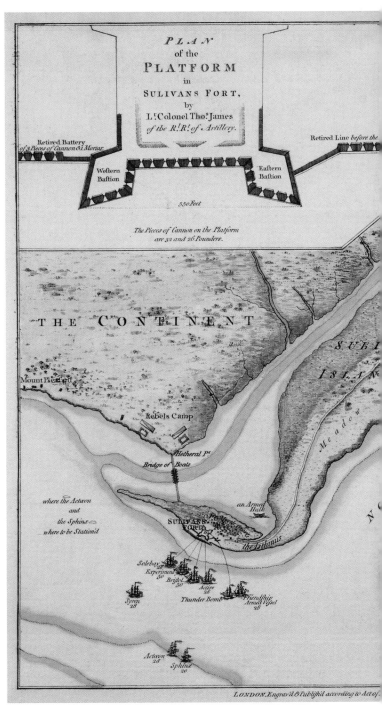

A Plan of the Attack of Fort Sulivan, near Charles Town in South Carolina, by a squadron of His Majesty's Ships, on the 28th of June 1776. London: William Faden, 1776. The Robert Charles Lawrence Fergusson Collection, the Society of the Cincinnati, Washington, D.C. Reproduced with permission.

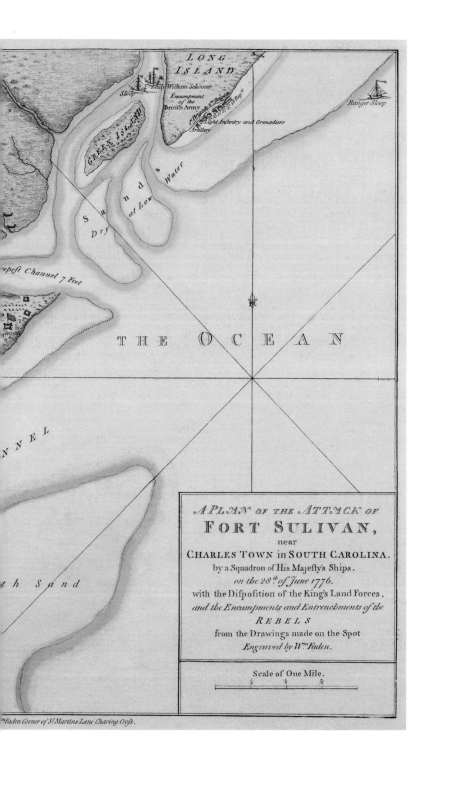

LONG ISLAND

Lady William Schooner

Sloop

Encampment of the British Army

1 st Brigade 2 nd Brigade 33 & 21 Reg t

Light Infantry and Grenadiers

Artillery

Ranger Sloop

GREEN ISLAND

S a n d s

Dry   at Low   Water

epest Channel 7 Feet

THE OCEAN

N N E L

th Sand

A PLAN OF THE ATTACK OF
FORT SULIVAN,
near
CHARLES TOWN in SOUTH CAROLINA.
by a Squadron of His Majesty's Ships,
on the 28 th of June 1776.
with the Disposition of the King's Land Forces,
and the Encampments and Entrenchments of the
REBELS
from the Drawings made on the Spot
Engraved by W m. Faden.

Scale of One Mile.

Faden Corner of S t Martins Lane Charing Cross.

The blue regimental flag of the Second South Carolina Regiment. Lewis Butler, *The Annals of the King's Royal Rifle Corps*, vol. 1. *"The Royal Americans,"* (London: Smith, Elder & Co., 1913), 217.

13.

An Army Mostly
Composed of Militia

Judging from the November 1778 correspondence between William Moultrie and Rawlins Lowndes, the strained relationship between the general and the president during Howe's East Florida expedition gradually warmed. This reconciliation may have been prompted by recent reports that the British in New York were assembling a formidable force to attack South Carolina. Moultrie offered Lowndes several ideas designed to place the state in a stronger defensive posture. First he would provision the militia and distribute the companies among three camps, each located within a two-day march of Charlestown but close enough to each other to lend mutual support in case of an overland attack from the north or south. To give the troops more mobile defensive firepower, he suggested that some of the large cannon could be mounted on field carriages. Building materials in town such as brick and lime should be collected for public service, and implements such as hoes, axes, spades, and saws should be sent to Forts Moultrie and Johnson.[1]

To accomplish the work necessary to build or improve fortifications, he proposed the drastic measure of impressing five hundred black men for manual labor. One hundred wagons would be needed to transport ammunition, and he recommended sending four hundred or five hundred head of cattle and a stockpile of Indian corn to Haddrell's Point to feed the troops posted there and at Fort Moultrie. Furthermore, to deny the British forage if they landed, Moultrie advocated slaughtering some of the cattle on the sea islands and driving off the rest. Mindful that the waterways could provide the enemy with inland access,

Moultrie also advised Lowndes to take a number of small boats into state service to transport troops and cannon wherever needed and to prepare armed vessels to patrol the Ashley and Cooper Rivers to prevent the British from running in troops or crossing those rivers to land on the Charlestown Neck.[2]

Military victories in the North had failed to subjugate Great Britain's North American colonies. Cognizant that France's entry into the war on the American side could break the stalemate, in March 1778 Parliament passed conciliatory acts devised to end hostilities, restore trade, and revive mutual affection between the colonies and the mother country. These measures would reunite Great Britain with the colonies, while granting the "British States throughout North America" freedom of legislation and internal government. Military forces would not be maintained on the continent without the expressed consent of the Continental Congress or the provincial assemblies. In essence Great Britain was ready to concede all that the Americans demanded except independence. The Continental Congress rejected Britain's peace overtures and called upon the states to field their quotas of Continental troops as soon as possible.[3]

Reconciliation thus having failed, military strategists in London formulated a plan to bring the conflict to a successful and speedy martial conclusion. They envisioned a second invasion of the southern colonies, a coordinated effort between regular troops from New York and Loyalists in East Florida. Like his predecessor Lord Dartmouth, His Majesty's American secretary, Lord George Germain, subscribed to the premise that the large numbers of Loyalists in the southern colonies, particularly Georgia, would facilitate the restoration of royal control. This strategy was substantively the same as the basis of the disastrous 1776 campaign against the Carolinas.[4]

The Continental Congress demonstrated its determination to strengthen the Southern Department on September 25, 1778, by passing resolutions to send three thousand troops from North Carolina and one thousand troops from Virginia to the assistance of Georgia and South Carolina. The force was to be composed of both militia and Continentals. The militia was to be paid by the Continental establishment, and the entire force was to be commanded by a Continental officer. The militia of South Carolina and Georgia called to arms during the present emergency were to be in the pay of the United States, a stipulation by Congress that would have important repercussions.[5]

It was not General Howe who would command this reinforced southern army. He had been sharply criticized by the military and civil authorities of South Carolina and Georgia for his conduct of the last East Florida campaign. By resolution of Congress, Howe was ordered to report straightaway to George Washington's headquarters. Maj. Gen. Benjamin Lincoln was directed to take command of the Southern Department and to repair immediately to Charlestown.[6]

Lincoln, born in 1733, had risen through the ranks of the Massachusetts militia to command troops in the environs of Boston in 1776. Lincoln reinforced Maj. Gen. Horatio Gates's command at Saratoga in August 1777, and during the subsequent battle, he was severely wounded in the right ankle by a musket ball. For his part in the pivotal victory, he received the well-deserved thanks of Congress. Lincoln had a reputation for administrative capability, a proven record of effectiveness in exercising independent command, and a reputation for leading militia. He appeared to be an ideal choice to replace Robert Howe in the Southern Department. Lincoln accepted his new assignment with optimism.[7]

Sir Henry Clinton, commanding British forces in North America, selected the seasoned lieutenant colonel Archibald Campbell to lead a thirty-five-hundred-man British invasion of regulars, Hessians, provincials, and Royal Artillery from New York to Georgia. Under orders to take Savannah, Campbell and his flotilla of transports and warships commanded by Cdre. Hyde Parker weighed anchor at Sandy Hook on November 26 and sailed south. In anticipation of Campbell's arrival, British and Tory raiders from East Florida launched a two-pronged sortie into Georgia during November to forage cattle and other provisions. An overland thrust against the settlements Newport and Midway was coordinated with an attack on Sunbury via the inland waterways.[8]

An anguished Howe learned of the change of command on October 9, well ahead of Lincoln's arrival in Charlestown. A second British invasion of the South offered Howe one last opportunity for redemption. When he heard reports of British devastation and pillage, the lame-duck general hurriedly set out from Charlestown on November 18 with a small force of Continentals to counter the threat. Writing from Zubly's Ferry on November 27 to bemoan the dreadful situation in Georgia, Howe urged Moultrie to send him men, powder, horses, and wagons.[9]

Moultrie acquiesced to Howe's requests for men and materiel, but he did so reluctantly. The cloud from New York had not disappeared but still hung over their heads in Charlestown. There was a consensus that the attack on Georgia was merely a diversion or prelude to an invasion of South Carolina. But the point became moot. Before Howe could reach the Savannah River, the British defeated a small, badly outnumbered Continental force at Midway and occupied Sunbury, choosing not to attack the Continentals who held nearby Fort Morris. With their aims more or less accomplished, the raiders withdrew back to East Florida.[10]

When Lincoln arrived in Charlestown on December 4, 1778, he received a warm welcome but found was a situation that was far worse than he had previously thought. He had inherited the same problems that had plagued General Howe: the number of promised troops failed to materialize; money, munitions, and provisions were lacking; and the militia was disobliging. Nonetheless he immediately began to prepare troops to march south to Howe's assistance. On December 27 he and Moultrie set out at the head of the First and Second South Carolina Regiments and a body of North Carolina militiamen. Altogether the force numbered about twelve hundred strong, but Moultrie and Lincoln did not reach Howe in time to put them to use.[11]

Two days before Christmas, the British expeditionary force arrived off Tybee Island at the mouth of the Savannah River. With only six hundred South Carolina and Georgia Continentals and one hundred Georgia militiamen to command, Howe believed that Savannah was indefensible. But when a British fleet of transports maneuvered upriver and disembarked troops at Girardeau's plantation on December 28, Howe and his council of war elected to defend Savannah against heavy odds rather than abandon the city to the British without a fight.[12]

On December 29 seven hundred Americans faced at least four times their number—professional soldiers commanded by experienced and capable British officers. Howe held a strong position and his troops were well disposed, but luck was on the British side. Guided by a slave who showed British scouts an obscure footpath through the swamp, Campbell's light infantry launched a surprise attack on the American right and rear followed with an assault on the main line. Howe's force collapsed almost at once and disintegrated into a desperate mob fleeing for its life. American losses were 83 killed and wounded and 453 captured. The British also seized seventy-one pieces of artillery and a considerable quantity of gunpowder, food, and other supplies.[13]

Stuck in Charlestown, Moultrie termed the decision of Howe's council of war to defend Savannah to be "the most ill-advised, rash opinion that possibly could be given; It was absurd to suppose that 6 or 700 men, and some of them very raw troops, could stand up against 2 or 3,000 as good troops as any the British had, and headed by Col. Campbell, an active, brave, and experienced officer." Howe should have retreated, opined Moultrie, especially since "he had certain information, that Gen. Lincoln was marching with a body of men, to join him, and actually did arrive at Purisburgh [sic], on the 3d day of January, only 4 days after his defeat."[14]

Moultrie also criticized the way that Lincoln and Howe managed the immediate aftermath of the battle, offering the view that if they had joined in the backcountry, their combined army, with the addition of reinforcements from Augusta and Ninety-Six, would have been large enough to dislodge the British from Savannah before they could fortify or receive help from General Prévost coming up from East Florida. (Lincoln considered this option.) From a strategic standpoint, however, the American disaster had a more pervasive effect than merely the loss of a provincial capital and important seaport.[15]

With Savannah, said Moultrie, "we lost the aid of almost all the citizens of that state as the British immediately encamped the troops along the Savannah River up to Augusta." Many Loyalists came out for the British, and the ardor of many Georgia Patriots was dampened for a time. "Sometimes the most trifling circumstance of error in war brings about great events; and the loss of Savannah was the occasion of the [ultimate] fall of Charlestown," he remarked in his memoirs, adding his belief that that the disaster at Savannah lengthened the war by a year.[16]

Lincoln and Moultrie left Charlestown on December 27 at the head of an army of twelve hundred mixed North and South Carolina troops—three hundred men of the First and Second Regiments from his brigade, and the rest mostly militia. They were too late to be of any help to Howe. The column reached Purrysburg on January 3, where Moultrie and Lincoln were joined by Howe and the remnant of his defeated army. Over the next two weeks, Lincoln's strength increased to about twenty-five hundred men, an army that was well-positioned and now large enough to counter any British thrust across the Savannah River, the primary defensive barrier between Georgia and South Carolina.[17]

It was at this time that Moultrie began communicating privately with Sen. Charles Pinckney. Pinckney was a cousin of Charles Cotesworth Pinckney and a longtime friend who had been very active in support of America's actions against the British government. He had been elected president of the Senate and to the Privy Council, and it was Moultrie's intent, through Pinckney, to promote the free exchange of intelligence between the military and government. During the winter and spring of 1779, while Moultrie was in the field, he and the senator carried on voluminous correspondence.[18]

In January 1779 Moultrie apprised his friend that the men were in good spirits and ready to receive the enemy but that they were not strong enough to take the offensive until reinforcements arrived. He also commented on the large number of refugees—"women, children, and negroes of Georgia . . . [a spectacle that even moved the hearts of the soldiers] travelling to they knew not where." The British conquerors, on the other hand, were not only stronger, they were close enough to the American outposts that their drums could be heard in the mornings; even the cough of a British sentry was audible if one listened carefully. Moultrie reported to Pinckney the loss of Sunbury. Although the officer in command at Sunbury with 120 Continentals had received orders to evacuate, Moultrie wrote with disgust that, "Don Quixote-like, [he] thought he was strong enough to withstand the whole force the British had in Georgia for which I think he deserved to be hanged."[19]

With his confidant Charles Pinckney, Moultrie had the freedom to unburden himself, and he did. "For God's sake let not your legislative or executive economy border too much on parsimony," wrote Moultrie regarding the militia, encouraging the South Carolina civil government to be generous and give the militia everything necessary to take the field. "It is now time to open your purse strings . . . and grant what the officers shall ask for that purpose," Moultrie said, adding a rare note of restrained emotion: "I cannot help being warmed when I think how ill the officers of this state have been treated, in being refused almost every necessity they applied for. . . . I shall say no more on this head as my warmth might carry me too far."[20]

Notwithstanding his remarks about equipping the militia, Moultrie greatly preferred regular troops over the necessity of relying on the unreliable and often uncooperative militia (though he commented on one occasion that a body of North Carolina Continentals were every bit as undisciplined as militia). But even if large bounties were paid to enlist Continental regulars, in the long run they were less expensive to maintain than militia. Moultrie made the dubious argument to Pinckney that if the regiments had been full, Savannah would not have been captured, or at the very least, the city would have been recovered. Perhaps recalling Howe's trouble during the last East Florida expedition, he correctly concluded that it would be dangerous to move into enemy territory relying too much on militia.[21]

Pinckney reported the contents of Moultrie's letters to the civil authorities, "to some of our great men," as he called them. Moultrie's observations had generally been very well received, except when Pinckney "gently touched on the strings of parsimony," of which Moultrie and too many others had often complained (Pinckney included). With this Moultrie had struck a raw nerve. The civil authorities were indignant over the implicit accusation of stinginess and argued that without South Carolina's money and provisions the army could not have marched into the field in the good condition that it did. Certainly, they said, South Carolina had provided more money than had ever flowed from the united treasury. Pinckney suggested that this discordant matter be dropped.[22]

Lincoln was aware of General Howe's difficulty managing the militia, and he soon gained firsthand experience of his own. An incident in camp demonstrated how recalcitrant the militia could be and how little power the Continental Army could wield to bring the militia under proper military discipline. It started when a soldier in Col. Joseph Kershaw's Camden Militia was absent from guard duty for several hours. When he finally returned to his post, he received some good-natured chiding from the captain of the guard, which provoked the truant guard to use insolent and abusive language.[23]

Now angry, the captain of the guard ordered the man's arrest. The offender grabbed his musket and, cocking the hammer, aimed at the captain and threatened to shoot. It took several other guards to overpower and disarm the struggling man. At Kershaw's request, General Lincoln convened a court-martial, drawing the officers from the militia and ordering Col. Richard Richardson to preside. Under military law the crime was punishable by death. To Lincoln's utter astonishment, seven members of the court refused the oath proscribed by the Continental Congress under the pretext that militia could be tried only under state militia law.[24]

The incident thoroughly vexed Lincoln, who laid the entire chain of events before Moultrie. Moultrie, though thoroughly sympathetic to Lincoln's frustration, maintained that by the letter of the law, the militia could not, in fact, be tried under the articles of war. Not only were the militiamen ignorant of the articles, but Moultrie argued that they would not take the field on such footing unless the legislature passed a law to that effect. Lincoln in turn countered that the militia from other states serving jointly with Continental troops and receiving Continental pay were indeed subject to the articles—the South Carolina militia should be as well. Lincoln and Moultrie put the question to an assembly of Moultrie's brigade field officers assembled at his quarters to hear both sides of the debate.[25]

Lincoln was astounded when the officers unanimously took Moultrie's side of the debate. They were just as frustrated by the militia, but like Moultrie they clearly understood that, like it or not, the militia constituted a large fraction of their numerical strength and that these troops had been very useful in the past. Lincoln and Moultrie's military reputations and the safety of the country depended on companies and regiments that could seemingly come and go at will. The militiamen did not lack in spirit, but they easily tired of camp life and would leave homesick, knowing that their dereliction would be punished only by a pittance of a fine.[26]

Pinckney took the opportunity to offer his opinions about the militia. First and foremost they were not nor did they want to become professional soldiers. The militiamen were free men who had never formally and voluntarily resigned the rights of citizens to the benefits of civil law, as in the case of the soldier in regular service. Furthermore the relationship between the Continental Congress and the states was yet to be clarified, and likewise the authority of Congress and of the officers of the Continental Army over the militia was yet unsettled.[27]

Pinckney expounded on his broad and lenient view of the militia, reminding Moultrie of their potential value and advising his friend to exercise forbearance: "I cannot help thinking with a little proper management, such as treating them as you would a coy maid, by gentle methods, you may at last expect a soldier-like performance of their duty; have patience and try to bear the misconduct of the

refractory militia with the military philosophy every general ought to be possessed of." It was counterproductive, Pinckney said, to try to punish free men
by applying "the halter [hangman's noose], or perhaps the receipt of a bullet
by the sentence of a court martial, for practices which they cannot be convinced
are crimes."[28]

General Lincoln, on the other hand, held tightly to his position, a stance
supported by the congressional mandate of September 25, 1778, that placed
militias in South Carolina under Continental command. Furthermore he had
received a letter from President Lowndes verifying that the militia was indeed in
the pay of the Continental establishment. But since the militia would not allow
themselves to be governed by Continental authority, Lincoln declared that he
would no longer provision them and that they were at liberty to go.[29]

Moultrie was alarmed by Lincoln's actions. The American troops were in
close proximity to the enemy, and he was concerned that if the British learned of
the divisiveness in the American camp, they might very well cross the Savannah
River. With this in mind, Moultrie again urged Pinckney to make recruiting for
the Continental regiments his first priority, even by conscription from the districts if necessary. Meanwhile Moultrie would use the militia to the best possible
advantage—to cover river crossings and protect their own country. This strategy
was tenuous at best, because the militia had already abandoned two important
posts without giving the least notice.[30]

Lawmakers in Charlestown were debating a revision of South Carolina's militia law, but Pinckney did not expect much progress to be made, particularly on
the matter of discipline, and he harbored no expectation that the militia would
be made subject to the articles of war. Wanting nothing more to do with the
militia troops, Lincoln turned them over entirely to Moultrie in the hope that
they might be more amenable to his orders as South Carolina's senior Continental officer. Lincoln's optimism was unfounded. Moultrie found that the militia
continued in their stubborn refusal to obey orders or remain at their posts. In a
pique Lincoln asked the now equally frustrated Moultrie to ride to Charlestown
to acquaint recently elected governor John Rutledge with the weakened condition of the army and to impress Rutledge with the obstinacy and ineffectiveness
of the militia. These unreliable soldiers had become an insurmountable obstacle
to every offensive operation they had contemplated.[31]

Moultrie and Lincoln were now of one mind. They had discussed at length
what must be done, and the majority of Lincoln's recommendations were much
the same as those Moultrie had already voiced in recent letters to Pinckney. First,
if the militia would not act *with* the army, it must act separately; Lincoln and
Moultrie wanted fifteen hundred militia sent to Purrysburg to cover the border
so that the Continental Army could resume offensive operations. Second, if the

first recommendation was unacceptable, the militia should be used for the defense of the backcountry. Third, provision must be made for the South Carolina militia to take the place of troops from North Carolina, whose terms were about to expire. Finally, Lincoln and Moultrie wanted all of South Carolina's Continentals to be sent to the army in the field, even those in garrison at Forts Moultrie and Johnson. Moultrie had long thought that the militia could be used to garrison the forts in their places.[32]

Moultrie (the Continental officer) and Pinckney (the militia officer) harbored fundamental philosophical differences of opinion as far as the proposed militia law was concerned. Pinckney informed Moultrie that the bill had met with great opposition in the House of Representatives, and he hoped that his fellow senators would continue to share his view that the proposed law, with its rigorous obligations and harsh penalties, infringed too much on the essential rights and privileges of their fellow citizens as free men.[33]

Pinckney had read law on the American continent instead of studying abroad, but he was thoroughly versed in the English legal system. To strengthen his case, he cited a spirited answer given by the members of the House of Commons to the king of England when they were told that it was improper to debate about rights and privileges when reports had been received that an enemy was about to land an invading army in the kingdom. "The answer was to this effect if I remember right, from the parliamentary history, 'that if they were sure the enemy had an army in the heart of the kingdom and were marching with hastened strides to Westminster, they would not part with one of the least rights and privileges of the people.'"[34]

Moultrie feared that without substantive change, the militia law would ruin the country's hope for attaining independence. His was a pragmatic viewpoint, and he countered Pinckney's argument by warning that "in contending too much for the liberties of the people, you will enslave them at last." He added, "Remember my friend, it has always been the maxim of all communities, to abridge the people some of those liberties for a time, the better to secure the whole to them in the future."[35]

Moultrie reached Charlestown by February 16, 1779, and with the aid of Colonel Charles Cotesworth Pinckney, he laid all of the facts concerning the militia before the governor and both houses of the legislature. The civil authorities were admittedly ignorant of certain details, and Moultrie's passionate presentation "aroused the spirit as well as the indignation of the House so much at the conduct of their fellow-citizens" that they reconsidered their former position regarding the militia. Although the legislators had recently rejected the idea of subjecting the militia to martial law, they now proposed a new law that passed both Houses unanimously.[36]

A cursory reading of the new law gives the impression that the extraordinary powers vested in the governor of South Carolina to do with the militia as he saw fit would allow him to place the militia under Continental articles of war if circumstances warranted. Such action would give Lincoln the statutory authority he wanted. But in application this never happened, and the relationship between the Continentals and militia remained as contentious and fractious as ever.[37]

14.

Port Royal to Briar Creek

To capitalize on their success at Savannah, British general Augustine Prévost sent Lt. Col. Archibald Campbell on an inland march to rally backcountry Tories. Campbell's ambition was to be the first British officer to "rend a Stripe and a Star from the Flag of Congress," and his army consisted of slightly more than a thousand British regulars and Loyalist militia—a quarter of the total British force in Georgia. With the second largest town in the state firmly under British control, Georgia would be lost to the Patriots and restored to full colonial status. After a 120-mile expedition upriver that met only token resistance along the way, the mission culminated with the occupation of Augusta, Georgia, on January 31, 1779.[1]

Results were disappointing. The response to Campbell's call for Loyalist recruits was lackluster, and a buildup of Patriot militia on the Carolina side of the Savannah River compelled Campbell to abandon Augusta after only two weeks. On February 15 the British contingent headed south to rejoin General Prévost at Ebenezer, a small community twenty-five miles upriver from Savannah where the British had established a staging area for backcountry operations.[2]

Lincoln and Moultrie sought a new opportunity to challenge Campbell in the backcountry—a chance to strike a decisive blow—and they were emboldened by the January 27 arrival of Maj. Gen. John Ashe with eleven hundred men of the North Carolina militia. Lincoln summarily dispatched Ashe from Purrysburg toward Augusta to rendezvous with Brig. Gen. Andrew Williamson's South Carolinians. He planned to trap the British between two armies: the combined forces of Generals Ashe and Williamson on the east side of the Savannah and Moultrie's corps of Continentals and militia, who would cross the Savannah below Augusta. Once surrounded, Campbell would be forced either to surrender or to fight an American army that outnumbered him three to one. Moultrie set out to put Lincoln's plan into effect, but after he had proceeded for only six or eight miles upriver, a messenger brought orders from Lincoln for him to turn around and return to base. Lincoln had decided to send him to Beaufort, South Carolina, on Port Royal Island instead.[3]

In the meantime Charlestown was in a perpetual state of alarm over reported British depredations along the South Carolina coast. New rumors that the town of Beaufort on the eastern side of Port Royal had fallen into the hands of the British fueled the general anxiety that General Prévost was attempting to gain a foothold from which to operate against Charlestown. Either way more troops were needed. Committees of both houses of the South Carolina legislature reacted to the emergency by passing a resolution to raise an army of three thousand men for the defense of Charlestown. Charles Pinckney informed Moultrie of the measure and his reservations—he could not fathom from where the legislature would raise such a large number of men without adversely affecting Continental recruitment. Moultrie did not respond to Pinckney's urgings for him to come to Charlestown to straighten out the mess. There were more pressing matters to deal with first.[4]

Prévost had taken advantage of British naval superiority and sent a small flotilla up the South Carolina coast from Savannah to make an amphibious assault on Port Royal. Aboard several privateers and transports were two hundred regulars and a four-inch howitzer, all commanded by Maj. William Gardner. The sight of the British entering Port Royal Sound on January 31 so unnerved the local militia that they refused to remain on Port Royal Island. Not long afterward the Continental garrison of Fort Lyttelton near Beaufort spiked their guns and hurriedly abandoned their fort. From all appearances an occupation of Port Royal and Beaufort would be uncontested by American forces.[5]

Moultrie and his aide-de-camp, Capt. Francis Kinloch, traveled as quickly as possible to reach the Port Royal ferry on January 31, but despite their exertion they were too late to prevent the spiking of the cannon at Fort Lyttelton. At the ferry they met Brig. Gen. Stephen Bull, who had gathered together 270 militiamen plus the handful of Continentals from Fort Lyttelton. Moultrie considered himself lucky to have them. The outlook brightened further when a contingent of the Charlestown Artillery arrived bringing two six-pound field pieces. The Charlestown Artillery was no run-of-the mill corps of militia. This elite battery had been organized and drilled by Christopher Gadsden, and the detachment sent to Port Royal was led by two notable captains, Edward Rutledge and Thomas Heyward Jr. Both Rutledge and Heyward were signers of the Declaration of Independence and delegates to the Continental Congress.[6]

Moultrie's presence greatly heartened the militiamen. A writer to the *South Carolina and American General Gazette* declared Moultrie's arrival at camp to be "an event that gave general joy, as it inspired us with a well founded confidence that he would lead us to honor and victory." Moultrie readily consented when the militia asked him to cross over to Port Royal at their head, and together they methodically traversed Whale Branch on the morning of February 2. The civilian ferry crossed Whale Branch, a waterway connecting the Broad and Coosaw Rivers about ten miles north of Beaufort, and was itself little more than a single flatboat, but by one o'clock in the afternoon all of the men and the artillery were across. At a cedar causeway north of Beaufort, Moultrie sent out Capt. John Barnwell's horsemen to find the enemy while the men rested and replenished their canteens from a freshwater spring.[7]

Moultrie had no indication of any British activity other than columns of smoke that had been observed while crossing the ferry. The smoke came from the western or Broad River side of Port Royal, and Moultrie and Bull learned of the source from Barnwell. General Bull's elegant mansion at Laurel Bay had been shelled by the armed British vessel *Germaine* before being looted and burned by a scouting party sent ashore the previous day. It was a customary practice of the British army to destroy the homes of prominent rebels to punish their treason. Laurel Bay was the largest plantation on the island, and by burning the house and every other building on that and several neighboring plantations, the British hoped to intimidate the South Carolinians. Instead the arson had the opposite effect of invigorating the militiamen who were now ready to defend their homes and hearths.[8]

The Americans picked up the march again at 8 P.M. and trekked the darkness for three hours until they reached John Mulryne's plantation less than a mile from Beaufort. Moultrie allowed the exhausted men to sleep on their arms at Mulryne's while Barnwell's troopers scouted the area. Barnwell reported that Beaufort was quiet—no sign of enemy—so Moultrie roused up and marched his small army the remaining distance, entering town just before sunrise on February 3. Beaufort was practically deserted, as most of the townspeople had fled for fear of the British.[9]

After a brief pause for rest, Moultrie and Bull set off to inspect the ruins of Fort Lyttelton. This small, tabby-walled stronghold was situated about a mile and a half below Beaufort on Spanish Point. Construction began during the French and Indian War, but the fort was not completed until 1764. Moultrie and Bull discovered the fort to be in shambles, although most of the stores were still intact, most importantly the fort's gunpowder. Capt. John L. De Treville, the fort's commandant, had no knowledge that Moultrie was coming to his aid, and when the invasion force appeared in Port Royal Sound, he ordered the fort's twenty-one cannons spiked and the bastion blown up to make the fort unfit for enemy occupation. Moultrie found that the fort's guns were so lightly spiked that that the spikes could be drawn from the touchholes with a pair of pincers.[10]

Major Gardner landed his force at Laurel Bay early on the morning of February 3, not long after Moultrie and his South Carolinians marched into Beaufort. Like Moultrie, Gardner was unaware of any significant enemy presence on Port Royal until he marched his redcoats to the ferry at Whale Branch. Hearing that Americans were camped at Beaufort, he turned his column toward the town and pressed forward.[11]

By 11 A.M. Moultrie and Bull had scarcely been at Fort Lyttelton a few moments when a rider brought word that the British were five miles away and moving rapidly toward town. Moultrie sent Bull back to Beaufort to call out the troops, and when he arrived in town less than an hour later, Bull had the troops formed and ready to march. The South Carolinians advanced in a column with light infantry forming the vanguard and flankers. Moultrie and Bull rode behind the van, just ahead of the rest of the column, and they continued west for two miles before a scout reported that the British were four miles away—not nearly as close as Moultrie had first thought.[12]

Now that he had a little breathing room, Moultrie proceeded slowly while he looked for a suitable position to await an attack. After another hour's delay, the British still did not show. A rider brought word that the redcoats were not coming their way at all—they were heading toward the ferry instead. Moultrie continued his roundabout pursuit northward for three miles on the road between Beaufort and the ferry and was halfway there when horsemen reported that the British had changed course again. They were coming from the ferry in full march right toward them.[13]

Moultrie sent Captain Kinloch ahead to reconnoiter. Kinloch returned to confirm that the British were not more than a mile distant. Spotting a wooded swamp to his front, Moultrie urged his men forward to gain the covered position. Evidently Gardner saw it as well and got his men there first. Moultrie halted his men on a slight rise called Gray's Hill, in an open field near the Halfway House Tavern, two hundred yards shy of the British position. He redeployed his marching column into a line of battle facing north astride the road. The two six-pounders of the Charlestown Artillery he placed in the center of his line, and he posted Captain De Treville and his few Continentals in the woods on the American right with their brass two-pounder to cover the enemy's near approach.[14]

During his reconnaissance Kinloch happened upon Gardner, who waved a white handkerchief from his sword and promised that Kinloch would not be fired on if he came close. Gardner told Kinloch that he knew the American strength and that General Moultrie was in command. Out of regard for Moultrie's brother (East Florida's royal lieutenant governor, John Moultrie) and to prevent the effusion of blood, Gardner offered to negotiate. He demanded possession of Fort Lyttelton, but in return he would permit Moultrie's army to leave Port Royal Island with the honors of war. After he conferred with Moultrie, Kinloch replied that the Americans had "too much English blood" in their veins to consent to Gardner's proposal or "to surrender any port without first fighting for it." These were strong words considering the recent behavior of the militia, but Moultrie was willing to test their mettle against well-trained, professional British soldiers.[15]

About 4 P.M. the British emerged from the trees with fixed bayonets. As they came within range, Moultrie ordered Captain Heyward to open with his guns. The Charlestown Artillery's second shot disabled the lone British howitzer. Moultrie advanced his right and left wings a hundred yards to meet the enemy, and the firing became general on both sides. The tactics were, as Moultrie noted, "reversed from the usual way of fighting, between the British and Americans; they taking to the bushes and we remaining upon the open ground." Fearing his men were getting the worst of it in the open, and aware of the bad consequences that could attend a retrograde movement with unseasoned troops, he ordered them to take cover in the trees alongside the road. Neither side could turn the other's flank, and after about forty-five minutes of firing, the American infantry-men had expended most of their cartridges and were calling for resupply. Captains Heyward and Rutledge reported the same predicament—the field pieces had fired almost forty rounds apiece, and their limber chests were nearly empty.[16]

Moultrie decided to order a slow withdrawal, but before the Americans began to pull back, the redcoats started retreating. Barnwell and his fifteen-man troop of light horse rode around the enemy formation in a display of hot pursuit that nearly turned the British retreat into a rout, but Moultrie could not press his advantage without ammunition. He directed the artillery to retire slowly and instructed the infantry to keep the pace of the artillery to cover their flanks in case the British mounted a counterattack.[17]

The affair was small from a numerical standpoint, but Moultrie won a crucial tactical victory against the British while at the head of a small army composed of the very type of soldiers that had so bedeviled the Continental command. When the battle was over, the South Carolina militia had vanquished British regulars who were forced to take to their boats and return to Savannah. The total number of British casualties is unknown, but the redcoats abandoned their position in such haste that they left behind fourteen dead and wounded.[18]

One American officer and seven privates were killed at Port Royal. Moultrie was particularly saddened by the death of Lt. Benjamin Wilkins, whom he deemed a most valuable officer. Four officers and eighteen privates were wounded, including Thomas Heyward. In all Moultrie was very proud of the behavior of the militia. The men had been orderly in their maneuvers and steadfast under fire in the open against British regulars. The Charlestown Artillery had performed like veterans, handling their field pieces like professionals and directing their fire with the utmost accuracy.[19]

In his report to General Lincoln, Moultrie lauded Barnwell and his cavalrymen, who had kept him informed of the British movements, captured a number of prisoners, and brought off twelve stand of arms. He later learned that the British expressed their admiration of the bravery of the officers on horseback. Moultrie was an old horseman himself, and the battle sparked in him a renewed interest in recruiting cavalry. Newly enlisted horsemen, he told Pinckney, should be sent directly to camp without delay for training. If sufficient numbers of horsemen could be raised, Barnwell would be an excellent choice to lead them, and he strongly recommended Barnwell for promotion to field officer.[20]

Moultrie also won fresh laurels during the engagement: "To attempt an encomium of General Moultrie would be unnecessary," wrote an officer to a Charlestown newspaper, explaining, "He acted like himself, and his countenance inspired everyone." Overall he was quite pleased with the outcome, but the whole affair had wearied the forty-eight-year-old Moultrie, causing him to express to Pinckney a sentiment that he shared with many of his revolutionary contemporaries: "I find my old bones yield much to fatigue; I hope, however, they will carry me through the war; then I will set me down in peace, and indulge myself the remainder of my days."[21]

Before departing Port Royal for Purrysburg, Moultrie ordered Lt. Col. Barnard Beekman to transport the cannons and stores from Beaufort and Fort Lyttelton to General Bull's camp on the mainland, which was safely out of reach of the British if they returned from Savannah with reinforcements. Moultrie worried that the militia would not remain on Port Royal once he returned to Purrysburg, and he issued orders for them to march to Purrysburg with him. Word passed up the chain of command from Captain Heyward on February 10 that the men of the Charlestown Artillery were displeased with their orders and that they would not stay away from Charlestown after March 1. The fickleness of the militia greatly disappointed Moultrie, who believed that he had restored their spirits by convincing them that the redcoats were not invincible and could be beaten with a slight numerical superiority if led by competent officers.[22]

On his return to Purrysburg, Moultrie applied to Lincoln for permission to travel to Charlestown. The lowcountry inhabitants remained nervous over the threat of a British invasion. Moultrie was of a different opinion. He was confident that if the British returned to capture Beaufort, they could easily be prevented from crossing over to the mainland by the militia. He wanted to go to Charlestown to put the troops on solid defensive footing himself. This would inspire the men and calm the locals. Lincoln, however, had other plans and informed Moultrie that he could not be spared. Lincoln intended to march three

thousand men from Purrysburg to Augusta on February 10 to interrupt communications between Augusta and disaffected backcountry Loyalists.[23]

The expedition had barely begun, Moultrie having only marched his troops
seven miles from Purrysburg, when he received word of large numbers of enemy
troops forming at Ninety-Six and Saluda, South Carolina. Of a more proximate
concern were reports of a planned British offensive aimed at Purrysburg. The
Americans were, in Moultrie's words, "greatly embarrassed to know which way
to move." If Lincoln moved his force upcountry, the British might cross the
Savannah and advance in the direction of Charlestown with the advantage of a
three- or four-day head start on any pursuit. Moultrie returned to camp again to
wait for Lincoln to consider the options.[24]

During the winter of 1779, Lincoln's army of Continentals and militia steadily
grew from the remnant that escaped the debacle at Savannah. From Purrysburg
the Americans could monitor British movements in Georgia or move to parry
any British attempt to cross the Savannah River. By March, Lincoln had perhaps
seven thousand men spread among camps from Augusta to Purrysburg. Having
returned from addressing the legislature at Charlestown, Moultrie commanded a
strength of two thousand Continentals at Purrysburg. He would be yet stronger
when his old Second Regiment joined him and when Governor Rutledge sent
fifteen hundred more militiamen to Purrysburg. Rutledge also planned to establish a new camp for up to five thousand men at Orangeburgh, South Carolina.[25]

Moultrie was surprised when Rutledge procrastinated. He had received information from an exchanged prisoner that Prévost had moved most of his force
to Ebenezer, obliquely to the northwest opposite Purrysburg, about six miles
away. Word was that Prévost would cross into South Carolina by the end of
March or first part of April. Even without reinforcements from Rutledge, Moultrie was cautiously confident. "I fancy they [the British] will think better of it; if
they do not they may get a good drubbing," he wrote with optimism. In fact the
Americans might save them the trouble and cross over to Georgia first to fight
the British on their own ground. Moultrie assured Pinckney that his men were
longing to have at them, "but this you may depend upon, we shall do nothing
rashly or inconsiderately; we well know what we have at stake."[26]

At this juncture Lincoln decided to make an offensive thrust at the British on
the Georgia side of the Savannah. He called a council of war for March 1 at Black
Swamp, the camp of Brig. Gen. Griffith Rutherford's North Carolina militia,
about twenty-five miles north of Purrysburg. Lincoln, Moultrie, and Rutherford
were joined by Major General Ashe. The council agreed to leave a rear guard
at Purrysburg and march the rest of the army to Black Swamp. The Americans
would then cross to the west side of the Savannah and unite with Ashe at Briar

Creek while General Williamson brought his militia down from Augusta. Ashe had taken his position fifteen miles north of Ebenezer near the confluence of Briar Creek with the Savannah River after shadowing Campbell's retreat south from Augusta, and he assured the council that the place was secure. The British were greatly misinformed of his numerical strength and would not dare think to attack him.[27]

Ashe returned to his camp on March 2. The next day his mix of about 1,500 North Carolina and Georgia militiamen and Continentals were surprised and completely routed at Briar Creek. The American disaster was perpetrated by a British column of 900 redcoats and Loyalist militia under Lt. Col. Jacques Marcus Prévost, the younger brother of Gen. Augustine Prévost. General Prévost had anticipated Lincoln's plan and attacked before the junction between Ashe and Lincoln could be made. Aside from the 450 men that rejoined Lincoln after the battle, Ashe's force virtually ceased to exist due to casualties and desertions on the part of militiamen who ran straight home to their firesides. The irreplaceable loss of a thousand stand of arms and seven field pieces was a catastrophe all by itself.[28]

Moultrie learned about the calamity from Maj. Peter Horry of the Second South Carolina Regiment. Since leaving Charlestown with Lincoln, Moultrie had been lobbying to have the Second Regiment transferred to him in the field. At first Pinckney and some of the other legislators in town refused on the grounds that the defense of Charlestown would be too greatly weakened, but they finally relented. Horry happened to be leading a detachment of the Second to Purrysburg and was about twenty miles away at Bee's Creek Bridge when he saw two or three hundred men retreating in a hasty and confused manner, mostly unarmed, and coming his way. General Ashe rode up to Horry and asked the captain to try to stop the fugitives. Horry formed his men with fixed bayonets and threatened to fire if they did not halt, which had the desired effect.[29]

Moultrie presided over Ashe's court of inquiry on March 10. The court faulted the North Carolinian for negligence for failing to secure his camp properly and to obtain adequate intelligence of the enemy but absolved him of cowardice. Moultrie summed up the effect of the calamity: "This unlucky affair at Brier-Creek, disconcerted all our plans," he wrote, "for it is not to be doubted that had we have crossed the river with our army, and joined Gen. Ash[e], which we were preparing to do, we should have had a body of 7,000 men; besides strong reinforcements were marching to us from every quarter sufficient to drive the enemy out of Georgia."[30]

Charles Pinckney tried to keep a positive outlook on the turn of events when he wrote to Moultrie that "this stroke I am hopeful will ultimately turn out to our common advantage, by making the militia more careful to prevent surprizes [sic]." Pinckney was inclined to lecture Moultrie on generalship from time to time and did not let this opportunity pass: "I well know your zeal and active spirit will spur you on, as you hint, to change posts; but, my friend, steady! Remember the Fabian policy . . . for the stake at risk is too great to lose, and Generals should never act from heat or revenge to punish a momentary insult . . . have patience."[31]

The Fabian policy mentioned by Pinckney was a reference to Quintus Fabius Maximus, the third-century B.C. Roman politician and general who was well known to classical scholars. When Hannibal and the Carthaginians invaded Italy during the Second Punic War (218 to 201 B.C.), Fabius refused to engage Hannibal in pitched battles with his weaker Roman army. Instead he instead employed the strategy that now bears his name, an approach that made use of harassing raids, delaying tactics, and attrition to exhaust the enemy over time and to gain victory by avoiding defeat.* Moultrie understood the major drawback of a Fabian policy—the demoralizing effect of frequent retreats and lack of major victories—and he reminded Pinckney that "the Fabian maxim does not agree altogether with American dispositions and undisciplined troops; they soon grow tired and desert."[32]

* After losing battles in 1776 and 1777, Generals George Washington and Nathanael Greene adopted this strategy despite its political unpopularity. Washington was given the sobriquet "American Fabius."

15.

"Let us Burgoyne them"

The American disaster at Briar Creek and the buildup of British forces at Ebenezer on the Georgia side of the Savannah River induced Lincoln and Moultrie to relocate their headquarters to Black Swamp, a more secure position and better staging area about twenty-five miles north by northwest of Purrysburg. Large-scale military operations against the British in Georgia were temporarily postponed in March and April 1779 while Lincoln reconsidered his options. In the interim the Americans replenished their clothing, arms, and ammunition from supplies sent south by Congress, seated in Baltimore, and from the Dutch West Indian island colony of St. Eustatius, the principal source of munitions purchased for the rebellious states.[1]

The British army in the southern theater was not reinforced, and this allowed Lincoln's army to achieve numerical superiority, largely due to successful recruiting on the part of Governor John Rutledge. The governor concentrated his newly enlisted militiamen at a central camp near Orangeburgh, where he hoped eventually to assemble up to five thousand men. By personally commanding the state militia, Rutledge showed his determination to exercise his executive power fully.[2]

Moultrie found himself in an uncomfortable position as spectator to the meddling of civil authorities in military affairs when Rutledge issued orders that were contradictory to policy set by General Lincoln. Moultrie expressed concern to Charles Pinckney that the governor's zeal would cause trouble: "I think I see matters brewing that may bring on misunderstandings between the Governor and Gen. Lincoln; such as orders issued from two commanders; which may perhaps run retrograde to each other; this may be of dangerous consequences at this critical juncture," he warned. Rutledge had ordered General Williamson to send raiding parties into Georgia to harass the British and to destroy livestock, provisions, and anything else that might be useful to the British. Rutledge also gave Williamson permission to order the Georgia militia to cooperate with him when necessary.[3]

Unknown to Rutledge, Lincoln had sent word into Georgia that any inhabitants who were loyal to the American cause and could not escape into Patriot-occupied territory would be left alone by the army if they remained quietly at home. Moultrie interjected himself into the situation by firmly but gently admonishing the governor that orders to the military could come from no one but General Lincoln. Not only should Rutledge's orders concerning the Georgia militia be considered void, but regarding the destruction of private property, Moultrie exclaimed, "what must become of the poor widows, orphans, and helpless old men should the order be indiscriminately put into execution?" The issue was amicably resolved, but this would not be the last time Moultrie would be entangled in controversy between the civil authority and military command.[4]

Benjamin Lincoln called a council of war on April 19 to formalize a plan that had been under consideration for weeks—a strategy to cross the Savannah River with five or six thousand men, leaving twelve hundred behind to protect the lowcountry. Moultrie had foreknowledge that he would command the rear defensive element and whatever action he saw, if any, would depend on the British reaction to the movement of the main American army. Pinckney was justifiably anxious that with both the American and British armies in motion, Charlestown would be vulnerable to attack, and he told Moultrie that he should not expect reinforcements from that quarter. Any detachments sent to strengthen Moultrie at Black Swamp would have to come from Governor Rutledge at Orangeburgh. In the meantime the defensive works that were being raised across the Charlestown Neck were nearing completion, a fact that pleased Moultrie, who told Pinckney, "I hope we never shall have occasion to try the goodness of the works: should you be attacked you may depend some of us will hasten to your assistance."[5]

The council of war consisted of Lincoln and Moultrie, Brig. Gen. Isaac Huger, and Brig. Gen. Jethro E. Sumner from North Carolina. American troop strength amounted to roughly five thousand men. The council approved leaving a thousand at Black Swamp and at Purrysburg and marching the remainder up the east bank of the Savannah to cross the river and take a strong position near Augusta. This plan offered several advantages. Communication with backcountry Loyalists and the Indians would be disrupted. Lincoln's advance would provide a measure of security for Augusta, where the reconstituted Georgia legislature was slated to convene on May 1. And an American descent down the west bank of the Savannah would likely force the British to give up their post at Ebenezer and retreat to Savannah.[6]

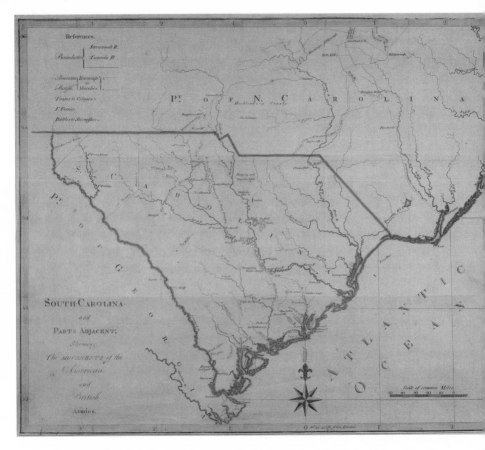

South Carolina and Parts Adjacent; Showing the Movements of the American and British Armies. The Robert Charles Lawrence Fergusson Collection, the Society of the Cincinnati; Washington, D.C. Reproduced with permission.

Lincoln marched from Black Swamp on April 20 with 2,000 light infantry and cavalry. After reaching the vicinity of Augusta two days later, he directed Moultrie to send the rest of the Continental troops and the artillery to join him, excepting 220 men of the Second and Fifth South Carolina Regiments and a light two-pound field piece. As predicted Moultrie was ordered to remain at Black Swamp and keep an eye on the British with these few remaining Continentals and a body of militia. If the British were to cross the river and move toward Charlestown, Moultrie would cover the fords and bridges over the rivers and creeks between Purrysburg and Charlestown to delay the British, giving Lincoln time to come to his assistance.[7]

Lincoln's ambitious plan had a major flaw. Compared to the size of the British force at Ebenezer, Moultrie's force was too small, and if it were swept aside by the British, the overland path to Charlestown would be clear. Gen. Andrew Williamson's militia was sufficient to secure the Georgia backcountry, and the danger posed by backcountry Tories was not enough to warrant Lincoln taking the better part of the southern American army upriver while leaving South Carolina exposed. Lincoln failed to grasp the British strategic situation. If he had remained at Purrysburg, the British could not mount another expedition into the interior without risking their line of communication with Savannah. Lincoln held Moultrie at Black Swamp as a precaution, but the void created by his absence would place Charlestown in serious jeopardy.[8]

Lincoln had been gone from Black Swamp for less than a week on April 25 when Moultrie received word that the British were in motion. It was paramount for Moultrie, then without knowledge of British strength and direction, to obtain timely intelligence. Maj. Peter Horry was on outpost duty at Purrysburg with a hundred men of the Second Regiment, and Moultrie ordered him to stay vigilant and to keep his horsemen on constant patrol. If Horry's scouts were to discover the enemy landing on the east bank of the river, he was to pull back to the Coosawhatchie Bridge and immediately notify Moultrie of his retreat by sending two or three riders to guarantee delivery of the message.[9]

Most of the Continentals and the best of the militia had gone with Lincoln on his foray to Georgia, and Rutledge was fully involved with organizing the militia in Orangeburgh. With Lincoln and Rutledge so occupied, Moultrie's concerns over troop strength were compounded by a lack of settled authority in Charlestown. Fortunately Lt. Gov. Thomas Bee had assumed authority in Rutledge's absence and fully supported Moultrie. When Moultrie took stock of his munitions and realized that he had only five hundred pounds of musket powder on hand, he ordered deputy quartermaster general Lt. Col. Stephen Drayton to apply to Bee for a thousand pounds from South Carolina stores. Bee informed Moultrie that he was daily expecting additional arms and powder from Baltimore sent by the Continental Congress, and he would send Moultrie powder by pack train as soon as possible.[10]

Moultrie did not know that Lincoln received advance warning of the British intent to cross into South Carolina at about the same time he did, perhaps even a day earlier. Lincoln acted on the premise that the British movement was only a feint intended to prevent a detachment led by Brig. Gen. Isaac Huger from joining his force. Consequently he did little more than caution Huger to be alert to the possibility of a surprise attack. This was a grave error. The British movement was not a diversion at all. It was thrust toward the heart of South Carolina.[11]

General Prévost began to land his redcoats on the South Carolina side of the Savannah River on April 29, crossing at Purrysburg and at Two Sisters Ferry near Black Swamp. The British were in dire need of forage, and Prévost saw the movement of the greater part of the American army toward Augusta as an opportunity to obtain badly needed lowcountry rice and beef for his army in the field and the garrison in Savannah. And once Prévost comprehended that Moultrie's small holding force constituted the soft underbelly of the American army, he realized that Charlestown could be his for the taking if he struck quickly.[12]

Prévost took two days to move his army across a rain-swollen Savannah River. Lt. Col. Alexander McIntosh had taken the place of Major Horry in rotation at the Purrysburg outpost, and once Moultrie confirmed that the British were indeed crossing the river, he recalled McIntosh from Purrysburg to Black Swamp. At the same time, he sent a dispatch rider to Gen. Stephen Bull asking him to send all available men and artillery to the Coosawhatchie River. On April 30 Moultrie sent a post rider to inform Lincoln of the British advance and that he was withdrawing from Black Swamp to Coosawhatchie. By the time Moultrie reached his new position, the British had reportedly occupied Purrysburg with fifteen hundred redcoats and several pieces of artillery. Information gleaned from deserters gave Moultrie the first indication that the British objective was Charlestown.[13]

The British occupied Black Swamp only three hours after Moultrie had left his camp on a fifteen-mile forced march to the Coosawhatchie River. "I cannot tell you their numbers, but I believe vastly superior to mine," he wrote Rutledge at Orangeburgh. Harkening to his relatively close brush with the British, he wryly added, "I escaped a trimming." He was right, and he knew he had made a lucky escape. Had he had remained at Black Swamp, he would have been attacked in force the next morning. Moultrie sent an express rider advising Lincoln to return immediately to South Carolina, but in the meantime he was in dire need of help from Rutledge: "I think it is absolutely necessary, that you [Rutledge] should send some reinforcements to meet me, as I am in hourly expectation of being alarmed by the approach of the enemy . . . be assured it requires your utmost exertions; as I am vastly inferior to them; they, by all accounts, 2,000, and I have not 1200 [all militia except 250 Continentals]. . . . You have not a moment to lose."[14]

Moultrie wrote to Lincoln and Rutledge from Coosawhatchie again on May 1—the third letter in two days to Lincoln and the second to Rutledge, hearing nothing from either in return. The poor communication and the lack of reinforcement frustrated Moultrie as he maneuvered to avoid confronting the British. If he could get a thousand troops and a few pieces of artillery from either Lincoln or Rutledge, he believed he could stop the advancing redcoats.[15]

By the late afternoon, Moultrie had withdrawn a couple of miles closer to Charlestown, taking position on a hill behind the Tullifiny River that he judged to be better ground on which to oppose the British. Once there he and Mr. Thomas Heyward Sr., a gentleman of the neighborhood, reconnoitered the area.

Finding several river fords very low as a result of a dry spell, Moultrie posted a guard at these places and sent out vedettes to warn of an enemy approach. By this time he had confirmed that General Prévost was commanding the British expeditionary force himself.[16]

General Bull also notified Moultrie on May 1 that he was bringing five or six hundred militia in two days. The trouble was that a British fleet had reportedly sailed from Savannah to support Prévost by threatening either Beaufort or Charlestown. For this reason very few of Bull's militiamen answered the call to come to Moultrie's assistance despite the fact that just a few months earlier he had come to their aid when the British landed on Port Royal. With their farms and families now in the path of the advancing British, home and hearth called more loudly than the clarion call to oppose the invasion with a united force. The militiamen either refused to leave home or else they removed their families to Charlestown or another secure area.[17]

By the morning of May 2, the British strategy was again in doubt. Deserters were now saying that Prévost had three thousand redcoats and that he intended to march them upriver after Lincoln. The accounts of the deserters were consistent with reports brought in by Moultrie's scouts. Moultrie hoped these reports true, because Lincoln's army was strong enough to oppose the British. Moultrie's army, still unreinforced, was too weak to meet Prévost in battle. He was outmanned and outgunned—his single two-pounder was no match for the six nine-pounders that the British had in tow. He had repeatedly asked for artillery to no effect, and his letters to Rutledge expressed a tone of unhopeful resignation.[18]

Moultrie finally heard from Lincoln, who gave a token response to his plea for help made on April 30. Lincoln was sending a detachment of 250 picked Georgia Continentals under Lt. Col. Francis H. Harris, and he would ask the governor to divert militia intended to reinforce the main army. Written on May 2, it is unclear exactly when this dispatch found its way into Moultrie's hands. Lincoln wrote it while at Silver Bluff, a place twelve miles from Augusta on the South Carolina side of the Savannah. In any case at the same time that Moultrie was preparing to defend Tullifiny Hill, Lincoln was staying put, confident that the British posed no serious threat to Charlestown.[19]

Rutledge also wrote to Moultrie on May 2 stating that he would soon march with reinforcements, but in the meantime he exhorted Moultrie to take every necessary step to procure all the men he could and to "throw every obstruction in the way, to annoy the enemy, and prevent their progress and ravages." The governor finally set out with his South Carolina militia, marching from Orangeburgh on May 4 and proceeding as quickly as the roads and weather would allow. Rutledge hoped to furnish four to five hundred men of horse, foot, and artillery. He was bringing all of his field pieces, a total of ten guns, and he was accompanied by a detachment of the Fourth Regiment Artillery commanded by Capt. Thomas Grimball. Thomas Bee in Charlestown promised to augment further Moultrie's artillery by mounting on field carriages as many guns as possible.[20]

Moultrie was obliged to abandon a number of sick soldiers to the British when the Americans hurriedly withdrew from Black Swamp because he did not have the wagons with which to transport them. Once he arrived at Tullifiny, however, he wasted no time in sending his senior physician, Dr. Peter Fayssoux, under a truce flag with a letter to General Prévost on May 2 asking for medical care and protection of the sick by the British. Moultrie reminded Prévost that Lt. Col. Archibald Campbell had claimed the same "offices of humanity" from General Williamson at Augusta and that he expected Prévost as an officer and a gentleman to comply. Moultrie waxed eloquent when he made his case, offering to Prévost that "to the humane, the distressed never plead in vain; his feelings, are not biased by party distinction . . . but actuated by the laudable motives of humanity, as well as Christianity, he generously supports and protects the weak and infirm."[21]

It made no difference to Moultrie if Prévost released the convalescents as paroled prisoners of war or detained them, so long as they were well treated. Prévost promised to do everything in his power to safeguard the captives "to the end that neither injury nor insult be offered to them," and he agreed to release them as paroled prisoners of war. The next day Moultrie sent sixteen wagons to transport them back to the American lines. Fayssoux was able to take a good look at the enemy position while he was behind British lines, and he reported to Moultrie that the camp extended for three miles from Two Sisters Ferry.[22]

As the Americans reluctantly gave ground in the face of an irresistible British force, promised reinforcements failed to materialize. By May 3 General Bull's militia was slowly trickling in, but neither a 150-man detachment of Col. Benjamin Garden's militia regiment nor the 250 picked Continentals sent by Lincoln had yet arrived. A band of Catawba scouts sent by Rutledge was also missing. The small numbers of militia and a few Indians would hardly count for much.[23]

Besides foot soldiers and infantry, Moultrie badly needed cavalry, and he complained to Rutledge that the British, "with parties of horse and Indians, were ravaging the countryside in a barbarous manner, killing people and burning a number of houses as they go on." Moultrie maintained that with a hundred horsemen he could put a stop to it. Bee in Charlestown did what he could, but it was not much. After some delay to equip them with saddles and carbines, Bee sent Capt. Isaac Du Bois and twenty-two of Col. Daniel Horry's cavalrymen to Moultrie on May 3.[24]

Moultrie was composing a letter to Rutledge at six o'clock on the afternoon of May 2 when Maj. John Barnwell (promoted after Port Royal) rode out of camp with twenty men to pursue a party of enemy horsemen. Before long Moultrie

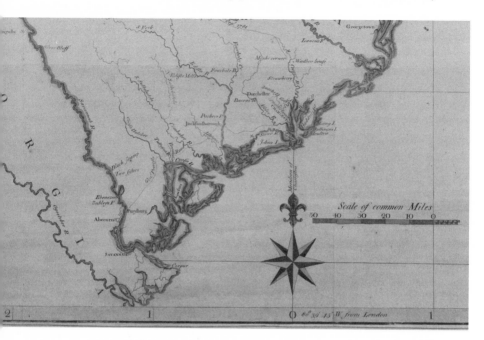

Detail of *South Carolina and Parts Adjacent; Showing the Movements of the American and British Armies.* The Robert Charles Lawrence Fergusson Collection, the Society of the Cincinnati, Washington, D.C. Reproduced with permission.

heard that Barnwell had engaged the intruders, and he put down his writing implements long enough to send reinforcements to Barnwell's aid. It was all for naught—the commotion amounted to only two guns fired at two soldiers, probably British scouts on reconnaissance. It was nearly dusk when Moultrie resumed writing. Continuing his letter to Rutledge, he reported to the governor that Lt. Col. John Laurens had returned from scouting the British lines on the Purrysburg Road. The redcoats had posted a field piece and a guard of Scots Highlanders in the middle of the road and extended their flanks so far to each side that Laurens could not get around them "to make discoveries." From all appearance, Laurens reported, the British did indeed intend to go to Charlestown.[25]

The British resumed their advance on May 3, compelling Moultrie to recall the hundred-man rear guard he had left to watch over the ford and bridge at the Coosawhatchie River. He was seeking an aide to carry out the mission when Colonel Laurens requested permission to go. John Laurens, the eldest son Henry Laurens, had only been in camp for three days. He had previously served with distinction on General Washington's staff and had just recently returned home to South Carolina. When Laurens learned of the British incursion into his home state, he hurried to the scene of the action and joined Moultrie's command.

Moultrie readily consented to young Laurens's request to bring in the rear guard. Laurens was a brave and experienced officer, and though he was a little too ambitious for his own good, Moultrie considered himself lucky to have him.[26]

Laurens left camp with a party of 250 that included a contingent of 150 picked riflemen and 100 men from the picket line. Once Laurens joined with the rear guard, his band would number 350, about a quarter of Moultrie's army, and he would be strong enough to cover his flanks if he encountered the enemy, who were believed to be in camp ten miles away. There is no evidence that Moultrie allowed Laurens discretion to do more than retrieve the rear guard and return to Tullifiny Hill.[27]

Instead of bringing off the rear guard at Coosawhatchie as ordered, Laurens found the British preparing to ford the river, and he decided use his detachment to oppose their advance in what would be the only delaying action fought by Moultrie's troops during the withdrawal of the army to Charlestown. Taking the rear guard with him, he crossed his troops to the west side of the river to confront the British vanguard and formed his men at the west end of a bridge. By doing this he put his line of retreat in jeopardy if the British got around his flank and into his rear. Laurens overreached; the British met his advance and pressed hard to destroy the Americans, occupying a plantation house and several outbuildings on a nearby hill from where they rained musketry and artillery on the Americans' exposed position. The Americans suffered two men killed and seven wounded. Laurens's horse was shot from beneath him, and he was wounded in the arm.[28]

As Laurens was carried from the field, Capt. Thomas Shubrick assumed command and wisely ignored Laurens's instructions to linger. He immediately withdrew, his quick action narrowly averting a worse disaster. Moultrie used the words *imprudent, rash,* and *impetuous* to describe Laurens, whom he had known from infancy, and he insisted that "had not Capt. Shubrick moved off at the very instant that he did, his party would have been cut off from their retreat and every man of them would either have been killed or taken prisoner."[29]

When Moultrie heard the firing from his camp at Tullifiny Hill, he supposed, albeit with some concern, that it was Laurens and his detachment coming in. Considering the circumstances, however, Moultrie's account of what happened next can hardly be taken as a full report. According to him, when the wounded Laurens was brought back to camp the general asked, exercising considerable restraint, "Well Colonel, what do you think of it?" "Why sir . . . your men won't stand," replied Laurens tersely. "If that be the case," said Moultrie, "I will retreat." Moultrie truly exercised an economy of words when relating the incident in his memoirs, for Shubrick's return to camp with the bloodied detachment unquestionably evoked a range of emotions in the usually even-tempered Moultrie. He was astonished and then furious that his simple orders had been disobeyed and utterly dismayed over the outcome of the skirmish, yet at the same time grateful that it was no worse than it was.[30]

Fortunately for Laurens, the state of affairs did not permit the convening of a board of inquiry, even if Moultrie had even considered taking such a measure. This, and Moultrie's reticence when recounting the event twenty-three years later, can be explained in part by the warm relationship that he had enjoyed over the years with the Laurens family. Furthermore John Laurens was considered a hero of the Revolutionary War, and in his memoirs Moultrie would say or write nothing that would sully that reputation. Perhaps Moultrie held himself responsible for sending Laurens on the mission. He did not let Laurens completely off the hook, however, stating emphatically: "had not Col. Laurens discouraged the men by exposing them so much and unnecessarily, I would have engaged Gen. Provost [sic] at Tullifiny."[31]

Moultrie began his withdrawal about midnight on May 3, abandoning Tullifiny Hill and crossing the Combahee River into Colleton County at the Salkehatchie Bridge. On May 5 he considered making a stand at Ashepoo but decided he was too weak to withstand British numbers. It took the Americans four days and nights of forced marches to cover the forty-five miles from Tullifiny Hill to Dorchester, where Moultrie halted to make camp on May 7. On the retreat from Black Swamp, Moultrie ordered all stores of rice and foodstuffs to be burned to prevent them from falling into the enemy's hands. Lt. Col. Johann Christian Senf, the state's engineer, eventually joined Moultrie from the governor's camp at Orangeburgh with about fifty horsemen. Moultrie ordered Senf and his men to keep in the rear and to burn boats and bridges, chop down trees, and throw every obstruction in the enemy's way to impede their march.[32]

Moultrie's army, outnumbered by more than two to one, was the only thing that stood between the British and Charlestown. In spite of the obstacles put in their way, the British pursuers followed closely enough to draw within four miles of their prey. Nor did the British confine themselves to chasing the Americans through the lowcountry. Tory militia accompanied by a band of Creek Indians burned houses and plundered at will, carrying everything away everything before them "with fire and sword."[33]

Aside from his few Continentals, Moultrie's army was now composed largely of Bull's militia from the Beaufort district through which they were retreating. Moultrie watched with helpless resignation as the dispirited militia melted away. Whole companies went home to take care of their farms and families, reducing the effective strength of his weakened army to six hundred soldiers, certainly no match for an enemy that he estimated to number three thousand.[34]

Moultrie took advantage of brief stops for rest along the route of retreat on the Ashepoo River and at Jacksonborough to write to General Lincoln and Governor

Rutledge, and as before, he desperately urged them to return to Charlestown with all possible dispatch. From Lincoln he had heard virtually nothing, nor did he know where Lincoln's army was except that it was not in the lowcountry where Moultrie needed it. From the governor he had received mainly empty promises of reinforcement and condescending instructions to delay the enemy. In a letter written by Rutledge on May 6 and probably not received by Moultrie until two days later, the governor indicated that he could not join Moultrie on the retreat but would take his militia to Charlestown via Dorchester.[35]

Still in the dark, Lincoln was planning to move down the Georgia side of the Savannah River with hope of diverting British attention away from Moultrie's army. How many if any of Moultrie's seven dispatches sent over the last seven days Lincoln received is unclear—he responded only twice—but Moultrie's best efforts to apprise him of the British advance and to urge his return to South Carolina were of no avail. Lincoln's letter from Jarrett's Ferry on May 6 indicates that he did not appreciate the gravity of Moultrie's situation or that Charlestown was the enemy's ultimate objective.[36]

Miscommunication, for whatever reasons, cost the Americans more than the lowcountry territory that was begrudgingly conceded to the British as Moultrie withdrew. A golden opportunity to trap Prévost between Moultrie's and Lincoln's armies was squandered, an idea that was not lost on Moultrie when he implored Lincoln to hurry: "I am retiring from them as fast as possible, pray follow them; and let us Burgoyne them."[37]

16.

"We will fight it out"

Moultrie halted his troops at Dorchester on May 7. He and his staff continued homeward for the remaining eighteen miles to Charlestown, expecting to return to camp the next evening. In Charlestown he was received with joyful open arms, but the celebration of his homecoming was short-lived. The town was in a state of great apprehension; in his words the townspeople were "frightened out of their wits." Their anxiety was justified—five armies were converging on Charlestown at the same time: Moultrie's army, reduced by desertion and attrition from 1,200 men to 600, followed by the 3,000-strong British army in close pursuit; General Lincoln and his army of 4,000 were either racing to Charlestown or stalking Prévost, but no one knew where they were; Lieutenant Colonel Harris's 250 Continentals and Governor Rutledge's 600 militiamen were hastening to reach Charlestown without being intercepted by the British. With the militia hurrying from the northern part of the country and from every parish to reinforce Charlestown, it looked as if the whole country was in motion. "In short," said Moultrie, "it was nothing but confusion and alarm."[1]

Moultrie had barely arrived in Charlestown when he learned that his pursuers were closer than he supposed. Instead of pausing at Salkehatchie Bridge on the Combahee River, Prévost had advanced as far as the Ashley River road. The Ashley River widened as it neared Charlestown, and with no boats of his own with which to cross anyplace he chose, Prévost had few options. He could march farther upriver and cross the Ashley at a point where it could be easily forded—at Dorchester. But if he took this course and Lincoln suddenly appeared and attacked from the rear as he came down the peninsula, he would have no way to escape back across the river. He would be trapped between Lincoln and the army in Charlestown.[2]

Prévost's other option was better, and it was a bit of sloppy generalship on Moultrie's part that unwittingly provided it for him. The British army could cross the river at Ashley Ferry, a narrow point eight miles above Charlestown, using boats left behind by the retreating Americans. This saved two days of marching that would have been lost if Prévost had moved his force upriver to ford the Ashley at Dorchester. If the thought of sequestering the boats on the east bank of the Ashley beyond the reach of British cavalry occurred to Moultrie, he did not follow through.[3]

Arguably Moultrie should not have given up Ashley Ferry without a fight. He could have used the three-day interval between his arrival at Dorchester and the British appearance at Ashley Ferry to establish and fortify a defensive position. If defeated at Ashley Ferry, he could have retreated through open country, saving what was left of his little army to join forces with Lincoln. True, his exhausted army of six hundred men had been retreating for days, becoming smaller with every passing hour. After being hounded by the British, the sanctuary offered behind Charlestown's defensive lines must have been irresistible.[4]

Moultrie found Charlestown in utter chaos—there was no unified command over the hodgepodge of South Carolina Continentals and militia in town. Fortifications that had been under construction by black laborers since February were far from ready. For this purpose Moultrie himself hired out ten of his slaves for twenty-eight days. The unfinished line extended from the Cooper River on the right to a tidal creek of the Ashley River on the left. The walls were only three or four feet thick in some parts, and the parapets were not yet complete.[5]

Yet once he had the opportunity to assess Charlestown's defensive works and review the troops that would occupy them, Moultrie concluded that the line could withstand a British assault. And while he still did not know Lincoln's whereabouts, he did know that Lincoln was coming. If he could hold his position long enough, the redcoats would be in an untenable position. It would be Prévost who would be trapped on the peninsula, not him. It was a calculated risk, and a wrong decision would mean losing his army and exposing the defenseless men, women, and children of Charlestown to the horrors of a siege.[6]

Moultrie had left Lt. Col. Daniel Horry in charge at Dorchester. When the British reached the Ashley Ferry on May 10, he ordered Horry to bring the American troops into town to avoid being cut off. Lieutenant Colonel Senf and his men were the last to come in before the town gates were shut. Senf certainly had good reason to avoid capture. The German-born engineer had come to America with Burgoyne's Hessian troops, and after being captured at the Battle of Saratoga in 1777, he defected to the American side. Once his army was safe inside the perimeter, Moultrie set about making his troop dispositions.[7]

He assigned the Charlestown militia to hold the right wing, and he positioned Lt. Col. Alexander McIntosh and the Fifth South Carolina Regiment in a lunette that anchored the right flank near the Cooper. The cannon along the right were manned by the Charlestown Artillery. On the left wing, he posted the country militia, supported by Col. Owen Roberts's Fourth South Carolina Regiment of Artillery. Lt. Col. Francis Marion and 100 men of the Second South Carolina Regiment occupied a redoubt on the extreme left of the line. An advanced redoubt forward and to the left of center was by manned by Lieutenant Colonel Harris and his 250 Georgia Continentals. The remainder of the Second Regiment and Brig. Gen. Casimir Pulaski's infantry were stationed in a redoubt at the center.[8]

Moultrie later explained why he included the details of his troop dispositions in his memoirs, stating that "by my being so particular in entering my orders; I might be thought by some of my readers to be too prolix: but while I am writing I have in remembrance my young countrymen, who may perhaps be called to the field some day or other; and by turning over a leaf or two of my book will find some form or precedent, which may be useful to them in their military career."[9]

He intended for General Pulaski's infantry in the center redoubt to function as a reserve corps, ready to sally against the British without having to disrupt the integrity of the defensive line. Polish nobleman Casimir Pulaski was an impoverished political fugitive living in Paris in 1775 when he was recruited to the American cause by Benjamin Franklin and Silas Deane, the United States envoys to the Court of Louis XVI. The flamboyant Pulaski spoke and understood so little English that he required the services of a translator, but unlike so many of the foreign opportunists that sought commissions in the Continental Army, Pulaski was an able soldier.[10]

Pulaski had acquired expertise as a cavalry commander in Europe, and his service in that capacity in Washington's army would earn him the sobriquet "Father of American Cavalry." He played a key role at the Battle of the Brandywine in September 1777, and his actions garnered him a promotion to brigadier general. During the spring of 1778, Pulaski proposed the formation of a legion of light infantry and cavalry to serve in unison, and hence Pulaski's Legion was born. In February 1779 Pulaski received orders to march his legion, now numbering about sixty cavalry and sixty infantry, south to Charlestown in support of General Lincoln. He had reached the outskirts of town on May 8, the same day that General Moultrie arrived from Dorchester. Pulaski left his infantry at Haddrell's Point and rode into Charlestown at the head of his cavalry.[11]

Prévost crossed the Ashley unchallenged on the morning of May 11 and began moving down the Charlestown Neck with nine hundred men. He left eleven hundred behind at the ferry to protect his rear against an approach by Lincoln, whose whereabouts were still unknown. His numbers were too few to conduct a formal siege and they lacked entrenching tools and sufficient artillery, but with audacity combined with luck and deception, he hoped to bluff the

Americans into surrendering Charlestown. Prévost made his opening play by sending a troop of dragoons and several hundred light infantry to reconnoiter the American lines.[12]

Pulaski's infantry had crossed the Cooper River that morning from Haddrell's Point. Now in response to the British aggression, Pulaski boldly formed and paraded his legion through the streets of Charlestown and unwisely ventured out beyond the lines and attacked the British advance. His 120 legionnaires accompanied by a few militiamen confronted the redcoats just beyond the Nightingale race course (New Market Course) above and east of present-day Line and Meeting Streets. Pulaski had bitten off more than he could chew. In full view of the townspeople and the American defenders, his tiny force was quickly overpowered; most of his infantry was killed, wounded, or captured, and the remainder scrambled into the cover of the advance guard in panic and great disorder. When Prévost brought his main army to within a mile of the town's gate, Moultrie opened on them with his cannon and halted their progress. All in all it was an inauspicious beginning for the Americans watching from behind the defensive works.[13]

Moultrie had witnessed the complications that had arisen when Generals Charles Lee, Robert Howe, and Benjamin Lincoln tried to conduct military operations in the face of civil interference. He was now about to experience this challenge to his command in an episode that would have both immediate and far-reaching consequences. Moultrie spent the evening of May 11 tending to his troop dispositions. Charlestown's defenders were at a high state of alert in anticipation of a nighttime attack by the British. About ten o'clock some men of the Charlestown militia on the American right thought they detected enemy movement in the darkness near the lines and opened fire, setting off a chain reaction of general firing of musketry and cannon along the line.[14]

Unbeknownst to Moultrie or anyone else on the line, Governor Rutledge had sent Maj. Benjamin Huger and a small party to repair a gap that had been left open for passage through the abatis. When the garrison set fire to tar barrels placed in front of the lines to give light and prevent a surprise, Huger and his party were spotted and mistaken for the enemy. Thirteen men were accidentally killed or wounded in the confusion, and Huger, a close friend of the Marquis de Lafayette and a gentleman characterized by Moultrie as "a brave and active officer, an able statesman, and a virtuous citizen," was one of the dead.[15]

Moultrie blamed the affair on the unsettled chain of command, principally that Governor Rutledge considered it his right to share military leadership. While riding in haste to the scene of the carnage, Moultrie happened to overhear one of the governor's aides issuing orders in the name of the governor and the Privy Council, and without stopping he shouted emphatically that these orders were not to be obeyed. Once fully apprised of the details of the accident that claimed the life of Huger, Moultrie was incensed, his ire fueled by the denial of the governor and the members of the council when he asked them who gave the order to send out Huger. Moultrie's anger was evident when he addressed them: "gentlemen, this will never do; we shall be ruined and undone, if we have so many commanders; it is absolutely necessary to chuse [sic] one to command."[16]

Giving the civil government this ultimatum was the logical course of action under the circumstances, but Moultrie went a step further when he agreed that if chosen, he would not interfere in any civil matters such as parleys and capitulations. Perhaps Moultrie was unwilling to take responsibility for a decision to give up the town if it became necessary to do so—it is impossible to divine his state of mind from the narrative in his memoirs. The governor and his Privy Council unanimously voted to concede all military command to Moultrie, who then returned to the lines. Moultrie would not know until later that he had erred in forfeiting to the civil government the right to treat with the enemy.[17]

About three o'clock on the morning of May 12, Moultrie was riding his defensive perimeter when he was approached by Governor Rutledge. The usually resolute Rutledge was losing his nerve and wanted to air his concerns with his old friend. Rutledge had been informed that the British numbered seven or eight thousand. How many soldiers were under Moultrie's command? Surely not more than eighteen hundred, thought Rutledge. Moreover the state's engineer, Lt. Col. Johann Christian Senf, had pronounced the defensive lines much too weak to withstand an assault. Should the lines be taken by storm, argued Rutledge, a great number of citizens would be put to death. Should they not parley with the enemy? Rutledge proposed sending a flag to General Prévost to see what terms of capitulation, if any, the British general might offer.[18]

Moultrie was not persuaded. He did not yet have returns from the various units now under his command, but he guessed his numbers to be upward of twenty-two hundred. As he and Rutledge debated the issue in the darkness, Moultrie insisted that the enemy could not force the lines—the men would hold. He was not at all interested in sending a flag in his name, but if the civil government chose to parley, he would not stand in their way, and if requested, he would send their messages through the lines. The governor assembled the Privy Council, and together they asked Moultrie to send the following message: "Gen. Moultrie perceiving from the motions of your army, that your intention is to besiege the town, would be glad to know on what terms you would be disposed to grant a capitulation, should he be inclined to capitulate."[19]

At about eleven o'clock in the morning of May 12, Moultrie received a reply from Lt. Col. Jacques Marcus Prévost, the victor at Briar Creek. Prévost commanded the British advance at Ashley Ferry, and writing on behalf of his brother, he offered peace and protection as an alternative to the "horrors attending the event of a storm" that he assured Moultrie would be successful. Those who chose not to take advantage of this so-called generous offer would be held as prisoners of war until their fates were determined by the outcome of the war. An answer from Charlestown was expected within four hours; silence would be taken as refusal of the terms.[20]

Moultrie showed the Prévost letter to Rutledge, who immediately called a meeting of the Privy Council at his house on Broad Street. Moultrie was invited to attend, and he brought General Pulaski and Colonel John Laurens with him. Rutledge opened the meeting by reading the letter aloud to his councilors, who debated the relative merits of surrender among themselves. The governor and a majority of the council favored capitulation. Moultrie, Pulaski, and Laurens argued that the American force was sufficient to repulse the enemy and that the town should not be given up without a fight. Without returns Moultrie did not know his exact numerical strength, but he gave his latest best estimate to be at least 3,180 men and approximated the British strength at between 3,000 and 4,000.[21]

Rutledge was closer than Moultrie on American numbers, stating emphatically that there could be no more than twenty-five hundred defenders. It is conceivable that Moultrie, convinced of the rightness of his position, exaggerated or deliberately inflated his estimates to strengthen his case for defense. On the other hand, the governor believed reports that the British force, actually only one thousand men in front of the lines and twelve hundred at Ashley Ferry, had grown to seven or eight thousand men by the addition of a large number of Tories from South Carolina, North Carolina, and Georgia. With time running short, Moultrie finally insisted that a decision be made so that he could return to the lines. The council in turn asked him to send a reply to Prévost rejecting unconditional surrender but instead suggesting that officers be appointed from both sides to negotiate more reasonable terms.[22]

On the way to the governor's house, Moultrie sent ammunition to the troops on the line and instructed Lt. Col. Louis Antoine Jean Baptiste de Cambray-Digny, a French engineer in Continental service, to work quickly to strengthen the weaker left side of the defensive perimeter. When Prévost observed the Americans working on their fortifications during the passing of the flags, he threatened to order an immediate assault if this work did not cease immediately. With the meeting under way at the governor's house, Capt. Thomas Dunbar of the Second Regiment briefly interrupted to report the situation to Moultrie, who then ordered Cambray to call a halt to the labor. Moultrie later admitted that the ongoing work was contrary to military rules governing truces and parleys.[23]

Now began what has been called one of the most controversial episodes of the Revolutionary War in the South, and what was certainly an extraordinary incident in the history of South Carolina. Debate continued on the American side as Rutledge and his councilors wrestled with an idea put forward to give up the town in exchange for neutrality. The subject of neutrality provoked strong emotions. When the Privy Council voted five to three in favor of surrender for neutrality, radical Christopher Gadsden became angry and disruptive, while John Edwards, a second of the holdouts for defending Charlestown, was reduced to tears. Moultrie later asserted that the deliberations had been kept quiet and that the townspeople remained calm, but in fact Gadsden instigated an uproar of a sort when he leaked news of the discussions to members of the General Assembly. Once the word spread, some of the men in town were ready to turn those who advocated neutrality over to the British, while others declared that they should atone with their lives for their disgraceful conduct.[24]

The governor and councilors adjourned from the governor's house and reconvened at Col. Barnard Beekman's tent on the line near the city gate, where they formulated their message to Prévost. Under the terms of their proposal, both South Carolina and Charlestown Harbor would become neutral territory for the duration of the war between Great Britain and America, and none of the citizens would become prisoners of war. The question of whether the state would belong to Great Britain or remain one of the United States would be determined at the end by the treaty of peace.[25]

Moultrie opposed the offer and would not have his Continentals included— even if it meant becoming captives of the British. His officers were in agreement, and when Moultrie sought one of them to carry the message from the governor and council across to the British, he met resistance. Colonel Laurens found the message offering capitulation to be so repugnant that he asked to be excused from delivery—he would do anything else to serve his country, but not that. Lt. Col. Alexander McIntosh of the Continental Army and Lt. Col. Roger Smith of the militia likewise attempted to beg off, but Moultrie pressed them into compliance.[26]

The whole affair begs the question of why Moultrie allowed the circumstances to devolve this far, and the answer is that civil authority trumped military control. This premise had been demonstrated over and over in South Carolina going back as far as the control of the provincial regiments by the five-man Secret Committee and Council of Safety in 1775. Moving forward to May 1779, Moultrie's giving over to civil authorities the right to negotiate with the British was at best misguided, but beyond that he merely allowed himself to be the conduit through which passed the messages between the British and the civil government. Even so, had the outcome turned out differently, the name and reputation of William Moultrie would not carry the same luster acquired by right of his heroism on June 28, 1776.

To understand his willingness to acquiesce if not actually participate in the governor's plan to take South Carolina out of the war merits consideration of a statement attributed to Moultrie, one that is not found in his *Memoirs of the American Revolution* but is probably reflective of the sentiments of the Charlestown leadership as a whole. On the word of John Laurens, Moultrie said that "although he was against it [capitulation] and would not have himself or the Troops under him included, yet he thought the other States have no reason to complain, as they had not fulfilled their engagements to [South Carolina] in giving it aid and assistance, from which promise that State came into the union." In other words South Carolina had been abandoned by her sister states and the Continental Congress.[27]

Moultrie's feelings of abandonment were likely exacerbated by a March 29 resolution of the Continental Congress. Acknowledging that the Continental battalions of South Carolina and Georgia were not adequate to their states' defense, that additional Continental detachments could not be sent to reinforce the Southern Department, and that the militia forces in service "ought not be relied on for continued exertions and a protracted war," Congress recommended a drastic solution. Georgia and South Carolina, "if they shall thank the same expedient," should take measures to raise a corps of three thousand black men commanded by white commissioned and noncommissioned officers. The corps of soldiers would be raised at Continental expense and be emancipated at the end of the war. Congressional delegates Henry Laurens and William Henry Drayton were proponents of the plan championed by John Laurens, who delivered the recommendation of Congress when he came home from Philadelphia. To Governor Rutledge and his Privy Council, the measure was not just inexpedient, it was wholly unacceptable.[28]

The issue of a negotiated neutrality soon became moot. General Prévost had appointed his brother to meet with Colonels McIntosh and Smith. The adversaries conferred at a spot a quarter mile from the American lines. Lieutenant Colonel Prévost would agree only to take the American proposal to his brother. He returned at noon with information that would prompt a great deal of consternation among the governor and Privy Council. Colonel Prévost stated peremptorily and emphatically that he "had nothing to do with the governor, that his business was with General Moultrie, and as the garrison was in arms, they must surrender as prisoners of war."[29]

The governor and council were downcast when McIntosh and Smith returned to the American lines bearing Prévost's final word. Moultrie had been unduly accommodating of the wishes of Governor Rutledge over the course of the proceedings, but now he grasped that the decision and responsibility to intervene was his and his alone. Moreover an equivocating civil government that was on the brink of abandoning its revolutionary ideals had wearied him beyond measure. He paused for effect before summing up the situation: "Gentlemen, you see how the matter stands, the point is this, I am to deliver you prisoners of war, or not." Few responses were muttered, some in the affirmative, but before anyone could say more, Moultrie settled the matter once and for all. "I am determined not to deliver you up prisoners of war," he announced, forcefully adding, "WE WILL FIGHT IT OUT."[30]

John Laurens, writing to his father, provided in a contemporaneous account more details than what Moultrie recollected for his memoirs. Laurens maintained that when informed that Prévost was not interested in treating with the civil authorities, Moultrie announced [Laurens paraphrasing], "that if that was the case . . . the conference was at an end—if he [Prévost] wanted the Town he must take it, that he [Moultrie] should not surrender it, but was ready for his attack whenever he [Prévost] thought proper to make it." Young Laurens noted that Moultrie's stand gave the garrison great satisfaction.[31]

In Moultrie's remembrance an overjoyed Laurens jumped up and exclaimed with relief, "Thank God! We are upon our legs again." Moultrie's decision had the immediate support of Christopher Gadsden, Thomas Ferguson, and John Edwards, the three "radicals" who had opposed capitulation every step of the way. Moultrie ordered the flag to be waved at the gate, the agreed-upon signal signifying to the British that there would be no more conferences to discuss the future of Charlestown and South Carolina. The fate of the town, the state, the civilians, and the soldiers would be settled by force of arms. After a while it became evident that the British had not noticed the flag waving, and so Moultrie sent Francis Kinloch to inform Prévost of his decision.[32] The Americans resumed in earnest their preparations to receive an assault, but when the sun arose on the morning of May 13, the British were gone.

17.

Lost Opportunity at Stono Ferry

The redcoats were indeed gone. Moultrie sent General Pulaski on horseback to try to verify their whereabouts. Galloping at full speed, the Polish count made two or three circuits before returning to report that the British were nowhere to be found. Moultrie sent Pulaski out again, this time with his cavalry and a party of militia. Venturing out further, Pulaski discovered that the British had crossed to the west bank of the Ashley. Moultrie then ordered Pulaski to search for General Lincoln and his Continental Army. By the time Pulaski covered the eighteen miles to Dorchester, most of the militia had abandoned his ranks. This left him with only about forty horsemen, barely enough to conduct patrols. There was still no sign of Lincoln, but even so Moultrie readied a detachment of almost eleven hundred men and two field pieces to reinforce Lincoln's army as soon its location became known.[1]

Communication between Moultrie and Lincoln had been sporadic since Lincoln departed Black Swamp for Augusta, and Lincoln's letter to Moultrie dated May 10 perfectly illustrates the point. This letter was written in response to Moultrie's communiqué of May 8, and Lincoln's intent was to inform Moultrie of his army's forced march to relieve Charlestown. "Do not give up, or suffer the people to despair" were the heartening words read by Moultrie on May 14, the day after the British had precipitously withdrawn. But a copy of the letter had fallen into British hands before Moultrie read the contents for himself. Foreknowledge of Lincoln's effort to relieve Charlestown by forced march caused

Prévost to abandon Charlestown and flee across the Ashley to prevent his troops from being caught between two fires.[2]

Moultrie sent a message to Lincoln on May 15 indicating that he was on the march from Charlestown with 400 Continentals, 350 militia troops, and 4 field pieces. He had persuaded the militiamen to accompany him by taking men who lived in the region that had suffered from predatory British raids. To get their co-operation, he had promised them that when parties were sent out to put a stop to British plundering, they would be among those chosen and would have a greater chance of recovering or protecting their own property. This expedition never left Charlestown. Conflicting intelligence of the enemy's location, along with the governor and council's fear of another British attack, prompted Moultrie to delay and finally to postpone the mission altogether.[3]

As Lincoln's Continental Army drew nearer to Charlestown, Prévost moved his force of twenty-five hundred regulars, Tories, and Indians across Wappoo Creek to James Island. The hunter had become the prey, and Prévost, who had outnumbered Moultrie during the pursuit to Charlestown, was now numerically inferior to the Americans. Prévost chose the coastal islands between Charlestown as his path of retreat. The swamps, creeks, and inlets offered a measure of security from attack. Badly needed provisions such as rice and beef were plentiful and there for the taking. Close proximity to the coast afforded the British army easy access to the Royal Navy for supply and transportation.[4]

Despite the British withdrawal, the populace of Charlestown generally believed that the British army encamped just across the Ashley remained a real threat to the city. Their fears were heightened when a British deserter brought word to Moultrie on May 16 that the entire British army was on James Island with enough artillery and supplies to maintain a close presence for an extended period of time. Even more unsettling was that the redcoats had scoured the region and collected a large number of schooners and row galleys that could be used to mount an assault against the town from that quarter.[5]

From atop the steeple of St. Michael's Church, the movements of the enemy a few miles away at Wappoo Creek and on James Island were plainly discernable making an attack from that direction appear to be imminent. Fort Johnson, on the Charlestown side of James Island, was vulnerable to capture, and Moultrie ordered Capt. John De Treville to remove as much of the fort's artillery as possible. Any cannons that could not be removed were to be dumped into the harbor or spiked. When De Treville and twenty-five armed Continentals went to the fort to secure the artillery, British raiders surprised the Americans before they could accomplish their risky mission, taking a few of them prisoner.[6]

Moultrie was obliged to reorder his troop dispositions, moving companies from the defensive works across the neck and redeploying them at various streets, bastions, and wharves on the harbor side of town. He considered his namesake fort on Sullivan's Island to be at risk of a seaborne attack from James Island, so he sent Francis Marion over there with part of the Second South Carolina Regiment. Moultrie also stationed a number of vessels at strategic points offshore of James Island and between the island and Charlestown to guard the waterways over which the British might come. The Charlestown garrison was especially alert to the threat posed by a nighttime attack, and Moultrie established signals for the ships guarding the waterways. Three cannon shots in succession would warn the town if a night crossing was discovered, and the ships' captains were instructed to "to keep up a brisk fire upon the enemy, to prevent their landing in town."[7]

Lincoln finally reached Parker's Ferry, seven miles west-northwest from Charlestown on the South Edisto River on May 17. He camped his army at Bacon's Bridge near Dorchester on the night of May 18. Over the next few days, Lincoln's Continentals shadowed the British army as Prévost continued his withdrawal. By month's end the redcoat army had moved from James Island to Johns Island. Lincoln, in turn, crossed Wappoo Creek from the mainland over to James Island on May 25. These movements, in tandem with Moultrie's realignment of the Charlestown defenses, somewhat lessened the apprehension of an attack on Charlestown and enabled Moultrie to send six hundred men and two field pieces to reinforce Lincoln on May 22.[8]

At this point Moultrie favored aggressive action, advising Lincoln, "if we can destroy them, it will be a great stroke." Accordingly an attack on the British position on the Stono Ferry was planned and put into motion on May 31. A reconnaissance in force by Count Pulaski revealed that the British position was too strong, and the operation was canceled. As part of the operational planning, Moultrie and Lincoln agreed that when communicating troop numbers, they would write double the actual number to deceive the British if a dispatch fell into the wrong hands.[9]

During the months of May and June 1779, a flurry of letters passed between Moultrie and Prévost concerning the exchange of prisoners of war. Both men exerted themselves to insure the safety and comfort of their captives, but at times their patience was sorely tried by the nuances and intricacies of negotiating with an enemy. At one point Prévost was frustrated by his inability to secure the return of a captured British navy captain. He threatened to end exchanges and send prisoners to New York to be confined on prison ships, where they would be susceptible to starvation, disease, and oftentimes death.[10]

"A little reflection must convince you of the injustice, as well as cruelty of such a proceeding," Moultrie wrote to Prévost with a warning: "I must observe to you also, that there are numbers of British prisoners in the United States, and that unnecessary hardships and severity shewn our people, unfortunate enough to be in your power, will demand a like treatment to such of yours as the fortune of war may have placed in our hands." Moultrie's admonition evidently caused Prévost to reconsider his options, for exchanges resumed.[11]

In the spring of 1779, the question arose over who would command the southern Continental Army. That March, not long after the debacle at Briar Creek, Benjamin Lincoln lobbied Congress asking to be relieved from duty as commander of the Southern Department. Lincoln reasoned that his leg wound sustained at Saratoga in 1777 had never completely healed, and he was worried that continued service in South Carolina during the summer months would aggravate the wound, perhaps enough to threaten fatal consequences. While Lincoln's request was under consideration by the Continental Congress, the delegates from South Carolina put forth a resolution to promote Moultrie to the rank of major general and command in Lincoln's place. Congress tentatively gave Lincoln permission on April 17 to leave South Carolina and rejoin George Washington's army and referred the matter of Moultrie's promotion to the Board of War.[12]

The Board of War recommended against Moultrie's promotion on May 13 —a decision based purely on political expediency. Other states, said the board, thought themselves entitled to a promotion of their own general officers. But lest it "excite uneasiness or difficulties unless a continental officer commands the army in the southern district," the board recommended Moultrie's appointment to commandant of the southern army contingent on the departure of General Lincoln. He would receive the allowances of a major general but without the elevation in rank. President of Congress John Jay wrote to Moultrie on May 15 offering his "best wishes, that this appointment may be productive of fresh laurels, and that you may again be the instrument of increasing the honors and security of your country."[13]

Lincoln was satisfied to leave the southern Continental Army under Moultrie's care, telling him, "From the attachment of the people to you, and your knowledge, judgment, and experience in military matters, I have great confidence, that you will command with honor to yourself, and with the approbation of your country." Moultrie accepted the appointment with great trepidation, notifying Jay on June 7 that under the present state of affairs he hoped General Lincoln would not take advantage of the opportunity to remove himself from the southern theater. He expressed similar sentiments to Lincoln but was far more frank, confiding, "I would not for the universe have the command fall upon me at this time. I am so unequal to the task, it would be placing me in such a point of view as might ruin my reputation forever."[14]

Moultrie and Rutledge were both convinced that Lincoln's departure would significantly hurt morale, and they told him so. In the end the entreaties of Moultrie and Rutledge persuaded Lincoln to stay and retain command. They were further encouraged by the news that Vice Admiral Jean Baptiste Charles Henri Hector, comte d'Estaing, commanded a French fleet of more than twenty warships and an army of four thousand French soldiers that were bound for South Carolina.[15]

At the heart of Lincoln's decision to leave the Southern Department was his belief that he had lost the confidence of the people of South Carolina. "Some ill natured persons had been casting reflections on him, for his having marched up to Augusta with the main body of his army; and leaving the low country exposed to the enemy; and putting Charlestown in such imminent danger," wrote Moultrie, who maintained that these aspersions were spread by persons who were ignorant of Lincoln's motives for going to Augusta. Moultrie had high praise for Lincoln and characterized him as "a brave, active, and very vigilant officer." He and his contemporaries viewed as a positive attribute that Lincoln was "always so very cautious, that he would take no step of any consequence; without first calling a council of officers, to advise with them on the measures."[16]

By mid-June 1779 Prévost was moving his army away from Charlestown toward Port Royal. After conferring with Rutledge and members of the Privy Council, Lincoln developed a plan to attack the British rear guard on the Stono River at a ferry that crossed from the mainland to Johns Island. Lincoln's strategy called for Moultrie to march a detachment of Charlestown militia to James Island in support of an attack by the Continental Army. On June 16 he ordered Moultrie to prepare the town's garrison to move at a moment's notice.[17]

The situation changed abruptly on June 19. Acting on fresh intelligence that the British were retreating to Savannah and that only a small rear guard remained at Stono Ferry, Lincoln ordered Moultrie to "immediately . . . throw over on James Island, all the troops which can be spared from the town; shew them to the enemy on John's-Island, in case an opportunity should offer without risking too much." Lincoln envisioned a joint operation against a divided enemy—a coordinated effort between his army striking from the mainland and Moultrie, who would bring a strong detachment of Charlestown militia by boat up Wappoo Creek to James Island. Once on James Island, Moultrie would be in position to cross over to Johns Island to attack the enemy's rear or to create a diversion to draw off reinforcements coming to support the main British position. Moultrie's force would consist of fourteen hundred militiamen drawn from Charlestown's eighteen-hundred-man garrison.[18]

Moultrie had almost 750 men with two field pieces and their ammunition ready to embark a little after eight o'clock on the evening of June 19. "If not prevented by want of boats," Moultrie told Lincoln, he should have them on James Island before daybreak. He worked in earnest toward that end, and Rutledge cooperated by directing the captains of the galleys and other public boats to follow Moultrie's orders.[19]

The Americans did have boats. The British had seized the boats at Ashley Ferry and the surrounding countryside, but the Americans still managed to collect a small fleet from areas unoccupied by the British. It was where the boats were on June 19 that was the problem. Lincoln had sent them eight miles upriver to Ashley Ferry on June 6, where they were moored under guard on the Charlestown side of the river. Moultrie ordered them back to Charlestown with all due haste, but he advised Lincoln at six o'clock on the morning of June 20 that they had been very slow to come downriver.[20]

Moultrie transported the Charlestown militia to James Island as soon as several batteaus and a galley became available, but high winds in the harbor thwarted his progress. The best he could hope for was to have his command in place by noon, but even this proved to be unrealistic. It really mattered little, however, because Lincoln did not wait for Moultrie to reach his position—his decision to press the attack when he did virtually precluded Moultrie's participation in the fight. By the time half of Moultrie's force finally arrived at the mouth of Wappoo Creek at 4:30 P.M., Lincoln had already been engaged in what Moultrie heard was a "small skirmish with the Enemy." He was sorry to have missed it, not realizing that Lincoln's assault on the British rear guard twelve miles away at Stono Ferry had developed into much more than a skirmish.[21]

Lincoln had marched his army from camp on the mainland about midnight on June 20. As he approached the British defenses in column, he found a rectangular stronghold approximately eight hundred yards wide and a hundred yards deep consisting of three redoubts in a line. The perimeter was formed by an abatis in front and around the flanks with the Stono River to the rear. A small marshy creek ran to the right front of the British line. Lincoln deployed his force of almost three thousand Continentals and militiamen from South Carolina, Virginia, and North Carolina into two wings, and an hour after daybreak he ordered them to advance against eight hundred redcoat defenders commanded by the Scottish-born Lt. Col. John Maitland. Lincoln hoped his superior numbers would be able to storm the enemy defenses, but once the two sides engaged, his attack stalled as both sides withstood furious musketry and four American field pieces dueled with their six British counterparts at relatively close range.[22]

After about an hour, it became apparent that Lincoln could not dislodge the enemy from their strongly fortified post. Maitland shifted troops within his interior lines, and it appeared that he would be reinforced from Johns Island. Mounting casualties convinced Lincoln of the futility of further sacrifice. The Americans withdrew in good order, giving the British a tactical victory. Despite the loss the Americans gained a moral victory of a sort—they had stood eye-to-eye and toe-to-toe with some of Britain's finest soldiers and had mostly behaved well. Victory and defeat at Stono Ferry were costly. One hundred thirty

British soldiers were killed, wounded, or missing. The Americans sustained 155 casualties, of which 26 were killed, including Col. Owen Roberts of the artillery.[23]

The details of the battle are not in dispute, but Moultrie's culpability in the American failure at Stono Ferry is a matter of controversy. Perhaps Lincoln believed that Moultrie was on schedule, for it is doubtful that he had received Moultrie's 6 A.M. letter when he launched the assault. However it is plain from his after-action report, actually a letter written to Moultrie on the day of the battle, that Lincoln had not fully reconnoitered the enemy position before opening the attack. In fact when relating his lack of knowledge of the ground in front of the enemy works, he uses the words "wholly ignorant."[24]

Historians who have criticized Moultrie for his tardy arrival on James Island fail to take into account that the boats he needed to transport his troops were moored upriver at Ashley Ferry instead of docked at Charlestown. Lincoln's decision to press the attack on May 19 did not allow sufficient time for Moultrie to gather the boats from upriver, ferry his men to James Island, and then march twelve miles to Lincoln's assistance. Furthermore it is conceivable that Moultrie's presence on the battlefield to create a diversion or to prevent British reinforcement would not have materially affected the outcome of the battle. It was not Moultrie's absence from the battlefield or British reinforcement that lost the battle for the Americans, but rather the strength of the British positions with their physical barriers and interior lines of communications, all combined with the failure of a few American units to follow orders. And it is telling that when the rushed, ill-planned, and poorly executed affair was over, Lincoln did not hold Moultrie blameworthy for the American defeat.[25]

A story circulated that Moultrie failed to collect the boats in Charlestown and proceed to James Island in a timely manner on June 20 because he hosted a soirée the evening before rather than attending to his duties. In 1851 Dr. Joseph Johnson of Charleston wrote that he considered the cause of the American defeat at Stono Ferry to be the result of timely British reinforcement just when the Americans had victory within their grasp. The British were reinforced, according to Johnson, because Moultrie and his troops were not there to prevent it.[26]

"But why could they not?" Johnson asked. "Because Moultrie did not leave the city at the time appointed; he lost his tide, and stuck aground in Wappoo. Moultrie was not a punctual man. He remained at his own house, with a convivial party of friends, until the tide had fallen too low for him to pass through the cut. [This was told to me by one of the expedition, Mr. Robert Dewar.] The expedition failed, and many valuable lives were sacrificed in vain." Johnson mentioned this "traditionary fact" as an object lesson for his young friends to demonstrate the dangerous consequences of procrastination.[27]

Johnson may have repeated a tradition, but evidence to establish the tradition as fact is lacking. No credible basis for substantiating Robert Dewar's claim has been uncovered. On the other hand, Moultrie's aforementioned letters of eight o'clock on the evening of June 19, 1779, and at six o'clock the next morning place him at work mobilizing and equipping his officers and men while awaiting boats. These dispatches should put to rest of any notion of him whiling away the evening hours in his cups.[28]

18.

"We were sure of success"

Apart from the failure of the Americans to accomplish their objective at Stono Ferry, coupled with the attendant loss of life and limb, the Battle of Stono Ferry was of little consequence, strategic or otherwise. Prévost had already decided to abandon the post on Johns Island. The British army was growing critically short of supplies, and general discontent was besetting his officers and men. In any event it took a week for the tactical situation on James and Johns Islands to stabilize as the British continued slowly to withdraw. Moultrie and Lincoln agreed that despite the setback, they would keep the belatedly arrived Charlestown troops on James Island, ready to cross the Stono over to Johns Island and attack the British if an opportunity arose.[1]

Without waiting to consult with General Lincoln, Moultrie seized the initiative on June 22, just two days after the Stono Ferry battle, when he sent three row galleys up Wappoo Creek and the Stono River to the ferry to destroy a pontoon bridge that General Prévost had reportedly thrown across the river. Moultrie also instructed the galley captains to sink, burn, or otherwise destroy any British vessels that they encountered on their return and, if necessary, to put troops ashore to support their mission. Count Pulaski would be available and ready to help if horsemen were needed. Moultrie wanted to disrupt the enemy's line of communications. He justified his actions to Lincoln by suggesting that if the raid was successful, an attempt to pursue and attack the British rear guard would be easier.[2]

The galleys headed upriver under the cover of darkness in the early hours of June 23. They made good progress in the face of a brisk fire from British field pieces and musketry from the bluffs that overlooked the river from Johns Island.

The expedition achieved its first measure of success when the galleys' return fire silenced the enemy, and not long afterward the Americans captured a schooner from under the British guns. The galleys anchored offshore to rest from their long night's work, but to their captain's astonishment the light of dawn revealed a nearby camp of almost twelve hundred redcoats supported by entrenched artillery. It was a close call. If they proceeded any farther upriver, they would be within easy pistol shot of the enemy entrenchments.[3]

Moultrie had maintained close operational contact with the expedition, but he also gave wide discretionary authority to Capt. James Pyne, who commanded the expedition from his galley *Rutledge*. Pyne wisely chose to return back downriver to friendly lines. Rowing with the current and with their prize schooner in tow, the galleys ran a veritable gauntlet of enemy guns and fortifications that had been thrown up during the night to oppose their passage. The foray cost the Americans six killed and several men wounded on the galleys, but Moultrie was pleased with the overall results.[4]

The British had held the strategic and tactical advantage from the commencement of their campaign into South Carolina until the time that Moultrie refused Prévost entry into Charlestown. Now despite the repulse at Stono Ferry, the momentum was shifting to the American side. The redcoats were on the defensive, outnumbered, and far from their home base to which they were connected by a rather tenuous supply line.[5]

"Rather unpleasant" was how Moultrie described the British situation on Johns Island in the preface to the second volume of his *Memoirs of the American Revolution*. "No doubt, they expected we should make some other movements towards them; they therefore thought it best to quit that place, and get to a place where they could be supported by their shipping," he said, adding that as a consequence, "they went from Island to Island, until they got to Port-royal, where they established a strong post at Beaufort." By sending the galleys upriver, Moultrie had given notice that American aggression would be unrelenting as long as the British were in close proximity to Charlestown.[6]

The British abandoned their post at Stono Ferry on June 24, a fact that went undiscovered until the next day. With the enemy retreating, Lincoln wanted Moultrie "to tread on their heels, if you can do it, without risking too much." Moultrie was again limited by the number of available boats, and he could transport only 320 men across the river from James Island to Johns Island at a time. This was too few to leave unsupported on the island while he made more trips if the British did a turnabout and attacked. Governor Rutledge did his best to have additional flats and other boats sent to Moultrie in time to strike another blow, but it was all to no advantage.[7]

Prévost successfully carried out his withdrawal before the Americans could act. The campaign was over; the time for fighting had passed. The oppressive heat and humidity of the season, the "attendant disorders of our summer," as Lt. Col. John F. Grimké called it, generally put an end to overt hostilities as the two armies retired into summer quarters. On June 28, 1779, Moultrie embarked his troops from James Island, and they landed in Charlestown around noontime. He barely stayed in town long enough to refresh himself. General Lincoln also wished to come to Charlestown, and he ordered Moultrie to take command of the main army on the Stono River in his place.[8]

Over the next few weeks, two issues occupied Moultrie's attention. First and foremost was the militia. Lincoln had been eager to press the attack at Stono Ferry on June 20, in part to get the best use out of militiamen from the two Carolinas, Georgia, and Virginia prior to the upcoming expiration of their terms of enlistment. Now a body of North Carolinians was about to leave camp for home, and Moultrie found it impossible to persuade Gen. Andrew Williamson's South Carolinians to continue to remain in the field. They also were determined to go home, and no argument could convince them otherwise.[9]

The salient problem was that there were no backcountry militiamen coming to replace them. The pretext given was that Indian unrest and incursions by North Carolina Tories obliged the backcountry militiamen to remain at home. This was an "old stale game they were playing" according to Moultrie, but he could not fault Williamson's 726 men for wanting to return to their families. They had been some of his best of the militia troops and had been in the field for five months.[10]

The concerned governor and his Privy Council ordered a draft of one-third of the South Carolina militia and ordered Williamson's men to remain in place until they were properly relieved. Williamson, on the other hand, told Moultrie that it would be best for the service if Moultrie discharged them rather than have them "discharge themselves" (Lincoln's words). Moultrie agreed with Williamson and issued orders to "to prevent the disagreeable necessity of their leaving camp without orders." Williamson promised to use his considerable influence at home to send relief from the backcountry as soon as possible.[11]

Moultrie received intelligence as early as July 2 indicating that the British intended to occupy Beaufort on Port Royal Island during the summer months, and Prévost did indeed consume most of the next three weeks moving his redcoat army to the safety of that location. Rumors circulated that Prévost also intended to establish and maintain a post on the mainland across from Port Royal with a garrison of one or two thousand men with which to challenge the Americans, but as time passed Moultrie came to doubt the credulity of these reports. He was correct; once across Whale Branch on Port Royal, the British stayed put.[12]

Moultrie did not quite tread on the heels of the British, but he certainly watched them closely. On July 5 he ordered three "brigades," one each from both Carolinas and one from Georgia, to march from their main camp near Stono Ferry to a new camp a little more than forty miles away at Sheldon, near the estate of Lt. Col. Benjamin Garden. The position was located about five miles northwest of the Port Royal ferry and fourteen miles northwest of Beaufort. The Americans marched in three columns to avoid crowding at the river crossings. Moultrie sent two field pieces with each column and sent the rest of his artillery back to Charlestown. He delayed his own departure for a few days to settle affairs with the militia whose times were expiring and then set off for Port Royal on July 11. From the vantage point of Sheldon, a force of about eight hundred Continentals could keep a close watch on the British on Port Royal.[13]

The British may have been in so-called summer quarters, but Moultrie sought opportunities for aggression on a small scale. He asked Lincoln to send twenty shallow-draft flatboats to use in making surprise attacks against the forward British posts on Port Royal. In mid-July Lincoln dispatched Sgt. William Jasper of the Second South Carolina Regiment along with a small party of men for Moultrie's discretionary employment in the conduct of partisan-type warfare. Moultrie eventually sent Jasper's contingent "to harass and perplex the enemy" in Georgia.[14]

Moultrie thought highly of Sergeant Jasper, who had recovered and re-mounted the blue provincial flag at the Battle of Sullivan's Island on June 28, 1776. He described the sergeant as a "brave, active, stout, strong, enterprising man." Moultrie had such confidence in Jasper's abilities in the field that he gave him a roving commission and liberty to pick his own men for covert action. Acknowledging Jasper's intrepidity, he wrote that "he seldom would take more than six: he went often out, and returned with prisoners before I knew he was gone."[15]

Prévost left Lieutenant Colonel Maitland in command of the Beaufort garrison and transported a major portion of his troops to Savannah, bringing the campaign to a close. Keeping watch over the British in July was hot and boring, and the situation in the American camp was not a good one. Provisions were running out. Moultrie's command diminished in size as militiamen departed for home when their terms expired. Those who remained became increasingly disgruntled. The Third Regiment mutinied for want of pay and clothing, as they had become used to regular pay but had received none over the last four or five months in the field. What little money was on hand was depreciated to near worthlessness.[16]

If Moultrie was apprehensive about the condition of the Continental Army and militia, he was downright critical of the Continental Navy for its absence during the campaign, and he made his feelings clear to Lincoln. "Is it not scandalous to America, that a handful of men, with two small men-of-war, should ride tri-umphant, and distress these southern states when perhaps our continental vessels are cruizing [*sic*] for the emolument of their commanders," said Moultrie, hot with indignation. "Should not this be represented to Congress?"[17]

Moultrie at first feared that the British buildup at Port Royal was a prelude to a new campaign, but it became evident rather quickly that the enemy was using the island to stage their withdrawal to Savannah. Anticipating a period of relative quietude on this front, Moultrie decided to attend the July session of the General Assembly in Charlestown. Matters of utmost consequence to the army were on the agenda, and as a senator representing the parishes of St. Philip and St. Michael, he wanted to take with him as many officers as could be spared, particularly since many of them were members of the House of Representatives. Together they would make sure that the General Assembly understood the dif-ficulty of maintaining the strength of the Continental regiments and the pure folly of depending on the militia, because they could not be kept in the field. In Moultrie's opinion "some other method must be fallen upon to raise an army, or else the country must be given up."[18]

The remonstrations of Moultrie and his officers fell short of the desired ef-fect. Instead on September 11, 1779, the South Carolina legislature passed an act that was calculated to bring the Continental regiments up to their full strength by offering increased bounties, thereby raising the existing force to five thousand men. But where the new law failed to meet Moultrie's expectations was the sec-tion that divided the militia into three rotating classes that would alternate into service for two-month stints, making it less efficient rather than more so. And despite the lobbying on the part of Moultrie, Lincoln, and others, the General Assembly again refused to place the state militiamen under the authority of the Continental articles when they were serving alongside Continental troops.[19]

A large French fleet commanded by the Comte d'Estaing upset the status quo on September 1 with its sudden and unexpected appearance off of the Georgia coast. Count d'Estaing, commander of the French expeditionary force in America, had not enjoyed success or popularity while cooperating in Rhode Island with Con-tinental forces led by Maj. Gen. Nathanael Greene in August 1778. But more recently he had led a victorious campaign to capture Grenada in the West Indies. Now responding to entreaties that emanated from Charlestown for help in driv-ing the British from Savannah, d'Estaing brought twenty-two ships of the line, ten frigates, one cutter, and enough transports to convey four thousand French troops to America. He hoped to make expiation for his failure in Rhode Island and to demonstrate his personal courage and fidelity to the American cause.[20]

Like everyone in Charlestown, Moultrie was elated when the French fleet anchored off the Charlestown Bar on September 4. A renewal of martial spirit caused a virtual suspension of everyday affairs. The legislature adjourned so that military officers could return to their regiments. Continental troops were brought in from the forts, and the militia was called out. Enlistments increased as volunteers mustered into service so that they would be present when the British gave up Savannah and marched out to deliver arms to their triumphant captors. "Every one cheerful, as if we were sure of success," Moultrie later wrote of the Americans' confidence, "and no one doubted but that we had nothing more to do, than to march up to Savannah; and demand a surrender."[21]

Moultrie would not be there to take in the grand spectacle. He would remain in command of the defense of Charlestown with a few South Carolina Continentals and militiamen. The specific reason for why Moultrie remained in Charlestown was never given. Perhaps it was illness; he only stated on September 26 that "the fates have forbid it." The expedition was expected to be of brief duration, and Lincoln considered inviting him to camp but hesitated because he thought that matters would be settled before Moultrie could possibly arrive. There was clearly no dishonor to being left behind.[22]

Lincoln's prediction was wrong. When d'Estaing demanded the surrender of Savannah, Prévost answered that he would defend the city to the last extremity. The British had constructed a formidable semicircular line of defenses that began near the riverbank above town and ended near the downstream riverbank. The campaign to retake Savannah now evolved in stages from rebuffed ultimatum to unsuccessful siege, to ineffective bombardment, and finally to an ill-advised frontal assault on a heavily fortified position. The epicenter of the allied attack was the Spring Hill redoubt, centermost of three redoubts on the right side of the British works.[23]

Before daylight on the foggy morning of October 9, 1779, some four thousand French and American soldiers stepped off. The thrust at the Spring Hill redoubt almost gained its objective without being discovered, but as the spirited Americans and Frenchmen converged on the position, the alert redcoats unleashed a torrential hail of musket balls, canister, and grapeshot. Through the abatis, up the glacis, and onward into the maelstrom they went—the struggle for Savannah would be won or lost at the Spring Hill redoubt, and it was up to the South Carolina Continentals and militiamen to turn the tide of battle. Finally reaching the redoubt, they fought with a desperate ferocity to wrench the stronghold from the British, who were obstinately determined to keep it. When the British counterattacked, brutal hand-to-hand combat filled the ditch in front with dead and wounded men.[24]

At the climax of the fighting on the Spring Hill redoubt occurred one of the more dramatic moments of the battle, the "high tide" of the American effort to breach the British lines. Lt. Col. Francis Marion bravely marched the Second South Carolina Regiment in good order toward the awaiting enemy. In the final rush to the earthworks, the two regimental color bearers planted their standards atop the British parapets. The blue flag and the red flag were the same banners presented in 1776 by Mrs. Susannah Elliott, to whom Moultrie pledged that they would be honorably supported and never tarnished. Moultrie's men gave their utmost to uphold his promise. Four color bearers were shot dead or mortally wounded, including Sergeant Jasper. The blue flag fell into the ditch with one of the fallen color bearers and was picked up by the British. The red flag was brought back to camp during the retreat.[25]

The October 9, 1779, Battle of Savannah was in fact one of the bloodiest battles of the Revolutionary War, comparable to the Battle of Bunker Hill, only in reverse. When the carnage was over, 58 Americans lay dead, and 181 Americans were wounded alongside 59 dead and 526 wounded Frenchmen. By comparison the British lost a mere 16 killed and 55 wounded. Casualties among the allied officer corps were remarkable. Count d'Estaing was wounded twice—once in the arm and once in the leg. Count Pulaski was mortally wounded while trying to rally the troops at the Spring Hill redoubt. Maj. Charles Motte was killed early while urging the Second South Carolina Regiment forward. Maj. Pierre Charles L'Enfant of the Continental engineers was badly wounded and left for dead on the field.[26]

Moultrie was convinced beyond any doubt that if the allies had attacked the incomplete and unmanned British works when they first arrived at Savannah, "they would have carried the town very easily . . . [the British] had only the Spring-hill battery completed and no abbettis [sic] round the town." In his opinion considerable time was wasted while the French and the Americans "employed themselves in throwing up batteries for their cannon and mortars . . . which gave the besieged three weeks to fortify themselves, and their success proves that they were not idle in that time." Historians have generally followed Moultrie's lead in criticizing d'Estaing for not acting promptly to compel a surrender or to drive the British forcibly out of Savannah.[27]

"This disappointment depressed our spirits very much," he reflected, "and we began to be apprehensive for the safety of these two southern states; it also depreciated our money so very low, that it was scarcely worth any thing." Moultrie had little else to say concerning the effect of the outcome of the campaign except that the militia behaved well under fire. And like many of his contemporaries, he also believed a false rumor that the battle's failure was due in a large part to British foreknowledge of the American plan of attack that was provided by an American deserter.[28]

19.

"I think they cannot pass this way"

From mid-July onward, throughout the legislative session and continuing through the abortive campaign to take Savannah in October, Moultrie took time from his public duties to tend to matters of a private nature. Whether or not his upcoming nuptials had influenced the decision for him to remain in Charlestown while the army marched to Savannah is unknown; however, William Moultrie remarried on October 15, 1779, at St. Philip's Church. The bride was Hannah Motte Lynch (born 1735), sister of Moultrie's close friend Col. Isaac Motte, widow of Thomas Lynch Sr., and mother of Thomas Lynch Jr., a signer of the Declaration of Independence. Thomas Lynch Sr. had died in 1776 of a stroke, a few months after the passing of Damaris Elizabeth Moultrie, while returning home from the Continental Congress.[1]

Thomas and Hannah Lynch had been married more than twenty years, and the couple moved in the same social and political circles as the Moultries. Moultrie and Hannah Lynch were quite likely acquainted for years prior to their first marriages, and like Damaris, Hannah was also of Huguenot extraction. Moultrie made no mention of remarriage in his memoirs, and the details of his courtship of Hannah Lynch remain obscure except that she was known to be "a lady of merit and beauty." Hannah brought one daughter to the Moultrie household from her previous marriage. The newly wedded couple's cup of joy was certainly mixed with the dregs of sorrow as they began their new life, for word of the disaster at Savannah was accompanied by the sad tidings that the bride's brother, Maj. Charles Motte, had lost his life in the battle only a few days before.[2]

The management of his personal funds had never been a source of concern to Moultrie. He had married into wealth and had been a good steward of his assets. But his memoirs are sprinkled with comments and footnotes relating to the poor financial condition of the state of South Carolina and the valuation of the state's currency. He wrote, "This great nation [Britain] we dared to oppose, without money." A chronic shortage of hard money in circulation for use in trade had certainly plagued the colony during the years preceding the Revolution, and the issuance of bills of credit had been tightly restricted.[3]

In 1775 the paper currency of the state of South Carolina depreciated to seven for one pound sterling. As Continental currency came southward, depreciation ran rampant, fueled less by military losses in the northern states and a diminishing popular confidence in the Patriot cause than by a progressive superabundance of bills. Charles Pinckney told Moultrie in January 1779 that new Continental recruits would be entitled to a five-hundred-dollar bounty if they enlisted within a month. In his memoirs Moultrie clarified for his readers that while this appeared to be a very high bounty, "the paper money had depreciated as low as 761 for one silver dollar." The devaluation led to profiteering on the part of unscrupulous post riders, who "being acquainted with the depreciation of the money, before we could possibly know of it, brought millions of dollars with them, which they gave for our property, to the ruin of a number of our honest and industrious citizens."[4]

By the summer of 1779, the paper money was practically worthless, "so depreciated," a cynical Lincoln wrote to Moultrie, "that I apprehend that unless something is done to increase its value, it will not long answer the purpose of carrying on the war; if that fails us, our only resource is the virtue of the people; how far that will avail us at this day, I leave you to judge." To answer what Charles Cotesworth Pinckney called "the present extraordinary exigencies of government," meaning that the state government was desperately short of the funds it needed to function, the General Assembly passed an ordinance in September 1779 authorizing the state of South Carolina to borrow money from private individuals. Moultrie was one of the several individuals who disregarded the recent military disappointments and stepped forward to risk his personal funds, loaning his government nine thousand pounds at the legally prescribed term of ten percent per annum.[5]

Since his disastrous call on Charlestown with Sir Peter Parker in 1776, Lt. Gen. Sir Henry Clinton had become commander-in-chief of the entire British army in North America. Clinton remained convinced that Charlestown was an attainable prize despite the previous two failed attempts to capture the coveted southern seaport. Clinton's strategic goals in 1780 were little different from that of his 1776 campaign—to capture Charlestown, rally southern Loyalists, reestablish royal authority in the southern colonies, and then march His Britannic Majesty's army victoriously from South Carolina north to the Chesapeake. But he would approach Charlestown differently this time. General Prévost's 1779 campaign, combined with intelligence gleaned from a thorough reconnaissance of the inland waterways, had revealed that the best approach to Charlestown was by passage through the inlets and sea islands to the rear of the town.[6]

An uncomfortable stalemate existed in the northern theater at the end of 1779. As was customary, military operations were for the most part suspended during the inclement winter months. George Washington's American army endured the worst winter of the war in Morristown, New Jersey. Clinton's British army was comfortably ensconced in New York. The British commander realized that timing was of the essence if he was to venture south with a part of his army. The condition of the Continental Army in the South was deplorable, both in size and in spirit. The southern army under General Lincoln had suffered defeats at Briar Creek, Stono Ferry, and Savannah.

The South Carolinians felt abandoned by the French, whose fleet had recently sailed away from the southern coast, and relief promised by Congress was slow to arrive if it arrived at all. The pervasive sense of isolation had nearly led the South Carolina civil government to give up Charlestown and withdraw from the rebellion when Prévost threatened the town in May 1779. Moultrie and his steadfast officers had prevented this calamity by their determination to fight, yet there remained a divided political sentiment in South Carolina upon which the British might capitalize.[7]

It was Prévost's victory in Savannah and the departure of the French fleet that persuaded Clinton to proceed with his plan to invade South Carolina. As before, Lt. Gen. Charles Earl Cornwallis was Clinton's second-in-command. A fleet of fourteen warships and ninety transports commanded by Vice Admiral Mariot Arbuthnot sailed from New York on December 26, 1779. Aboard the transports were more than eighty-seven hundred British, provincial, and Hessian soldiers—the flower of the British army in North America—embarked on a harrowing month-long journey to Savannah that was beset by such stormy weather that a number of the transports foundered and a part of the fleet was scattered. Four-fifths of the army's fourteen hundred horses were lost, as well as some of the army's heavy artillery, before the fleet straggled into Georgia waters on the first day of February.[8]

The Americans were not oblivious to the British plan for a third invasion of the South. Reports of the expedition assembling in New York were transmitted to General Lincoln, and there was no doubt that the mission's objective was Charlestown. Defensive preparations had been under way for weeks, and in January when Lincoln received notice of Clinton's departure from Sandy Hook, he intensified the fortification of the Charlestown Neck. Shaken from its inertia over southern affairs by the disaster at Savannah, Congress sent badly needed munitions and other war materiel from Philadelphia, and to bolster Charlestown's military manpower, Congress ordered the Virginia and North Carolina Continental Lines serving with the northern army to proceed on a long march southward.[9]

To help defend the harbor from the British navy, Cdre. Abraham Whipple cruised to Charlestown from Bermuda heading a flotilla of three Continental Navy ships: the twenty-eight-gun frigates *Providence* and *Queen of France* and the eighteen-gun sloop *Ranger*. *Providence* and *Ranger* had been captained in the past by John Paul Jones. Though lacking the charisma of Captain Jones, Whipple, born in 1733, was truly one of the great but largely forgotten American naval heroes of the Revolutionary War. He enjoyed an illustrious career full of daring exploits. On one occasion in 1779, Whipple and his squadron captured eleven cargo-laden British merchantmen bound from Jamaica without firing a single shot. Unfortunately the usually intrepid Whipple would turn in a disappointing performance at Charlestown.[10]

About the time the British reappeared off the South Carolina coast, the General Assembly adjourned, but not before bestowing Gov. John Rutledge with dictatorial powers. Rutledge soon afterward issued a proclamation calling for the militia and the inhabitants of the town to rally immediately to the defense of Charlestown under pain of confiscation and imprisonment. Ironically a similar counter-proclamation made by Sir Henry Clinton offered amnesty and protection for repentant rebels, but it also warned of the dire consequences of defiance. These two opposing proclamations would force the populace to choose between the greatly diminished Continental Army and the military might of Great Britain.[11]

Never before had a general officer allowed a Continental Army to be shut up in a besieged town. Rather all experience was to the contrary—Washington had evacuated the cities of New York and Philadelphia in 1776 and 1777 rather than be trapped. But Lincoln was pressured from Congress and South Carolina to defend the town. Judgment and experience notwithstanding, Lincoln believed that Charlestown was defensible, or that it could be held at least long enough for reinforcements to lift a siege. Moreover he was afraid that if he abandoned the post that he had been sent southward to defend, his reputation would suffer as a result. Lincoln therefore resolved to remain in Charlestown instead of withdrawing the American army into the countryside to fight another day. His abandonment of a Fabian strategy would have far-reaching consequences.[12]

As for what to do while awaiting Clinton's next move, Lincoln posed the question to a council of war held on February 12. Should the Americans strike before Clinton could consolidate his force outside of Charlestown? With the exception of one dissenter, the council answered Lincoln with a resounding "no."

Moultrie was among those who believed that the venture was too risky and that the Continental Army was too weak to take on a superior enemy force in the open.[13]

After two weeks of repair and refitting off Tybee Island, the British fleet sailed northward along the South Carolina coast to North Edisto Inlet, twenty miles southwest of Charlestown. Troops landed without incident on the night of February 11 on Simmons Island (present-day Seabrook Island) and continued disembarkation the next day on Wadmalaw Island.[14]

Taking advantage of the rivers and creeks that connected the coastal islands to transport troops and supplies by flatboat and encountering little resistance, the British took possession of Johns and James Islands, occupying their old defensive works at Stono Ferry and seizing Fort Johnson. From James Island's eastern shore, the redcoats could look across the harbor at Charlestown, on the peninsula to the northwest about two and a half miles away. They were within sight of their objective, but the Ashley River remained a formidable barrier that would have to be traversed. On February 16 the redcoats crossed over to the mainland via a bridge over Wappoo Creek. Meanwhile part of the British fleet sailed farther north from North Edisto Inlet and took station off the Charlestown Bar to blockade the harbor. For the third time in the war, Charlestown was under serious threat of attack.[15]

On February 19 Lincoln sent Moultrie with detachments of cavalry and light infantry totaling six hundred men to Bacon's Bridge on the Ashley River, two miles above Dorchester and twenty miles from Charlestown. It was here that Lincoln believed that the British, for lack of boats, would attempt to cross the Ashley River onto the Charlestown peninsula. At Bacon's Bridge Moultrie established a camp to receive incoming militia. Accomplishing that, he sent skirmishers out to gather intelligence, to harass the enemy flanks, and to impede the redcoats' progress in any way possible. In the interim he took pains to secure all manner of livestock, carriages, and boats—anything that would be useful to the British on their march, especially the horses. Moultrie erected strongly fortified works on the high ground commanding Bacon's Bridge, but if the British tried to force a crossing, he would have to destroy the bridge before retiring.[16]

At his disposal were 227 light infantrymen drawn from the regiments of the South Carolina Continental Line and commanded by Francis Marion. Moultrie's 379 horsemen consisted of Pulaski's Legion, now led by Maj. Pierre François Vernier, and the First Virginia Continental Dragoons under Lt. Col. William Washington (George Washington's cousin). The numerical advantage of cavalry allowed Moultrie the freedom to send out sorties to skirmish with the enemy at in the vicinity of the Stono River, and American aggressiveness kept the enemy close to their lines. The horsemen were quite active, and Moultrie kept Lincoln well supplied with fresh intelligence and prisoners.[17]

Moultrie notified Lincoln on February 22 that the militia had once again failed to respond to the emergency: "I have not one militia-man doing duty here. I am informed they are patroling [*sic*] in their different districts." This time a fear of contagion was preventing the militia from coming into town, said Moultrie, who explained, "they are afraid of the small-pox breaking out, when they are cooped up, which they say, will be worse to them than the enemy."[18]

Lincoln was indignant—"much surprised to find the militia so unreasonable as to wish to avoid this town . . . the safety of the town depends upon their coming to its assistance . . . they must be brought down; they ought to have been here before now, for they have nothing to apprehend from the small-pox." It was true that an outbreak of smallpox had occurred the previous November, but Lincoln had diligently inquired of the commissioners of the town, the surgeons of the hospitals, and the officers of the army, who all reported that smallpox was nowhere to be found in Charlestown.[19]

A late February storm that temporarily disrupted the British intercoastal supply line made Moultrie less wary of an enemy approach overland toward his position at Bacon's Bridge. To Lincoln he wrote, "The rains have filled our rivers and swamps so much, that it is almost impossible for the enemy to drag their cannon and artillery stores along. I think they cannot pass this way; it therefore becomes us to look out, and expect them from some other quarter."[20]

Instead Moultrie suspected that Clinton would transport his army on flatboats and galleys down the Stono River and Wappoo Creek to land west of town. Alternatively the British might perhaps "draw their flat-bottomed boats from Rantowle's [Creek] to Ashley-river, drop down, and land near our lines; or cross at Ashley-ferry and land on the causeway." The causeway he referred to was a road built across swampy ground leading to Ashley Ferry. Moultrie proposed to cut the causeway within grapeshot distance of his field pieces so he could rake the enemy if they attempted to approach the bridge.[21]

Lincoln recommended that Moultrie consider dividing his cavalry into thirds, keeping one third at Bacon's Bridge and sending the rest to patrol the vicinity of the Stono River. The roving horsemen would be able to reconnoiter the area extending from Rantowle's to Wappoo Creek. Before acting on Lincoln's advice, Moultrie rode out on February 24 to inspect the enemy positions on James and Johns Islands. Indeed Clinton was establishing a large supply depot on James Island at the mouth of Wappoo Creek where it joined the Stono. When he reached Wappoo Creek, Moultrie found a good view of the whole quarter-mile-long British encampment. By observing the stacks of arms and number of men moving about, he estimated the enemy strength to be between one thousand and twelve hundred British and Hessians. He also noted the large number of galleys, schooners, and flatboats.[22]

Word reached Moultrie on March 1 that the British had crossed Wappoo Creek and were moving toward Bacon's Bridge. By March 7 a British reconnaissance in force was about three miles from Ashley Ferry, well below Bacon's Bridge. Moultrie's prediction that Clinton would not approach the west bank of the Ashley via an overland route had been wrong, and there was little he could do other than call in his cavalry, make ready to destroy the bridge, and prepare to send the light infantry into town. In fact he could do practically nothing at all, for he was ill and bedridden—his communiqués to Lincoln were written by his aide-de-camp, Capt. Philip Neyle.[23]

Moultrie did not specify the nature of his illness in his memoirs, but it was feared in camp that he had contracted "nervous fever," the archaic term for typhoid fever. This bacterial disease was not uncommonly a consequence of unsanitary conditions in camp, but it was not the likely etiology of Moultrie's indisposition, as he was on the road to recovery in about a week's time. However, his indisposition was severe enough to warrant his relief by Gen. Isaac Huger. Moultrie returned to town on March 9 for several days of convalescence at home, though whether he was recuperating from the fever or the two blistering treatments of mustard plaster administered by the Second South Carolina's regimental surgeon, Dr. Jeremiah Theus, is a matter of conjecture. In the eighteenth century, the treatment truly could be worse than the disease.[24]

20.

"Had Moultrie been in command"

Eighteenth-century military engineers combined physical barriers with concentrated artillery and small arms fire to discourage the most brave-hearted attacker from attempting a direct assault against fortifications. Indeed wise generals were unwilling to risk the carnage that accompanied an attack against a well-entrenched enemy unless all other options had been exhausted. Instead they employed siege operations. The five elements of the eighteenth-century siege were the investment, the bombardment, the construction of parallels and approaches, the breaching of the fortifications by artillery, and the final assault. Parallels and approaches were excavated trenches that enabled an army to advance slowly but systematically toward enemy fortifications while under cover from defensive fire.[1]

If the siege works brought the besiegers close enough to the ramparts for a general assault, and if it became evident that the fortifications could be breached while sustaining acceptable offensive losses, the besieged would usually capitulate. Two other dynamics argued in favor of a peaceable conclusion of a siege. When living conditions became intolerable for the defenders, starvation could become a factor. And when the lifting of the siege by the arrival of outside reinforcements had become doubtful, capitulation was the rational course of action.

To bring the Charlestown campaign to a close, Clinton first needed to envelop Charlestown completely to prevent American supply and reinforcement. The British solidified their position on the west bank of the Ashley by erecting a series of batteries facing the town. The first heavy cannon were mounted on March 12 at Fenwick's Point just north of Wappoo Creek. Sighting their six guns across the river from this position, the British artillerists commanded the length of Tradd Street in town.[2]

To the north advanced parties of redcoats crossed upriver unopposed at Drayton Hall above Ashley Ferry at dawn on March 29 using flatboats that had been secreted up the Ashley under cover of darkness from Wappoo Creek. Before sunset the main part of the British army was across and marching down the neck toward town. A small party of American light infantry and riflemen led by Col. John Laurens engaged the redcoats in a sharp skirmish on March 30 that did little to slow their advance. Clinton's army was soon deployed in front of the Charlestown defenses.[3]

The British held the numerical advantage from the outset, fielding a besieging force of British regulars, provincials, and Hessian soldiers that numbered approximately eighty-seven hundred men. Lincoln, by contrast, could muster only forty-two hundred Americans with which to garrison Charlestown, Fort Moultrie, and Lempriere's Point on the east bank of the Cooper River. A mere thousand militiamen had answered the call to join ranks with the meager Continentals. The Continentals were so reduced in number from losses at Savannah that Lincoln had found it necessary to consolidate South Carolina's regiments, merging the men of the Fifth and Sixth Regiments into the First, Second, and Third Regiments. Reinforcements trickling in from Virginia and North Carolina would eventually swell the ranks of the American defenders to nearly fifty-seven hundred.[4]

Work on the American defensive lines across the neck had proceeded more or less continuously over the preceding months, though with varied degrees of fervor depending on the perceived sense of urgency. There can be no doubt that once the enemy appeared at the gates, Lincoln, Moultrie, and their subordinate officers were tirelessly occupied with the construction of the fortifications, much in the same way that Maj. Gen. Charles Lee fretted over the town's defenses in 1776. The Americans utilized two Continental engineers, Lt. Col. Louis Antoine Jean Baptiste de Cambray and Col. Jean Baptiste Joseph de Laumoy, to supervise the work.[5]

Hundreds of slaves labored to extend the existing lines across the neck from the Cooper River marsh on the east side of the peninsula to the Ashley River marsh on the west. The workmen revetted the earthworks with palmetto logs and strengthened the line by the addition of earthen redans and batteries connected by ramparts topped with protected parapets. By the end of the siege, the muzzles of nearly eighty cannon bristled from their embrasures. Colonels Cambray and Laumoy would come to view the American defensive works with disdain, but General Clinton saw them differently, grudgingly conceding that the defenses were "by no means contemptible."[6]

To reach the earthworks, an approaching enemy would have to advance under fire while contending with a number of obstacles. First he would have to

A Sketch of the Operations before Charleston, the Capital of South Carolina, 1780. Thomas Abernathie, 1785. The Robert Charles Lawrence Fergusson Collection, the Society of the Cincinnati, Washington, D.C. Reproduced with permission.

traverse a broad expanse of approximately a mile of open country that had been cleared of trees and buildings to provide open fields of fire. After crossing this plain, he would reach an eighteen-foot-wide canal that was six feet deep. This "wet ditch," as it was called, was filled with water from tidal creeks that stemmed from the rivers and marshes on either side of the peninsula and ran parallel to the American lines 450 feet away. After the canal two rows of abatis would have to be negotiated. An attacker would then be confronted by a dry ditch that was twelve feet wide and six feet deep, located at the base of the ramparts. To cross the ditch, he would have to maneuver past two rows of sharpened stakes driven into the bottom of the ditch. Climbing from the ditch, the unfortunate assailant would then face a double-row fraise that projected from the ramparts.[7]

The American right flank was protected by a detached redoubt at the end of the main line. Another detached work called the advanced redoubt, or half-moon battery, was pushed forward to defend the wet ditch on the left. The center of the line was secured by a tabby and masonry hornwork set 300 to 350 feet behind the parapet. This fortification, constructed in 1759 and known as the Old Royal Works, housed eighteen heavy guns that wrecked havoc on the British batteries. Lincoln often used the hornwork as a command post during the siege, and he envisioned it as a fallback position if the British breached the main line.[8]

By occupying James Island, controlling the mainland west of the Ashley, and establishing their camps on the Charlestown Neck, Clinton's British army had invested Charlestown from the west and the north. A naval blockade would seal off Charlestown from the sea. The importance of denying the Royal Navy a seaward approach to the town was not lost on Lincoln and Moultrie. A successful naval defense of the Charlestown Bar was imperative. For this Lincoln and Moultrie depended on Cdre. Abraham Whipple and his squadron of four Continental warships.[9]

Lincoln and Moultrie expected Whipple to anchor the American ships in Five Fathom Hole to prevent the British fleet from entering the harbor. Whipple maintained that the anchorage in Five Fathom Hole was untenable. Conditions that would favor a British crossing of the bar—a rising tide and an east wind—would prevent American ships in Five Fathom Hole from maintaining position on station and coming abeam to aim their broadsides. Moreover if the British did cross the bar under full sail and maneuver between Fort Moultrie and the American ships anchored in Five Fathom Hole, the American navy would be cut off from town. On this particular point, Moultrie agreed with the commodore, and after sounding Five Fathom Hole himself, Lincoln grudgingly acquiesced to Whipple's judgment.[10]

Instead of waiting in Five Fathom Hole for the ships of the Royal Navy to cross the bar, Whipple and his captains decided that the American ships would anchor in the narrow channel between Sullivan's Island and the Middle Ground. This second line of defense blocking the entrance of Rebellion Road was within point-blank range of Fort Moultrie. Admiral Arbuthnot's ships would have to run the gauntlet single-file, one at a time, and if he dared, Moultrie was willing to wager that his friend Col. Charles Cotesworth Pinckney's artillerists inside the fort would rake the channel. No, the British could not pass without losing ships, and for that reason Moultrie doubted they would even try.[11]

Eight of Arbuthnot's smaller warships passed over the bar on March 20 and sailed virtually uncontested into Five Fathom Hole. The next morning Moultrie counted ten men-of-war, seven frigates, and twenty other ships anchored in Five Fathom Hole. This was a much larger naval force than the Americans had anticipated. The outnumbered and outgunned American navy had only nine ships with which to oppose the British trespassers: four Continental vessels, three French frigates left behind by d'Estaing, and two brigs belonging to South Carolina.[12]

Despite Moultrie's doubt of Arbuthnot's audacity, the prevailing sentiment was that Arbuthnot would rely on the superiority of his force to run his ships past the guns of Fort Moultrie as quickly as possible and take station above town in the Ashley and Cooper Rivers. From the rivers the British vessels could enfilade the American lines from the rear. Moultrie earnestly hoped that the batteries erected around the harbor would be able to keep the enemy ships clear of town it they did indeed try to pass upriver.[13]

The tactical situation in the harbor took an even more drastic turn for the worse for the Americans on March 21. A panicked Whipple and his captains reported that the British force was far too powerful for his squadron to resist, even from the favorable position near Fort Moultrie. In Whipple's opinion neither the American ships, nor Fort Moultrie, nor obstructions placed in the channel could prevent the British from sailing up to the town. Exasperated, Lincoln ordered the ships to withdraw up the Cooper River rather than engage the British fleet.[14]

The American fleet sent by Congress had been utterly useless in the defense of Charlestown. Their crews dismounted the cannon from their embrasures and dispersed them with the greatest dispatch to the batteries about the town. Several of the ships were scuttled in the Cooper River across from the Exchange, from where a boom of cables, chains, and spars was laid across the sunken hulks to the marsh on Shute's Folly in order to obstruct the upriver channel. Those few vessels still afloat anchored behind the barrier to serve as floating batteries. The virtually uncontested relinquishment of the harbor provoked one historian to declare, "Had Moultrie been in command, somebody would have been hurt before the harbor was abandoned."[15]

On March 26 Lincoln ordered Moultrie to see to the disposition of artillery among the batteries and works in and about the town. As he went about his work, he may have felt an odd sense of déjà vu that reminded him of the harried preparations that were made for the Battle of Fort Sullivan four years earlier. But this time Moultrie was assisted by the officers of the Brigade of Artillery, most of whom had seen action and knew what would soon be in the offing. There were

79 guns mounted in sixteen batteries across the neck, including 6 guns in the advance redoubt on the left. On the water side of town, 95 guns were mounted in ten batteries. By the time Moultrie finished, more than 220 guns faced menacingly outward from the defensive works around Charlestown. And now that the naval force was nonoperational, Moultrie was able to use twelve hundred sailors to help man the batteries.[16]

The British broke ground on their first parallel on the night of April 1. The Americans immediately brought up artillery, and the next day began firing at the redcoats as they worked. Moultrie remarked to a friend that the daily bombardment of the British became so much of a spectacle for the townspeople that many of the ladies would stroll out from town to the lines "with all composure imaginable" to watch the barrage. Once the enemy batteries joined the chorus, he knew that the spectators would make themselves pretty scarce. These artillery exchanges would be impressively loud, but in Moultrie's opinion they would not be not very dangerous, at least not from the distances over which the two sides would begin firing—about a thousand yards, perhaps a little less.[17]

Aside from harassing the workmen, the American bombardment did little damage to the British works. A line of six connected redoubts were completed during the first week of April. The British batteries were not yet ready to return fire, but the batteries at Fenwick's Point and the galleys in Wappoo Creek could fire back, and on April 5 Clinton ordered them to open on the town. A number of houses were hit, Governor Rutledge's house was struck twice, and several civilians were killed. In due course the British bombardment escalated as their batteries on the neck were brought on line. Few houses north of Broad Street escaped damage from British shot, shells, and incendiaries fired from their main lines. The houses south of Broad were likewise ravaged by the batteries on James Island and the galleys in the Ashley River. The redcoats rained iron and terror on the city, and the deaths of women and children brought home the harsh realities in ways the inhabitants had never experienced.[18]

Alexander Garden related an incident during which Moultrie was nearly killed in his bed. According to the story, Moultrie was so worn out from the "severe duty on the lines . . . that to renew his energies, he took up his quarters for one night, in Elliott's buildings, near the centre of the city, where there was the least chance of interruption, to the rest he sought for. A tremendous fire about the dawning of the day, roused him from his slumbers, he started from his bed, and was hurrying on his regimentals, when a shot striking the house, entered the apartment and lodged in the bed from which he had risen. The delay of a few moments," Garden concluded, "must have proved fatal to him." Garden was not there during the siege, so he must have gotten the story secondhandedly. Since Moultrie did not comment on this episode in his memoirs, its veracity cannot be positively confirmed.[19]

Moultrie hated to evacuate his namesake fort, a post that for so long stood as a symbol of South Carolina's defiance, but neither was he inclined to reinforce the fort using troops from town. In the end it made little difference. Eight British warships and a small assortment of other vessels sailed past Fort Moultrie and anchored near Fort Johnson on April 8, each man-of-war pausing only long enough to unleash a single broadside at the fort. Just as Moultrie predicted, Pinckney and the men of the First South Carolina Regiment refused to allow the enemy to pass unscathed. A hot fire from the fort's guns inflicted damage to the mast and rigging of several of the trespassers and caused a crippled British store ship to run aground in the cove. When it was all over, the Royal Navy had full possession of Charlestown Harbor, and the town was now completely invested on three sides. The only open lines of communication ran east across the Cooper River.[20]

By April 10 the British had cannon emplaced in two of the six batteries of the newly completed first parallel. Clinton and Arbuthnot decided it was time to query the Americans to see if a negotiated surrender could be obtained. "Regretting the effusion of Blood and distress which must now commence," the British commanders deemed it "conformant to humanity to warn the Town and Garrison of Charlestown of the havoc and devastation with which they are threatened from the formidable force surrounding them by Sea and Land." Clinton's overture was the first in a series of parleys that would eventually culminate in the town's capitulation. In spite of Clinton's assertion that any delay in giving up Charlestown would constitute "wanton indifference to the fate of its inhabitants," and without consulting with anyone on the matter, Lincoln summarily refused the call for the Americans to lay down their arms, declaring that it was both his duty and inclination to defend Charlestown to the last extremity.[21]

Clinton had overstated his case when he declared that the town and garrison were surrounded. With his cavalry and a series of outposts on the Cooper and Wando Rivers, Lincoln maintained all-important avenues northeast to the backcountry and a route through Christ Church Parish toward the Santee River and onward toward North Carolina. This American eastern flank, so to speak, was anchored by Fort Moultrie, a battery at Haddrell's Point that guarded the channel between Hog Island and Shute's Folly, and most important, a strongly fortified position at Lempriere's Point.[22]

Lempriere's Point, or Hobcaw Point as it was also known, was a small tip of land four miles across the Cooper from Charlestown just below the confluence of the Cooper and Wando Rivers. Batteries at Lempriere's Point would prevent the Royal Navy from gaining access upriver if British ships somehow got past the obstructions guarding the entrance to the Cooper River. Holding this point was crucial to keeping open the vital corridor by which communications traveled back and forth and provisions were brought in and through which any attempt to evacuate Charlestown would be made. Lincoln employed some of his best troops to defend it. On April 11 he sent a battery of six eighteen-pound guns from Fort Moultrie to strengthen the redoubt at the point. Moultrie and Brig. Gen. Lachlan McIntosh of Georgia were keenly interested in Lempriere's Point as a back door out of Charlestown as the British advanced their siege lines.[23]

Lincoln summoned his generals together on April 12 to sign a letter to Governor Rutledge urging him to leave Charlestown. The governor had so far objected to repeated requests that he and his Privy Council depart in this time of danger. Lincoln, Moultrie, and others, however, finally won out, and the letter was signed by Lincoln's war council to counter any public perception that Rutledge was deserting his post. Rutledge's fear for his reputation was thus mollified; he crossed the Cooper River at noon the next day and headed for the backcountry with three members of his Privy Council. Rutledge appointed Christopher Gadsden to the office of lieutenant governor in the place of Thomas Bee, who was away in Philadelphia attending the Continental Congress. He left Gadsden and the more radical members of the Privy Council in charge of the civil government of Charlestown for the duration of his absence.[24]

Moultrie and Rutledge were quite fond of each other. The two men had shared a lifetime of experience from boyhood, and it was Rutledge who backed Moultrie's decision to defend Fort Sullivan in 1776. Later when Moultrie reflected on the episode, he clearly saw the importance of the governor remaining free from British captivity when Charlestown fell, crediting Rutledge's presence in the country with giving spirit to the people and keeping alive the resistance against the British. "To have a man of such great abilities, firmness, and decision amongst them" was crucial, and in summarizing all that Rutledge accomplished both militarily and as the singular embodiment of civil authority, Moultrie emphatically stated that "in short, he did every thing that could be done for the good of the country."[25]

Rutledge did not leave Charlestown unaccompanied. Lincoln ordered a number of supernumerary officers and officers unfit for duty to move to the safety of the backcountry. Among the refugees was Lt. Col. Francis Marion. Marion had been a guest at a late-night soirée at the Tradd Street home of Capt. Alexander McQueen on March 19. Over the course of the evening, McQueen, who was Moultrie's adjutant general, locked the doors of his residence to prevent the untimely departure of his guests before the evening's rounds of toasts had been drunk. The temperate Marion, wishing neither to overindulge nor to risk offending his host, tried to steal away by dropping to the ground from a second-story window. Looking down from the window, Marion misjudged his fall and badly sprained or fractured his ankle.[26]

The incapacitation of so brave and valuable an officer appeared to be a calamity for the Americans, and it was certainly humiliating for Marion. But the twist of an ankle would prove to be a fortuitous twist of fate that prevented him from falling into the hands of the British. At first, recalled Moultrie, Marion "was so lame that he was obliged to sculk [*sic*] about from house to house among his friends, and sometimes hide in the bushes until he grew better; he then crept out by degrees, and began to collect a few friends." But with his freedom preserved by the escape, Marion went on to become one of South Carolina's great partisan leaders and an American folk hero. He revived the South Carolina militia and successfully opposed British incursions into the state from Charlestown during the latter part of the war. Marion earned the sobriquet "Swamp Fox" from his adversary Col. Banastre Tarleton because he and his irregulars often hid in the swamps to evade the British.[27]

Moultrie's wife, Hannah, also left Charlestown about this time. She may have been among the governor in exile's entourage, although this is not a certainty. After traveling to the Cape Fear River region of North Carolina, a long, distressing journey, Hannah safely arrived at the home of her daughter Elizabeth Harleston. There is no primary material from which to draw firm conclusions, but considering the circumstances, it is easy to conceive that concern for her security outweighed Moultrie's anguish and desire to have her close at hand. They had, after all, been married only six months, and what a tumultuous half-year it had been.[28]

Lincoln called his general officers to another council of war at his quarters on April 13, 1780, the same day Governor Rutledge left town. According to Lachlan McIntosh, it was at this council that Lincoln *first* (McIntosh's emphasis) laid out the condition of the garrison and the state of their supplies of ammunition and provisions. The commanding general at this point held little hope of outside intervention. Neither were the French engineers, Cambray and Laumoy, optimistic. They rendered an exceedingly scornful opinion of the defensive lines, calling them mere field works that could hold out longer than a few days more.[29]

Lincoln was prepared to evacuate the garrison, and he asked the council to consider the practicality of this course of action. Moultrie supported evacuation, as did McIntosh, who did not want to hesitate even an hour getting the Continentals across the Cooper River while an escape route remained open. The salvation of South Carolina and perhaps the other southern states depended on a breakout by the Continental Army. Quite a few of the officers present acquiesced to McIntosh's point of view, but no final consensus had been reached when a howling of incoming artillery rounds broke up the meeting.[30]

Lincoln's war council and Rutledge's departure notwithstanding, April 13 marked a significant change in the momentum of the siege. Between nine and ten o'clock in the morning, the British opened a furious, fifteen-hour bombardment from heavy guns and mortars on the neck acting in concert with the batteries and galleys at Wappoo. The British artillery demolished several American gun emplacements and killed at least two men. Noncombatants also suffered as incendiary shells fired from mortars aimed at the lines fell in town, igniting two houses, and several women and children reportedly lost their lives in the barrage.[31]

Dawn on April 14 revealed that during the night the British had opened their second parallel twelve hundred feet beyond the first parallel and only five hundred feet from the wet ditch and abatis. This new trench was also about nine hundred feet from the hornwork. The opposing lines were now within musket range of each other, and skirmishing by skilled marksmen on both sides made the contest increasingly hazardous. Exposing oneself to enemy fire, even briefly, could be a fatal error, a fact attested to by the rising number of casualties. Indeed American small arms and grapeshot exacted a toll on British working parties. British counterbattery fire, in turn, blasted the American artillerists while the Hessian jaegers kept up a withering fire of musketry from their trenches. The closing proximity of the combatants sometimes produced tragic and grisly results. Moultrie's aide-de-camp, Capt. Philip Neyle, found himself in the wrong place at the wrong time on April 18. Returning to the rear after delivering Moultrie's order to quicken fire upon the enemy, Neyle was partially decapitated by a cannonball.[32]

The smoke and thunder of the cannon was ferocious and lethal. Still, the danger of the artillery fire was not confined to the intended targets. Both sides suffered casualties from friendly fire and other tragic accidents. Two American cannoneers were badly injured when their twelve-pounder burst on firing. Ironically they were arguably the last casualties of the Battle of Sullivan's Island, since this was one of the guns belonging to the British frigate *Acteon* that ran aground while engaged with Fort Moultrie in 1776.[33]

The *Acteon* had become stranded in the shallows of the Lower Middle Ground in the initial battle on June 28, 1776, and set afire by her crew before they abandoned ship. The victorious South Carolinians later retrieved the ship's guns from the shallow water. The cannons were first thought to be a windfall for the Americans, but in retrospect the misfires led Moultrie to believe that they had been ruined: "It is remarkable that eight or ten of those guns [from the *Acteon*] which we weighed, and mounted on our lines, were every one of them bursted, after two or three rounds, which makes me suppose that their being heated by the fire of the ship, and suddenly plunging into the water while red-hot, destroyed their metallic parts, and left only the dross behind."[34]

21.

"It was our last great effort"

The mounting devastation wrought by British artillery and the advancement of the redcoat siege lines forced Lincoln, Moultrie, McIntosh, and the other American generals to reevaluate their prospects. Efforts to reconvene a council of war were thwarted by repeated interruptions at Lincoln's headquarters, so it was not until April 19 that the council could meet again, this time at Moultrie's quarters. Generals Lincoln, Moultrie, McIntosh, Woodford, Scott, and Hogun attended this meeting, joined by Col. Barnard Beekman of the artillery, the engineer Colonel Laumoy, and Col. Maurice Simons of the Charlestown militia.[1]

Charging the council with secrecy, the persistently indecisive Lincoln once again outlined the American situation and asked the council members to speak their minds as to what actions should be pursued under the present circumstances. A number of officers, including McIntosh and Moultrie, still favored an evacuation, despite the fact that a British force was now present on the opposite bank of the Cooper River. The threat awaiting on the other side of the river was actually greater than anyone in Charlestown fully realized until several days later when deserters reported that General Clinton had received twenty-six hundred reinforcements from New York. These additional troops allowed the British to strengthen their army east of the Cooper without having to withdraw troops from their siege lines. Clinton would later appoint General Cornwallis to command this detachment.[2]

Matters in the council were nearly settled when Lincoln committed a critical error—the same mistake Moultrie made when British general Augustine Prévost threatened Charlestown the previous year. Lincoln allowed the civil authorities a voice in proceedings that were solely the aegis of the military. Christopher

Gadsden appeared at the meeting, and Lincoln invited him to join the council. Gadsden was fundamentally opposed to both evacuation and capitulation, but if the council of war decided to surrender, he would provide terms amenable to the Privy Council on behalf of the town's inhabitants. In return Lincoln agreed not to act without the consent of the civil authorities.[3]

The council of war reconvened that evening at General Lincoln's quarters. Engineer Laumoy restated the deficiencies of the American fortifications, "if they were worthy of being called so," underscoring the improbability of holding out much longer and the impracticality of making a retreat. And like before Laumoy's vigorous arguments in favor of capitulation swayed the council toward negotiating for honorable terms.[4]

Gadsden suddenly entered, bringing with him the radical members of the Privy Council: Messrs. Ferguson, Hutson, and Ramsay. Rudely and vociferously protesting against the council with words that bordered on insurrection, the members of the civil government pressed hard for defending the town. Thomas Ferguson pointed out that the citizenry were aware that boats were being gathered for a Cooper River crossing, and he vowed that if evacuation was attempted, he would not only open the gates and allow the enemy to come in, but that he would assist in attacking the Continentals before they could board their transports.[5]

If Lincoln, Moultrie, McIntosh, and the others believed that they had suffered enough obnoxious treatment, they were wrong. Gadsden and the councilors exited, and deliberations continued further until Col. Charles Cotesworth Pinckney stormed in. Pinckney, who had somehow caught wind of the deliberations, had come over from Fort Moultrie, and "forgetting his usual Politeness," he addressed Lincoln "in great warmth and much the same Strain as the Lt. Governor [Gadsden] had done." Pinckney was incensed that any option other than defending Charlestown was under consideration.[6]

Lincoln called his council together again on April 20. The arguments were essentially the same. Evacuating the army across the Cooper River presented a number of "distressing inconveniences." First, the civil authorities had vehemently objected to evacuation and threatened to take active measures to oppose it. Second, evacuation would have to be accomplished using vessels that were at the mercy of wind and tide to cross a river "three miles broad" in face of a superior enemy. Third, a considerable enemy force had possession of the road to the Santee River, the only route of retreat. Finally, if a worn-down, fatigued, and starving Continental Army reached the Santee ahead of pursuing British infantry and cavalry, there would be too few boats with which to make a crossing.[7]

Laumoy insisted that the garrison could not possibly hold out much longer. To Laumoy the impracticability of retreat rendered immediate capitulation imperative. When the issue came to a vote, the council agreed to seek terms from the British before their affairs became more critical. But if acceptable terms could not be obtained from General Clinton and Admiral Arbuthnot, the council agreed to reconsider evacuation.[8]

Moultrie omitted details of the proceedings in his memoirs, and he avoided an explicit statement of his own opinion regarding retreat, surrender, or making a stand. He signed the minutes of the meeting, but according to John Lewis Gervais, Moultrie was the only general to disagree with the council of war. A lifelong lowcountry inhabitant with a definite stake in the outcome, he undoubtedly understood the desire of Gadsden and Ferguson to defend their town to the bitter end. But Moultrie was still the second-ranking Continental officer, and as such he took the pragmatic approach of trying to save the Continental Army if he could. When it became apparent that the army could not escape, he finally yielded to the decision to offer terms rather than subject the garrison and inhabitants of Charlestown to needless bloodletting and wanton destruction in the face of an assault.[9]

Like Lachlan McIntosh, Moultrie was offended by the insulting and abusive treatment that Lincoln had suffered at the hands of the civil officials, not to mention his close friend Pinckney's unbecoming indignation. The invective heaped upon Lincoln applied obliquely to Moultrie, McIntosh, and the other officers of the council. Moultrie and McIntosh were unwilling to face more direct criticism. While discussions were ongoing in the councils, the two men were preparing for their favored option—moving the Continental Army across the Cooper and into the backcountry. However once Ferguson's reaction to the gathering of boats made it clear that evacuation would be opposed by the civil officials, Moultrie and McIntosh met together privately and burned an April 17 draft of their evacuation plan.[10]

Once the decision to negotiate had been made, Lincoln and assistant inspector general Lt. Col. Jean Baptiste Ternant formulated the terms of capitulation that were offered to Clinton on April 21. Lincoln hoped to obtain concessions that would make surrender palatable to the civilian inhabitants of Charlestown, but in truth the terms proposed were far more lenient than Clinton would ever accept. Under the proposed articles of capitulation, the British would permit the Continental Army and militia thirty-six hours to retire from their works with the usual honors of war—with muskets at shoulder arms, drums beating and fifers fifing, and colors flying. After withdrawal across the Cooper River, the Americans would be allowed to march unimpeded cross-country for ten days. The French and American ships would be able to leave the harbor unmolested, and the inhabitants of Charlestown would be granted twelve months to decide to live under British rule or go elsewhere.[11]

Clinton's mission from the outset had been to quash the rebellion in the southern colonies, and that meant destruction of the southern Continental

Army. A capitulation that left the American army intact to fight another day would be a hollow victory. It is not surprising, then, that Clinton and Arbuthnot found Lincoln's proposals completely unacceptable, and they immediately rejected them, referring Lincoln to Clinton's original terms offered. Lincoln called his generals together to consider Clinton and Arbuthnot's reply. Rather than accepting British terms or proposing revised terms, the council recommended that a messenger be sent across the lines to inform the enemy that they might begin firing again whenever they pleased. They would fight on, trusting that reinforcements would eventually arrive to raise the siege or permit an escape.[12]

All the while the British continued their slow advance toward the American fortifications, steadily strengthening the second parallel by building batteries and bringing cannon up from the rear. On April 21 British sappers began digging the third parallel in front of the wet ditch about 20 yards away—a stone's throw from the abatis and about 750 feet from the American lines. The British trench works became increasingly sophisticated as workmen added gun emplacements, platforms, magazines, traverses, banquettes, and parapets. Progress came at a price, however. American gunners and marksmen did their best to annoy the redcoats and Hessians as they pushed their trenches forward.[13]

The Americans were not idle and improved their works while under fire. "When the enemy's third parallel was completed, we had sand-bags placed upon the top of our lines, for the riflemen to fire through," wrote Moultrie. He provided the most vivid description of the American defenses: "The sand-bags were about two feet long and one foot thick, we laid down first two of them, three or four inches one from the other, and a third laid upon the top of the two, which made a small loop hole for the riflemen to fire through, the British immediately followed our example: many men were killed and wounded through these holes."[14]

Attempting to turn the tables, in the early morning hours of April 24, the Americans launched a surprise attack against the forward British lines. The dawn sortie struck out across the wet ditch and penetrated beyond the third parallel on the British right and nearly reached the second parallel before being stopped by a British rally. When the detachment of two hundred Virginia and South Carolina Continentals commanded by Lt. Col. William Henderson advanced on the enemy's approaches from the advance redoubt, they caught the British completely unaware. The bloodthirsty Americans killed at least fifteen redcoats with the bayonet, likely more, and brought back twelve prisoners, seven of whom were wounded. The British counterattacked, but Moultrie had ordered his artillerists to load with grapeshot during the night, and a few shots of grape sent the enemy reeling back into their trenches.[15]

For Moultrie tragedy marred the success. Only two Continental soldiers were wounded, but his youngest half-brother, Capt. Thomas Moultrie, was killed while returning to the American lines. It is likely that Moultrie saw the terrible event unfold before his eyes as he watched the outcome of the affair. The whole army mourned the highly regarded young officer, who was Francis Marion's messmate. In a letter to a friend written three days after the incident, Moultrie was unable to give full voice to the depth of his staggering private loss, saying little more than "my poor brother Tom was killed on his return into our lines." Thomas was buried in St. Philip's churchyard on the day he fell.[16]

The death of General Moultrie's younger brother gave rise to a brief flurry of correspondence between estranged brothers. But it was Alexander Moultrie, a captain of the Charlestown militia, instead of William who conveyed the sad news to Dr. John Moultrie Jr., who still held the post of royal lieutenant governor of East Florida. Notwithstanding the family rift caused by the war, John loved and mourned his younger half-brother after learning of Thomas's tragic death. In his return letter to "Sandy," as Alexander was known to family and friends, John stated that Thomas's participation in the revolutionary movement was not voluntary, that he was at best a conflicted Patriot who had succumbed to peer pressure when he accepted his commission.[17]

The word *brother* had for five long years been a term of reproach and real sorrow for John Moultrie, who said, "How unhappy & sad must that man be who dares not ask a blessing on the most publick & interesting endeavors of his brothers, but on the contrary with deep sorrow & concern pray to the Almighty to confound all their devices." John closed his letter to Alexander as "your affectionate but distressed brother." Absent was any mention or inquiry into the well-being of William, a sign that the division between the oldest two brothers may have been the widest among the siblings. Indeed recall that early in the war, William Moultrie seemed to relish the idea of an expedition against St. Augustine, telling Maj. Gen. Charles Lee that he would not at all object to bringing brother John under attack.[18]

Brig. Gen. Louis Lebèque Duportail arrived in Charlestown overland from Philadelphia on April 26, sent by Congress to assist Lincoln in Charlestown's defense. Duportail was the bearer of bad news on two accounts. First, reported Duportail, reinforcements from Washington's army would not be forthcoming—the Americans defending Charlestown were on their own. Second, after a review of the Charlestown defenses, Duportail declared them to be untenable, confirming the negative opinions given beforehand by Cambray and Laumoy. When a council of war again deliberated on evacuation, a group of citizens who Moultrie did not name individually but may have consisted of the aforementioned radical members of the civil government "expressed themselves very warmly, and declared to General Lincoln, that if he attempted to withdraw his troops, and leave the citizens; that they would cut up his boats, and open the gates to the enemy."[19]

On May 1 the Americans kept up "a Smart Bombardmt. during the day." Moultrie escalated the shelling by ordering that the firing from the flanks, advanced works, and other batteries that could be brought to bear on the enemy should commence immediately after dark and continue every night until countermanded. The barrage of round shot, scrap metal, and shards of glass, combined with musketry, inflicted casualties and slowed the British as they labored under fire to advance their lines. The redcoats, watchful for another sortie like the one in the wee hours of April 24 that claimed the life of Thomas Moultrie, replied in kind with their guns and mortars, but after a few nights a Hessian captain begrudgingly complimented the American gunners: "It is customary everywhere for the fire of the besieging army to be more severe than that of the besieged in order to dismount the latter's batteries. Only here the opposite is true."[20]

The men on the lines were constantly on the alert for the frequent incoming shells, and the constant strain was exhausting. "The fatigue in that advance redoubt, was so great, for want of sleep," said Moultrie, "that many faces were so swelled they could scarcely see out of their eyes." He set out to relieve Maj. Ephraim Mitchell, who commanded the battery in the advance redoubt, a position that Moultrie admitted was quite exposed to the enemy and was by far the most dangerous post on the lines. He had not rounded on this battery for a few days, and to reach the position, he took the usual way in by crossing a bridge that traversed a ditch. But since his last visit, he found that "[the British] had advanced their works within seventy or eighty yards of the bridge, which I did not know of; as soon as I had stepped upon the bridge, an uncommon number of bullets whistled about me."[21]

Looking to his right, Moultrie could see the heads of about twelve or fifteen British soldiers firing their muskets at him from behind their breastworks. He quickly sought cover: "I moved on and got in; when Major Mitchell saw me, he asked me which way I came in, I told him over the bridge, he was astonished, and said, 'sir it is a thousand to one that you were not killed,' and told me, 'that we had a covered way to go out and in,' which he conducted me through on my return." Moultrie remained in the battery only about a quarter of an hour, just long enough to give necessary orders. During that brief interval, he and the battery's occupants were "constantly skipping about to get out of the way of the shells" fired from British howitzers that were not more than one hundred yards away from the American works. The British were, in Moultrie's words, "throwing their shells in bushels on our front and left flanks."[22]

On May 7 a thirteen-inch British shell exploded within ten yards of the old magazine located two hundred feet north of St. Philip's Church on Cumberland Street. Moultrie realized how close to disaster the town had come. The magazine contained ten thousand pounds of powder, and an explosion caused by a direct hit would certainly have resulted in catastrophic devastation and loss of life.

Moultrie had the powder removed from the magazine, farther back from the front to the safety of the cellar of the Exchange located at the junction of Broad Street with East Bay.[23]

The cellar was constructed of thick, brick, barrel-vaulted walls and ceiling. At some point before the British gained possession of Charlestown, Moultrie ordered workmen to brick up the compartment where the powder was stored. So safe was the powder in the Exchange, Moultrie remarked in his memoirs, that even though the British had possession of Charlestown for so long, "they never discovered the powder, although their provost was the next apartment [room] to it." When the Continental Army reclaimed the town at the end of the war, the powder was found just as Moultrie had left it.[24]

British activity east of the Cooper River rendered pointless any further discussion of evacuation. Lt. Col. Banastre Tarleton's cavalry had surprised and routed Continental horsemen and North Carolina militiamen at Biggin Bridge near Monck's Corner on April 14. Moultrie called the affair "shameful." The victory allowed a detached British force of twenty-three hundred men under Cornwallis to operate east of the Cooper virtually unopposed. This American defeat sealed the doom of the Charlestown garrison.[25]

A domino-like effect followed: the British captured the three-gun American battery at Haddrell's Point on April 26, and under threat of attack, the American force manning Lempriere's Point abandoned their defensive works on April 27 in great disorder. The Americans were completely invested. The escape route and communications with the outside were completely closed, and Moultrie knew it. "We are closely blocked up," he confided to a friend. Duportail's assertions to the contrary, Moultrie still desperately clung to the hope of outside relief.[26]

Greatly annoyed by Commodore Whipple's unwillingness to engage the British in Charlestown Harbor, Moultrie earlier predicted that the timidity of the Continental Navy would result in Fort Moultrie being tamely given up without a contest. "After the British fleet had passed Fort Moultrie," admitted Moultrie, "it was no longer of use to us, but rather a dead weight." Pinckney marched the better part of the First South Carolina Regiment into town on April 24, leaving behind Lt. Col. William Scott with three Continental companies and some militia.[27]

The British landed five hundred sailors and marines on Sullivan's Island during the night of May 4. They were preparing to take the fort by storm on May 6 when Scott realized the futility of his situation and negotiated a surrender. Scott and his garrison marched out of Fort Moultrie with the usual honors of war on May 7. When the victors marched into the fort, they "leveled the thirteen Stripes with the Dust, and the triumphant English Flag was raised on the Staff."[28]

From his vantage in town looking across the harbor, Moultrie could see the British flag flying from Fort Moultrie's flagstaff. Even though it was no surprise that the fort was lost, he was displeased that it surrendered without firing a shot in its own defense, a vast contrast to the gallant stand he had made nearly four years earlier. The loss of the men and the dispiriting effect was compounded by the forfeiture of forty-one cannon, a ten-inch mortar, and a considerable quantity of ammunition and other provisions that could not be removed from the fort and taken to town.[29]

For a third time, General Clinton called for the Charlestown garrison's surrender on May 8. The situation was indeed bleak when the council met in the hornwork. The British had drained the wet ditch, and the breach batteries in the third parallel of the British siege lines had opened on the Americans during the night of May 7. The beleaguered American soldiers and sailors had been subsisting on reduced rations of sugar, rice, and coffee for several days, but now the provisions had run out. Of the sixty-one Continental and militia officers in attendance, Moultrie and forty-eight others agreed that terms should again be offered by Lincoln. Among the dissenters who still wanted to oppose the British were Pinckney, Beekman, and Laurens.[30]

Throughout the day of May 8, Lincoln and Clinton worked out the details of the cease-fire that would be in place while terms were proposed and considered. Under the terms that Lincoln now proposed, the Continental soldiers would march out as prisoners but with the honors of war. The militia would be permitted to return home unmolested. The town's inhabitants would be given a year to decide whether to live under British rule or relocate elsewhere. Moultrie noted that during the Lincoln-Clinton negotiations, the defensive lines became ever more vulnerable to an assault: "While these flags were passing, the militia looked upon all the business as settled, and without orders, took up their baggage and walked into town, leaving the lines quite defenseless."[31]

After a series of back-and-forth exchanges of terms that surely bedeviled both besieger and besieged, Lincoln and Clinton reached an impasse; neither party's alterations to the terms proposed were acceptable to the other. On May 9 negotiations broke down altogether, and hostilities resumed at eight o'clock that evening. After waiting for about an hour, American gunners shattered the dead calm of night, giving three cheers and ending the cease-fire by opening with an artillery barrage that that was immediately answered by the British.[32]

The nearly simultaneous firing of 180 to 200 guns was deafening. Moultrie described the scene that was at once both beautiful and terrible, "a glorious sight . . . like meteors crossing each other, and bursting in the air; it appeared as if the stars were tumbling down. The fire was incessant almost the whole night; cannon-balls whizzing and shells hissing continually amongst us; ammunition chests and temporary magazines blowing up; great guns bursting, and wounded men groaning along the lines; it was a dreadful night!"[33]

Moultrie considered that night to be the Americans' "last great effort," but it was all to no effect, and their martial ardor faded. "We began to cool, and we cooled gradually, and on the eleventh of May we capitulated," he wrote dispassionately in his memoirs. The Americans had had enough. Their spirits were broken, their stomachs were empty, and many parts of town were in ruin from solid shot and incendiary shells. Moreover the British had drained and crossed the wet ditch and first abatis and were within twenty-five yards of the main American line. And by now Clinton had grown tired of waiting. He appeared to be preparing for a general assault.[34]

Lincoln received petitions from officers of the militia and a number of townspeople on May 11 informing him that they were willing to accept Clinton's terms and asking him to surrender. The civil authorities were also willing to abandon their belligerent stance. A hopeless situation became desperate as military order began to erode, and Lincoln's hand was forced. At two o'clock in the afternoon, a large white flag was raised above the parapets. The drums beat parley, and the guns firing from both sides of the line fell silent.[35]

The terms that Lincoln agreed to accept were essentially the same terms offered by Clinton on May 9. None of the desired concessions were obtained for the militia or civilian populace, but at that point no one seemed to care. The Continental soldiers and sailors would remain as prisoners of war on parole until duly exchanged. The militiamen would be allowed to return home on parole. Officers could retain their sidearms but had to give up their horses. Any citizen who bore arms during the siege would be held as a prisoner on parole under the same terms as those offered to the militia. In a move that would later haunt General Cornwallis at Yorktown, Clinton denied Lincoln's request that the Americans be granted the honors of war during the surrender ceremony. Lincoln signed the articles of capitulation on May 12, 1780.[36]

With the stroke of a quill, Lincoln effectively removed fifty-six hundred Continental soldiers and sailors from the conflict, including one major general and six brigadier generals. The British also captured South Carolina's lieutenant governor, three members of the Privy Council, and an assortment of other civil officials. The lost war materiel included more than two hundred cannon and fifty thousand pounds of gunpowder. Lincoln's decision to defend Charlestown and the ensuing American defeat resulted in fourfold consequences: the effectual dissolution of the southern Continental Army, a succession of American defeats in the backcountry, British occupation of the state of South Carolina, and years of bitter and bloody partisan warfare.[37]

22.

Prisoner of War

On the morning of May 12, 1780, Charlestown belonged wholly to the British. At eleven o'clock the Continental soldiers marched out of their works in formation with colors cased, some fifteen hundred to eighteen hundred men. Clinton did not allow his vanquished foe to march in step with an English march, and so the American drummers beat the mournful "Turks's March." One by one they stacked their arms and colors in a large pile. A Hessian soldier described their captives as "thin, miserable, ragged and very dirty. Their officers appeared to be primarily young people and poorly dressed, each in a different colored uniform and with different facings." Many remained defiant to the Hessians, and "chagrin and anger were seen in all their faces." Moultrie was devastated by the American defeat and could barely contain his emotions as tears spilled down his cheeks.[1]

Expecting a second division of Continentals, the British were astounded to learn that excepting five or six hundred sick and wounded hospitalized in the city, there *were* no more Continentals. The Continental lines of three states, South Carolina, North Carolina, and Virginia, had virtually ceased to exist. A British captain of artillery complimented General Moultrie, remarking that the Americans had made a gallant defense, but then he mentioned, almost in passing, that they "had a great many rascals among you . . . who came out every night and gave us information of what was passing in your garrison." The British officer named names, but Moultrie provides no clue in his memoirs as to whether or not retribution was exacted.[2]

The militia turned in their weapons the day after the surrender. On the afternoon of May 15, British artillerists transported these weapons by wagon to a storehouse containing four thousand pounds of fixed ammunition. Ignoring warnings from Continental officers that some of these arms were still loaded (and some were rumored to be intentionally cocked), the British carelessly threw them into the storehouse, causing several to fire. The discharging firearms set the powder ablaze, causing a tremendous detonation that killed sixty or seventy British soldiers and perhaps twice that many bystanders, scattering carcasses and body parts over several parts of town. "One man was dashed with violence against the steeple of the new independent church, which was at a great distance from the explosion," Moultrie noted, adding the graphic detail that the impact "left the marks of his body there for several days." A Hessian captain wrote that he had never witnessed a more horrible spectacle of war.[3]

The resultant conflagration spread to six neighboring houses, including a brothel and a poorhouse, and the militia worked alongside the British to extinguish the inferno. All labored under the apprehension that the fire would spread to the nearby magazine. If the ten thousand pounds of powder stockpiled in the magazine were ignited, there would be, in Moultrie's words, "a hell of a blast." At the time of the explosion, Moultrie was in a house that adjoined St. Michael's Church. The building shook, and the windows rattled as if they would tumble out of their frames. Walking to the safety of South Bay Street, he was accosted by an angry Hessian officer who accused the rebels of having set the fire on purpose as happened in New York. Moultrie denied the charge, but the Hessian placed him under armed guard. When he learned of it, Maj. Gen. Alexander Leslie, who was appointed by Clinton to take initial command of Charlestown, quickly sent an apology and an order for Moultrie's release.[4]

The enlisted men of the Continental regiments were confined to barracks in the city of Charlestown. After collecting their baggage and signing their paroles, the Continental officers were sent to Haddrell's Point, where they maintained a headquarters at the Hibben House. Officers were required to report in at intervals to validate their parole. The officers at Haddrell's Point were allowed to range within six miles of the barracks (twelve miles for general officers) but were prohibited from crossing rivers, creeks, or other bodies of water. With some exceptions this kept them isolated from the enlisted men and noncommissioned officers in town. Moultrie was allowed to go to Charlestown when he pleased, and he often went there to look after the welfare of his men, although he wrote of his perplexity when, about seven weeks into captivity, his mobility was temporarily restricted on account "of some misconduct in our officers . . . , escape, or some caprice, I cannot tell which."[5]

Moultrie was the senior officer at Haddrell's Point, and on May 18, six days after the surrender, General Lincoln assigned him the responsibility for arranging quarters for the paroled officers while they awaited exchange. Most lodged in a barracks consisting of three brick buildings constructed in a U-shaped formation about a mile from the harbor on land acquired by Moultrie, Charles Cotesworth

Pinckney, and others acting under legislative fiat in 1777. The 274 officers were more than the available barracks space could hold, and so quite a few found quarters in private homes within the limits of their paroles. Some of the more junior officers built huts in the woods and planted gardens in the sandy soil, making themselves as comfortable as they could under the circumstances. The water at Haddrell's Point was poor, but the offshore breezes somewhat alleviated the humidity.[6]

Moultrie found housing with Pinckney at Pinckney's uncle's plantation called Snee Farm, five miles away in Christ Church Parish. The British allowed him to retain his horse and three servants, and until security was tightened at the end of June, he enjoyed a limited degree of freedom to come and go to and from town as he pleased. Otherwise he was permitted to receive visiting friends and family. Tended by his body servant named Fortune, Moultrie had access to mail (generally opened), books, and newspapers. It is said that he regularly received copies of the gazette published under royal authority so that he and Pinckney "could read every misfortune of their countrymen, and the jeers of the garrison wits at their woes." Pinckney would be Moultrie's constant counselor, a calming influence on those occasions that the British provoked his ire.[7]

Captivity was tedious, but the accommodations were comfortable enough. Time was passed in conversation with other officers or listening to Pinckney playing his cello. His wife, home from Cape Fear, presumably resided in Christ Church Parish or in town for a time, but if she shared the same misfortune as the Pinckney family, she was eventually ousted from her home in town and evacuated to the countryside. Though far from any battlefields, detention still carried some risk, posed in part by the climate and in part by the large number of captives confined within a relatively circumscribed area. Pinckney reported to his sister in October that the general and Mrs. Moultrie had neglected to take quinine-containing bark and consequently had suffered a relapse of malarial symptoms. Neither had Moultrie or his wife been inoculated against smallpox, the illness that would claim Pinckney's infant son in December.[8]

Early in June, Benjamin Lincoln departed for Philadelphia under the terms of his parole. Moultrie became de facto commanding officer and the principal advocate for the captive Continental force—not just for his fellow parolees at Haddrell's Point, but also for the enlisted men in Charlestown. The acquisition and rationing of beef, flour, and other foodstuff was a major problem from the onset of the internment. After only ten days at Haddrell's Point, insufficient quantities of provisions had arrived with such irregularity that starvation threatened. The officers, Moultrie included, resorted to catching crabs and fish to supplement their meager sustenance.[9]

The same paucity of provisions equally applied to medications and other necessities of life needed for the sick, and Moultrie considered it his duty to inform

Congress of the distressing situation of the Continental hospital specifically and the prisoners of war in general. Money and credit were needed to purchase what was required. Moultrie's appeals for relief to both his captors and the president of the Continental Congress met with only a small measure of success. Fortunately he was on good terms with Brig. Gen. James Patterson, the first British commandant of Charlestown, to whom he freely made application for relief of whatever deficiencies were to be found. Patterson, who provided assistance when he could, defined himself to be entirely a soldier, and in turn depended on Moultrie's advice concerning certain civil matters in Charlestown.[10]

The responsibility of supply rested with Capt. George Turner. Turner, who had commanded a company of the First South Carolina Regiment, was not without administrative experience. He had served on detached duty as aide-de-camp to Gen. Robert Howe in the northern army. Before leaving for Philadelphia, Lincoln appointed Turner deputy commissary general of prisoners for the Southern Department. As a consequence Turner had the troublesome and thankless job of trying to provide supplies for the captured garrison, particularly the sick and wounded.[11]

Lincoln had tried without success to establish a line of credit for Turner to draw upon for the purchase of provisions. To make ends meet, Turner obtained loans in the form of bills of exchange, promissory notes that he became personally liable for, in the amount of fifteen hundred pounds sterling, half of which he was able to use before the merchants refused to accept them altogether. To make matters worse, some of the creditors began to demand repayment of the bills, something Turner could not manage without funds from a perpetually broke Congress in Philadelphia.[12]

Moultrie appeared at first to be willing to work with Turner. But when Moultrie sought information from Turner regarding the availability of supplies and hard currency, Turner chaffed at the prospect of being answerable to an authority other than Congress, the commander of the Southern Department, or the commissary general of prisoners. This angered Moultrie, who was not fully apprised of the obstacles that had been thrown in Turner's way, and he threatened to replace Turner with an officer of his own choosing. Claiming no disrespect or personal pique, Turner openly considered himself beyond Moultrie's authority and asserted that Moultrie had no right to replace him with another officer. Moultrie proved Turner wrong. As commanding officer of the captive southern Continental Army, he would not tolerate what he perceived to be insubordination. In this he was supported by Congress, who dismissed Turner from the office of commissary of prisoners.[13]

It is unclear whether or not Moultrie suspected Turner of any malfeasance. Rather the clash between Moultrie and Turner was more a result of the two men's intransigence combined with Moultrie's misunderstanding of the financial difficulties encountered by Turner: the captain's inability to obtain hard money for purchases and the failure of American credit in Charlestown. The outcome of the episode, beyond Turner's dismissal and replacement, was that a supply system that had been hobbling along pitiably now broke down completely, grinding to a halt during the four months that Moultrie and Turner engaged in their squabble. A court of inquiry called by Moultrie at Turner's request on December 19, 1780, examined Turner's accounts and absolved him of any financial misconduct.[14]

Gen. Henry Clinton departed Charlestown for New York on June 5, 1780, leaving Gen. Charles Cornwallis in overall command of the British troops in the South. As a parting shot, Clinton issued a proclamation on June 3 that altered the terms of capitulation by revoking paroles of all inhabitants of the "province" except those men in Continental service. Clinton declared that all other persons must submit their allegiance to Great Britain or be considered enemies and rebels. Clinton's proclamation was a source of great despair and consternation. Combined with the wave of anguish and blood thirst that followed in the wake of Tarleton's massacre of Col. Abraham Buford's Virginia Continentals at the Waxhaws on May 29, the decree galvanized for independence a large number of South Carolinians who might have otherwise waited out the duration of the war in the relative neutrality afforded by their parole.[15]

As commanding officer General Moultrie's concerns were not limited to provisions. He was also responsible for discipline. He found some of the officers at Haddrell's Point to be ungovernable, and despite attributing uncivil behavior to the close confinement of 250 men from different states with differing dispositions, he had to admit that some were "uncouth gentlemen," thereby unwittingly coining an oxymoron. The senior American officer residing at Haddrell's Point was General McIntosh, and the officers had only been at Haddrell's Point for a month when McIntosh complained of the disorderly conduct, continual disputes, and frequent duels among the officers. The Charlestown summer heat and humidity, boredom and inactivity on the part of the men, and perhaps the application of alcoholic libations were contributing factors. To restore military discipline, Moultrie authorized courts-martial for the offenders, with the results to be transmitted to Congress. Lord Cornwallis fully approved the plan.[16]

The British were sticklers to the letter of the law, often to the complete disregard of its spirit. Parole violations, whether real or perceived, were a recurring source of friction between the British and Americans, and Moultrie labored earnestly and relentlessly to resolve them. On June 29 he attempted to intervene on behalf of Dr. John Houston, a Continental officer paroled in Charlestown but given permission to travel to Georgia on private business. Houston was arrested in Georgia by the Crown's civil authorities on charges of treason. With the permission of General Cornwallis, Moultrie wrote to Georgia's royal governor, Sir James Wright, threatening "of the consequences of proceeding on the trial, as should any injury be done his person, retaliation will certainly be made by Congress and their allies, on the subjects of his Britannic majesty. . . . I therefore, require his releasment [*sic*] from you." Through the efforts of Moultrie and other intercessors, Houston was promptly released.[17]

The British arrested civilians and soldiers on the slightest pretense. The offenders frequently requested Moultrie's assistance, and he was variably successful in obtaining their release. During the thirteen months that he was a prisoner, he discovered that the British, when dealing with both soldiers and civilians, could be quite inventive, frivolous, peremptory, and sometimes mean for the sake of meanness. On one occasion a civil official violated his parole and left Charlestown for fear of his life at the hands of Loyalists. In an interview with Moultrie, Cornwallis condescendingly intimated that other prisoners might suffer consequences if Moultrie did not order the man back to Charlestown. Moultrie did not back down and told Cornwallis that "he might do as he pleased, but that his lordship was too much of a soldier to know that every one was accountable for his own parole, and for no other." Besides, Moultrie argued, he had no authority over a civilian official.[18]

The goodwill between Moultrie and General Patterson was severely tested when a British captain complained about the American officers' celebration of their supposed independence at Haddrell's Point on the evening of July 4, 1780. Music and illuminations were permitted, but it was the American officers' discharge of firearms that caused an uproar—"an indecent abuse of lenity," said Patterson, expressing his mortification and great displeasure. The commandant ordered that the officers should immediately and without exception relinquish their firearms, and he notified Moultrie that he planned a court-martial to investigate the incident.[19]

Moultrie, who had attended the party, recalled no indecent abuses or gross outrages, attributing the noise to "exhilaration of spirit which in young men is too frequently the effect of convivial entertainments." Other than two or three fifers who played the call for dinner, there was no music other than what had been provided by a British soldier, who with two others and some women had danced for two or three hours and were gone an hour before Moultrie returned to Snee Farm at five o'clock. Moultrie reminded Patterson that British prisoners in American custody had been allowed to celebrate the anniversary of St. George's Day and the birthday of His Britannic Majesty without harassment, and he saw no inconsistency in their paroles for the Americans to do the same.[20]

Under the articles of capitulation, officers were allowed to keep their pistols, and while Moultrie apologized for the shots fired, he assured Patterson that no affront was intended. He attributed the nature of the celebration "to the warmth of a cause which the continental officers at Haddrell's Point have embraced through principle; in which some of them bled and for which all of them are now suffering." Though Moultrie held the high moral ground, Patterson had the upper hand and therefore the last word, arguing that as captors the British had a right "to expect from them, a decent behavior; far short of illuminations, and other irregular demonstrations of joy." In the end Moultrie was able to negotiate a compromise that allowed the officers to retain their pistols, but as a show of his disapprobation of the American officers' conduct, Patterson demanded that they turn over their fowling pieces.[21]

The confinement of American prisoners of war was a troubling issue for both captor and captive. For the captives, particularly the South Carolina officers who as members or progeny of the lowcountry elite were unaccustomed to privation, the scarcity of food, clothing, medicines, and accommodations could pose serious hardships. For the captors, keeping prisoners on land was more than just a little inconvenient and expensive: feeding, housing, and providing sufficient guard for the prisoners created immense problems. Security notwithstanding, escapes occurred with alarming frequency. According to Article III of the articles of capitulation, Charlestown prisoners were to await exchange at a place agreed upon, which happened to be on dry land. But when an influx of American captives flooded into Charlestown in after the American debacle at Camden on August 16, 1780, a large number of captives were moved to prison ships in Charlestown Harbor.[22]

Conditions onboard all British prison ships were horrific beyond most imagination. The mortality rate was so great that more American soldiers died of starvation and disease in these floating hulks than in all battles of the war combined. The ships in Charlestown Harbor were no exception to the rule. General Patterson's replacement, Lt. Col. Nisbet Balfour, confided the lethality of the prison ships to a British comrade, remarking coldly that "the rebel [*sic*] Prisoners die faster even than they used to desert." The issue of prison ships surfaced again in November 1780. Moultrie received a report of the shocking mortality rate from jail fever (probably typhus) onboard the *Concord* in Charlestown Harbor from Dr. David Oliphant. Balfour, referring to Moultrie's protest and appeal to Balfour's humanity as pathetic, denied the presence of fever on the ship, but he moved the prisoners to shore nonetheless.[23]

Balfour was one of Cornwallis's most trusted subordinates. Prior to coming south for the campaign to take Charlestown, he saw action at Bunker Hill (where he was wounded), Long Island, Elizabethtown, Brandywine, and Germantown. In August 1780, when Cornwallis took the field and moved northward into South Carolina, he appointed Balfour commandant at Charlestown to replace Patterson. Moultrie described Balfour as a "proud and haughty Scot, [who] carried his authority with a very high hand; his tyrannical disposition, treated the people as the most abject slaves." Balfour's violent and arbitrary administration caused a sincere wish among the populace for an American force to liberate them from his ill treatment and oppression.[24]

Friction developed between Balfour and Moultrie right away. On August 29, while reading the newspaper, Moultrie was outraged to find that thirty-three of the most respectable men of South Carolina had been dragged from their beds during the night and sent, by order of Cornwallis, aboard the prison ship *Lord Sandwich* under suspicion of plotting insurrection. The truth was that these powerful and influential men were, by their silent example, restraining many citizens from exchanging their paroles for the protection of the Crown and the return of privileges afforded British subjects. They may have indeed encouraged the spirit of rebellion, but they did so only within the constraints of their paroles. Included among the prisoners were Thomas Heyward Jr., one of the signers of the Declaration of Independence; Christopher Gadsden, South Carolina's lieutenant governor; and Thomas Farr, Speaker of the House; but also the general's younger half-brother, Alexander Moultrie.[25]

Exercising considerable restraint under the circumstances, Moultrie demanded that Balfour immediately return the prisoners to their paroles. If Balfour refused to comply, Moultrie would ask Congress to intervene. True to character, Balfour summarily dismissed the protest as exceptionable and unwarrantable and refused to accept any renewed applications from Moultrie on the subject. The prisoners were subsequently shipped to St. Augustine, East Florida, where they remained in exile, and others followed in November. Undeterred by Balfour's intransigence, Moultrie vigorously protested the sending of Continental soldiers to the prison ships, invoking the precedents under the terms of the articles of capitulation for quartering prisoners set by Clinton, Cornwallis, and Patterson. Moultrie predicted that his complaints would fall on deaf ears, so he was hardly surprised when Balfour sent word that he "would do as he pleased with the prisoners . . . and not as General Moultrie pleases."[26]

Moultrie fired another series of broadsides at Balfour during late January and early February 1781 when he discovered the British actively recruiting American soldiers from the hospital. It began when during a town visit Moultrie was informed that British officers had been frequenting the American hospital for the purpose of enlisting American soldiers into British service. Later while on his way to the boat that would convey him back to Haddrell's Point, he saw an officer escorting a gentleman dressed in clergyman's attire who was leading a number of Continental soldiers down to the wharf. Moultrie immediately protested to Balfour, who denied complicity. Lord Cornwallis was against the recruiting of prisoners of war. Balfour, however, was willing to allow the practice, short of blatant disobedience to his commanding general, and his actions, while not authorized, were certainly condoned further up the chain of command by Sir Henry Clinton and Lord George Germain.[27]

Hospital conditions were deplorable due to overcrowding and the practically nonexistent eighteenth-century understanding of disease and its transmission. One conservative estimate is that more than eight hundred prisoners died of smallpox, dysentery, malaria, yellow fever, and other diseases during the British occupation of Charlestown, and the death toll may have been significantly higher. Making matters worse, as punishment for interfering with furtive recruiting of hospitalized prisoners, the British denied American physicians and surgeons full access to the sick. This practice of enlisting soldiers from the American side (a threat of transfer to a prison ship was an effective recruiting tool) soon led to one of the most famous exchanges of correspondence of the war.[28]

Balfour constantly vexed Moultrie with a series of violations of the articles of capitulation and contemptuous responses to the American general's objections. Moultrie felt honor and duty bound to remonstrate against every violation and grievance committed by the British, whether they were attended to or not, and the meager satisfaction that he could derive in many instances was the secure knowledge that he could never be charged with neglect. Meanwhile Moultrie sent a packet to the Continental Congress in Philadelphia on March 21 that contained correspondence and intelligence from St. Augustine. About two weeks later, he followed with copies of his exchanges with Nisbet Balfour. The Continental Congress now possessed information outlining in detail the shameful infractions and cruelties committed against the citizens and captive soldiers in South Carolina, and it was Moultrie's desire that "the person who so unfeelingly distressed our fellow prisoners may be called to some account."[29]

The Committee of Intelligence, to whom Moultrie's letters were referred, confirmed "that outrages abhorrent to Civilized Nations have been practiced and sanctioned by the British General Cornwallis and the Officers and Men which compose the banditti under his command." Citing acts of unrestrained barbarity and malice perpetrated by the British navy on American mariners and other enumerated offenses, Congress resolved in June 1781 to retaliate by confining and treating British and German prisoners "in a manner as will be most conformable to the usage which American soldiers in captivity receive from the enemy."[30]

Balfour attempted to squelch Moultrie's advocacy through the power of intimidation by accusing Moultrie of breaching his own parole. Under the terms of the capitulation, Moultrie was allowed to exchange communications with the Continental Congress so long as outgoing letters and dispatches were first inspected by British authorities. In January 1781 he entrusted General Duportail with a packet meant for delivery to Southern Department commander Maj. Gen. Nathanael Greene. The French engineer had been exchanged and was departing

Haddrell's Point for Philadelphia. Moultrie left the packet unsealed for inspection before Duportail left British lines.[31]

Moultrie expected Duportail to seal the packet after inspection and then forward it onward to Greene from Philadelphia. There was nothing about the contents of the packet to arouse suspicion, merely a return of prisoners to be exchanged and an accompanying cover letter to Greene. "I had not the least idea of sending a letter to the American camp, or anywhere else, in a clandestine manner, and contrary to my parole," Moultrie wrote to Balfour in response to the accusation that he had violated the proscribed practice.[32]

Moultrie did have foreknowledge that Duportail might detour to Greene's camp to procure money and horses needed to complete the trip to Philadelphia, but he trusted the Frenchman to act within the bounds of his parole. Duportail, Moultrie told Balfour, was a gentleman of the strictest honor and would not willfully commit an impropriety. In the end Moultrie apologized for what he considered to be a misunderstanding. Balfour informed Cornwallis of the matter, but nothing further seems to have come of the episode.[33]

Wealthy or prominent supporters of the Patriot cause risked losing everything if the newly formed United States failed to gain independence. With this in mind, the British employed flattery, bribery, gentle persuasion, and sometime direct pressure to induce or coerce prominent individuals to place themselves under the Crown's protection. Lord Charles Greville Montague, past royal governor of South Carolina and old acquaintance of Moultrie, returned to Charlestown after the city's capitulation to raise a regiment for service in the West Indies. Nearly four hundred Continental soldiers from the prison ships were persuaded to enlist in this regiment after Montague guaranteed them that they would not serve against their former comrades.[34]

Lord Montague sought to persuade Moultrie to lead this regiment. Writing on February 9, 1781, he reminded Moultrie of the warm feelings of friendship shared by the two men and expressed his desire to meet with the captive general. Whether or not this meeting took place is unknown, but in a follow-up letter on March 11, Montague laid out his agenda, citing a sincere wish that Moultrie would take advantage of Montague's patronage. At the same time, he earnestly hoped that Moultrie would not be offended at the offer he was about to make.[35]

In the past Moultrie and Montague had cordially put aside differences of opinion regarding the commencement of what Montague termed "this unfortunate war." But stooping to abject sophistry, Montague attempted to convince Moultrie that the general had done his duty: "You have now fought bravely in the cause of your country. . . . You have had your share of hardships and difficulties . . . younger hands should now take the toil from you."[36]

The former colonial governor recommended that Moultrie quit his present service and go with him to Jamaica to fight the French and the Spaniards. In Montague's eyes Moultrie's honor and reputation would remain untarnished. His actions would be attributed to his friendship with Montague, and by leaving the country for a time, Moultrie would avoid any disagreeable confrontations in Charlestown. Once Britain had won the war, Moultrie could return to take possession of his estates. So strongly did Montague desire that Moultrie accept his offer that he agreed to relinquish command to Moultrie and serve as a subordinate. Finally Montague assured Moultrie that his proposal was completely confidential, as would be any reply. "Think well of me," he offered in closing.[37]

Moultrie would have none of this devil's bargain, and writing from the Hibben House on the following day, he expressed astonishment that Montague could possibly conceive that he would accept such an offer. After taking Montague to task for seducing American soldiers to enlist in the British army, Moultrie made it clear that he had not yet fulfilled his duty to his country "while it is still deluged with blood and overrun with British troops, who exercise the most savage cruelties." He was prepared to sacrifice his life and fortune and promised to continue to "encourage the youth of America to stand forth in defense of their rights and liberties."[38] The strongest words of outrage were reserved for the very idea of going into British service and emerging with reputation and honor intact:

Good God! Is it possible that such an idea could arise in the breast of a man of honor? I am sorry you should imagine I have so little regard for my own reputation as to listen to such dishonorable proposals; would you wish to have that man whom you have honored with your friendship play the traitor? Surely not. You say by quitting the country for a short time I might avoid disagreeable conversations, and might return at my own leisure and take possession of my estates for my self and my family; but you have forgot to tell me how I am to get rid of the feelings of my injured honest heart, and *where to hide myself from myself.*[39]

In closing Moultrie sardonically suggested that Montague should instead recommend to his superiors that they withdraw British forces from the continent and allow independence. Once that was accomplished, Moultrie would then persuade his commanders to accept terms and allow Great Britain free trade with America. He even discretely suggested in a manner that would not violate his parole that Lord Montague should defect to the Patriot side. And as a parting shot, Moultrie countered Montague's *think well of me* with "Think better of me."[40]

Perhaps Lord Montague acted in collaboration with Colonel Balfour, who was weary of Moultrie's constant complaints on behalf of Charlestown's prisoners of war and would have liked to silence the general. Even before the Montague-Moultrie exchange of letters, Balfour made an overture to Moultrie's son William, playing on the son's interest in the family estate since he was his father's only heir. If Moultrie were to resign his commission, as British officers could at any time and place, Balfour promised that the estate would be restored, all damages paid, and that William Jr. would never be asked to bear arms against his father.[41]

Henry William DeSaussure, who as a youth in 1780 was captured by the British at Charlestown and spent time floating in the harbor in the hull of a prison ship, remarked that only four months prior to Balfour's proposal to bring Moultrie over to the British side, Benedict Arnold had yielded to greed and British allurements. What the British could not win with warfare, they would attempt to purchase with gold. "But while in Arnold they found a traitor, in General Moultrie they met a true patriot who rejected with scorn the offers to abandon that struggle for liberty and independence."[42]

23.

Exchange and Repatriation

Reports were sketchy, but it is doubtful that Moultrie and his Continentals in Charlestown were completely in the dark regarding events as they occurred in the countryside beyond the limits of their captivity. The grisly Waxhaw Massacre of Col. Abraham Buford's Continental force of about 420 men (sent for the relief of Charlestown) at the hands of Lt. Col. Banastre Tarleton took place on May 29, 1780. On August 16 Continental troops commanded by Maj. Gen. Horatio Gates suffered another catastrophe at the Battle of Camden. After being routed by Cornwallis, Gates led the headlong retreat and rode for more than three days to cover the 180 miles to Hillsboro, North Carolina, before he stopped to gather himself.

Conversely the officers at Haddrell's Point were elated and their downtrodden spirits restored by the Overmountain Men's stunning victory of over Maj. Patrick Ferguson and his Loyalist militia at Kings Mountain on October 7, 1780, and Brig. Gen. Daniel Morgan's crushing victory over Cornwallis and Tarleton at Cowpens on January 17, 1781. Moultrie found his British captors, usually smug and haughty, to be "chagrined and disappointed." In between defeats and victories, the captives surely heard of the exploits of brigadier generals Thomas Sumter and Francis Marion as they masterfully waged partisan warfare in the backcountry.[1]

Though decisively defeated at Cowpens, Cornwallis hounded Gen. Nathanael Greene's army of Continental troops and militia as the Americans retreated into North Carolina. The pursuit ended at the Battle of Guilford Court House on March 15, 1781. The British held the field at the end of the day, but it was a pyrrhic tactical victory—Cornwallis lost a quarter of his army. A few weeks after the battle, the British marched to their destiny at Yorktown where Cornwallis, denied the honors of war, surrendered his army to George Washington on October 19, 1781. The British march into Virginia left Greene's army free to move back into South Carolina, where it relentlessly engaged British and Loyalist forces, successfully wresting control of the state from the British, except for the immediate vicinity of Charlestown.

When General Washington appointed Greene to command the Southern Department in late 1780, Washington's trusted Quaker friend became a successor in a line of failed commanding generals: Robert Howe, Benjamin Lincoln, and Horatio Gates. Greene, who had also served as quartermaster of the army, took an immediate interest in the situation in Charlestown, and he wrote to Moultrie from Charlotte in December 1780 to inquire about the condition of American prisoners of war in the Southern Department. It was Greene's impression that the southern states were furnishing supplies for their own men held captive. The sad truth, Moultrie informed Greene, was that Virginia and North Carolina had provided some clothing and a few necessities but that the men of the South Carolina Line "have had no supplies, are destitute of everything, and a great number of them are entirely naked." The British occupation of South Carolina rendered the state incapable of sending aid to Charlestown.[2]

Moultrie had written Congress several times about the matter and was assured that provisions would be sent in October 1780, but nothing arrived. Congress finally sent two ships from Philadelphia to Charlestown in early 1781, both loaded with flour to be sold and the proceeds used for the benefit of the prisoners of war. The income from the first shipload of flour was expended solely to benefit the hospital, but the funds gained from the disposition of the contents of the second ship, when distributed among the Continentals and militia, did not go very far. Moultrie requested additional aid, and Congress authorized the shipment of six hundred hogsheads of Virginia tobacco for sale in Charlestown in April.[3]

A tempting opportunity for escape arose at one point during Moultrie's captivity. In late March 1781, Lt. Col. John F. Grimké and Maj. John Habersham faced a British court-martial in Charlestown for trumped-up parole violations. The men spent five weeks in close confinement under utterly miserable conditions in the city jail or provost, which was a part of the cellar under the Exchange. Moultrie strongly protested Grimké's and Habersham's mistreatment, but to no avail. After release from the jail to his barracks, Grimké escaped from Haddrell's Point and made his way through the lines to join General Greene's army. Grimké subsequently requested a court of inquiry on his conduct, which unanimously found that it was warranted and that he had not broken his parole by leaving Haddrell's Point.[4]

Greene approved of Grimké's conduct and opined that the British had acted in such bad faith and violated the terms of capitulation so many times that the officers were free from their paroles. Greene later consented to a plan to allow Grimké to lead a raid on Haddrell's Point to free his brother officers. When apprised of the plan, General Marion fully concurred and provided Grimké with a detachment with which he did successfully liberate many of the officers at the barracks. A number of fugitive officers making their escape stopped at a church near the Snee Farm, where Moultrie was quartered, and offered to take Moultrie and Pinckney with them. Moultrie and Charles Cotesworth Pinckney, in the firm belief that the officers were justified in their actions, wished them good luck but declined to risk themselves, expecting soon to be exchanged.[5]

Moultrie became involved in the prisoner exchange process on a limited scale before a formal cartel was arranged. In early January 1781, as he prepared to begin exchanges, he sought the guidance of General Greene. The five Continental brigadier generals captured at Charlestown—Moultrie, McIntosh, Scott, Hogun, and Woodford—had decided on the order of exchange, giving preference to those who had been held captive the longest and were the senior officers of the ranks proposed. At the end of January, Moultrie asked Greene if he should continue to exchange in this fashion and on a larger scale, as he had heard that General Washington and General Clinton had agreed on a general exchange that would begin soon.[6]

By the end of February, Moultrie had exchanged a number of Continental officers. But he was also having second thoughts about the process, being unsure of the custom of the Continental Army. Was he to "adhere to the old customs of war; exchanging cavalry for cavalry, infantry for infantry, artillery for artillery," he asked Greene, or should he "go on as hitherto, by seniority and the longest in captivity"? It would take months before Moultrie would receive a definitive answer in the form of a proper exchange cartel, but in the interim the whole business of prisoner exchange was nearly derailed by his nemesis, Nesbit Balfour.[7]

At the end of March 1781, Moultrie began yet another letter to Balfour: "You cannot possibly be more tired with reading my letters than I am of writing them." Moultrie protested what he deemed "a most violent and inhuman breach of the capitulation," referring to the forcible impressments of American soldiers onboard prison ships for service in the West Indies or elsewhere. He received no reply from Balfour until ten days later, when Balfour notified him that that General Cornwallis had ordered *all* prisoners of war to be loaded aboard transports bound for the West Indies. This proposed move was supposedly prompted by the inability of Cornwallis to reach an acceptable prisoner exchange agreement with General Greene and was also purported to be in retaliation for alleged mistreatment of Loyalist militia captured by Francis Marion.[8]

Moultrie demonstrated considerable restraint under the circumstances. Regardless of any differences of opinion between Cornwallis and Greene, he had in fact received word that Congress had proposed an exchange plan that was approved by Sir Henry Clinton. So far as Moultrie knew, official exchange of prisoners might have already begun, and he explained to Balfour that sending Continental prisoners to the West Indies could disrupt negotiations and at the same time would do nothing to alleviate the suffering of Marion's captives. At worst Cornwallis could expect full retaliation from General Washington for any such mistreatment of the unfortunate souls so misused by the British.[9]

As for Marion, Moultrie emphatically told Balfour that to misuse prisoners "is contrary to [Marion's] natural disposition." There can be no doubt of the high esteem that Moultrie harbored toward Marion as an officer and a gentleman. Nonetheless he informed Marion that he had heard allegations of improprieties on the part of Marion's troops. Moultrie knew his friend to be generous and humane, but at the same time he understood that Patriot and Loyalist militiamen were fierce enemies. He admonished Marion that while he knew his friend was "well acquainted with the customs of war, and that your disposition will not countenancesuch cruelties [murders were alleged], . . . I am therefore to request the favor, you will give such orders as will prevent private animosities from taking revenge at this time by such unwarrantable practices as can only serve to disgrace the generous and the brave."[10]

Weeks passed, and nothing happened. Then on May 1 Moultrie was apprised that the prisoners would be transferred to Long Island, New York, rather than the West Indies. Moultrie considered the transfers of prisoners to represent a complete dissolution of the capitulation and said so to Balfour. Fortunately the prisoners went nowhere. The articles of the exchange cartel for the Southern Department, known as the Pee Dee River cartel, were finally agreed upon on May 3, 1781. The cartel stipulated that prisoners should not be sent from the continent while the articles of the cartel were in force. According to the terms of the cartel, the American prisoners at Charlestown who were slated for exchange were to embark by mid-June and sail on a British truce ship to Jamestown, Virginia. They would then proceed from Jamestown into Virginia, to Philadelphia or, if sick, to the hospital. Exchanged or paroled British prisoners would sail to New York or to Charlestown.[11]

The families of the exchanged soldiers and exiles certainly felt relief to at last be free of British obduracy and great joy to be repatriated with their husbands and fathers, but their voyage to Philadelphia was not voluntary and not without a price. Balfour issued a cruel edict, published on June 27 in the *Royal Gazette,* banishing from Charlestown the wives and families of those who adhered to independence and refused to swear allegiance to the Crown. He added insult to injury when he mandated the seizure of "rebel" homes and property for use by the British, turning more than a thousand out of their houses without any means of subsistence. Moultrie's family was among the 741 Charlestown refugees who, in obeisance of Balfour's orders, gave up their homes and left Charlestown for Philadelphia.[12]

Article VI of the cartel specified that officers not exchanged for want of similar ranks to apply were to be immediately paroled to their homes to await exchange. This was not feasible for Moultrie and his fellow southerners; their home was under British occupation. Therefore while on parole in July 1781, Moultrie and his family boarded the small British cartel brig *Burton* to sail for Philadelphia. There was room for others, so upward of ninety persons, Continental officers and militia with their families, accompanied the Moultries for what turned out to be a mostly pleasant trip. Charles Cotesworth Pinckney and his family were among these passengers. At some point Moultrie was joined in Philadelphia by his brother Alexander and his family, who traveled from St. Augustine after Alexander's exchange.[13]

After their release from confinement, many of the exchanged and paroled officers found themselves in serious financial straits, having not been paid for many months. Most had resorted to borrowing from friends and associates in Charlestown and now had little if any money to sustain themselves, far less for the repayment of debt. Exchanged officers could return to their regiments, but near-destitute parolees, who could not immediately return to duty, had no recourse but to petition the Continental Congress in Philadelphia to request back pay and reimbursement of expenses.[14]

Moultrie once again found himself in the position of advocate for members of his former command. He received an August 13, 1781, letter from twenty-four distressed refugees from South Carolina and Georgia who requested that he present their grievances to Congress. Among the aggrieved officers were Pinckney, Col. Barnard Beekman, Col. Jean Baptiste Joseph de Laumoy, and Col. Louis Antoine Jean Baptiste de Cambray. The petitioners recounted the details of their captivity at Haddrell's Point, where they were generally in want of the essentials for living, and maintained that while now they were no longer subject to British oppression, they were "in a strange country, without money, some of us almost without cloaths [*sic*]." What little pay the officers had received was far from adequate, and to add insult to injury, they were not allowed firewood to cook their food—the Board of War had issued an order that wood was to be refused to any person not on active duty.[15]

Moultrie endorsed his officers' petition and sent it on to Congress with his personal request for their relief. Congress responded by immediately ordering that the officers be supplied with rations of firewood, and on September 29 Congress voted three months' pay for officers of the South Carolina and Georgia Continental Lines who were not supplied from their states. Three days later Moultrie and Lachlan McIntosh called on superintendent of finance Robert Morris to collect the money. It is hardly surprising that the officers received no supplies from home considering the devastation the British had brought to South Carolina and Georgia, and it was well that Moultrie's brothers in arms requested his intervention when they did. Congress had become so overburdened with similar requests that it resolved in December to accept no more petitions.[16]

At no point in his memoirs does Moultrie reveal his own circumstances, but considering that he had his family with him in Philadelphia, he may have been in a similar state of affairs as his fellow refugee officers. Even so he may not have been completely devoid of resources. On June 22, 1781, before he progressed from Charlestown to Philadelphia, he was named as a partner, along with South Carolina congressman Thomas Bee and others, in the ownership of a privateer. The one-hundred-ton ship *Columbia,* captained by William H. Sargeant, carried eighteen guns and an eighty-man crew. No correspondence regarding the arrangement of this partnership has been located, nor has a record of the ship's success or failure been found.[17]

Moultrie made Gen. George Washington's acquaintance for the first time on August 30, 1781. Washington was en route from New York to attack Cornwallis at Yorktown, Virginia, when he rode into Philadelphia at about one o'clock in the afternoon. The French generals Jean-Baptiste Donatien de Vimeur, Comte de Rochambeau and François Jean de Beauvoir, Marquis de Chastellux accompanied Washington, who paid his respects to Congress at the Pennsylvania State House before attending a dinner at the home of Superintendent of Finance Robert Morris. Moultrie joined Washington and the French generals for dinner, as did Brig. Gen. Henry Knox and several other gentlemen.[18]

In January 1782 Washington pressed for Moultrie to be exchanged for Lord Francis Rawdon, a British colonel who had been acting in the capacity of brigadier general prior to his capture at sea by the French. Before that could transpire, however, Moultrie and Pinckney were part of an exchange for Maj. Gen. John Burgoyne, who surrendered his British army three and a half years earlier at Saratoga on October 17, 1777. After months of negotiation, on February 19, 1782, General Moultrie's formal exchange and release from parole was consummated in a deal for Burgoyne that included Moultrie and Pinckney, 32 other officers, and 433 rank and file.[19]

By order of General Washington, brigadier generals were required to wear a blue coat with buff facings and lining, yellow buttons, white or buff underclothes, two epaulets with one star on each, and a white feather in the hat. Washington considered it important "for the sake of appearance and for regularity of service that the different military ranks should be distinguished from each other." It is not hard to conceive that Moultrie's clothes had become somewhat worn and tattered during his period of captivity, and he apparently acquired a new uniform coat while in Philadelphia. Once his coat was ready, Moultrie sat for the Philadelphia portraitist Charles Willson Peale.[20]

On February 21, 1782, Moultrie submitted a letter to John Hanson, the president of the Continental Congress, informing him that he had been formally exchanged. His earnest desire was to contribute further to "the establishment of this Freedom of America, a Cause which I have hitherto exerted every nerve and still hope to have it in my power to go on." Even so circumstances had arisen during his captivity to cause him a degree of uneasiness. He had been superseded in rank by three junior brigadiers: William Smallwood, Henry Knox, and Louis L. Duportail.[21]

Moultrie did not question these men's ability, and he seemed to grasp the political expediency of Frenchman Duportail's promotion. However it was the promotion of Smallwood of Maryland to major general that he found to be disagreeable. Smallwood had received the well-deserved thanks of Congress and promotion to brigadier general in recognition of his critical role in keeping what was left of the Continental Army together after Gates's debacle at Camden. The Marylander had unfortunately followed his successes by behaving rather badly over issues of seniority and by refusing to serve under Maj. Gen. Friedrich Wilhelm Augustin von Steuben in Greene's southern army. Moultrie reminded Congress that he too had received their thanks in 1776 and been given command of the southern army in 1779 with the emoluments of a major general. Certainly he was entitled to elevation in rank as well. He expressed his wishes along with his hope that Congress would enable him to return cheerfully to his duty.[22]

A congressional committee composed of Ezekiel Cornell from Rhode Island, Samuel John Altee from Pennsylvania, and Thomas Bee considered Moultrie's position and found his request to be reasonable. The committee offered a resolution to Congress on March 22 authorizing his promotion to major general. Two separate votes failed to approve the measure. Some congressmen felt that additional major generals were unnecessary, while others were willing to reward Moultrie's patriotism and service.[23]

Moultrie had long been serving in the capacity of a major general, and in fact there had been talk of his promotion back in 1779. What seemed to lie at the crux of the matter was a longstanding and ongoing debate about the promotion of general officers that began with an October 1780 plan to reorganize and consolidate the army. There was agreement in Congress that there were more than enough general officers to command the armies at a time when the nation's finances necessitated the strictest economy. Therefore the rule of promotion of colonels to brigadier general and of brigadiers to the rank of major general adopted by Congress was that of apportioning those officers according to the number of troops that the states had in the field. Congress had established this as a fixed principle, not to be deviated from except in cases of particular merit or when services rendered such deviation proper.[24]

Even so the secretary at war, Maj. Gen. Benjamin Lincoln, recognized that the policy of proportioning the number of general officers according to the number of men raised by the states had wounded the feelings of many senior officers. Several of the states had been so overrun and plundered by the British that these states could no longer furnish troops, leaving officers without commands. What may sound trivial or petty by modern standards posed a serious question of honor in the late eighteenth century. Congress therefore established that these officers could be employed in a staff capacity, be assigned other necessary duties in the army, or be considered retired, retaining rank, pay, and privileges until their recall became necessary.[25]

If Moultrie felt rebuffed by congressional inaction, he left no comment on the matter. Was he retired, or would he receive new orders? In August 1782 when General Washington was finalizing arrangements for several commands, he might have found Moultrie something useful, but Moultrie never notified him as to whether he intended to return to the field or resign his commission. Greene had matters well in hand in the South, and more to the point, there were no South Carolina Continentals in Greene's army for Moultrie to lead. On the other hand, Charlestown was still occupied by the British, so he could not go there. Perhaps he could act in an advisory capacity or use his presence to help rally the militia and inspire the populace.[26]

Expecting that he would soon depart for home, Moultrie wrote to Pinckney from Philadelphia on March 3, 1782. Charles Cotesworth Pinckney and his brother Thomas had already taken their families to South Carolina, and though at the time Moultrie was uncertain of exactly where his friend was, he reckoned that the letter, with Pinckney's certificate of exchange enclosed, would eventually find its way into the hands of its intended recipient. Moultrie used the opportunity of writing to inform Pinckney of the latest turns of events. For one thing Gen. Lachlan McIntosh had been exchanged—that much was good. But further exchanges had been temporarily halted while commissioners negotiated an exchange of Lord Cornwallis for Henry Laurens, who had been imprisoned in the Tower of London since being taken at sea in 1780.[27]

Moultrie and his family departed Philadelphia in early April 1782 with high hopes that by the time they reached Charlestown they could march directly in "without obstruction and sit [them]selves down quietly." Getting home, however, would not be so simple. In June they arrived at Capt. William Alston's Waccamaw plantation near Georgetown, South Carolina, where he deposited Hannah before proceeding onward. With no South Carolina troops to command, he struck out to find General Greene, whose Continental Army was camped on the Ashley River quietly awaiting the British evacuation of Charlestown. The hundred-or-so-mile journey to Greene's camp was the most dull, dreary, melancholy ride he had ever taken. The land had been stripped bare, wasted by war, and was completely destitute of the many wild and domesticated animals that had previously abounded in the region. "The dragoons told me, that on their scouts, no living creature was to be seen, except now and then a few camp scavengers [turkey buzzards], picking the bones of some unfortunate fellows, who had been shot or cut down, and left in the woods above ground."[28]

Along the way Moultrie visited General Marion's encampment at Peyre's plantation on the Santee River in St. Stephen's Parish. British foraging parties had been ranging from Charlestown, and at Marion's camp Moultrie picked up an escort of twenty infantry and a like number of cavalry to augment the volunteers who had accompanied him from Georgetown. In the direct route between Marion's camp and Greene's camp was North Hampton, Moultrie's plantation at St. John's Berkeley.[29]

The estates of the most "violent absentees" had been under sequestration in accordance with a proclamation issued by Cornwallis on September 1780 that allowed commissioners and overseers to manage the plantations for the use and benefit of the British army commissaries. Moultrie's slaves did not necessarily view the British as liberators. "I then possessed about two hundred slaves, and not one of them left me during the war," he set down in his memoirs. "Although they had had great offers, nay, some were carried down to work on the British lines, yet they always contrived to make their escapes and return home."[30]

Considering his two-year hiatus from home, it was logical for him to stop at North Hampton for the night, but when he arrived he found the place desolate, "stock of every kind taken off, the furniture carried away." All was quiet at first, but once he was recognized, the scene came to life: "It being Sunday the Negroes were all dressed in their best, and received me with the greatest gratitude and joy that can be imagined with everyone shaking hands, with tears of joy; my old Peggy (a new negro) came and kissed my cheeks, and to close the scene, old Boston and Simon came hand in hand, singing their country song, with the greatest demonstrations of joy; and one, and all, thanking God that I was come back again." For several hours the slaves hung around the courtyard fence, frequently turning their eyes in Moultrie's direction, "and with a loud exclamation, of [']Ky![']* and [']thank God my Master was come,['] I assure you I was obliged frequently, to leave them and retire to the chamber to wipe my Eyes. [John F.] Grimkie [sic] was so affected, that he could not refrain from taking out his handkerchief —[Johann Christian] Senf also can tell you of his feelings [on] the occasion."[31]

Another hard day's ride brought him to the headquarters of Greene, located at Ashley Hill, about sixteen miles from Charlestown. Moultrie was wholly

---

* "Ky!" is supposedly "an African interjection, showing a delighted astonishment, equivalent to "is it possible?—can the good news be really true!" Griswold, Simms, and Ingraham, *Washington and the Generals of the American Revolution,* 2: 56.

impressed with the unbearable stench of the camp, detectable from a distance. Under ordinary circumstances Greene would have moved his camp at frequent intervals during the summer months, but he had allowed the army to remain on the same ground since August in expectation of Charlestown's evacuation. Camp conditions may have been a factor in Moultrie's decision to return to North Hampton after a visit with Greene, who apparently had no role for Moultrie to fulfill right then.[32]

It was at Gov. John Mathews's Uxbridge plantation on the Ashley River just north of Middleton Place that Moultrie wrote a letter to his wife, Hannah, on August 17. He had longed to hear from her, and it was his first opportunity since he had arrived there to express hope that they would soon be reunited in town. He did not believe that the enemy would vacate Charlestown until after the autumnal equinox in late September; their fleet had not yet reached Charlestown.[33]

He also reported that Susannah Elliott had been so kind as to offer the Moultries the right of first refusal of the use of one of her houses in town and had informed him that some of their personal effects were safe with friends. This included their crimson bottomed chairs, a desk, a box of china, Hannah's commode, and a trunk of curtains. The drawing room, dining room, and bedroom furniture was still in the house with another box of china and most of his books, but he reassured her that it was all in good hands. The plantation grounds were desolate, stripped of livestock, but an orchard with a number of fine young trees was in tolerable shape.[34]

Assured by Marion that he was safe while at home, Moultrie intended to remain at North Hampton until either Charlestown was evacuated or until summoned by Greene. He stayed there for part of October and November, but before the end of November he found new quarters with a part of the army camped at Middleton Place, just to the north of Ashley Hill. Middleton Place was the home of Henry Middleton, president of the First Continental Congress. With the British evacuation of Charlestown imminent, Moultrie could not be drawn away from the army, not even by the death of his sister-in-law Charlotte Huger Motte, the wife of John Huger.[35]

Moultrie explained in a letter to Hannah, "I heartily console you, on the death of your poor sister Huger, and sincerely pity John's distressing situation; could I be of any service, I would endeavor to come to comfort him, but matters are now so arranged, that I cannot leave the Camp, as 'tis expected with the greatest [ ], that the British are to leave the Town on Monday [December 2, 1782]." By this time Hannah was on the eastern side of the eastern branch of the Cooper River at Hagan plantation, home of her sister's father-in-law, Daniel Huger. Moultrie thought she should remain there for the time being, but he promised to come for her or send for her soon.[36]

The British finally evacuated Charlestown on December 14, 1782. The Continentals moved in to take possession as the redcoats withdrew from the redoubts of the defensive works and marched down King Street to Gadsden's Wharf. It was a slow process, but the movements of the two armies were conducted with great order, and the transition proceeded without incident. Moultrie was the only officer of the South Carolina Line to accompany Greene into town as the British loaded transports for departure. No South Carolina militia were present, not even Marion, perhaps because they were thought to be "*too* irregular, too ragged of raiment, to be permitted to share this triumph! They were not too ragged to *fight,* only too ragged to show."[37]

Moultrie recalled the touching scene with great satisfaction: "At 3 o'clock, P.M. General Greene conducted Governor Mathews, and the council, with some other of the citizens into town: we marched in, in the following order: an advance of an officer and thirty of Lee's dragoons; then followed the governor and General Greene; the next two were [Brigadier] General [Mordecai] Gist and myself; after us followed the council, citizens and officers, making altogether about fifty: one hundred and eighty cavalry brought up the rear: we halted in Broad-street":

> It was a grand and pleasing sight, to see the enemy's fleet (upward of three hundred sail) laying at anchor . . . and what made it more agreeable, they were ready to depart from the port. The great joy that was felt on this day, by the citizens and soldiers, was inexpressible: the widows, the orphans, the aged men and others, who, from their particular situations, were obliged to remain in Charlestown, many of whom had been cooped up in one room of their own elegant houses for upwards of two years, whilst the other parts were occupied by the British officers, many of whom where a rude uncivil set of gentlemen. . . . I cannot forget that happy day when we marched into Charlestown with the American troops; it was a proud day to me, and I felt myself much elated, at seeing the balconies, the doors, and windows crowded with the patriotic fair, the aged citizens and others, congratulating us on our return home, saying, "God bless you, gentlemen! you are welcome home, gentlemen!" Both citizens and soldiers shed mutual tears of joy.[38]

"This fourteenth day of December, 1782, ought never to be forgotten by the Carolinians," proclaimed Moultrie, who added that "it ought to be a day of festivity with them, as it was the real day of their deliverance and independence." Moultrie had an additional cause for gratification. While waiting with Greene's army for the British to evacuate Charlestown, he would have learned of his promotion by Congress to the rank of major general. On October 15, 1782, he became South Carolina's highest ranking officer of the Revolutionary War.[39]

Major General William Moultrie, from a painting by John Trumbull (1756–1843). The Society of the Cincinnati, Washington, D.C. Reproduced with permission.

Part III

24.

Restoring Civil Government

The end of the war closed the last chapter of William Moultrie's military career as a general officer in the Continental Army, and he promptly resumed his duties in the South Carolina political arena. He had served in the Provincial Congress and the General Assembly during the war; however his tenure as a legislator was eclipsed by the many pressing military matters. South Carolina had emerged from the war in political chaos, and Moultrie and his contemporaries were determined to restore order.

His detention in Charlestown by the British had enabled Moultrie to stay abreast of the vicious and vindictive civil war in the backcountry. No other state had witnessed the extent of partisan animus between Whig and Tory that was experienced by the inhabitants of South Carolina. "Each party oppressed the other as much as they possibly could, which raised their inveteracy to so great a height, that they carried on the war with savage cruelty: although they had been friends, neighbors and brothers they had no feelings for each other, and no principles of humanity left," recalled Moultrie in his memoirs. "When the British party prevailed; after the surrender of Charleston, [the Tories] gave full scope to their interested and malicious passions . . . and committed the most violent acts of cruelty and injustice [against the so-called rebels], which was sanctioned by the British, provided they called themselves friends to the king."[1]

The Loyalists found their situation reversed when Gen. Nathanael Greene's Continental Army returned to South Carolina in 1782. As the British army withdrew from their backcountry posts, the returning Patriots found their families starving and their homes wrecked by pillage and fire. "Sweet revenge comes now to reek [*sic*] her vengeance on those infamous, merciless, bloody villains that had gone before," wrote Moultrie, who also knew of the numerous depredations committed by the Whigs upon the Tories. He remarked that "the conduct of those two parties was a disgrace to human nature, and it may with safety be said that they destroyed more property, and shed more American blood than the whole British army."[2]

To restore the state's civil government, excepting of course within the bounds of British-occupied Charlestown, Gov. John Rutledge called for new elections. Accordingly he convened the General Assembly in January 1782 at Jacksonborough, about thirty miles west of Charlestown on the Edisto River. The British occupation of Charlestown had prevented many parishes from holding elections, and many lowcountry leaders were either in captivity or in exile. A result was that compared to other South Carolina legislative sessions, the backcountry was relatively overrepresented at Jacksonborough. If Moultrie was present, he was there only as an observer and not as an elected legislator, but his son, William Jr., and his half-brother Alexander were participants.[3]

The Jacksonborough Assembly addressed a number of important issues. John Mathews was elected to succeed Rutledge as governor. Financial and military matters required immediate attention, yet it was the actions taken against Loyalists for which this legislative session is best remembered. Acting out of revenge, but also motivated by the state's poor financial condition, the Jacksonborough Assembly passed acts that gave the state the power to banish Loyalists, to confiscate their property, and to assess financial penalties (amercement) on those whose British loyalty did not rise to a level that warranted confiscation. The Confiscation and Amercement Acts also applied to a significant number of Patriots who willingly submitted to British protection after the surrender of Charlestown.[4]

Relative to the hard-liners with their punitive judgments, Moultrie was rather conciliatory to some who had taken protection, understanding that many of them had been compelled by family circumstances. Several gentlemen he knew accepted commissions in the Loyalist militia to protect their friends and neighbors from ill treatment. Others took protection and remained quietly at home; that was no great offense, was sometimes unavoidable, and Moultrie had advised several of his friends who were not in the Continental Army to take that step after the fall of Charlestown and to wait patiently until the Continental Army liberated them. But some had crossed over the line between necessity and loyalism. Moultrie reserved harsh judgment for those who chose "to take protection, then a commission, and then to treat their countrymen worse and with more rigor than enemies themselves." Their offense was unpardonable.[5]

Notwithstanding his conciliatory stance, the Confiscation Act provided Moultrie with the opportunity to add to his already extensive land holdings. In June 1783 he acquired a plantation named Kent, confiscated from the Colleton family for the crime of being absentee loyal British subjects. This property consisted of two tracts totaling seven hundred acres in St. John's Berkeley that had been a part of the twelve-thousand-acre Wadboo Barony granted to Landgrave James Colleton, a former governor. Colleton was the third son of Sir John Colleton, who was one of the eight original proprietors of Carolina under the reign of King Charles II. Moultrie eventually made Kent his country seat.[6]

The voters of St. John's Berkeley sent Moultrie back to the House of Representatives in 1783 and 1785 and to the Senate in 1787, 1789, and 1791. Meeting for the first time in Charlestown since the British evacuation, the 1783 General Assembly faced a number of serious challenges. The reinstitution of stable civil government was crucial. Dealing with the consequences of the Confiscation and Amercement Acts passed by the Jacksonborough Assembly was necessary, and trying to establish a modicum of financial stability in the face of South Carolina's war debts was a third issue. The House appointed Moultrie to serve on its Ways and Means Committee. He was also appointed to a commission tasked with concluding a peace treaty with the Cherokee Indians and establishing a plan to regulate trade between South Carolina and the Cherokee Nation.[7]

By happenstance, before the close of the legislative session that sat from July until August 13, 1783, a report was brought to the House of Representatives that a large quantity of gunpowder had been discovered under the Exchange. This was the same gunpowder that Moultrie had hidden from the British shortly before the capitulation of Charlestown in May 1780. The estimated quantity was fourteen thousand pounds, much more than Moultrie recalled in his memoirs, and to the legislators' pleasant surprise, not only had they outwitted the redcoats, but most of the powder was still usable.[8]

Moultrie chaired a joint House and Senate committee appointed in February 1784 to consider the petitions of persons who had been subject to the Confiscation and Amercement Acts. He commented on the gradual shift of the legislature toward their Loyalist South Carolina countrymen, many of whom he thought had suffered arbitrarily: "The Jacksonborough assembly was much censured by some, and thought to have been very severe and cruel to their fellow-citizens, in passing the confiscation, banishment and the amercement laws. . . . When they had got possession of their country again, and peace was restored, [the legislators] were softened with pity, and had compassion for their fellow-citizens, and listened with cheerfulness to the prayer of their petitions." "After sitting several weeks and giving everyone a fair and impartial hearing," he recounted, "a report was made to the separate houses in favor of a great majority; and a great part of those names which were upon the confiscation, banishment and amercement lists, were struck off."[9]

A disagreeable situation developed when the legislature allowed British and Tory merchants who had set up shop during the British occupation to remain in Charlestown. These merchants enjoyed an unfair financial competitive advantage over impoverished Patriot merchants by supplying the material wants of the lowcountry planters and wealthy inhabitants of Charlestown who availed themselves of the available British credit. Protests by Charlestown's Patriot merchants and artisans against the legislative favoritism toward the British traders ultimately devolved into mob activity that sank further into abject violence and rioting against British merchants during the summers of 1783 and 1784. One positive effect of the civil unrest was the realization that a separate municipal government was warranted to administer local affairs. In August 1783 the General Assembly acted to incorporate the city that would henceforth be called Charleston. A popularly elected city government was established that consisted of wardens (city councilmen) who chose an intendant (mayor) from their own number.[10]

Moultrie came closest to serving his state on the national stage on February 10, 1784, when his fellow legislators named him to represent South Carolina at the Continental Congress. This honor would have required him to relinquish his seat in the South Carolina House. His selection to Congress was preempted, however, by his February 16 election by the General Assembly to become lieutenant governor, which also required that he relinquish his assembly seat. The functions of the office of lieutenant governor were not well delineated by the South Carolina Constitution of 1778 except that the lieutenant governor would succeed the governor if he had to vacate his office for any reason. Moultrie would attend meetings of the Privy Council under Gov. Benjamin Guerard and play an advisory role. He served in this capacity for one year.[11]

Moultrie was reelected to the House for the 1785–87 term by St. John's Berkeley and the parishes of St. Philip and St. Michael. He again gave up his seat, however, when the legislature elected him to the office of governor of the state of South Carolina on Thursday, February 10, 1785. The installation of a new governor called for pomp and ceremony. On the appointed day, Monday, February 14, preceded by the sheriff bearing the sword of the state and accompanied by the members of the Senate and the House, Moultrie made his way to the balcony of the Senate room, where he was formally proclaimed governor. The gentlemen then collectively moved in solemn procession to the Exchange, where the commencement of Moultrie's gubernatorial term was publicly announced. Moultrie had held positions of great responsibility during wartime, and now he took on the heavy mantle of leadership as "His Excellency," vested with the executive authority of his state's civil government.[12]

Under the constitution of 1778, Governor Moultrie functioned as an adviser to the legislature, in which role he periodically recommended issues for consideration. He also served as an intermediary between the state's delegates to the Continental Congress and the other state governments. Because the governor was elected by the legislature, Moultrie's independence and executive authority was weakened, and he possessed no veto power. But this did not mean that the prestige of the office was diminished. "On the contrary (barring the selfishness and political scheming inevitable in human affairs), there was a strong tendency to regard the governorship as a sort of civic crown with which to honor public men who had fairly earned such a high distinction."[13]

Limitations aside, a number of important issues demanded Moultrie's attention during his first term, including the state's domestic and Continental debt, the ongoing sectional friction between the lowcountry and backcountry, Indian relations, boundary disputes with neighboring states, immigration, inland navigation, and improving the state's defensive posture. It was a matter of course that a former major general, now governor and commander-in-chief of the state militia, should be concerned about defense. This subject had been an object of great import from the time the British had evacuated Charlestown. On March 13, 1783, six months before the signing of the Treaty of Paris, Governor Guerard notified the legislature that General Greene had received orders from General Washington to march his Virginia, Maryland, and Pennsylvania Continentals northward. Greene planned to leave behind only three hundred cavalry and a like number of North Carolina, South Carolina, and Georgia Continentals to defend the three southernmost states.[14]

The House had appointed Moultrie, Andrew Pickens, and Thomas M. Hyrne to consider the consequences of Greene's withdrawal. Based on their recommendations, the General Assembly subsequently requested that in addition to the cavalry and small number of infantry, Greene also leave behind a small artillery detachment, all of the ordnance, and the ordnance supplies. Washington had allowed Greene some latitude to exercise his own prudence and discretion if the state appeared to be in imminent danger. Unaware that a negotiated peace was in effect, Greene was reluctant to leave the South vulnerable.[15]

Now in the absence of any long-term Continental presence, Moultrie stood as a staunch advocate for strengthening the state's militia. In his first message to the legislature in February 1785, he emphasized the need for local preparedness. But without a war to fight, the militia existed more on paper than in reality. A militia law passed at Jacksonborough in 1782 had been replaced by a 1784 act that reduced the militia from a wartime footing to a corps that mustered by regiment only once every twelve months (once every six months for Charleston companies). "However distant or improbable a War may seem to be," Moultrie reminded the General Assembly, "a policy requisite to be served in Peace, is to prepare for the event."[16]

Moultrie remembered that it had been the well-established militia that had contributed to the state's military preparedness in 1775 and 1776. To bolster the militia's state of readiness, he petitioned the legislature for the acquisition of cannons for harbor defense, arms and ammunition, and "a proper Train of Artillery, Tents and other Camp necessities, Sufficient for our Militia to take the

Field on the shortest notice." He was intent on avoiding what he called "the many inconveniences we experienced in our late Contest," when military operations were thwarted by inadequate equipage. Unfortunately the poor condition of the state's finances rendered the legislature incapable of acting on Moultrie's recommendations.[17]

In his first message of 1786, Moultrie restated the importance of reorganizing and regulating the militia, suggesting that an inspector general, answerable to the governor, should be appointed to review the regiments throughout the state, to coordinate musters, and "to take such other Steps for the Training and exercising them as shall be thought proper." Complaining that his efforts to bring the militia into serviceable condition had failed, he faulted the legislature for their neglect and blamed the defective militia law for frustrating those officers who aspired to military service. No amount of goading on Moultrie's part could persuade the legislature to address the militia problem. The legislature would maintain the status quo until 1792, when the militia law was brought up to the standard set by the congressional mandate.[18]

Peace did not ensure economic prosperity. To the contrary circumstances worked the opposite as the state emerged from the wreckage of war. It cost money to restore the agricultural infrastructure and to replace the slaves that had either fled from their masters or were carried off by the British. Unfortunately there *was* no money. Conditions were exacerbated by a succession of bad rice harvests that further depressed the economy. To fund rebuilding and the maintenance of their lavish lifestyles, the Charleston elite and the land-poor lowcountry planters relied on the aforementioned British merchants, who were happy to extend easy credit at high interest rates. But as debt accumulated, the acute shortage of circulating currency rendered repayment of the debts impossible. Many of the British creditors themselves were on the brink of financial ruin, and when they appealed to the courts for relief, smoldering public sentiment against them increased. In the backcountry landowning debtors, who were angry that valuable properties auctioned to satisfy legal judgments were bringing only a fraction their worth, protested by closing the courts to prevent foreclosures and sheriff's sales.[19]

Moultrie had been in office only a short time when the debt crisis came to a head. To his Privy Council in July 1785 he warned of "the great and many dangers arising from the present pressing lawsuits by the inhabitants against each other at this time of calamity, when they are not able to settle with each other, owing to the present scarcity of money and the last failure of crops throughout this State." After due consideration the council unanimously supported Moultrie's plan to call a special session of the legislature to "put a stop to the dreadful situation."[20]

When he convened the legislature on September, 26, 1785, Moultrie praised the members for putting aside their convenience for the good of their constituents. Then he laid out his concern over the matters that he deemed oppressive and contrary to the happiness of the people of South Carolina. It was with great reluctance that he proposed legislative interference in private contracts, but without intervention, the debtors faced ruined. The problem, he said, was not limited to a few individuals, but rather "it has become General, it is not Confined to one or two families, but exists throughout the State, a few, very few excepted."[21]

Moultrie went on to summarize the cascade of events that had precipitated the crisis: "The Scarcity of a Circulating Medium in some degree have Created the Action of the Creditor[;] the will of Providence by destroying Several following Crops, and a total want of Confidence furthered the Injury." The crux of the matter was that if a debtor complied with the demands of his creditors and sold his estate to raise money to pay his debt, he might only receive a quarter of the property's value from the sale. The power of the law, if allowed to run its natural course, would forcibly "transfer the whole Property of a large part of your Own Citizens, into the Hands of Aliens, and this at much under its real worth." Legislative interference was justifiable, and Moultrie implored the legislature "to remove, or at least alleviate the Evil."[22]

Before adjourning in October, the legislature passed two measures that provided Moultrie's desired debtor relief. The Sheriff's Sale Act of 1785 (also known as the Pine Barren Act) stipulated that land could be tendered for payment of debt in lieu of cash, but for not less than three-quarters of its appraised value. The legislature also authorized the printing of paper currency, based on loans collateralized by land mortgages, gold, or silver. This currency served as a circulating medium that was not legal tender except for payment of taxes, but it was in fact widely accepted as payment in business transactions.[23]

The British merchants were not at all happy with the legislature's actions and voiced their objections to their own government. The British foreign secretary, the Marquis of Carmarthen, had already accused South Carolina of violating the fourth and fifth articles of the Treaty of Paris by passing a debtor-relief act in 1784 that placed a moratorium on lawsuits to collect debts contracted prior to February 26, 1782, and by passing the Sheriff's Sale Act. The first act prevented loudly complaining British merchants from having judicial means to recover their losses, and the second act saddled the debtor with potentially worthless land instead of a liquid asset. In contrast Article IV of the treaty stated that "creditors on either side shall meet with no lawful impediment to the recovery of the full value in sterling money, of all bona fide debts heretofore contracted." Article V of the treaty pertained to the restoration of confiscated estates.[24]

Secretary of Foreign Affairs John Jay queried Moultrie on the matter in June 1786, and Moultrie defended his state's actions with vigor. Regarding the fourth article, Moultrie informed Jay that British subjects had encountered no more difficulties or impediments in the recovery of their debts than had American citizens. And while the situation of the state was such that the legislature had found it necessary to pass laws tantamount to the shutting of the courts, British property owners had enjoyed the same protection and "were saved from ruin equally as those of America." Regarding the confiscation of Loyalist properties, Moultrie pointed out to Jay that South Carolina had complied very liberally with the recommendations of Congress pursuant to the fifth article of the treaty and had restored most of the estates that were under confiscation. In justifying confiscation Moultrie reminded Jay that the value of the "property [slaves] carried off by the British and belonging to the Citizens" far exceeded the value of the property that had lawfully been confiscated or sold.[25]

The debt crisis would be a recurring, complicated, and controversial issue that would vex the General Assembly for years to come. The Installment Act replaced the Sheriff's Sale Act in 1787 and allowed debtors to pay debts in three annual payments beginning in 1788. A provision of the Installment Act prohibited the importation of slaves for a period of three years beginning in 1787, not for the sake of antislavery sentiments but because importing slaves would cost money and increase debt. Later in the Senate after his term as governor, Moultrie would support the Installment Act. He and his cohorts who championed debtor relief were not motivated purely by altruism, however. The debt crisis affected the inhabitants of both the lowcountry and the backcountry, but debtor-relief legislation benefited the well-established wealthy coastal planters more than those in the backcountry. Moultrie's actions could be construed, in part, to be self-serving because he himself was one of the lowcountry debtors.[26]

The threat of hostile actions on the part of the state's resident Native American populations was always a matter of concern to the governor, and Moultrie occasionally found himself in the role of diplomatic intermediary between the government of South Carolina and the state's Indian tribes. Notified by Indian commissioners Benjamin Hawkins and Andrew Pickens of ongoing treaty violations, in February 1786 he informed the legislature that large surveys of vacant tracts for white settlement in the northwest part of the state were causing encroachment on the towns of their old adversaries the Cherokees. Moultrie was greatly concerned, and he cautioned that if this continued there would be disagreeable consequences. His warning was referred to committee, but no action was taken. The confiscation of Cherokee land was viewed as a natural consequence of Cherokee support of the British during the late war.[27]

The Catawba tribe, on the other hand, had been American allies against the British in the war. Moultrie's paternalist attitude toward the Catawba Indians is revealed by his recommendation to the legislature that their vacant lands, fourteen square miles on the northern boundary of the state, should be leased to white settlers. The rent money, Moultrie believed, would be useful "for the establishing of Schools among them for the Education of their Children; by this they will become an enlightened Civilized People and useful Inhabitants to the State." Moultrie feared that "if they are Suffered to live in their present Ignorant uncivilized manner; they will be a burthen to the state," and their land would remain an uncultivated, useless forest.[28]

In March 1786 Moultrie forwarded to the legislature a petition he had received from the Catawba Indians voicing a complaint that they were being abused and prohibited from hunting deer on land belonging to white people. This, they said, was their principal means of supporting themselves and their families, and as loyal friends and good soldiers, they asked for relief from this imposition. With the approval of the legislature, Moultrie subsequently issued a proclamation stating that the Catawbas had a right by treaty to hunt in any part of the state provided that they did not hunt within any fenced property or cause injury to any of the state's white inhabitants.[29]

In mid-February 1786 a small party of Choctaws wandered into Charleston. They had come from signing the treaty at Hopewell, Andrew Pickens's plantation on the Keowee River near Seneca Old Town, and were making their way home to what is now lower Alabama and Mississippi. Having no linguist capable of understanding the Choctaw language, and therefore not knowing their wishes, Moultrie had them taken care of while he sought an interpreter, which he finally found. The Choctaws presented a ragged appearance, and the legislature furnished each Indian with a blanket, a coat, a shirt, a pair of leggings, and other articles necessary for their comfort.[30]

When the whites and natives were finally able to converse in an intelligible manner, the Choctaws requested a formal audience with the governor, and a meeting was set for March 17. Tinctimingo, also known as Red Woodpecker, was the head of the Choctaw delegation. He opened the proceedings by addressing Moultrie: "I have come here to see you, to take you by the hand, and to be brother to you. . . . we are all your friends, and we will take up the hatchet for you, and be on your side always."[31]

Red Woodpecker explained that on the way home from treaty negotiations, the Choctaw had been harassed by a party of Creeks. The Creeks, whose territory consisted of what is now parts of southwestern Georgia and southeastern Alabama, tried to induce the Choctaws to join in a war against the whites. When the Choctaws refused, a fight broke out, and several Choctaws were killed by the angry Creeks. The trouble with the Creeks, Red Woodpecker said, "made us to come a great way round to see you and to tell you, if the Creeks will make war upon you, we will fight your battles, and shall look for your support in powder and bullets and good guns. Tell us what we shall do and we will do it." Moultrie promised them an answer the next day.[32]

When Moultrie met with the Choctaws at the appointed time, he ceremoniously greeted them as old friends and he complimented their prowess as warriors. Expressing regrets that they had suffered at the hands of the Creeks, he assured them that if the Creeks wanted to make war, "our beloved men at the northward will send us a great many men to fight, and we shall soon kill a great many of them and drive them from their country." Moultrie really did not want to be drawn into an Indian war and thanked the Choctaws for their offer to fight the Creeks, but he refused to allow young Choctaw warriors to be killed while the whites sat still. Rather "if we want you we will send for you and give you good powder and bullets and good guns, and we will go and fight together and then we shall be brothers and love one another." As a show of goodwill, Moultrie presented the Choctaw with rifles and smoothbore muskets with a supply of powder and bullets before he sent them on their way.[33]

With Moultrie's term as governor nearing expiration, the voters of St. John's Berkeley elected him to represent them in the South Carolina Senate. On February 24, 1787, he relinquished the reins of the executive branch to Thomas Pinckney, younger brother of Charles Cotesworth Pinckney. During his administration he had not received the legislative support needed to strengthen the state's militia, principally due to budget considerations, but he had initiated measures that would help to alleviate the debt crisis. The issue of debt, both the Continental debt and domestic debt, would continue to challenge succeeding governors and general assemblies, as would sectional division.[34]

From the earliest days of backcountry representation in the assemblies of South Carolina, legislative apportionment was based on taxable wealth and therefore overwhelmingly favored the lowcountry. By the 1760s, however, the white population of the backcountry had become disproportionately greater than that of the coastal area. The relative disenfranchisement of the backcountry was the root of discord, even antagonism, between the two regions. It was not a result of any action on Moultrie's part, but it is worthy of mention that over the course of his first gubernatorial term, the lowcountry-dominated General Assembly gradually began to pass more laws that benefited the backcountry.[35]

Change was slow, and a number of lowcountry legislators were resistant to the very end, but over time the tension between the two regions began to abate. Bills were passed that divided backcountry districts into counties and establishing a long-desired system of courts. Perhaps the greatest concession to the long-standing wishes of the backcountry was the legislature's decision in 1786 to move the state capital from Charleston to the middle of the state—to a site on the Congaree River where a new town named Columbia would be established.[36]

25.

South Carolina's Cincinnatus

The surrender of Cornwallis to Washington at Yorktown, Virginia, on October 19, 1781, set in motion a chain of events that culminated in the formal end the Revolutionary War by the Treaty of Paris on September 3, 1783. The British abandoned Charlestown in December 1782, but it was November 1783 before the redcoats finally withdrew from New York City. During this interval former Boston bookseller Maj. Gen. Henry Knox carried through an idea that he had been contemplating for years—an organization or society of officers that would satisfy several purposes. The primary purpose of the society would be to perpetuate the bonds of friendship between brothers in arms and provide charity for destitute officers, widows, and orphans. On the political side, the organization would operate as an advocacy group to protect the interests of the solders after the army disbanded.[1]

At a meeting at General von Steuben's headquarters at the Fishkill-on-Hudson in New York on May 13, 1783, members of the Continental officer corps constituted themselves into a hereditary, benevolent, and fraternal society that they named after a figure who was well-known to classically educated men of the eighteenth century: Lucius Quinctius Cincinnatus, a Roman nobleman of the fifth century B.C. who left his farm to lead Rome to victory against a powerful invader. When the crisis passed, Cincinnatus relinquished his power and returned to his plow. The Continental officers elected George Washington president general of the newly formed Society of the Cincinnati on June 19, 1783. Washington gave the nascent brotherhood an added measure of prestige. He epitomized the Roman model of the selfless patriot, a veritable American Cincinnatus who answered his country's urgent wartime call to command the Continental Army during the Revolutionary War and then returned home a private citizen to his beloved Mount Vernon.[2]

William Moultrie had exhibited the Cincinnatus ethos in 1779 when he wrote to Charles Pinckney, "I find my old bones yield much to fatigue; I hope, however, they will carry me through the war; then I will set me down in peace, and indulge myself the remainder of my days."Moultrie had no foreknowledge of the plan for the Society of the Cincinnati that Henry Knox and the other officers in New York put into play, so it is an interesting coincidence that he expressed these sentiments in a letter to Nathanael Greene on May 5, 1783: "I believe there is scarcely an American officer but most cheerfully lays by his sword and uniform. I most sincerely do, and with heartfelt joy return to the callings of a country life free from the tumultuous busy scenes of war. Cincinatus [sic] himself never returned to his plow better pleased."[3]

Under the aegis of its general society, the Society of the Cincinnati would consist of fourteen component societies: one for each of the original thirteen states and France. Sometime during the summer of 1783, Moultrie received letters from von Steuben and Maj. Gen. William Heath informing him of the establishment of the organization and asking him to organize the component society in South Carolina. Moultrie set about assembling the Continental officers residing in the state. The first of three meetings to organize the Society of the Cincinnati of the State of South Carolina occurred at the City Tavern (formerly Dillon's) on the northeast corner of Church and Broad Streets in Charleston on August 29, 1783. Moultrie presented Heath's letter with the enclosed copies of the northern proceedings and the proposed institution.[4]

After discussion the forty-three officers present voted to accept the invitation to become a branch of the society. Moultrie was elected president of the state society on the first ballot, and Isaac Huger was elected vice president. Moultrie presided over subsequent meetings at the tavern on September 13 and October 6, during which bylaws were adopted and other organizational details were worked out. The October meeting set a precedent for upcoming meetings: it would begin precisely at eleven o'clock in the morning, and dinner would be on the table at three.[5]

Moultrie forwarded copies of the proceedings of the newly formed South Carolina Society of the Cincinnati and the state's rules and bylaws to von Steuben on October 13, 1783. He was enthusiastic about the society and promised to give it his utmost support. "So Laudable, so Honorable, so Virtuous a Society cannot but meet with the approbation of every good Man," he wrote to the baron, hardly realizing the firestorm he had unleashed by discussing the formation of the society in the presence of a gentleman who was ineligible for membership.[6]

The organizing members of the Society of the Cincinnati, Moultrie included, did not predict the hostile reaction to their so-called One Society of Friends. Opponents feared that the Cincinnati would wield undue political influence and that the hereditary provisions of membership were meant to establish an American aristocracy contrary to the republican character of the United States. These concerns formed the basis of a public backlash that ignited in South Carolina. Chief among the society's antagonists was Judge Aedanus Burke.[7]

Judge Burke was present when Moultrie initiated the formation of the South Carolina component of the society. He did not like what he heard, nor did he like what he read when he obtained a copy of the society's institution. Burke was an Irish immigrant who had served as a lieutenant in the Second South Carolina Regiment. He resigned his commission to take a judicial post but later held the rank of captain in the militia. Like Moultrie, Burke became a prisoner of war when the Charleston garrison surrendered in 1780. Now he served as the state's chief justice. He was well connected with the former officers who would become members of the society in South Carolina, and he seems to have been on friendly terms with them, but he had not served long enough in Continental service to qualify for Cincinnati membership.[8]

Whether honestly motivated to action or just peeved that he was ineligible for membership (which he vehemently denied), Burke devoted himself to denouncing stridently the new organization. In October 1783, he published under the pseudonym Cassius an anti-Cincinnati polemic titled *Considerations on the Society or Order of Cincinnati*. This pamphlet first appeared in Charleston, but by the spring of 1784, it had been reprinted in Philadelphia, New York, and other northern cities and published in a number of northern newspapers.[9]

Fueled by Burke's diatribe, disapproval of the Society of the Cincinnati grew into a general alarm that played out in private correspondence and in newsprint. Among the society's more prominent detractors were Thomas Jefferson, Benjamin Franklin (who later accepted honorary membership), James Madison, John Adams, Samuel Adams, and John Jay. South Carolinians did not seem to care much one way or the other. As an electorate they "refused to be panicked into disavowing men who they knew had won independence," and they favored neither Cincinnati nor anti-Cincinnati for elected office. A few members backed away from the society, but the vast majority of members, however surprised by the outcry, were undeterred. The society not only weathered the storm of disapprobation but flourished. Over time the concerns of the society's detractors proved to be completely unfounded.[10]

In January 1784 George Washington called for the first general meeting of the society to be held in Philadelphia on the first Monday in May, and it has long been held that Moultrie attended. He was indeed elected to be a delegate and intended to go. On February 10, 1784, the South Carolina General Assembly chose him to be a delegate to the Continental Congress but then six days later elected him to the office of lieutenant governor of South Carolina. Moultrie altered his travel plans accordingly. He remained in Charleston, and other delegates attended the Cincinnati meeting in his stead. To make up for his absence, Moultrie sent a packet of correspondence to the general meeting that contained the details of the establishment of the Society of the Cincinnati in South Carolina.[11]

George Washington presided over the first general meeting of the Society of the Cincinnati at Philadelphia from May 4 to May 18, 1784, during which he was unanimously reelected president general. He did not intend to attend the triennial meeting to be held at Philadelphia in May 1787 and was determined not to stand for reelection. In October 1786 he sent a circular letter to the presidents of the state societies explaining the logic behind his reluctance to be president general, mainly his desire to retire to private life.[12]

After showing Washington's circular to the South Carolina Cincinnati on February 12, 1787, Moultrie wrote to Washington lamenting the causes that the president general had given for his disinclination to continue as president general. But as Moultrie noted, an important event would place Washington in Philadelphia at the time of the 1787 triennial meeting. Virginia had chosen him to be a delegate to the constitutional convention that would convene at Philadelphia in May. The Cincinnati of South Carolina were thus cautiously optimistic that with the triennial meeting coinciding with the constitutional convention, Washington would attend and acquiesce to reelection.[13]

Washington did indeed come to Philadelphia in May 1787, and while he was not present at any of the society's formal sessions, he dined with members on May 15. Not necessarily due to Moultrie's urging, he also agreed to remain the society's president general, a position he held until his death in 1799. He never attended another general meeting, but he maintained an active interest and continued to support the society. Concurrent with the meeting of the Society of the Cincinnati that began and ended in May, Washington presided over the Constitutional Convention that ran through mid-September.[14]

In accordance with the articles of the new U.S. Constitution ratified in 1788, Washington was elected first president of the United States in 1789. At the behest of the South Carolina Cincinnati, Moultrie composed a letter congratulating him on his election and inauguration. "Possessed of every feeling that can act on grateful hearts," Moultrie began, "the Society of the Cincinnati in the State of South Carolina, beg leave to congratulate you on the happy occasion which has once again placed you in a situation of rendering general good to their country." The South Carolina Cincinnati concurred with the people's choice and expressed their most sincere wishes for his success and the hope that they would all enjoy "the fruits of a government which has for its basis, the good of the people of America."[15]

Moultrie's letter and Washington's reply were widely published in the newspapers. The president accepted the congratulations of the South Carolinians with characteristic graciousness. As Federalists most of the Cincinnati favored a strong central government, and Washington was gratified to have their commendation, which he could not receive "without emotions of peculiar satisfaction."[16]

Ironically it was the badge of the society that very nearly caused a rift between Moultrie and the South Carolina Cincinnati on one side and General von Steuben and Maj. Pierre Charles L'Enfant on the other. The idea of a hereditary badge for Continental officers seems to have predated the Society of the Cincinnati. Henry Knox was allegedly overheard in 1776 speaking of his "wish for some ribbon to wear in his hat, or in his button hole, to be transmitted to his descendants, as a badge and a proof that he had fought in defense of their liberties." If so then Knox did not pursue the matter until he began to draft his proposal for the society's institution.[17]

Enter French engineer Pierre L'Enfant, a veteran of campaigns in both the northern and southern theaters who survived grievous wounding at Savannah and would later become famous for his plan for the District of Columbia. L'Enfant designed an eagle of gold, with miniaturized medallions on the eagle's breast bearing scenes on the obverse and reverse depicting Cincinnatus's ascent to power and his return to the plow. The eagle was suspended by blue ribbon edged in white that symbolized the bond between America and France.[18]

The trouble between the South Carolina Cincinnati, von Steuben, and L'Enfant began in December 1784 when Capt. William Thompson, a South Carolina member and owner of the City Tavern, received payment of $27.50 (approximately $625 in 2012 dollars) from each of twenty-five other South Carolina members to procure Cincinnati eagles. Presumably these eagles were to be fabricated in Philadelphia. Instead Thompson obtained eagles made in France from Major L'Enfant and delivered them to the members who had paid him in advance. Unfortunately for the financially distressed L'Enfant, he never received payment from Thompson.[19]

General von Steuben wrote Moultrie a strong letter addressing the subject in July 1786. On a previous visit to Charleston, von Steuben had made his opinion abundantly clear that the South Carolina society would be disgraced if measures were not immediately taken to reimburse Major L'Enfant for the medals. Von Steuben acquainted Moultrie with the fact that L'Enfant was in arrears for a very large sum and had been prosecuted in France on this account. He implored

Moultrie to use his influence to save L'Enfant's credit and thus extricate them all from this disagreeable situation.[20]

Moultrie told von Steuben that he was "extremely anxious to extricate L'Enfant from his embarrassed situation and to remove the Odium that might fall upon several of the Officers of our Society by a misrepresentation of their contract with Captain Thompson." As a result he had called a special meeting to investigate the matter. But after a full inquiry, it appeared certain that the contract for the eagles was made between the members of the South Carolina Cincinnati and Captain Thompson. The members were unaware that L'Enfant was even involved in the transaction.[21]

The South Carolinians unanimously agreed that there was no legal or moral obligation to L'Enfant on the parts of those gentlemen who had contracted with Thompson to obtain eagles, and that there could be "no impropriety or indelicacy imputed to them . . . for refusing to reimburse Major L'Enfant for losses sustained in private Contracts made with a Man who betrayed his confidence." That was not all. The South Carolinians wanted to wash their hands of the whole affair. Thompson, it seems, had not delivered all of his contracted eagles in South Carolina. Some he had sold in Georgia, where he had recently relocated. Thompson was now beyond the reach of the South Carolina society. All present and future correspondence relating to Thompson and L'Enfant would be referred by Moultrie to the president of the Georgia Society of the Cincinnati.[22]

This did not satisfy von Steuben, who put L'Enfant's case before the society's general meeting in Philadelphia in May 1787. The meeting devoted a substantial amount of time to considering L'Enfant's requests for reimbursement of debts incurred while procuring eagles from France. The general meeting accepted a recommendation to "take every arrangement within its power to settle all claims which Major L'Enfant can have either on the justice or generosity of the Society." This would include an appeal to the states on which L'Enfant had existing claims to make a speedy accommodation.[23]

L'Enfant subsequently reapplied to the South Carolina society for relief in March 1788. Contrary to their previous remonstrations, the South Carolinians had reconsidered their position. In a letter to L'Enfant, Moultrie could not help but recount the particulars of Thompson's fraudulent acts; nevertheless he reassured the major that the South Carolina Cincinnati would reimburse him for their eagles and that payment, with interest, would be transmitted forthwith.[24]

At the same time that Moultrie served in the capacity of president of the South Carolina Cincinnati, he also became president of the St. Andrew's Society. He had joined this organization in 1758 by virtue of his Scottish descent, with the support of his father, who had been president, and perhaps the encouragement of his older brother John. The Revolution had interrupted the regular meetings of the St. Andrew's Society, but it was never dissolved, and though its archives and insignia were mislaid, they were later found to have been carefully preserved. Because of its Loyalist character, the society was unpopular immediately after the war, but by 1787 "the thickness of Scottish blood had overcome the tenuity of the bitter waters of civil strife." Former Whigs and Tories met together in the fraternal bonds of Scottish brotherhood on St. Andrew's Day in 1787 and elected Moultrie to be president of the revived organization. He held this position until 1790.[25]

26.

Canals, Constitutions, and Commissioners

The agricultural economy of South Carolina changed dramatically in the years following the Revolutionary War. Without the former British subsidy, indigo declined in value as a cash crop, as did rice, and both staples were gradually replaced by cotton. That cotton could be grown lucratively in the backcountry gave impetus for the westward extension of the state's population. Lowcountry plantations in close proximity to Charleston had easy access to market via navigable streams and rivers; however backcountry plantations, some more than a hundred miles away, had no such accessibility by water. Conveying cargo from the backcountry by road was difficult and at times impossible. The connection of South Carolina's river systems with a series of canals to facilitate the transport of backcountry agricultural produce to Charleston was studied in 1770, but the idea of an inland waterway was shelved during the war.[1]

The Santee Canal was the first of the state's large-scale canal projects. Cognizant of the economic devastation suffered by their state and their personal fortunes as a consequence of the war, on November 10, 1785, a number of "thoughtful and enterprising men" convened at the State House in Charleston to consider a proposal to open inland navigation by means of a canal with locks between the Santee and Cooper Rivers. After a discussion the committee decided to petition the state legislature for incorporation during the next session.[2]

Gov. William Moultrie's name was not listed among the gentlemen who petitioned the General Assembly on February 7, 1786, but his stance on the matter was well known. The previous year he had emphasized to the legislature the importance of inland navigation to convey produce to market, "particularly in that Valuable but Bulky Article of Tobacco which is now of so much Consequence to our Trade, and by its Very great increase will in a few years be one of Our first Staples."[3]

The General Assembly granted incorporation to the Company for Inland Navigation from Santee to Cooper River on March 22, 1786. Immediately following incorporation, the circle of men that had applied to the legislature met to organize formally the Santee Canal Company, as it was called. Moultrie's role in the earliest of meetings is unknown. As governor he was not precluded from participating in what was hoped would be a profitable venture, but he remained in the background, at least publicly, while his business partners lobbied the General Assembly for incorporation. That changed when the board of directors formed and the company chose him to be president and John Rutledge his vice president.[4]

Moultrie immediately sought an engineer to oversee the first stages of the project. George Washington had long been interested in a canal connecting the Potomac River with the Ohio River valley and was president of the Potomac Company chartered in 1785. Assuming that he was personally acquainted with a reputable and capable engineer named James Brindley, Moultrie wrote to Washington in April 1786 to ask of Brindley's whereabouts and availability. If Brindley was engaged, Moultrie suggested, then perhaps he could be spared to advise the Santee Canal Company on how to proceed so as to "prevent us from beginning wrong." He closed with a rare mention of his Mrs. Moultrie, who tendered her best respects to General and Mrs. Washington.[5]

Washington was pleased to learn of the South Carolinians' endeavors, admitting to Moultrie that it gave him "great pleasure to find a spirit of inland navigation prevailing so generously." Washington had located Brindley, who was presently committed to the Susquehanna Company, but he inquired to see if Brindley's services could be dispensed with long enough to satisfy the needs of South Carolina. In the meantime Washington suggested that a competent and capable engineer could be obtained in Europe. In fact he had taken the liberty of sending letters of inquiry to France and England on Moultrie's behalf. Their old friend the Marquis de Lafayette had since responded that one of France's civil engineers could be hired for a reasonable fee. Washington concluded his letter with a personal touch: "Mrs. Washington joins me in compliments and every good wish for Mrs. Moultree [sic] and yourself."[6]

Brindley spent about four months during the winter of 1786–87 in Charleston as a consultant. But to find an engineer to carry forth the project, the Santee Canal Company had to look no further than its own backyard. Johannes Christian Senf, the South Carolina state engineer who had served his adopted land so well during the Revolutionary War, was hired to plan and supervise the canal's construction. Senf was a member of the Society of the Cincinnati and was well known to the board of directors, and Moultrie and Senf definitely held each other in high esteem. Brindley and Senf likely collaborated on the siting of the canal and the construction of masonry locks while Brindley was in Charleston.[7]

Moultrie and his partners had trouble raising capital in an economically depressed postwar economy, and so construction of the canal did not actually begin until May 1793. Nonetheless in July of that year, the *City Gazette* referred to the Santee Canal Company as "flourishing," its prospects "so flattering," and predicted that the speedy completion of the canal would "ensure immense advantages both to the country at large, and the stockholders in particular."[8]

Senf was forced to deal with a number of obstacles during the construction of the canal: the limited availability of artisans and tradesmen such as bricklayers, stonecutters, blacksmiths, and carpenters; the escalating cost of hiring thousands of slaves for manual labor; and the brutally hot, humid summer weather and typhoid fever endemic to the region (termed "canal fever" in this context) that contributed to a high attrition of the workforce. Frequent freshets on the Santee slowed progress, and a flood in 1796 devastated the lowcountry, ruining a substantial portion of completed work. Senf had first estimated the cost of the project to be more than fifty-five thousand pounds sterling, but he later claimed that the actual cost was more than double this amount. By some estimates the actual cost was even higher.[9]

Moultrie stepped down as president of the company in 1794, but he remained active as a member of the board of directors. To raise additional capital, the directors authorized a series of four public lotteries in 1795. The newsprint advertisements designed to encourage public patronage in the lotteries dramatically expounded on the economic benefits that would be realized by everyone in the state, particularly the backcountry farmers. However the directors tended to exaggerate the progress of construction and the rapidity with which Senf and his workmen were moving toward completion. In March 1796 Moultrie was a member of a committee that examined the canal from end to end. The committee reported a "fair prospect of speedy and complete success in the great undertaking," but in 1797 the company was forced to secure loans and sell shares for less than par value to secure more capital.[10]

After seven years of construction, the canal finally opened in May 1800, and though it was later profitable, the Santee Canal Company never paid a dividend during Moultrie's lifetime. Once finally finished, the Santee Canal traversed twenty-two miles from the Santee to the Cooper River, ascending thirty-four feet from the Santee to its summit level and then descending sixty-nine feet as it flowed to the Cooper, a process that required a total of ten locks built of brick and stone. The canal itself was thirty-five feet wide with a water depth of four feet. This enabled horse-drawn boats fifty feet long and nine feet wide bearing loads of up to twenty-two tons to navigate the canal. Lack of profitability aside, in its day the Santee Canal was said to be at least equal to any work of the kind in the United States, and it did certainly convey economic benefits to the upcountry farmers and planters as well as the Charleston merchants by lowering the cost and accelerating transportation.[11]

In 1787 Moultrie and another group of gentlemen petitioned the state legislature for the incorporation of another company to dig a canal from the Edisto River to the Ashley River. What role he played in the management of the Edisto Canal Company is unknown. In 1789 the Santee Canal Company and the Edisto Canal Company joined with the Catawba Company and the Broad River Company in an unsuccessful bid to the legislature for financial assistance, their funds "not being adequate to carry the purpose of their institution into effect." The Edisto Canal Company never accomplished much, nor did the Catawba and Broad River companies, and these chartered private companies eventually became defunct. Of the four only the Santee Canal Company remained viable, and although it was not the profitable enterprise envisioned by Moultrie and his fellow shareholders, the Santee Canal was effectively used for inland navigation until 1840.[12]

The first government of the United States was based on the Articles of Confederation that were established by the Articles of Confederation and Perpetual Union, an agreement proposed under wartime conditions in 1777 and ratified in 1781. Under the Articles of Confederation the government had no executive or judicial branches, could not impose taxes, and lacked the authority to regulate foreign and interstate commerce. Governor Moultrie was among many who advocated for the necessity of a stronger federal government. "I trust," he replied to Massachusetts governor James Bowdoin's urging for a federal convention to revise the articles, "that this state, with every other in the confederation, are well convinced their existence as a nation depends on the strength of the union. Cemented together in one common interest, they are invincible; but ruined when divided, and must fall a sacrifice to internal dissensions and foreign usurpation."[13]

Moultrie demonstrated his willingness to relinquish certain state powers to Congress in February 1786 when he laid before the Senate correspondence received from several other states that contained copies of their legislative acts: "I beg leave to recommend to your serious reflection the propriety of Vesting the Congress of the United States with full power to regulate our Commerce and Navigation, and I take the liberty to observe that, although such powers may be attended with some disadvantages to ourselves, as a State, yet I trust We shall not be so wanting in our Attachment to our Sister States in the Union, but that we will Sacrifice some local advantages for the general good."[14]

Prior to 1786 South Carolina had ceded the power to Congress to regulate trade with the West Indies in response to Britain's 1783 prohibitions against American trade with the British island ports in the Caribbean. The General Assembly now responded to Moultrie's entreaty by granting Congress power to regulate trade with the West Indies and all other external or foreign trade of the states, for a limited time, and provided that nine of the thirteen states would do the same. "This State has taken every step in its power to support the Union," Moultrie informed Secretary of Congress Charles Thompson.[15]

In February 1786 Virginia governor Patrick Henry sent a packet from Virginia containing a legislative resolve to appoint commissioners to meet and discuss the regulation of trade. The session of the South Carolina General Assembly, however, was already under way when Moultrie received Henry's communication. Moultrie informed the Virginian that being close to adjournment, they had already determined to receive no new matters for consideration, "and in this case the Executive [has] no power to appoint [commissioners]." In any event, Moultrie was pleased to report, his state had "already passed an Act giving Congress full power to negotiate trade." Moultrie delayed his reply until June, and he begged Henry's pardon for the tardiness, explaining that "immediately on adjournment of the Legislature, I was obliged from my want of health to retire into the Country a few weeks."[16]

Delegates from five states met in Annapolis, Maryland, in September 1786. The result was a call for a convention of all of the states to meet the following May in Philadelphia. Submitting a report of the Annapolis convention with his January 1787 message to the South Carolina General Assembly, Moultrie characterized the upcoming convention of the states as indispensible, and he urged the legislators to select delegates to meet with those of the other states. The legislature chose John Rutledge, Charles Pinckney, his cousin Charles Cotesworth Pinckney, and Pierce Butler to represent South Carolina when the convention convened in Philadelphia in May 1787. Instead of modifying the Articles of Confederation, however, the delegates drafted the Constitution of the United States. The convention subsequently sent the new Constitution to the states for ratification.[17]

Debate in the South Carolina legislature between the Federalists, who favored a strong central government, and the opposing Anti-Federalists began on January 16, 1788, and lasted for four days. The two Pinckneys, Rutledge, and Butler presented the document, argued its merits, and answered opposition voiced by Judge Henry Pendleton and Rawlings Lowndes. Moultrie had completed his first term as governor the previous February and now represented his own St. John's Berkeley Parish in the Senate. He undoubtedly attended the sessions and listened to the animated debates. At length the 151 legislators agreed by a one-vote margin to put the question of ratification to a convention of the people to be held in Charleston the following May. The location of the convention would give a decided advantage to the wealthy lowcountry merchants, lawyers, and planters who favored ratification.[18]

South Carolina's convention, "called for the purpose of considering, and of ratifying or rejecting, the Constitution framed for the United States by a Convention of delegates assembled at Philadelphia," convened on May 12, 1788, at the Exchange. Delegates chose the new governor, Thomas Pinckney, to preside. Most but not all of the opposition came from upcountry delegates. Deliberations lasted until May 23, when the question of ratification was put to a vote, and South Carolina became the eighth state to ratify by a two-to-one margin. The coastal centers of Beaufort, Charleston, and Georgetown were nearly unanimous in support of ratification, other lowcountry parishes were divided in their support, and the backcountry was overwhelmingly against ratification. Senator Moultrie aligned himself with the Federalists and voted in favor of ratification. Whatever remarks he made during the deliberations were not recorded.[19]

With the federal government reconfigured, South Carolina was in need of a new state constitution. When the South Carolina General Assembly convened for the first time in the new capital, Columbia, the legislators decided to call for a state constitutional convention to meet in the capital on May 10, 1790. A thorough examination of the Constitution of 1790 is beyond the scope of this work, but suffice it to say that the lowcountry elite, through the apportionment of delegates skewed in their favor as was done in the past, deepened sectional hostility by adopting a new constitution that virtually ignored the postwar economic growth and increasing prosperity of the backcountry. Moultrie again represented St. John's Berkeley. He was one of thirty-two delegates appointed to the committee of privilege to certify that delegates were properly elected and to adjudicate any complaints of breach of parliamentary rules or procedure.[20]

Moultrie became a widower for a second time in December 1789 when wife Hannah died at the age of fifty-four. They had been married for a decade. Only a few affectionate wartime letters reveal the nature of their marriage. But an anecdote (of unknown origin) was published in the *News and Courier* in 1929 with the express intent of giving an interesting sidelight on his domestic relations. "A friend was passing his house in Charleston and noticed the old general working out in the garden with the hot sun pouring down on his head. The friend inquired if it were not too hot to be working out in the open on a day like this, whereupon the general, straightening up and mopping the sweat from his face, then looking toward the house where his wife was watching him replied, 'The temperature is hotter up there than out here in the sun.'"[21]

From the end of the Revolutionary War in 1783 and through the rest of the 1780s, the South Carolina state treasury existed in a state of disarray. Previous House committees had failed in their attempts to untangle and reconcile the state's finances. Physician and historian David Ramsay recalled that "many frauds were committed without detection and much was lost from neglect and mismanagement. No man in or out of office could tell with any precision the amount of the debts and credits of the State."[22]

As an afterthought the legislature amended the Constitution of 1790 to stipulate that the commissioners of the treasury were to expedite the balancing of the books. The old books were to be closed and new books opened in 1791. To this end in February 1791 the General Assembly elected three commissioners to settle the public accounts prior to 1791. Senator Moultrie was the first commissioner selected, and of the eighteen legislators whose names were placed in nomination, he received the most votes. The other commissioners chosen were Senator John Lewis Gervais, a backcountry planter and Charleston merchant, and senator and Charleston intendant Arnoldus Vanderhorst.[23]

Moultrie, Gervais, and Vanderhorst vacated their Senate seats to work at the herculean task, and the legislature entrusted them with broad powers to achieve their purpose. As commissioners they were authorized to "adjust and settle the accounts of the present and all former commissioners of the treasury, and all tax collectors and receivers, and of all and every other agent or agents, board, person or persons, who have at any time heretofore been entrusted with the collection and disbursement of public money in any way or manner whatsoever." Not even the accounts of the deceased were immune from scrutiny. The commissioners were empowered to give discharges on final settlement and to cancel bonds or other obligations, file lawsuits against defaulters, and prosecute them to final judgment and execution. In addition they had the power of subpoena and the authority to imprison anyone who refused to cooperate with their endeavors.[24]

When the books and other records arrived in Charleston from Columbia, the commissioners conducted a complete inventory. "This proved a difficult piece of business and took up a good deal of time, as we found them in great Confusion," Moultrie wrote in a report to the legislature after ten months of investigation. Moultrie attributed the condition of the records to their frequent removal from place to place, particularly during the war. The number of missing records and the poor, sometimes fraudulent record keeping convinced the commissioners that the books could never be balanced.[25]

The work led Moultrie, Gervais, and Vanderhorst down a number of different avenues. An inspection of the papers of the state treasurer revealed accounts due the state that antedated the Revolution. They turned these and other dormant notes over to the treasurer for collection. They also performed a painstaking review of the state's indents (interest-bearing promissory notes issued to fund the Revolutionary War debt), assisted the commissioner to settle the accounts of South Carolina with the United States, and examined the records of the agent for the foreign debt and the tax collectors. At one point they discovered $22,047 in Continental dollars and a quantity of other paper money in an old chest. The commission encountered some unexpected foot-dragging to the point of recalcitrance on the part of the state attorney general, but they were reluctant to compel his cooperation by legal means without the express permission of the legislature. Perhaps this is because the attorney general was Moultrie's half-brother, Alexander.[26]

The commissioners presented their findings to the legislature a year later. Their detailed ten-page report, supported by dozens of pages of compiled ledgers, addressed a very wide range of financial instruments: indents that were appropriated for the interest of the commutation of Continental officers; bonds, notes, and accounts due the public; and the amercement and confiscation of Loyalist estates. While sorting through their state's financial anarchy, they uncovered instances of perjury and fraud, and in the most flagrant cases they instigated criminal prosecutions. The number of accounts and receipts of paper that Moultrie, Vanderhorst, and Gervais sorted through nearly defies comprehension. Moultrie informed the legislature that it was "impossible to go through such a complication of business without the assistance of clerks" and that he and his fellow commissioners had found it necessary to hire two full-time clerks at their own expense. Despite the best efforts of the commissioners, it would take many years of work to satisfy the legislature's mandate to bring order out of chaos.[27]

27.

"The honor of being one of your family"

The Society of the Cincinnati held its general meeting in Philadelphia on May 4, 1791. Conspicuously absent from the assembly were the society's president general and the delegates from South Carolina. By accident rather than by design, the gentlemen who missed the Philadelphia reunion, including the president general, met together elsewhere on the same day—but in Charleston instead of Philadelphia.[1]

George Washington began to contemplate a tour of the thirteen states soon after his April 23, 1789, inauguration. He completed a tour of New England in October and November 1789, but it was 1791 before he was able to visit the South. A southern tour would allow him to assess postwar economic conditions and evaluate agriculture, commerce, and manufacturing in the region. He was also determined to learn how the new federal government was regarded in the South, especially since Congress had just passed an unpopular excise tax on distilled spirits. This so-called Whiskey Act was the first tax on an American domestic product. But there were personal reasons as well. He had suffered from poor health in recent months. A southern tour would further increase his physical activity and ease the burden of his executive duties—measures all endorsed by his personal physicians. And finally he would be able to establish personal relationships with his former Continental officers and other regional leaders that he knew only by reputation or through correspondence.[2]

Washington planned his trip in intricate detail, much like a military campaign, remarking in a letter to Thomas Jefferson, "I shall halt one day at

Fredericksburgh and two at Richmond; thence I shall proceed to Charlestown by the way of Petersburg, Halifax, Tarborough, Newbern, Wilmington, and George Town." The president thus departed Philadelphia on the morning of March 21, 1791, and headed to Mount Vernon whence he left on April 7, setting off through southern Virginia and down the North Carolina coast.[3]

Charleston was the most important city Washington would visit on his tour, and her citizens made lavish preparations for the entertainment of the nation's chief magistrate. William Moultrie and the leaders of the South Carolina Society of the Cincinnati involved themselves in the planning of nearly every public aspect of Washington's visit, and they anticipated his arrival with enthusiasm. An announcement appeared in the *City Gazette* on April 19: "The members of the Society of the Cincinnati established in this State intend to pay every respect and honor due the president of the United States on his arrival in this city; it is therefore to be hoped that those members who may be in the country, will make it a point to be in town at or before the 10th instant, the time when the president may be expected." A notice in the May 2 issue reminded the Cincinnati's committee of arrangements of the meeting set for ten o'clock that morning at Edward McCrady's Tavern on East Bay Street. Dress for the occasion was full uniform, undoubtedly because Washington was expected that very day.[4]

After passing through Virginia and North Carolina, Washington crossed the border from North Carolina into South Carolina on the afternoon of Wednesday, April 27. Two days later he reached Clifton, a rice plantation on the Waccamaw River that was home to Capt. William Alston. It was at Alston's that Washington encountered the delegation that had come to escort him to Charleston: his distant cousin and acclaimed cavalryman Lt. Col. William Washington, South Carolina's preeminent Continental officer and former governor William Moultrie, and John Rutledge Jr.,* son of the Revolutionary War governor of South Carolina and former U.S. Supreme Court justice. If the intention was to greet the president at the border, they were late, principally because of poor communications in the remote areas through which Washington traveled. Nonetheless Washington would have their company for the remainder of the journey.[5]

When he learned that Moultrie, William Washington, and young Rutledge were riding to Alston's, Moultrie's wartime confidant Gov. Charles Pinckney sent with them a letter containing the itinerary for Washington's stay in Charleston. "You may be assured," Pinckney informed the president, "that the people of this country feel themselves on this occasion so strongly bound by every principle of gratitude and affection that no exertion will be wanting on their part to render your stay among us as agreeable as possible." When Washington toured New

---

* John Rutledge Jr. represented his father, who had been elected chief justice of South Carolina in February of that year and was engaged with the court's spring session.

England in 1789, he was kept quite busy with engagements in the important cities that he visited, but nothing matched the scale of the reception that he would receive in Charleston. In the meantime Moultrie assumed the role of Washington's personal chaperone, and he became the president's constant companion for the better part of this leg of his tour through South Carolina. This gave Moultrie and Washington an opportunity to renew an acquaintance with each other that had been briefly established in Philadelphia while Moultrie awaited exchange in 1781.[6]

Moultrie likewise took on the responsibility for ensuring that the remainder of the southward course ran smoothly. For instance it took two ferries and a mile-long causeway to traverse the north and south branches of the Santee River and the marshy delta that lay between. This stretch was often troublesome for travelers. Fortunately Thomas Pinckney's Fairfield plantation was on the south bank of the south branch of the river, and Moultrie asked Pinckney to have his boats on hand at the ferries to help carry the president's horses across the river. The Santee, however, was perhaps more than just an obstacle to be negotiated on the road to Charleston. While making their way across the Santee River, Moultrie's and Washington's attention was probably diverted to a subject of mutual interest—the canal that would form an upstream connection between the Santee and Cooper Rivers. Moultrie was a driving force behind this project, which Washington had heartily endorsed.[7]

Washington covered as many miles as possible between large towns and cities in a day, and his coterie traveled the nearly sixty miles from Alston's to Charleston in six days. At Governor Pinckney's behest, Moultrie requested a stopover at Snee Farm, Pinckney's little farm in Christ Church Parish. This was the same house where Moultrie and Charles Cotesworth Pinckney resided as British captives after the fall of Charlestown. Washington obliged and stopped for breakfast there on the morning of Monday, May 2.[8]

Moultrie may have used the delay to allow a messenger time to cover the last five miles to Haddrell's Point to alert Charleston of Washington's imminent arrival. Washington's carriage rolled into Haddrell's Point shortly before noon. One of the first things that came into view was the old barracks that housed the Continental officers who became prisoners of the British when Charlestown fell in 1780. He had hardly glimpsed Charleston across the Cooper River when the fanfare and pageantry began. Awaiting his arrival at Haddrell's Point was a small contingent of Charleston's most influential men: Brig. Gen. Charles Cotesworth Pinckney, Maj. Edward Rutledge, and Col. John Sandford Dart.[9]

Moultrie and the others joined Washington aboard a twelve-oared barge manned by thirteen splendidly uniformed American sea captains who ferried them across the mouth of the Cooper to Prioleau's Wharf. More than forty vessels accompanied the barge, including a boat bearing a musical ensemble who serenaded the presidential retinue with vocal and instrumental selections as they made way toward town. South Carolina governor Charles Pinckney and Lt. Gov. Isaac Holmes, Intendant Arnoldus Vanderhorst, the city wardens,* and members of the Society of the Cincinnati welcomed Washington as he disembarked from the barge onto the wharf. Forming a procession, with the Cincinnati men bringing up the rear, the dignitaries led the president down East Bay Street to the Exchange as onlookers cheered them on.[10]

Perhaps as Washington mounted the steps of the Exchange, he was aware of the building's rich history. Or perhaps not. In any event the building had played a central role in Moultrie's experience over the previous two decades. Patriots protested the oppressive acts of the British Parliament there. The provisional and state legislatures had met in its upper rooms. Confiscated British tea was stored in the same cellar where Moultrie successfully hid Continental gunpowder. Independence had been proclaimed at the Exchange, yet the British had quartered troops there during the occupation and used the basement as a provost dungeon. More recently the 1788 convention that ratified the U.S. Constitution met there. Standing on a platform raised within the grand balustrade facing Broad Street, Washington watched the procession pass in review.[11]

Once past the Exchange, the parade reversed its course and proceeded to the president's lodgings at 87 Church Street. The wardens had selected the three-story brick mansion of Judge Thomas Heyward Jr., a signer of the Declaration of Independence and captain of the Charlestown Artillery during the war. A short respite allowed the weary guest time to rid himself of the dust of the road and to prepare for a private dinner given by Governor Pinckney at the governor's home on Meeting Street. Pinckney's dinner party included a small company of gentlemen, and Moultrie was assuredly one of the invitees, for it was he who had delivered the invitation to Washington on the governor's behalf.[12]

From the very moment George Washington set foot in Charleston, he was subject to a full itinerary of balls, banquets, tours, and private dinners. Nearly every civic group sought to address, feed, raise a glass, or otherwise entertain—it was an exhausting schedule by any standards, particularly when one considers the amount of wine that must have been consumed in drinking round after round of toasts. The gentlemen who attended these events given in honor of the president were well documented in contemporary newsprint, whether they were government officials, members of the military, clergy, Cincinnati, or even "gentlemen strangers." Moultrie was not only present and accounted for on the majority of these occasions, he seems to have kept pace with the best of them. But when one considers that Washington's southern tour was ostensibly for the benefit of his health, it would not be surprising to learn that he was more fatigued when he left Charleston than when he arrived.[13]

---

* From 1836 onward the city intendant and wardens were known as mayor and aldermen.

The Cincinnati came front and center on May 4–5, and their own president, General Moultrie, was at the head. On the morning of May 4, Moultrie escorted Washington on a riding tour of the remnants of the defenses that had been erected across the Charleston Neck between the Ashley and Cooper Rivers during the 1780 British siege. The British had filled in many of their trenches after Gen. Benjamin Lincoln's American force surrendered, but they had also strengthened the former American defenses during their two-and-a-half-year occupation. Eleven years later there was still much to see, and Washington was keenly interested in viewing the battlefield to understand better what had transpired during the siege.[14]

Washington and Moultrie were in good company. Along for the tour were Gen. Charles Cotesworth Pinckney; Maj. Edward Rutledge, who had served in batteries along the American lines as a captain of the Charlestown Artillery; and Washington's private secretary, Maj. William Jackson, who was Lincoln's aide-de-camp at the time of the siege. The outing got off to an early start, so it was good that the magnificent banquet at the Exchange on the evening before had ended its toasts (typical of the Charleston entertainments) shortly after eight o'clock. As they rode circuit across the ground, Moultrie pointed out the positions of the British batteries, approaches, and parallels. The landscape had changed, but the ruins of the hornwork remained, and time had not erased all traces of the American redoubts and the wet ditch. Along the way each of the other former officers offered his own distinct perspective of the greatest American disaster of the war.[15]

Publicly Washington expressed his great satisfaction at the gallant defense made by the Charleston garrison during the siege, but his private thoughts were somewhat different. He confided to his diary that he "was satisfied that the defence was noble & honorable altho' the measure was undertaken upon wrong principles and impolitic." Whether he said as much to Moultrie in private is not known, but even in 1780 Washington had been of the opinion that Lincoln should have evacuated the American garrison as soon as the British fleet entered Charleston Harbor.[16]

That evening the South Carolina Society of the Cincinnati hosted a formal dinner in Washington's honor in the upstairs Long Room at McCrady's Tavern. As the South Carolina Society's president, Moultrie presided over the occasion, assisted by Vice President Charles Cotesworth Pinckney. The Cincinnati were resplendent in their uniforms with their eagles pinned to their breasts. It was an important affair, and the Cincinnati had broadened their guest list to include a number of other dignitaries. Governor Pinckney and Lieutenant Governor Holmes attended, as did South Carolina's congressional delegation. On hand were several French and Spanish diplomats, as well as Intendant Vanderhorst and the other city wardens.[17]

Once the gentlemen were seated and the banquet got under way, the members enjoyed "a very sumptuous dinner" while being serenaded by a choral ensemble. It was after dinner that the toasts began, and if nothing else, in the giving of toasts the Cincinnati were masters of the art. The gentlemen raised their glasses a total of fifteen times to the exclamations of "hear, hear," and the Charleston Artillery, with their field pieces unlimbered nearby, in turn answered each salute by discharging one of their guns. The ceremony began with a toast to the United States and ended with a tribute to the "Patriotic Fair of America." In between they drank to the honor of Louis XVI, King of France, Counts Rochambeau and d'Estaing, and the officers of the French army and navy, as well as the members of President Washington's cabinet.[18]

The rounds of toasts included a salute to the French monarchy but also included a toast to the French National Assembly that had recently come into being as a result of the nascent French Revolution. Toward the end Washington rose and proposed that the Cincinnati drink to the memory of the late Gen. Nathanael Greene (who died in 1786) and all of their brother officers who fell in America's defense. This certainly was a solemn toast that may have been drunk in silence. The banquet finally concluded, and the Cincinnati men, full to the brim with the brotherly affection that can only be known by comrades in arms, proceeded to a splendid ball hosted by the city corporation at the elegantly illuminated City Hall.[19]

Early the next morning, Generals Moultrie and Pinckney, with Majors Rutledge and Jackson along, resumed their battleground exploration by taking Washington on a boat tour of Charleston Harbor. The group landed first on James Island, where they enjoyed "an exceeding good breakfast" served at the house of Fort Johnson's commandant, Capt. Michael Kalteisen. After breakfast Kalteisen walked the group through the fort's ruins. From this vantage point, Washington had an excellent view of Charleston about two and a half miles to the northwest and Sullivan's Island about the same distance across the harbor to the east.[20]

The party then boarded their boat and crossed the harbor to Sullivan's Island. There was little to see of the remains of Fort Moultrie or the bridge to the mainland constructed by Christopher Gadsden in 1777. Any of the fort's palmetto wood that had not rotted away after the war had been carried off by scavengers. Nonetheless Moultrie amply compensated his audience for the dearth of ramparts and battlements. He was known to be an animated and entertaining conversationalist, and when he recounted South Carolina's valiant and victorious stand against the overwhelming might of Sir Peter Parker's British fleet on June 28, 1776, Washington listened intently. Charles Cotesworth Pinckney had only observed the battle from Fort Johnson, but he had commanded the fort during the 1780 siege and offered his own valuable insights. While on the island,

Washington, Moultrie, and the others were treated to a light lunch of wine, fruit, sweets, and cold cuts before they returned to town.[21]

Washington enjoyed, or perhaps endured, a continuous round of tours, banquets, concerts, receptions, and dinners, accompanied by what the *City Gazette* called on one occasion "a select party of respectable gentlemen." It stands to reason, then, that by the end of the week, Washington, Moultrie, and everyone in Charleston were exhausted by the seemingly endless festivities. But May 8 was the Sabbath, and the two namesake churches of the parishes of St. Philip and St. Michael invited the weary president to join them in worship. In typical Washington fashion, to avoid giving offense the president attended services at both churches, St. Philip's in the morning and St. Michael's in the afternoon.[22]

Moultrie and his family were communicants at St. Philip's, and he had served on St. Philip's vestry, but he had once been a pew holder at St. Michael's. On this particular Sunday, he attended only the morning service at St. Philip's. Although the inhabitants of Charleston were not necessarily strict adherents to the Sabbath as a day of devotion and rest, there were no banquets, receptions, or balls in honor of the president on that day.[23]

At the conclusion of the service at St. Michael's, the city wardens conducted the president to the home of General Moultrie. Washington was to be Moultrie's guest for a quiet private dinner. Moultrie's in-town residence at 60 Meeting Street was but a short southward stroll from St. Michael's and was not at all far from Judge Heyward's house on Church Street. The nearly three-quarters of an acre lot was surrounded by a wall of brick and stone. The main dwelling, "six rooms neatly finished, wainscoted, and papered," connected to a new brick addition of two large, elegant rooms. Typical of the residences of many of Moultrie's contemporaries, several outbuildings served the main house: a kitchen, a pantry, a wash house, a storehouse, stables, and a coach house. Tile shingles covered the roofs of the main house, addition, and outbuildings. Well-tended gardens made the property a lovely and genteel setting for entertaining an honored guest.[24]

Washington's cool and sometimes detached public demeanor contrasted sharply with Moultrie's affable and gregarious nature. They were, on the surface, polar opposites. Washington generally presented a reticent and dignified exterior that belied his underlying emotions. On the other hand, Moultrie was an open book who tended to wear his heart on his sleeve. But privately, when among friends and especially when relaxed by a few glasses of wine, Washington would drop the facade and enjoy the jokes, good humor, and hilarity of his companions. It has been said that if Washington "ever unbent anywhere [in Charleston], it was probably at that hospitable board" where the host, an acknowledged raconteur, was known to "set the table in a roar." It is fair to assume that the two gentlemen enjoyed a most agreeable evening, and from their ensuing correspondence, it is clear that Moultrie and Washington had indeed developed a comfortable friendship.[25]

As the evening wore on, the two old soldiers had much to discuss. The topics were likely wide ranging and far reaching, perhaps touching on the late war, their nation's young constitutional government, and Indian unrest on the frontier. They may have shared opinions about the evolving revolution in France and the effects that political situation might have on their nation and their Cincinnati brethren abroad. One historian speculated that the subject of horticulture occupied a significant portion of the dinner conversation. As planters, both men had a great interest in the topic, and as Moultrie showed Washington around his residence, there can be no doubt that the president took an interest in Moultrie's garden greenhouse and the fruit trees imported from the West Indies. Washington's pursuit of gardening is well documented: the plants he grew, his greenhouse constructed at Mount Vernon between 1784 and 1787, even his failed attempt to grow palmetto trees in his experimental garden.[26]

It was Moultrie who facilitated Washington's desire to obtain plants from South Carolina for his garden. Moultrie sent a shipment of plants to Mount Vernon in December 1791 so that they would arrive in time for spring. Winter ice prevented delivery to Mount Vernon by way of Baltimore, with the cargo arriving in Norfolk instead, a situation that caused Washington much anxiety for the plants' safety and viability. He was relieved when the eight boxes containing sweet shrub, Italian myrtle, opopanax, oleanders, and royal palmetto arrived from Norfolk in good condition. Moultrie assured Washington that all of the plants could withstand the Charleston winters except the opopanax, which would need the shelter of a greenhouse. Moultrie also sent his friend some seeds of the Indian creeper. Washington was most appreciative. "Were I not assured of the pleasure which you take in obliging me," he wrote to Moultrie with affection on March 14, 1792, "I should be at a loss how to express my acknowledgments for the kind attention which you have shewn to my wishes in sending these plants."[27]

On the morning of Monday, May 9, Washington departed Charleston for Savannah. Astride his white stallion, Prescott, he rode up King Street at six o'clock in the morning, accompanied by Moultrie and Sen. Pierce Butler. At the outskirts of town, the party was joined by "most of the principal Gentlemen of the city," including Governor Pinckney, Sen. Ralph Izard, Intendant Vanderhorst, the city wardens, the Cincinnati, and the militia. Appropriate formalities and remarks were exchanged, and the Charleston Artillery, drawn up some distance away, saluted the president with a fifteen-gun federal salute, after which the German Fusileers fired a volley of musketry in his honor. The assemblage proceeded northward up the peninsula for about nine miles to the bridge that now spanned the Ashley River. After crossing the river, the gentlemen breakfasted at a tavern on the south side of the river—the same tavern to where Henry Laurens and Moultrie delivered a Cherokee delegation for a conference with Lt. Gov. William Bull in 1760.[28]

It required four days for Washington's cavalcade to traverse the eighty or so lowcountry miles from Charleston to Purrysburg, fifteen miles north of Savannah. At Purrysburg the president was to rendezvous with the Georgia delegation that would escort him downriver to the Georgia seaport and former capital city. As they made their way toward the Georgia border, Moultrie surely gave Washington an account of the British pursuit of his small, ragtag Continental Army through this region during the spring of 1779. Just the rivers they crossed—the Edisto, the Ashepoo and Combahee, the Tullifiny and Coosawhatchie—gave the former commander of the Continental Army an appreciation of why military maneuvers in the Carolina lowcountry had been so logistically complicated.[29]

After covering twenty-eight miles on the first day, Washington and a "select party of particular friends," counting Moultrie and Pierce Butler, spent the night at Sandy Hill, the plantation of Washington's cousin William Washington. The next morning most of the cortege turned back for home, and now only Moultrie and Butler guided the caravan. Along the way they lodged at Duharra, the home of Mr. O'Brian Smith, a known Anti-Federalist and close associate of Cincinnati nemesis Aedanus Burke. Despite political differences Smith welcomed Washington, Moultrie, and Butler with the open hospitality befitting South Carolina lowcountry tradition.[30]

On Thursday, May 12, Moultrie relinquished his friend to the care of the waiting Georgians at Purrysburg. He knew he could not have left Washington in better hands, for among the prominent men from Savannah was his old comrade and friend Gen. Lachlan McIntosh. Butler accompanied the Georgians to Savannah, and thus Moultrie stood alone on the riverbank as Washington boarded the eight-oared barge that would carry him downriver.[31]

By all accounts Washington's 1791 southern tour was a resounding success. By the president's own calculations, he covered 1,887 miles by the time he returned to Philadelphia on July 6. But of all of the towns and cities that Washington visited on his southern tour, he was most impressed with Charleston. Nowhere else was he received more graciously and warmly, but perhaps his blossoming friendship with Moultrie colored his feelings about the South Carolina seaport. The extent of the amity that developed between him and Moultrie is evident in their exchange of correspondence after Washington returned to Philadelphia. Moultrie wrote him on July 10, 1791, congratulating the president on his safe homecoming and wishing him health, peace, and happiness. "And be assured, Sir," Moultrie added, "while I had the honor of being one of your family,* I have set it down in the catalog of my life among the very happy days which I have enjoyed."[32]

In his return letter dated August 9, Washington commented on the hospitality that he had enjoyed in South Carolina when he wrote, "My happiness has certainly been promoted by the excursion, and nowhere in a greater degree than while resident among my fellow-citizens of South Carolina. To their attentions (yours in particular) I shall always confess myself much obliged." Washington had given Moultrie an open invitation to visit him in Philadelphia, and expressing his affectionate regards, he stated that he looked forward to Moultrie's promised visit with sincere satisfaction. Neither Washington nor Moultrie could know that within a few years their friendship would be severely tested.[33]

---

* In the military context, the *family* consisted of Washington's headquarters staff. In the context of Moultrie's usage, *family* refers to a small, select group of friends and advisers, or employees in the case of William Jackson, who served the president during his South Carolina tour.

28.

Security Without and Within

In 1792 in the capital of Philadelphia, a search was begun to name a successor to Maj. Gen. Arthur St. Clair as the commander-in-chief of the United States army. Candidates for the post included generals Benjamin Lincoln, von Steuben, Lachlan McIntosh, Daniel Morgan, Anthony Wayne, Charles Cotesworth Pinckney, and surprisingly, William Moultrie. According to a memorandum from a March 9 meeting of President Washington's cabinet, the merits of the candidates were noted. Lincoln was judged to be "sober, honest brave and sensible, but infirm; past the vigor of life." Von Steuben received high praise for his discipline and expertise with tactics, but he was rejected as a foreigner. Pinckney was "of unquestionable bravery . . . a man of strict honor, erudition and good sense: and it is said has made Tactics a study," but he was relatively unknown in the northern part of the country.[1]

The memorandum acknowledged Moultrie's bravery and accommodating temper, and his experience fighting the Cherokees was viewed as a virtue. If selected Moultrie would have commanded the Legion of the United States, a force that combined the arms of cavalry, infantry, and artillery to operate against Native Americans in the Northwest Territory. But if Washington was the author of the memorandum, as his editors suggest, he must have compiled this list of generals prior to his 1791 southern tour. His comments ("What the resources or powers of [Moultrie's] mind are—how active he may be—and whether temperate or not, are points I cannot speak to with decision, because I have had little or no opportunities to form an opinion of him") certainly seem to predate his long visit with Moultrie in Charleston. After deliberating Washington gave the post to Anthony Wayne. General Wayne served with distinction until he died from complications of gout in 1796.[2]

In February 1791 Moultrie ran for a second term as governor of South Carolina. In a joint session of the Senate and the House, incumbent Charles Pinckney easily defeated him by a margin of 49 of the 125 votes cast. Moultrie ran again on December 4, 1792. This time he prevailed over John Ewing Colhoun and Arnoldus Vanderhorst by a narrow margin. A bicameral committee paid a formal call on the governor-elect to notify him of his election and inquire when he would attend the House to qualify himself as governor. Moultrie replied that he would appear at noon on the next day.[3]

Moultrie's investiture was very similar to the ceremony that inaugurated his first term. When he arrived at the State House at noon on December 5, an escort led him to a joint session in the House chamber for formal introduction as governor-elect by the Speaker of the House, who administered the oath of office. Camden District sheriff Wade Hampton ceremoniously proclaimed Moultrie to be "Governor and Commander-in-Chief in and over the State of South Carolina." The new governor, preceded by Hampton bearing the sword of the state and accompanied by the members of the Senate and House, made his way to the portico of the State House, where the sheriff presented him to the gathered crowd.[4]

The turbulent political environment within which Moultrie began his second term was a far cry from the relative calm that prevailed during his first. Almost immediately Governor Moultrie was forced to endure the embarrassment of the political downfall of his half-brother Alexander, who was South Carolina's attorney general. Alexander Moultrie was impeached by the House and convicted by the Senate of embezzling sixty-five thousand pounds of state funds to speculate in the South Carolina Yazoo Company. This company was involved in shady dealings to acquire and settle land belonging to Georgia, a scheme that would be a part of the Yazoo Land Scandal.[5]

When the facts came to light, Alexander Moultrie submitted his resignation to his brother the governor on December 18, 1792. During the course of the proceedings in the House of Representatives, the former attorney general admitted his wrongdoing, but he denied criminal intent. His friends in the House tried unsuccessfully to mitigate the consequences of his actions by proposing a motion to allow the accused to resolve the issue by surrendering his real and personal estate as security pending repayment of the debt. The Senate found the defendant guilty and disqualified him from holding any state office of public honor, trust, or profit for a period of seven years.[6]

Vacant South Carolina lands were initially opened to purchasers in 1784. The General Assembly discouraged land speculation by limiting the size of grants and requiring cultivation within two years. Despite these precautions land speculation became rampant. Moultrie was not complicit with his brother in the Yazoo Land Scandal, but he was not above a certain amount of speculation in land. He had already used the advantage of his position as commissioner to settle the boundary between South Carolina to acquire 10,500 acres in Craven County in 1772 and 1773, and 5,100 acres in Tryon County, North Carolina, in 1775. Before the war he accumulated an additional 4,200 acres mostly in the South Carolina backcountry. During the land grab that occurred after the war, he obtained another 3,700 acres in the Ninety-Six District. One can only wonder if his thoughts were on using these lands to settle his debts in 1785 when he pressed the General Assembly to enact debtor relief legislation.[7]

Moultrie was obliged to confront the abuses of large-scale land speculation when Secretary of State Peter Freneau asked him to sign several grants containing surveys for very large quantities of land. "As some of these Surveys are laid in parts of the State that are thickly inhabited, where I do [not] conceive that such large Bodies of Vacant Land [can be], I have declined the most of them," he informed the legislature on November 30, 1793. The plats in question were so poorly drawn that they bore little relation to the actual terrain. At stake were nearly two million acres in sixty-one plats surveyed for thirty men. To curb "this spirit of Land Jobbing [that was] Exceedingly Mischievous to the Good people of this state," the House and Senate halted the delivery of grants surveyed during the previous legislative session and ordered Freneau to publicize the names of those with pending grants exceeding two thousand acres to warn settlers who had prior claims to the land.[8]

The General Assembly subsequently passed an act in May 1794 to curb the land jobbing abuses and excessive surveys. The law closed the land office for four years, restricted the size of grants to five hundred acres for any one person during that interval, and put in place punitive legal remedies for excessive surveys, unlawful grants, and "iniquitous schemes" that posed a threatened poor, uninformed small landholders. In reference to excessively large grants that Moultrie did sign in 1793 (not the aforementioned surveys presented by Freneau), the legislature declared "that the Governor must have been deceived when he signed the same." Before leaving office in December 1794, however, Moultrie signed still more of these excessive land grants, some of them for friends and political allies, and all were clearly contrary to the spirit and meaning of the law. Upon discovery of Moultrie's indiscretions, the legislature called for a judicial review of these grants in circuit courts to be to determine their individual legitimacy and legality. This seems not to have occurred, and notwithstanding the General Assembly's criticism of his actions, there apparently were no repercussions for the former governor.[9]

If Moultrie vacillated on the issue of land grants, he had a strong opinion about those who speculated in land bounty grants given for military service. In 1788 the U.S. government belatedly rewarded its Continental soldiers with western land, and Moultrie's rank of major general entitled him to eleven hundred acres. Needing liquid assets, he assigned his bounty land warrant to Philadelphia merchant, broker, and land speculator David Cay, probably for far less than the land was really worth. This action was apparently born of necessity, and though quite common in occurrence, it did not sit well with Moultrie and his comrades in arms, many of whom were impoverished.[10]

Moultrie called a meeting of former Continental officers on the evening of Monday, January 7, 1793. Acting for themselves, the noncommissioned officers, and the private soldiers residing in South Carolina, they adopted a statement to Congress complaining of the wrongs they had suffered. Moultrie was the author of the memorial, in which he noted that at the close of the war the government lacked the resources to pay its soldiers. But now that the country was at peace and flourished under a respectable constitution, it was proper for Congress to redress the injustices. Moultrie emphasized to Congress that the losses and attendant poverty of the solders "have not proceeded from dissipated morals, nor from any culpability in themselves; they proceeded from the necessities which followed them in consequence of devoting their whole time to the service of their country."[11]

They had taken to the field as soldiers out of duty and love for their country and had expelled their enemies. They had "experienced in the arduous struggle, hunger, sickness, nakedness and penury. . . . Our families for a great portion of this time were neglected, our private property ruined." They had secured peace, established freedom in the land, and were, "from the assurances of congress, possessed with the pleasing hope of returning each to his own home, and being enabled by the justice of that congress to enjoy a competency. These hopes soon vanished like a dream." Instead they received commutation and pay certificates that carried no specific worth. Pressed by want and destitute of resources, many ruined, they were obliged to part with their hard earnings at a depreciated value.[12]

The South Carolina officers were late with their remonstrations. Committees from New Hampshire, Massachusetts, Pennsylvania, Delaware, and Georgia had registered protests during the latter part of 1792. It was all for naught. When Congress considered a measure to discriminate in favor of the original holders of Continental paper over speculators who had paid the original holders perhaps as little as twelve cents on the dollar, it lacked sufficient support to pass.[13]

During Moultrie's second term as governor, the security of South Carolina was a major concern. In his first message to the General Assembly on December 14, 1792, he expressed apprehension that an Indian war would soon break out, and for that reason Moultrie continued his predecessor's policy of providing arms and munitions for the backcountry militia. In the past the militia had been poorly organized, undersupplied, and poorly led, but even though the legislature had not enacted a militia law, the exigencies were forcing the state's militia to emerge gradually from its decrepit condition on its own. But it still had a ways to go.[14]

In a letter to George Washington penned in February 1793, Moultrie requested six brass three-pounders from the arsenal of the United States. To strengthen his case, he apprised the president that a "spirit of emulation seems to be taking place rapidly among the Militia of this state, by forming themselves into Volunteer companies under respectable officers, and in neat uniforms, several of which are Artillery." Washington was pleased at the progress being made, but he was unable to fulfill Moultrie's request for artillery.[15]

Acting on the belief that an Indian war was inevitable, in July 1793 Moultrie recommended Andrew Pickens to Washington to command an expedition of four or five thousand South Carolina, Georgia, and North Carolina militiamen against the Creeks. Only then, Moultrie opined, could a firm and lasting peace be established. Pickens agreed and also pushed for a military campaign. Many Georgians were spoiling for a fight with the Creeks, but President Washington understood that a Creek war could bring on a war with Spain, whose Florida territory "was in the neighborhood of the Creeks." Washington sanctioned only defensive action, giving Moultrie approval to send South Carolina militia across the state line into Georgia in the event of an invasion of a large force of hostile Indians. Fortunately a diplomatic solution was found, and an Indian war on the frontier was averted.[16]

The defense of the frontier did not draw attention from the tumultuous political developments in Europe. The French Revolution that began in 1789 would have dramatic implications for Moultrie's second governorship. The new French republic declared war on Great Britain in February 1793, and Moultrie rightly worried that the United States would be drawn into a European war as Great Britain, the Netherlands, Spain, and Portugal aligned against revolutionary France. To the South Carolina Senate and House, he later explained, "Not Knowing how this War might affect us, I thought it advisable in our Defenseless Situation, in order to place us on a respectable Footing to have the Command of the port of Charleston, and to secure us from Insult to cause a small but respectable Battery to be raised on the spot where Fort Johnson stood." The House considered worthy of their approbation Moultrie's initiative in erecting coastal defenses to counter any warring forces that might approach the South Carolina coast.[17]

Moultrie fully comprehended the consequences of allowing an enemy fleet to enter the harbor. He had learned that lesson in 1776 and again in 1780, and so fortifying the harbor became a major priority. He planned to erect batteries at Fort Johnson and Fort Moultrie and on the point of a marsh across from Fort Johnson called Shute's Folly. For instructions as to how he should conduct himself in case any of the warring powers appeared in Charleston Harbor, Moultrie queried Washington late in April 1793. "I have taken as my guide the Treaties which subsist between the Several powers and the United States; and as in some instances these will clash, I am to request your instructions." Washington's answer came in the form of a neutrality proclamation on April 22 specifying that the United States would "with sincerity and good faith adopt and pursue a conduct friendly and impartial toward the belligerent Powers." Washington warned the citizenry "carefully to avoid all acts and proceedings whatsoever, which may in any manner tend to contravene such disposition."[18]

Moultrie subsequently released the salient points of Washington's proclamation to the newspapers in the form of a proclamation of his own in which he enjoined the citizens of South Carolina to be vigilant in their compliance with the conditions of neutrality. At first blush it would appear that Moultrie was marching in step with Washington, but in fact he was in a predicament. French privateers had been operating out of Charleston with his knowledge, and he considered the Franco-American alliance formed in 1778 to remain in effect. The declaration of neutrality by the Washington administration forced Moultrie to bring South Carolina in line with national policy despite the fact that he was partial to the revolutionary French republic.[19]

A by-product of the French Revolution was a very bloody free black and slave revolt in the French colony of St. Domingue on the Caribbean island of Hispaniola in 1791. It was feared that the revolt would be the catalyst for a slave revolt in the southern states. The exodus of white refugees from St. Domingue to the United States had other consequences as well. Many of the French refugees had contracted yellow fever, a mosquito-borne illness hallmarked by fever, jaundice, and oftentimes, death.

When Moultrie learned that a "pestilential disease" was prevalent in the Caribbean islands, he ordered incoming ships from the West Indies into quarantine under the guns of Fort Johnson until the passengers and crew were examined by the port physician, his nephew Dr. James Moultrie. Crews and cargoes were subsequently allowed to land at the lazaretto, or quarantine station, on Sullivan's Island to wait out their period of isolation. This greatly alarmed those who had built houses on the island for the occupation of themselves and their families during the summertime to avoid the diseases that could become rampant during that time of year. Fortunately with these precautions a yellow fever epidemic was averted in Charleston.[20]

Philadelphia was not so fortunate. Infected refugees brought the causative virus, and mosquitoes vectored the disease to the city's population. Consequently during the unusually hot and dry summer of 1793, several thousand Philadelphians succumbed to yellow fever, then known as the "black vomit." The fear and dread that accompanied word of the catastrophe in the nation's capital prompted Moultrie to call for a day of fasting, humiliation, and prayer so that the citizens of Charleston "may with unified hearts and voices . . . offer up our joint supplications to the All Wise, Omnipotent and Merciful Ruler of the World, humbly beseeching Him to . . . remove from our fellow citizens, the calamities which attend them, and to implore Him to avert the like and all other evils from this our land."[21]

Like Moultrie during his first gubernatorial term, Gov. Charles Pinckney had been stymied by an inability to prod the legislature to improve the state's militia. Consequently Pinckney was unable to bring the South Carolina militia into compliance with the Uniform Militia Act of 1792, enacted by Congress to standardize structure, training, and equipage of the states' militias. In 1794, despite a declared neutrality, British interference with American merchantmen on the high seas threatened to pull the United States into the conflict on the side of the French. Frustrated by legislative inaction, Moultrie called the General Assembly into special session in April 1794 where he warned of "the necessity of expediting energetic Measures or otherwise our preparations may be of little avail." The two chambers of the General Assembly eventually worked out their differences and agreed to a militia bill.[22]

Moultrie was absent for the opening of the April special session owing to a severe attack of gout that delayed his departure from a stopover at North Hampton. Nevertheless he sent word via his secretary that President Washington had ordered him to fortify Charleston and Georgetown with batteries and redoubts. Congress would furnish seventy-two large-caliber cannon and eleven thousand dollars to complete the work. Moultrie was grateful for the guns, but he informed the legislature that the funding was inadequate. Since the coastal inlets and harbors could not be fortified in their entirety, he intended to construct galleys that could be rowed to whatever points they were most needed. The legislature concurred with his plan and pledged to cover the congressional shortfall.[23]

Moultrie had not yet reached Columbia from North Hampton when a band of Cherokee chiefs and warriors appeared in town. The legislators were at somewhat of a loss as to how to deal with them in his absence. When Moultrie arrived a day or two later, he found that the Indians were a delegation traveling to Philadelphia to negotiate a treaty of peace with Congress. The Cherokees had journeyed to Cambridge in the Ninety-Six District, arriving there on April 25 to confer with James Seagrove, the agent for the Southern District. But after several days of fruitless waiting for Seagrove, they trekked onward to Columbia. Moultrie explained to the legislature that the Cherokees had come to Charleston "in order that they might communicate their Intentions to the Governor of the State, and also solicit his Opinion with Regard to the manner which would be most advisable for them to adopt in proceeding to Philadelphia with the great-est Dispatch." Moultrie suggested that the Cherokees remain in Columbia until they heard from Seagrove, but they were unwilling to delay, so he advised them to travel onward to Charleston, whence they could obtain sea passage to their destination.[24]

The Cherokees agreed to Moultrie's plan, but they also "signified a Wish and Expectation that some pecuniary Supply would be furnished them for the purpose of defraying their travelling Expenses, and those of the Water passage." Moultrie understood that Indian affairs fell under the aegis of the federal gov-ernment. Nonetheless he informed the legislature that as "it would not be good policy in us to suffer them to leave this disatisfied [sic], I have promised them to procure their passage to Philadelphia, and would recommend it to your House to Vote them such a Supply of Money, as you may deem necessary for the pur-poses they have mentioned, and whatever it may be, I should apprehend it will be reimbursed to the State by Congress." The General Assembly concurred and provided the sum of $250.[25]

At the end of November 1794, Moultrie reported that the fortification of Charleston under his direction had sufficiently advanced. Money and laborers generously contributed by the citizenry had combined with "the Patriotic Exer-tions of the Mechanics . . . , who undertook the Erection and Completion of the Work," to finish "one respectable Battery mounting ten heavy Pieces of Can-non." The structure that faced eastward into the harbor from a site near the tip of the Charleston peninsula was given the name Fort Mechanic in honor of its builders. Fort Johnson was almost complete and boasted fourteen heavy cannon. Fort Moultrie was in a state of "forwardness," but workmen had not begun the battery on the marshy island Shute's Folly. As for the frontier posts, Moultrie questioned the need to maintain them in light of the fact that Secretary of War Henry Knox had recently sent an agent to live among the Cherokees.[26]

Arnoldus Vanderhorst superseded Moultrie as governor on December 17, 1794. Once he retired from public life, Moultrie assumed the attitude of a gentleman farmer, although he clearly depended upon income derived from agriculture. This was unfortunate. After the war Moultrie had become increasingly debt-ridden, his credit so poor at one point that he needed assistance from his fam-ily to remain solvent. To help him obtain a large loan in 1784, his stepdaugh-ter Elizabeth Lynch Harleston put up twenty of her slaves as security and later mortgaged several tracts of land. Now a series of bad crop years along with a postwar agricultural shift in South Carolina contributed to Moultrie's economic duress. The war ended the British bounty paid for indigo, and by 1798 indigo had yielded to cotton as South Carolina's main cash crop, an ascent aided by the invention of the cotton gin in 1793.[27]

Moultrie was not the first to plant long-staple cotton in South Carolina, but he was one of the first to attempt to cultivate it on a large scale by planting 150 acres at North Hampton in 1793. Regrettably the experiment was a dismal failure, a result of Moultrie's inexperience and unfamiliarity with the proper management of cotton cultivation combined with an unfavorable crop season and depleted soil. Consequently Moultrie lost a full year's income from that acreage.[28]

Moultrie's Kent plantation, forty-two miles north by northwest from Charleston, became his country seat. The seven-hundred acre tract obtained in 1783 by virtue of the confiscation act was bounded by Biggin Creek and the lands of Charles Cotesworth Pinckney and Edward Rutledge. Kent's rich, high ground abounded with hickory, and the soil was loose and gravelly, good for corn, indigo, and cotton. More than half of the acreage was a swamp filled with a mixture of cypress, ash, white oak, and tupelo. Coincidentally the Santee Canal ran through the swamp, and as a consequence the swamp could be flooded any time, even during the dry season. The canal was advantageous as a conduit to transport harvested timber to Charleston.[29]

Moultrie wrote more about Kent than North Hampton or any of his other properties because in his later years, he had fewer distractions and became more contemplative about his agrarian pursuits. He began to make observations in small ways, and only for his own satisfaction, recording when and how much he planted of certain seeds and roots, without any intended design, "but being in the country, and having little else to do (after reading part of the day) I did this in order to amuse myself; and every days observations brought on new Ideas 'til at length I employed a good deal of my time that way particularly on Sundays. I walk in my fields quite alone; and as there were no works carrying on left me intirely [sic] to myself, to contemplate and observe the progress of everything in the field which I did very attentively, and set down my observations on my return home." Unfortunately this man who had devoted the better part of his life to public service, whether military or civil, would not be able to maintain this idyllic existence.[30]

29.

The Governor and Citizen Genet

The effects of the French Revolution (1789–99) on American politics and foreign policy cannot be overstated. The 1789 formation of the National Assembly by the middle-class bourgeoisie, the storming of the Bastille in symbolic revolt against royal authority, and the subsequent adoption of the Declaration of the Rights of Man and of the Citizen preceded the imposition of constitutional government on the French king Louis XVI. The constitutional monarchy subsequently failed and devolved by stages into a regicidal republic that beheaded its king and queen and embarked on a war against the other monarchal powers of Europe in 1793. During a thirteen-month Reign of Terror beginning in September 1793, the ruling radical Jacobins led by Maximilien Robespierre violently purged France of political opposition by sending to the guillotine rival moderate Girondins and tens of thousands of other suspects from every social class.[1]

In parallel with the evolution of the French Revolution was the gradual emergence and divergence of two political parties in the United States. Not to be confused with the Federalists and Anti-Federalists of the constitutional debates, the two factions, the Federalists and the Democratic-Republicans (or just Republicans), were personified in George Washington's cabinet by Secretary of the Treasury Alexander Hamilton and Secretary of State Thomas Jefferson, respectively. The two parties differed philosophically on the size and role of government, fiscal policy, and foreign affairs, particularly concerning relations with Great Britain and France. The elitist Federalist Party favored a strong central government that would assume the states' Revolutionary War debt, a national bank, and improved relations with Britain. The more egalitarian Republicans were constitutional constructionists who opposed the fiscal policies of the Federalists and championed states' rights. The Republicans were closely aligned with the United States' wartime ally France.

The Federalists and Republicans viewed the early, constitutional stages of the French Revolution as a logical extension or consequence of their own successful revolution against Great Britain. By late 1793, however, the revolution had taken a decidedly ugly turn. The monarchs and many of the aristocrats and French members of the Society of the Cincinnati had been executed. Most of the rest had been imprisoned or had left the country. By 1794 Europe was at war, and blood ran in the streets of Paris. In America the rift between the Federalists and the Republicans widened into a chasm. The Republicans somewhat condoned the bloodshed in France as an inevitable price for French liberty and wanted the United States to support its ally. Conversely the Federalists found abhorrent the fratricidal Jacobin atrocities and were determined to keep their fledgling and militarily impotent nation out of the conflict—hence their support of Washington's April 1793 neutrality proclamation.[2]

William Moultrie, it would seem, fit the Federalist mold. As a first-term governor, he advocated the transference of certain state powers to the national government, and he voted in favor of South Carolina's ratification of the U.S. Constitution. He was a member of the typically Federalist, socially elite landowning and slaveholding planter aristocracy. The Society of the Cincinnati, in which he played such an important role, had an aristocratic French component, and many of his close Federalist friends were members. Many of his business associates in the Santee Canal Company were Federalists.

By the time of the French Revolution, however, Moultrie had adopted a decidedly Republican stance. If it was a love of France that caught him up in the spirit of the French Revolution and sent him down the path of republicanism, his sentiments reflected the feelings of many South Carolinians, particularly those from the backcountry, who still resented the dominance of the lowcountry elite and the influence of British merchants in Charleston. Perhaps the French Huguenots were a factor. Both of Moultrie's dearly departed wives and members of his extended family were of Huguenot extraction, as were quite a number of his lifelong lowcountry associations. The Huguenots were happy to see the decline of the French monarchy and the Roman Catholic Church, under whose rule they had suffered religious and political persecution before being driven from France.[3]

It is also possible that Moultrie's republicanism was not driven by pure political ideology. Perhaps he was dissatisfied with the status quo and disappointed over not receiving patronage from President Washington, who he venerated. Whatever the reason (or reasons), Moultrie embraced the French Revolution beyond the point that the radical French revolutionary government eventually disillusioned the Federalists and quite a few pro-French Republicans. As a consequence his support of the policies of the French diplomats sent to the United States would bring him into conflict with Washington's foreign policy.[4]

On September 3, 1792, the French consul to the Carolinas and Georgia arrived in Charleston. The thirty-year-old Michel-Ange-Bernard Mangourit found two factions in the city. The first comprised a large number of white aristocratic French refugees from St. Domingue who had been displaced by the slave revolt. These émigrés, most of whom were avowed bitter enemies of the new French Republic, had the support of the Federalists. In contradistinction were the prorevolutionary Republicans, the governor of South Carolina among them, from whom he received a warm welcome. Moultrie and Mangourit formed a warm friendship soon after Mangourit came to Charleston, and Moultrie would become France's most important friend in South Carolina.[5]

The extent to which the French Revolution and the representatives of the French Republic enthralled many South Carolinians was in evidence on January 11, 1793, when Mangourit hosted a grand *fête nationale* to celebrate the "auspicious events" that had taken place in France. In honor of the occasion, Governor Moultrie called out Charleston's military units to parade on Broad Street. At ten o'clock the consul, resplendent in full uniform and accompanied by a company of French naval officers and sailors, began a procession that wound through the streets of Charleston. Marching up Broad to the chant of "La Marseillaise," Charleston's corps of artillery, regiment of infantry, and troops of cavalry fell in and joined the march that turned down Church Street and proceeded to William's Coffee House on Tradd.[6]

It was at William's Coffee House that Moultrie and other local dignitaries joined the procession, with Moultrie taking his place at the front with Mangourit. When passing the French Huguenot Church, Mangourit halted the procession, and "as an expiation for the persecutions of Louis the XIVth against the church, he took off his hat, and saluted it with the national colors." A service at St. Philip's followed, and afterward the participants returned to William's Coffee House, where Mangourit presented Moultrie, Christopher Gadsden, other distinguished gentlemen of Charleston with laurel branches in recognition of their past military glory.[7]

At the elegant banquet given that evening, a total of nineteen toasts were offered and drunk "with loud and generous applause" as the celebrators reveled in radical revolution and republicanism. The fourth, fifth, and sixth toasts honored the United States, the U.S. Congress, and George Washington, respectively, but the rest espoused French revolutionary ideology in some form. Moultrie proposed the seventh toast to Jean Pethion, first president of the French Republic.[8]

Mangourit's sphere of influence extended from Charleston only as far as North Carolina and Georgia. On April 8, 1793, another Frenchman landed in Charleston aboard the thirty-two-gun frigate *L'Embuscade,* and his presence thrust Moultrie on to the national political stage. Edmond Charles Genet, addressed as Citizen Genet, was the recently appointed first minister plenipotentiary to the United States. Franco-American relations had suffered since the Franco-American alliance of 1778. Genet's mission was ostensibly to restore amicable fraternal, political, and commercial relations between the two countries, by treaty if possible. But he was also instructed to insist on the application of the articles of the 1778 alliance. If properly enforced, this would permit French privateers to bring their prizes into U.S. ports while preventing those of Great Britain from doing the same. In addition to commissioning privateers, Genet was expected to raise an army of Americans to liberate Florida and Louisiana from Spain.[9]

Republicans in Charleston received Genet with open arms, and he remained there for nearly two weeks before setting off for Philadelphia. During his time in Charleston, Genet met with Governor Moultrie and other leading Republicans of the city, and he reveled in an outpouring of sympathy for the French Republican cause. Between dinner engagements and social occasions, he commissioned four privateers and put Consul Mangourit in charge of plans for an invasion of Spanish Florida, all without the approval or foreknowledge of the U.S. government. Taking these actions, or any actions for that matter, was a serious diplomatic faux pas that would taint his relations with President Washington.[10]

A week after he made landfall, Genet reported to Minister of Foreign Affairs Pierre Lebrun that he and Moultrie had established a close and trusting relationship. The venerable veteran and sincere friend of the Revolution had been eager to assist him in every capacity. Moultrie helped the young French minister procure provisions for the French Republic's colonies and military, and he furnished information and letters of introduction to those who might also be interested in Genet's undertakings. What would turn out to be Moultrie's most controversial move was that he allowed Genet to recruit, arm, and operate French privateers out of Charleston. Moultrie shared the Republican rationale that the Franco-American alliance of 1778 was still in effect and that French vessels should be accorded the same privileges enjoyed by American ships in French ports during the Revolutionary War. It was also Genet's impression that Moultrie was going through the motions of fortifying Charleston Harbor to keep up appearances of neutrality while he (Moultrie) aided the French.[11]

Moultrie's actions outraged Charleston's pro-British Federalists, who tried to hamper Genet's recruiting of Americans. Announcements inserted in the newspaper by propagandists on both sides kept the public guessing about the facts. A piece appeared reporting that Moultrie had ordered "all houses of rendezvous for volunteers in the French service, to be immediately shut up, and that he [was] determined to exert his power and influence to prevent the fitting out of privateers in this port." According to the author, neither Genet nor the French

Republic wanted American citizens involved in such "unwarrantable business." This of course was patently false, and a Federalist writer quickly retorted that Moultrie had done nothing to stop French volunteers from organizing, nor had he exerted his power and influence to prevent the arming of French vessels. The Federalist writer summarily dismissed Genet's "pretended declarations" as groundless, based on his procurement of provisions for the French military prior to his departure for Philadelphia.[12]

The uproar over French privateers hinged on the fact that Charleston's economy was dependent to a large degree on credit and commerce with British merchants. Hence the success of French privateers would disrupt British shipping to South Carolina. Moultrie's opponents decided to call a meeting of concerned pro-British citizens for April 29 at the City Hall to demand that he take measures to prevent French privateers from fitting out in Charleston. A confrontation was avoided when the meeting was postponed. Local remonstrations aside, when French privateers began taking English prizes, British minister George Hammond vigorously protested through official channels, prompting the president to request that Secretary of War Henry Knox inquire into Moultrie's conduct.[13]

On the morning of April 18, 1793, Genet set off for Philadelphia. Moultrie escorted the young diplomat out of town, and before they parted company, the governor provided Genet with a letter of introduction to President Washington. The letter was more of an expression of Moultrie's esteem for Washington than a recommendation of Genet. While Genet was traveling the post roads between Charleston and Philadelphia, Washington and his cabinet were grappling with the validity of the Franco-American alliance in the context of the overthrow of the French monarchy and whether or not Washington should receive Genet as a fully credentialed minister from France.[14]

Federalists Alexander Hamilton and Henry Knox maintained that the alliance of 1778 had been made with (the recently decapitated) Louis XVI and was now void; Genet should not be received. Republican Thomas Jefferson argued that the alliance had been made between nations, not individuals, and that the treaty remained in force. By the time Genet arrived on May 16, Washington had proclaimed neutrality, but he accepted Jefferson's interpretation of the Franco-American alliance and reluctantly received Genet.[15]

In Philadelphia Genet attempted to rationalize what he had done while in Charleston. Relating his version of events in Charleston to Jefferson, Genet claimed that he had reminded Moultrie that "liberty consisted in doing what the laws did not prohibit." Genet said that Moultrie knew of no law contrary to arming and outfitting privateers in Charleston Harbor, but also that he "begged that whatever was to be done, might be done without consulting him, that he must know nothing of it &c." Genet was prone to exaggeration, but if he was correct, then Moultrie must have thought that the maintenance of plausible

deniability would help safeguard American neutrality or perhaps his own culpability. What was said and done in secret eventually came to light, and it became
common knowledge that the South Carolina governor had condoned French
privateering.[16]

Moultrie was excoriated in the Federalist press for having allowed French
privateers to sail from Charleston after customs officials refused to grant them
clearance to depart, and rumors eventually began to circulate in the press that
he would face impeachment for his actions. A Republican who wrote in Moultrie's defense tried to explain the behavior of "a man who has grown grey in one
uninterrupted honorable pursuit, by devoting his services to the establishment
of liberty, order and good government in his country." Moultrie's detractors, the
writer maintained, had been guilty of sophistry, rank aristocracy, party politics,
and gross misrepresentation. He went a step further to excuse Moultrie's allowing
the French privateers to embark without clearance from the port collector, using
a technicality as his reason to explain that "in the collector's office, all vessels
must clear out for a certain place, before a permit is granted; and as a privateer
may not always choose to inform a collector of his destination, his only alternative is to get a pass from the executive to clear the harbor."[17]

It was suspected that when Moultrie issued a quarantine proclamation in
August 1793 to prevent yellow fever from entering the state, he was really acting
to impede British shipping in Charleston Harbor. Moultrie's favoritism toward
the French against the British was patently clear to Washington's cabinet, a fact
Jefferson acknowledged in his notes about French privateering—that the South
Carolina governor was "winking at it." But Washington's neutrality proclamation
combined with a strong letter from Secretary of War Knox obliged Moultrie to
end his open support of French privateering. Not only was he to withdraw his
assistance of the French, but he was also to use the South Carolina militia to
enforce federal policy, interdicting the privateers when warranted, and to notify
Washington for instructions concerning the disposition of any detained French
vessels. These were the real circumstances under which Moultrie issued his neutrality proclamation on June 7. No matter how much he disagreed with the spirit
of the policy, he complied with Washington's directives.[18]

The enthusiastic crowds that greeted Citizen Genet at the stops along his
route to Philadelphia contrasted sharply with his cool reception by President
Washington on May 16. Over the next several months, Genet's defiant and in-
temperate behavior toward Washington, his unwavering persistence in commissioning, arming, and operating French privateers out of American ports contrary
to Washington's orders, and his ongoing plans to invade Louisiana and Florida
further alienated him from the executive branch, even Jefferson. Genet gravely
misunderstood the American form of constitutional government by thinking
that the president was answerable to Congress and that Congress was directly

answerable to the people. He threatened to circumvent presidential authority by appealing directly to the people of the United States to rally public opinion in support of his mission. With this he went too far. In August an angry and exasperated Washington requested that the French Republic recall their minister.[19]

Notwithstanding his support of the French and his personal regard for Genet, the news of the young French minister's indiscretions appalled Moultrie. "Through the medium of the northern newspapers," he privately wrote to Genet on September 5, "we in this state have been informed, that a dispute had taken place between the President of the United States and yourself . . . and that upon your differing therein, you said, with a degree of warmth, that you would appeal to the people. Viewing it here represented, many real friends to the republic of France have taken great offense, as it conveys insult to a character highly respected by his country, independent of the station which he fills." Moultrie asked Genet to provide him with a detailed account of the dispute, giving the young diplomat an opportunity to give his side of the story while admonishing his friend that "opinions lead people more often astray for want of knowledge of the particulars."[20]

Moultrie did not expect Genet to publish his letter, along with a reply, in the newspapers. Nor did he foresee that Genet would use these letters as a springboard to mount a defense. This is exactly what he did, denying all allegations against himself—accusations that he attributed to a dark and deep intrigue. He stated emphatically that he would not condescend to the level of men he despised to prove the absurdity of their charges. He maintained that the representative of the great and good French people should not conduct himself that way. This was an interesting proposition considering that he had behaved rather badly since he arrived in Philadelphia. Still failing to comprehend the workings of the U.S. form of republican government—that the president was the sole executor of the law and was not subservient to Congress—Genet proposed rather disingenuously that instead of circumventing the president, he wished to make his appeal to Congress using the president as his medium. Washington, of course, would have none of this tack, nor would Jefferson, who like Washington was by now entirely vexed by Genet's intransigent behavior.[21]

The appearance of Moultrie's letter in the press provoked public commentary by a pseudonymous Federalist. "Americanus" laboriously lambasted Moultrie and questioned his motives for writing to Genet. Criticizing Moultrie for meddling in foreign affairs, he posed a series of rhetorical questions designed to cast Moultrie in a most unfavorable light. And he accused the governor of giving the French minister an opportunity to "vent that spleen against the public officers of government, which has so long been confined, and now bursts forth, impatient of longer restraint"?[22]

Failing to discern Moultrie's intentions, Americanus dismissed him by stating "that the mountain has been in labor and brought forth a mouse!" Americanus judged Moultrie's conduct to be both improper and indiscreet, and he proposed that Moultrie, "by his future conduct, endeavor to make amends to a nation that has already felt the ill consequences of his imprudence." He could best accomplish this by minding his own business "and by leaving to others the direction of matters which do not need his extraordinary interposition."[23]

A Republican correspondent writing to the *City Gazette* under the name "A Carolinian" countered Americanus point by point and insisted that the pseudonymous attack was unjust since Moultrie had written to Genet as a private citizen. "No man," he said, "by being a public officer, becomes thereby divested of his right, in common with the rest of his fellow-citizens, of enquiring into, and being interested in whatever concerns the public welfare of the community of which he is a member." Still another writer calling himself "Bob Short" offered that "the criminality which Mr. Moultrie has incurred by entering blindfolded into a correspondence with Mr. Genet . . . was not an unpardonable sin."[24]

Taking exception to the old proverbial allusion employed by Americanus, Bob Short carried the argument to a level that would no doubt have resulted in a meeting on the bloody field of honor if his identity were made known, remarking, "'That the mountain has been in labor and brought forth a mouse!' says Americanus; which is more than his mother could say, poor woman, when she brought him forth!" Moultrie's supporters were many and vocal. The distinctly Republican Palmetto Society celebrated the American victory of June 28, 1776, in 1794 by toasting Governor Moultrie with the wish that any attempt to asperse his character would be "sir peter parkered."[25]

The polarization of Charleston during the French Revolution led to the formation of two opposing political societies. With the help of their supporters, the Domingan refugees, or colonial aristocrats as these émigrés were called, formed the French Patriotic Society to oppose the policies of the Republican French revolutionary government. Mangourit, in turn, fostered the formation of the Republican Society. The membership roll of the Republican Society included planters, lawyers, merchants, and artisans—a cross-section of Charleston's inhabitants. Many of the Republican Society's members would become intimately involved in Genet and Mangourit's schemes to invade Spanish-held Louisiana and East Florida. Moultrie was not a member of this society, although quite a few of its members were Cincinnati men, including his son, William Jr. The president of the Republican Society was Stephen Drayton, who had served Moultrie as secretary during his first term as governor, secretary of the Santee Canal Company, and secretary of the Society of the Cincinnati. William Tate was the society's secretary, and former attorney general Alexander Moultrie was a member.[26]

For all of the partisan rhetoric, the Society of the Cincinnati managed to remain above the political and ideological fray. For the 1793 observance of the Fourth of July, the Cincinnati assembled at General Moultrie's house at ten o'clock in the morning for a procession to Harris's hotel on East Bay Street, where they were joined by the American Revolution Society. The men proceeded onward to St. Philip's for prayers and anthems, followed by an oration delivered by Drayton. Afterward the Cincinnati returned to Harris's hotel for a meeting during which Federalist and Republican members reelected Moultrie as president of the South Carolina Cincinnati.[27]

Moultrie never retracted his support of Genet. According to Mangourit, who arranged to have Genet's translated correspondence published in the *City Gazette* in November 1793, Moultrie had been enchanted by the boldness and dignity of Genet's letters. Lamenting Genet's recall, Moultrie blamed the French minister's failure on "our infant government, quite unaccustomed with Europe politics, having no other idea than plain honest republican principles." Moultrie believed that the United States "were sliding fast in the vortex of British influence. Their trade, their gold and mercantile interest would have soon swallowed us up." In his mind Genet's best intentions in trying to cement the two republics had been "construed into faction, and into a design of drawing us into a war."[28]

30.

"Brother love to the brave Republicans"

While Moultrie's conduct was bandied in the press, a crisis developed in Charleston. One by-product of the French Revolution was the aforementioned free black and slave revolt. The inhabitants of South Carolina were acutely aware of the numerous atrocities committed against white slave owners in St. Domingue by an army of rebellious slaves after the sacking of Cap-Français in July 1793. Now they were anxious about an insurrection at home. Someone overheard slaves on Blake's Wharf saying "there are not many soldiers[,] we need not be afraid of them," and indeed Moultrie had received credible outside intelligence of a slave insurrection fomenting in South Carolina. In August 1793 he received a packet from Virginia and a chilling letter from a black in Charleston informing him that his state could be on the threshold of a massive slave uprising.[1]

The packet sent by Lt. Gov. James Wood of Virginia contained three letters of importance. One letter, discovered by pure serendipity in the streets of Norfolk, was a conspiratorial missive to the "Secret Keeper" in Norfolk from the "Secret Keeper" in Richmond. The Secret Keeper in Richmond claimed knowledge of six thousand blacks in Charleston with access to arms and powder. In another letter a Norfolk militia commander estimated that more than two hundred black people brought by French refugees from Cap-Français would be ready to join the scheme proposed by the Secret Keeper in Richmond.[2]

In the third letter a gentleman from Virginia warned Charleston's intendant, Arnoldus Vanderhorst, that six thousand black people in South Carolina were "determined on the 15th of October next in concert with others of the Different

States to massacre the Inhabitants without discrimination." To draw attention from their bloody work, they would set fires to houses as a diversion while they carried out their murderous scheme. It was rumored that the black people of Cap-Français had gained their liberty in this way.[3]

Equally disconcerting was an enigmatic letter that Moultrie received on the morning of October 10, 1793, from "A Black" who warned of intrigue in Charleston. "Altho I am one of those too unpopular characters here, a free black," the letter's author prefaced, "yet tis my love to a people among whom I have been all my life, would urge me to tell you personally what I do in this way [clandestinely by letter]." The informant was being watched, and he feared for his life if he was discovered speaking directly to the governor. He advised Moultrie to "be on your guard against certain strangers, don't let your attention be directed to Frenchmen alone, . . . we also have enemies to the northward . . . keep up the military duty till after the 10th February next at least—don't be lulled by the seeming humility of those about you." These reports steeled Moultrie's resolve to prevent an uprising if he could and to suppress a revolt if it happened. He placed the backcountry districts on alert and ordered the militia to keep up patrols and to mount extra guards.[4]

Moultrie's precautions did not allay apprehensions in Charleston, whose populace had become increasingly alarmed over accounts of black depredations in St. Domingue. As the date for the rumored revolt drew near, their fear was exacerbated by a rising number of acts of murder and arson in the city for which blacks were suspected of committing. Right or wrong, it was the free blacks that suffered the consequences of the escalating paranoia.[5]

Acting under pressure from a citizens' committee of Domingans, English merchants, and Federalists who wanted, among other demands, to have free blacks expelled from the state, Moultrie issued a proclamation on October 15, 1793, the day the revolt was rumored to begin. Among the free black people (some racially mixed) lately arrived from St. Domingue, he declared, there were purportedly many characters who were dangerous to the welfare and peace of the state. He therefore ordered all people of color and free blacks who had arrived from St. Domingue or elsewhere during the preceding twelve months to leave South Carolina voluntarily within ten days time. Those who disobeyed this order would be subject to close confinement while they awaited deportation.[6]

Moultrie found himself in the midst of another political quagmire when the schooner *Maria* crossed the bar into Charleston from St. Domingue. Constrained from docking by the governor's quarantine proclamation, the ship anchored under the guns of Fort Johnson; supplies could be delivered to the ship, but disembarkation and intercourse between ship and city was prohibited. It was acknowledged that French soldiers and civilians from Cap-Français were aboard the *Maria,* but the exact circumstances that brought the ship from St. Domingue and the intentions of the passengers upon landing in Charleston were not known, and the city was awash with rumors. Mangourit at first suspected that those aboard the *Maria* were counterrevolutionaries, but he was wrong. The Domingan émigrés believed that slave agitators were aboard or that the French soldiers had come to arrest and deport them to France.[7]

At this point Moultrie became embroiled in a plot to discredit Mangourit by implicating the consul in the purported slave revolt conspiracy. A group of émigrés brought Moultrie a packet of incriminating documents—copies of correspondence proving that Mangourit was complicit with passengers on board the *Maria* as instigators of slave insurrection. Calling on the consul at his quarters, an angry governor demanded the truth from Mangourit and insisted on seeing the original letters. Mangourit had always referred to Moultrie as his "venerable friend," but now that Moultrie was questioning his culpability, the consul was livid at the "weakness of the old man." Mangourit was on the defensive, but he wisely held his peace. The friendship and cooperation of the governor was vital to the success of certain plans that he and Genet had devised to invade Spanish-held territories in North America.[8]

To prove his innocence, Mangourit suggested that Moultrie examine the original correspondence, and within a few days Lt. Col. G. Josnez, ranking French army officer on the *Maria,* presented the letters to Moultrie at his residence. Moultrie was careful to exercise due diligence—he had already endured criticism for his pro-French stance. Now he was caught between the French consul on one hand and the Domingan émigrés and the Federalists and on the other. The consul's adversaries would like nothing better than to alienate Mangourit from his Republican support. Therefore even though Josnez maintained that he had no more correspondence for Mangourit, the governor insisted on a search of Josnez's personal belongings by members of his staff.[9]

The search turned up nothing, and to make amends to Mangourit and Josnez for doubting their word, Moultrie had them join him for dinner, after which the trio raised their glasses in toasts to the French Republic. Moultrie treated Josnez with his usual relaxed conviviality and even waxed maudlin before sending the colonel back to his quarantine camp on Sullivan's Island.[10]

Mangourit was exonerated and the St. Domingan refugees on board the *Maria* absolved of collusion, but it was left to Moultrie to convince the citizens' committee that he had matters under control. A deputation arrived on Moultrie's doorstep while he met with Mangourit and Josnez to propose the organization of Domingan émigrés into a counterrevolutionary military battalion to counter any landing of the shipboard French soldiers. Moultrie had just demonstrated that his friendship with Mangourit, and his pro-French sympathies, did not interfere with his obligation to ensure public safety. Stretching the truth almost to the breaking point, Moultrie convinced the deputation that the author of the letter signed "A Black" purported that the French soldiers aboard the *Maria* had come to help put down the rumored slave revolt. This, Moultrie said, proved that the *Maria's* passengers were not involved in a conspiracy. Moultrie accomplished this feat of deception without actually allowing the deputation to see the letter. Mangourit, who overheard the exchange, was surprised and impressed by the governor's diplomatic dexterity.[11]

By this time Moultrie was clearly annoyed by the *Maria* affair, and he flatly refused the request of the émigrés to form a military unit. Any military action required to keep the peace would be managed by the Charleston militia. It was also the intent of the citizens' committee to prevent the French soldiers from coming ashore and to force the *Maria* to leave Charleston, and in this the deputation got its way. As Josnez was taking his leave of Moultrie, the governor recommended that rather than endure the inhospitable quarantine conditions on Sullivan's Island—brackish water, lack of provisions, and rampant disease—it would perhaps be best if the *Maria* left Charleston. Josnez heeded Moultrie's advice, and the ship soon hoisted sail for a friendlier harbor.[12]

Was the slave insurrection plot real, or was it a conspiracy? The preponderance of the evidence points to a conspiracy. That a secret revolt involving a large numbers of insurgents could be coordinated across several states is doubtful. But a scheme hatched by Domingan refugees and Federalists, acting separately or together to cast the French consul Mangourit as a party to a slave uprising, would certainly drive a wedge between Moultrie and the officials of the French Republic and dampen the ardor of South Carolinians who supported the French Revolution.

Thomas Jefferson also received a report that slave insurrection was being imported to Charleston as part of a radical French plan, "the first branch of which has been carried into execution at St. Domingo." When he relayed the information to Moultrie, he made it clear that he doubted the reliability of the information and the informant. Moultrie prudently treated the threat as credible—to do otherwise was just too risky. Even if there was a question of the veracity of reports that reached Moultrie in 1793, public safety demanded that he take the matter seriously until the threat had been resolved one way or another. The prevention of a slave revolt was the one issue on which Federalists and Republicans agreed.[13]

From the moment Genet came ashore in Charleston, he meant to carry out his instructions to export republican revolution into Spanish-held territories. Mangourit worked quietly but tirelessly in Charleston to organize expeditions to accomplish this part of the Genet mission. The consul sought Moultrie's assistance early on, and he convinced the governor that a successful conquest of Spanish territories would benefit both nations. The liberation of Florida and Louisiana would weaken Frances's enemy Spain, he argued. The United States would gain western territory, population, increased security from Indian attack, and freedom of navigation. Mangourit communicated his dialogues with Moultrie to Genet, reporting that Moultrie was so wholeheartedly in favor of the idea that he was working on a plan of his own.[14]

Moultrie proposed sending French merchants as envoys to the Indian tribes to encourage their old allies, by bribe if necessary, to fight against the Spanish. This idea was not unprecedented. European powers had used the indigenous people of North America to make war against each other for as long as whites had contended for the continent. Mangourit did not favor the plan at all. "Ce projet est petit Impraticable dangereux," the consul informed Genet. He knew of no traders that would be willing to go among the Creeks, Choctaws, and Chickasaws for such a purpose. If French traders incited the Indians to commit hostile acts—"to scalp a few heads and steal horses," Mangourit said—it would alert the Spanish to strengthen their borders in preparation for an attack.[15]

The plan might indeed benefit Georgians, who were always looking for an excuse to mount an Indian campaign, but it was of no use to France. In his final analysis, Mangourit had no doubt of Moultrie's valor, but he questioned his venerable friend's strategic and tactical abilities. As Mangourit's plans evolved, he walked a fine line with the governor, careful to maintain Moultrie's interest in Louisiana and the possibility of acquiring western acreage. But Moultrie was a high-profile figure, and public knowledge of his involvement could have disastrous consequences. Hence Mangourit became very circumspect, telling Moultrie only what little was necessary, particularly concerning the Florida invasion.[16]

Heedless of violating U.S. neutrality, in 1794 Genet and Mangourit developed and put in motion ambitious plans to invade Louisiana, West Florida, and East Florida. William Tate received a colonel's commission and command of the Revolutionary Legion of America that he raised in the South Carolina backcountry. His second-in-command was Stephen Drayton, president of the Republican Society. The South Carolina contingent, joined by men recruited in Georgia, would rendezvous in Kentucky with George Rogers Clark and his Independent and Revolutionary Legion of the Mississippi. The combined force would descend the Mississippi River and attack New Orleans. In conjunction with the campaign into Louisiana, Col. Samuel Hammond would advance from Georgia with his Revolutionary Legion of the Floridas to take St. Augustine. Either of the two expeditions, if successful, would send detachments against West Florida.[17]

Genet and Mangourit had initially planned for Tate's legion to be transported by a French naval squadron to New Orleans for the attack. Genet thus ordered Tate to have the recruits travel to Beaufort or Port Royal. "I conferred with the governor [Moultrie]," Mangourit informed French minister of foreign affairs François Deforgues. "We agreed that the corps would march through in inconspicuous groups as far as Beaufort and that there as in all places in the United States where one finds scarcely one person on a square league, it would be supposed [that they were] arriving there either out of curiosity or to exchange supplies of the country for our money." When French naval support for the mission evaporated, the plan was abandoned for the overland route.[18]

Moultrie was Mangourit and Genet's connection to Drayton and Tate. Both men were former Continental officers and members of the South Carolina Society of the Cincinnati. Moultrie and Drayton had a longstanding and close relationship. Moultrie was so impressed by Tate's military ability that he later endorsed Tate to French Republic's Council of Safety for service in Europe as an American worthy of trust and confidence. His letter recommending Tate, full of his effusive wishes of "health and brother love to the Brave Republicans of the Council of Safety," demonstrated the extent to which Moultrie had embraced republican ideology. He closed the letter, "Citizens believe me to love all Republicans."[19]

The invasions depended on money, French naval support, and an element of secrecy for success. For Genet and Mangourit, all three were lacking. The French diplomats were confident that by having ordered officers to recruit outside of the United States, they could avert charges of violating U.S. neutrality. But when word leaked that they were quietly organizing armed troops within the borders of the state, the South Carolina House of Representatives ordered an investigation. A thorough inquiry revealed that a number of the gentlemen of the state had accepted military commissions from Genet.[20]

Prominent among the identified South Carolinians were Drayton and Tate. Both houses of the Federalist-dominated General Assembly agreed that they were guilty of high crimes and misdemeanors for contravening the neutrality policy of the United States and referred them to Attorney General John Julius Pringle for prosecution. Drayton was subsequently indicted in federal court for his actions, but the case was dropped when government witnesses failed to appear to testify against him. Thankfully for Moultrie, his involvement went unnoticed, although his pro-French sympathies and ties to Drayton and Tate were no secret.[21]

The report of the House investigatory committee was scathing in its condemnation of Genet and Mangourit, calling Genet's plot "a daring and dangerous attempt by a Foreign Minister to intermeddle in the Affairs of the United States, to usurp the powers of Government, and to levy Troops in the Bosom of the Union . . . contrary to the express sense of the Government of the United States. The direct tendency of these measures of the Foreign Minister, is to disturb the internal tranquility of the United States, and to involve them in hostilities with nations with whom they are now at peace, which sound policy requires should be preserved."[22]

Moreover the committee suggested that the governor issue a proclamation forbidding the enrolling of citizens of the state into a military organization and prohibiting the citizens from enlisting in a military organization for any purposes not sanctioned by the United States or the state of South Carolina. All unlawful assemblages of troops unauthorized by the government should be forbidden. The committee recommended that the governor "exert the whole public Force to the utmost extent, if necessary, to ensure obedience to his proclamation."[23]

In a message to the governor that was laced with sarcasm intended to remind Moultrie of his place, the House set forth its stern expectation. "It is to You, Sir, as the Chief Magistrate of the State, who have been chosen to watch over her Honor, her Tranquility, and her Interest, that We cheerfully commit the faithful Execution of the Resolutions; and in a concern of such infinite Importance, We trust that neither Time or Opportunity will be lost in carrying them into the fullest effect." Moultrie had no choice but to comply, and two days later he issued a proclamation, drawing the text almost verbatim from the report of the House investigative committee. And on the recommendation of the General Assembly, he sent to President Washington in Philadelphia the resolves of the legislature and copies of the affidavits submitted as evidence against those found to have been organizing men for French service. To avoid retribution Moultrie requested that that the names of witnesses be kept secret.[24]

It was not Moultrie's finest hour as governor, but at least the full extent of his collaboration had not come to light. He avoided the type of stinging criticism in the press that had followed the publication of his letter to Genet, but more important, he avoided possible impeachment. Despite his chastisement Moultrie continued to work behind the scenes to assist Mangourit, who does not seem to have given up the idea of attacking Spanish territories. On January 14, 1794, just a month after his proclamation, Moultrie paid a visit to the consul. He scolded Mangourit (and Genet in absentia) for not having money to pay those who had accepted French commissions. Speaking on behalf of several officers who formerly were generals in the American army, Moultrie informed Mangourit that they were dissatisfied with their commissions as mere lieutenant colonels. Once the conquest was over, Mangourit promised, the officers would receive honors in line with their military talents.[25]

Mangourit pursued his plans to invade the Spanish territories until the new minister, Jean Fauchet, canceled the expeditions in March 1794. His successor arrived in Charleston a month later, prompting Mangourit's return to France. In a parting letter to the former consul, Moultrie praised the upright character of his sincere friend, who he characterized as a zealous and patriotic defender of the rights of his republic who had suffered criticism and calumny at the hands of malicious persons who hated the two republics.[26]

Genet and Mangourit were out of the picture and French intrigues on the North American continent ceased, but the war in Europe between France and Great Britain and her European allies waged on. Desiring to maintain the fragile neutrality, President Washington sent John Jay to London to negotiate a treaty that would improve diplomatic and trade relations between the United States and Great Britain. Lauded by the Federalists as a reasonable compromise and denounced by the Republicans who argued that the 1778 alliance with France was still in effect, the Jay Treaty was ratified by a two-thirds vote of the Senate in 1796. This outraged the French, who vehemently protested that the treaty was unfair to France and flagrantly pro-British in the context of American neutrality.

Federalist candidate John Adams narrowly defeated Thomas Jefferson in the course of the second U.S. presidential election held in 1796. Jefferson practically swept the South and received all of South Carolina's electoral votes for president, but the election served as a veritable referendum on the French Revolution and an apparent repudiation of Republican politics. There were transatlantic repercussions as well. An angry French government suspended diplomatic relations with the United States and instructed the French navy to harass American shipping.

Moultrie's friend Charles Cotesworth Pinckney joined John Marshall and Elbridge Gerry as part of an American commission sent to negotiate with the French. Pinckney had been a good choice as minister to France. He was a veteran Revolutionary officer, and though he was politically aligned with the Federalists (he preferred not to be associated with either party), he was sympathetic to the French and spoke their language fluently. But when Pinckney had arrived in Paris in December 1793, he was most inhospitably received. Not only did the French Executive Directory refuse to accept his credentials as minister, but in retaliation for perceived grievances, the Directory threatened Pinckney with imprisonment and expelled him from the country.[27]

The growing rift between the United States and France turned into a frank rupture in October 1797 when French ministers refused to receive or negotiate with the U.S. delegation without payment of bribes. Rejecting the demand, Pinckney was adamant: "The answer is no! No, not a sixpence!," a response which was popularized by the newspapers as "Millions for defense, but not one cent for tribute!" The three French agents who suggested the bribes were referred to in dispatches as X, Y, and Z, hence the name of the incident became the XYZ Affair. The episode resulted in a severe anti-French backlash that further strengthened the Federalists to the detriment of the Republican Party, which was determined to support France to the bitter end. Neither Federalists nor Republicans, however, wanted what seemed to be an unavoidable military conflict with France. President Adams and Congress began to prepare the country for war.

Nationalism and patriotism now trumped Moultrie's love for France. His friend Pinckney had suffered, and his country was offended by French arrogance and aggression. Using the presidency of the South Carolina Society of the Cincinnati as his bully pulpit, Moultrie praised Adams's temperance and conciliatory stance adopted during negotiations with France but stated for the record that the men who formed the front ranks in their country's establishment of independence could not possibly be expected to be lukewarm when that liberty was in jeopardy.[28]

It was true that Moultrie felt a poignant sense of anguish that offensive actions emanated from a quarter from which Americans expected acts of friendship, but if it came to war with their former ally, the Cincinnati stood ready to offer their service and experience: "We have maturely weighed in the balance *tribute* and *dependence,* against *war* (with which in its most calamitous shape we are not unacquainted) and we have no hesitation in declaring . . . that we are prepared to support the Government of our choice, and to repel the unjust aggressions of *France* at every hazard."[29]

France initiated an undeclared war against American shipping, preying on hundreds of unarmed merchantmen in the Caribbean and along the southern coast, effectively nullifying the Franco-American alliance established in 1778. The so-called Quasi-war, also known as the Franco-American War, began when Congress rescinded U.S. treaties with France on July 7, 1798. One positive consequence of the war was the rebirth of the United States Navy, which though small in size, enjoyed good success against marauding French privateers. Most of the hostile actions between the belligerents were fought at sea, one notable exception being the landing of a contingent of marines and sailors from the *USS Constitution* that captured a French privateer and a Spanish fort in the harbor of Puerto Plata on St. Domingue in May 1800.

31.

The Lion in Winter

The end of William Moultrie's second term as governor signaled his retirement from public life. Leisure and ease was not to be his lot—rather sorrow and financial difficulty. In December 1796 his family was again reduced when Moultrie's only son, William, died at his Windsor Hill plantation at the age of forty-four. The general had outlived two wives and both of his children. His immediate family now consisted of a daughter-in-law, also named Hannah, his grandchildren and their families, and his half-brother Alexander's family. The untimely loss of his only son and namesake was devastating, as father and son had always been very close.[1]

During 1796, in his sixty-sixth year, Moultrie began his memoirs. His stated motivation was a dissatisfaction with what had thus far been published on the subject of the Revolutionary War. He did not refer to specific titles, but several treatises on the subject had originated in England. Perhaps he wanted an American point of view, particularly respecting the southern campaigns, for he titled his work *Memoirs of the American Revolution, So Far as It Related to the States of North and South-Carolina and Georgia.* Moultrie felt an obligation to preserve for posterity the particulars of this great event. Hence he dedicated himself to the task of giving the plain facts as they happened without embellishment or melodrama.[2]

Moultrie considered himself to be uniquely qualified for this laborious task, having had the honor of playing a very conspicuous part in the American Revolution involving the states of South Carolina and Georgia. Moreover he retained numerous documents of indisputable authenticity, materials possessed by no one else, and wherever the chain of events was broken, the still-lucid sexagenarian could rely on his memory and personal knowledge "to link them together and carry on the subject."[3]

Aaron Burr, a Republican and vice president of the United States in the administration of President Thomas Jefferson, visited the South Carolina lowcountry in 1802 to be present for the birth of his grandson Aaron Burr Alston, whose parents were William Alston's son Joseph and Burr's daughter Theodosia. While in Charleston Burr enjoyed the usual entertainments and elegant dinners held in honor of visiting dignitaries. Republicans and Federalists put their differences aside and celebrated their guest in harmonious conciliation. Moultrie, as a former civil and military leader, was of course included in the festivities, and his retirement from the banquets was followed by toasts in his honor.[4]

Burr was a member of the Society of the Cincinnati, giving him and Moultrie a prior basis for association. The two men discussed Moultrie's forthcoming memoirs. Burr was very interested in Moultrie's work and wrote to Sen. James Jackson in Savannah that Moultrie had given "a plain, direct and faithful account of matters which came within the General's knowledge and he dares to relate things as he saw and believes them. . . . A fair occasion now arises for correcting some errors and falsehoods which have been published and too long believed and the occasion ought not be neglected."[5]

In compliance with copyright law, Moultrie registered the title of his memoirs in the office of the clerk of the District Court of South Carolina in May 1802. He boarded the brig *Charleston Packet* bound for New York at the end of June to consult with David Longworth, who had agreed to publish *Memoirs*. Fortuitously when he checked into his lodging at Lovett's Hotel, he found that he had arrived just an hour before the New York Society of the Cincinnati was to dine there. A New York newspaper reported, "The day was spent with more than usual harmony. The unexpected arrival of Gen. Moultrie from South-Carolina, heightened the happiness of this band of patriot soldiers and brothers. The presence of this veteran recalled past scenes of American heroism and glory, and gave superior zest to the social enjoyments of the festive board."[6]

It went well with Longworth in New York. *Memoirs of the American Revolution* went to press on September 1, and Moultrie expected that books would be ready for delivery within three months. He returned to Charleston toward the end of November aboard the brig *Enterprise* without any books, however. It had been anticipated that an "enlightened public" would encourage publication through liberal subscriptions. By the time of publication, the price had doubled from the projected three dollars per copy. Perhaps for this reason subscriptions did not come in as rapidly as projected. In any event publication took until March 1803. Printer and bookseller William Conover finally received a shipment at his shop on Broad Street and announced on May 31 that Moultrie's long-awaited memoirs were ready for sale at six dollars per set.[7]

His Excell^cy William Moultrie, Late Governor of the State of South Carolina, Major General in the American Revolutionary War, pen and ink by Charles Fraser. The Walters Art Museum, Baltimore, Md. Reproduced with permission.

Moultrie's *Memoirs of the American Revolution* consisted largely of extracts, orders, official letters, journals, and correspondence with his friends that, "although private, yet they contain so much of the subject I am writing upon, that I cannot dispense with them, as they bring to light a number of anecdotes which happened in the war, that otherwise would have been intirely [*sic*] lost." He begged the pardon of his readers, adding the caution that the included documents were often written in the haste and confusion of war and were never intended for publication. Near the end of his preface, Moultrie insightfully con-cluded, "In the course of this reading, it will be found how ignorant we were in the art of war, at the commencement of our revolution."[8]

The two handsomely bound and printed octavo volumes, together more than nine hundred pages in length, began with an account of a May 13, 1774, nonim-portation meeting in Boston (that Moultrie did not attend) and concluded with the reoccupation of Charleston by the Continental Army in December 1783. Moultrie appended the second volume with public papers that he referred to in the body of the work. Between the front cover of volume 1 and the back cover of volume 2, he related, to a greater or lesser extent, "all the movements of the armies, battles, sieges, retreats, &c. which happened during the period; as well as a connected account of the transactions of the governments of the said three states, so far as they related to the military movements."[9]

An important primary source that is often quoted in other works and con-sidered one of the best of the personal accounts of the Revolutionary War, *Mem-oirs of the American Revolution* has nonetheless received criticism for Moultrie's focus upon his home state, a perceived emphasis on the preservation of the eco-nomic and political status quo of the lowcountry planter aristocracy in lieu of the greater principles of liberty, and his supposed if accidental representation of himself as an "unusually able commander reduced to a relatively minor role in the Revolution, like South Carolina herself."[10]

On the first point, it turns out that Moultrie was actually ahead of his time. The role of the southern colonies was largely downplayed by historians prior to the middle of the twentieth century, and it has even been suggested that in the aftermath of southern defeat during the Civil War, northern historians intention-ally dismissed the significance of the Revolutionary War in the South. Whether this bias is real or imagined, it is fair to say that only in the last three or four decades have historians truly recognized the overall importance of the southern campaigns to the final outcome of the Revolutionary War and hence given these operations the attention they deserve.

Second, Moultrie presented the facts from his singular perspective. If he is at fault for disregarding higher principles such as liberty in his narrative, it is only because he was committed to presenting documentary evidence and did not allow himself the luxury of waxing philosophic over abstractions. As for preservation of the status quo at the expense of liberty, South Carolina was in fact the wealthiest and most English of the North American colonies. The lowcountry planters had long enjoyed enormous economic benefit through trade with England and price supports of rice and indigo. Yet Moultrie and his peers risked their lives and their fortunes by joining their northern brethren in a rebellion for the sake of indepen-dence despite the fact that British oppression had not touched South Carolina in the way that it had affected the people of Massachusetts.

Lastly, while not a Washington or a Greene, Moultrie was indeed a competent commander, dilatory at times perhaps, but when aggressive action was required, he pursued his objectives with a purposeful vigor. His narrative is not at all self-aggrandizing. He did not gloat in victory, nor did he attempt to disguise his faults while covering the preparations leading to the Battle of Sullivan's Island on June 28, 1776, the campaign leading to the British siege of Charleston in May 1778, or the capitulation of Charleston in May 1780. Documentation of his efforts to obtain fair treatment for the Continental prisoners of war and his correspondence with Lord Montague, who urged defection to the British, was presented with little commentary. Whether intentionally or not, Moultrie also helped to salvage the reputation of Gen. Benjamin Lincoln, who had been sharply criticized for allowing the Continental Army to be trapped within the lines of Charlestown.[11]

The sale of his memoirs infused some badly needed cash into Moultrie's distressed finances. In October 1804 he thanked Baltimore merchant William Presstman for a payment of $125. "I hope they are approved by the Citizens of your State, many of whom must be good judges as they were privy to and will be acquainted with all of the transactions there related," Moultrie told Presstman, adding that he was optimistic that the books would be well received by the gentlemen of the military, "some of them I had the pleasure of being well acquainted with."[12]

It has been claimed that Moultrie penned his memoirs during a decade of imprisonment as an insolvent debtor when he occupied a small, two-story cottage on Magazine Street midway between Archdale and Mazyck (now Logan) Streets. Thus wrote John Bennett, reporting for Charleston's *News and Courier* in 1938: "The affairs of the hero of the battle of Fort Moultrie, after his second term as governor of the state, had become involved in inextricable confusion. Of his personal integrity there was no doubt. . . . Jail-bounds at that time included several blocks bounded by the lanes of ingress, egress and thoroughfare in the neighborhood of the Charleston county jail, or as it was spelled in the old days, gaol. In consideration of his position and in view of his many services to the state and to the community, a more decent dwelling than ordinary was allotted him. . . . While an occupant of this humiliating but not ignoble dwelling, General Moultrie's narrow fare, such as his constricted means provided, was generously supplemented by faithful friends."[13] In this piece Bennett related an anecdote that originated with his grandfather, Dr. William Harleston Huger:

At the close of the general's last administration as governor an unexplained discrepancy occurred in his accounts, of several thousand dollars.

When asked to explain this discrepancy all the old general could say was "God knows where it is, gentlemen. . . . I never touched it!"

Being himself in straitened circumstances owing to absent-minded management of his own property, and unable to adjust the deficit, he was consigned to prison as an insolvent debtor.

His residence was within jail-bounds, and his movement was so circumscribed; but he was occasionally permitted to go to his small plantation near Wantoot, in St. John's, Berkeley county, to oversee the management of that property.[14]

In another version it was war debts that caused Moultrie's insolvency: "His political enemies did not allow the State to repay the Revolutionary War vouchers he had signed—as commanding officer and in accordance with standard military practice of the day—to obtain food and supplies. In consequence, at the close of his second term he was consigned to debtors' prison on Magazine Street, where he lived in a two-story frame house as an insolvent debtor until his death. Doubtless, as president of the Society of the Cincinnati, he was allowed some freedom to attend its meetings."[15]

The case for Moultrie's imprisonment is based on hearsay and circumstantial evidence. Even though several printed sources maintain that he was imprisoned for debt, this has not been conclusively proven by an examination of the records of the Court of Common Pleas. Likewise no dates of confinement can be verified, if confinement occurred at all. Moultrie did reside on Magazine Street for a time up until 1802, boarding with a Mrs. Hall. While visiting New York to arrange the publication of his memoirs (How could he travel if he was so indebted?), he planned to send a shipment of pickled lobsters, oysters, and cheese to his landlady, a gift that would be most uncharacteristic for someone so financially destitute as to be imprisoned. Furthermore President Thomas Jefferson appointed Moultrie to be one of the South Carolina District's general commissioners of bankruptcy in 1802. It seems unlikely that he would have appointed Moultrie to this patronage post if the old general was, in fact, himself personally insolvent.[16]

This is not to imply that Moultrie did not have his full share of financial strain during his latter decades of life, and if he did not go to debtors' prison, he was constantly scrambling to meet his obligations. His penury took root during the war. Like many of his contemporaries, Moultrie had suffered financially as a consequence of his military service. He risked his money and property by hiring out his slaves during the war to perform manual labor for the Continental Army and by loaning money to the state during and after the war. His North Hampton plantation had been sequestered by the British, stripped of livestock and much furniture, and no crops were harvested from his neglected fields. And evidently during his postwar years, Moultrie was not very adept at managing his personal affairs while he concentrated on public service in the General Assembly, as a two-term governor, and as a commissioner to settle public accounts.[17]

Moultrie's chronic indebtedness is attributable to loans and expenditures made over a period of years to restore and maintain a lifestyle consistent with his status as a leading member of the lowcountry aristocracy. Crop failures and the perennial shortage of currency were also contributing factors. Like many of his cash-poor, land-rich contemporaries, he accepted the terms of credit that the British merchants eagerly extended. Prodebtor legislation enacted during the 1780s, on occasion at his request as governor, provided temporary relief from his creditors, but he continued his profligate spending, and likewise his debt accumulated. Matters would periodically come to a head when a merchant would decide to return to England. Prior to departure the merchant, frustrated and often nearly destitute from maintaining excessive accounts receivable, would advise his customers to settle their debts promptly or face litigation. And so it went, particularly after 1787 when the legislature did not extend the Sheriff's Sale Act and debtors lost some of the protection that they had heretofore enjoyed.

A broad examination of the judgment rolls of the courts of common pleas reveals that between 1785 and 1805, Moultrie was named as a defendant in lawsuits on more than forty occasions. As expected the vast majority of the plaintiffs were merchants, many of them British, all of whom were trying to collect their past due accounts. In his legal entanglements, Moultrie was not unique among his contemporaries, and Charleston lawyers who pursued these cases on behalf of the merchants undoubtedly made a good living. One can only wonder if the British merchants took peculiar pleasure in sending the American general and governor who championed debtor-relief legislation before a judge. This would be ironic, because Moultrie had also supported softening of confiscation and amercement of the estates of wealthy British planters and merchants.[18]

Three particularly interesting lawsuits serve to illustrate the depth and breadth Moultrie's ongoing financial difficulties apart from his indebtedness to Charleston's merchants. In 1772 he agreed, in exchange for a house on North Broad Street adjacent to St. Michael's Church, to pay his father's second wife, Elizabeth, an annuity of five hundred pounds. Of course during the war and especially after the capitulation of Charlestown in 1780, he was unable to meet this obligation. Consequently in 1786 Elizabeth Moultrie took her stepson to court and won a settlement. In 1798 Moultrie was sued by St. Philip's Church for failure to pay his rents over a period of thirteen years dating back to 1785 "for the use, occupation and enjoyment" of two pews, even after repeatedly promising to do so. In this case he confessed his fault and did not contest the charges.[19]

Last is the case of Pierce Butler versus William Moultrie and his grandson, William Ainslie Moultrie. While in New York seeing to the publication of his memoirs in 1802, Moultrie sought and obtained from his friend the former senator Pierce Butler a loan of one hundred pounds sterling. His grandson, who was traveling with him, cosigned the ninety-day note. "Ten thousand thanks to you Dear Major, your kindness has relieved me from much anxiety," he wrote to Butler, who resided in Philadelphia at the time. Moultrie must have incurred expenses in New York that he was unable to cover, for he immediately turned the funds over to the New York merchant house of Charles and Gulian McEvers. Nor did he have the funds with which to repay Butler ninety days later. In 1805 an exasperated Butler finally filed suit to recover his loss.[20]

To satisfy legal judgments against him, Moultrie was forced to divest himself of personal property such as slaves and many of his real estate holdings. Moultrie put up for sale his residence on Meeting Street where he entertained George Washington in May 1791. The property was finally sold in 1796 at a public auction held near the Exchange. North Hampton, the plantation most often mentioned in this narrative, remained in his possession until his death, but he mortgaged eight hundred acres of the property in May 1786. Moultrie also owned other plantations and tracts of land in different parts of the state and in Georgia. He placed his Kent plantation in St. John's Parish on the market with three other tracts in 1793, advertising the advantage of Kent's close proximity to the Santee Canal. Moultrie several times averted the sale of Kent under writs of *fieri facias* to satisfy judgments obtained in lawsuits. By 1801 he had sold the tracts of land, but a willing buyer for Kent was not found until 1802.[21]

If the old general was ever truly on the brink of commitment to debtor's prison, this embarrassment may have been averted by his grandson. The elder statesman eventually took residence with William Ainslie Moultrie, who seems to have taken responsibility for his grandfather's liabilities from about 1802 onward. He purchased two of the general's slaves who were being auctioned in a sheriff's sale in April 1800, and he also assumed liability for the aforementioned loan from Butler when Butler sued in 1805 and he was named as a codefendant.[22]

The beginning of the nineteenth century brought Moultrie's seventieth birthday. He remained as vigorous as his advanced age and gout would permit. There were meetings of the Society of the Cincinnati and journeys by ship to New York and the new seat of the federal government in Washington. On Wednesday, January 15, 1800, he marched from the Orphan House to St. Michael's Church as a pallbearer in an elaborate funeral procession in remembrance of George Washington, who died on December 14 of the preceding year.[23]

Perhaps to provide the aging Moultrie with income, the South Carolina legislature appointed him to the post of treasurer for the lower district of the state in December 1803. He tried valiantly to serve actively rather than as a mere figurehead, but he found that his duties required more attention than his increasing infirmity allowed him to give. He tendered his resignation to Gov. James Burchill Richardson after serving for six months.[24]

Moultrie died of natural causes on the morning of September 27, 1805, at the home of his grandson on Meeting Street. He was two months shy of seventy-five years old. A vast concourse of mourners turned out for his funeral at St. Philip's, which was conducted with full military honors rendered by the Charleston militia. The next day's *Charleston Courier* reported the news with a terse pronouncement that "the revolutionary services of this much beloved and revered patriot are so well known to every American, as to render any recital of them unnecessary." Gov. Paul Hamilton declared a month-long public period of bereavement, and at their meeting on the night of his death, the Society of the Cincinnati resolved to wear military mourning—a band of black crape or cloth around the left arm above the elbow and the shrouding of the sword-hilt—for two months as a mark of respect to their late venerable president. The Cincinnati then began to plan an elaborate ceremony in his honor.[25]

The memorial service centered on a funeral oration delivered by the Reverend Dr. William Hollinshead from the pulpit of the Independent or Congregational Church on Archdale Street at noon on October 15. A procession formed at the Carolina Coffee House on the corner of Tradd Street and Bedon's Alley at eleven o'clock and then proceeded to its destination less than three-quarters of a mile away. The Cincinnati invited the participation of a number of individuals and groups: the governor and his aides, Judge Heyward, the clergy of the city, the mayor and other civil officers, the Charleston militia, the American Revolution Society, and any fellow citizens who desired "to pay a respect to their late virtuous and patriotic General."[26]

In his oration Reverend Hollinshead used biblical references to portray Moultrie as an example of "the chosen servant of God, who fulfills the will of heaven in acts of public usefulness; whose life is a blessing to mankind; whose generous toils evince a spirit animated by celestial inspiration, and guided by the unerring eye of heaven to a successful accomplishment of its own purposes." But in the ordinary walks of life, Hollinshead depicted to his listeners, Moultrie was "a cheerful, manly, sincere and unaffected friend. . . . Unassuming and unostentatious, he was an easy, affable and agreeable companion. . . . Generously hospitable, his roof gave shelter to the weary traveler; the poor and the necessitous partook freely of his beneficence, and the worthy stranger found his habitation the sanctuary of merit."[27]

As a matter of course, Hollinshead touched on Moultrie's military career, giving special attention to his lopsided victory against seemingly overwhelming odds on June 28, 1776. He also recalled that Moultrie had indignantly spurned the British attempt to seduce him "from the standard of liberty" while he was their prisoner in 1781. "The volumes of fame will perpetuate the memory of his deeds," the pastor said, "and while the names of a Washington, a Greene, a Marion and a Gadsden are mentioned with honor, the name of Moultrie shall never be forgotten."[28]

Alexander Garden's eulogy of Moultrie, composed for the Society of the Cincinnati and printed in the Charleston newspapers, compared him with the Spartan king Leonidas (albeit more fortunate) who "defended the straight [*sic*] committed to his charge with heroic intrepidity, against a superior force, that had been deemed irresistible." Moreover Garden likened him to the incorruptible Roman consul Gaius Luscinus Fabricius, who could not be bribed, "to show to the admiring world how insignificant the power of gold, to shake the principles of a heart warmed with the genuine glow of heaven-born liberty." But when Garden discarded the hyperbole to describe the man that he knew well, he used generous terms: "In private life, [Moultrie's] disposition was frank, liberal, sincere; his manners simple and conciliating; duplicity and disguise were odious to a nature fixed on the firmest basis of candour and truth. As a husband, father, master, he was affectionate, gentle, most indulgent— in short, as has been said of a great statesman, and distinguished patriot, he was every thing to his family, but what he gave up to his country."[29]

Epilogue

The newspapers provided some details of General Moultrie's funeral at St. Philip's Church and burial on September 27, 1805, but nothing in the contemporaneous records mentioned his place of interment at Windsor Hill about sixteen miles northwest of Charleston. Moreover the grave was not marked, and as to why there was no memorial stone or epitaph erected at the grave, there is conjecture that "times were hard and the family reduced in means. A mural tablet was placed by the Society of the Cincinnati in St. Philip's Church and this satisfied family and friends who waited for more prosperous times." Within a few years of General Moultrie's death, there was hardly anyone left to pay tribute to his memory. With the death of William Ainslie Moultrie in 1811, the Moultrie name in direct descent from the general became extinct—only granddaughter Charlotte, the wife of Dr. Edward Brailsford, survived.[1]

In 1826 Alexander Garden made an impassioned appeal to the Society of the Cincinnati for the erection of a stone with a suitable inscription, but this never was accomplished. There was speculation in certain corners that Moultrie's grave was unmarked by a headstone because of his indebtedness at the time of his death and that his family kept the gravesite a secret to prevent its disturbance by creditors who might seize the remains. More likely, when Garden's generation passed, the location of the unmarked grave was simply forgotten.[2]

A commission was appointed in 1850 to find the grave, disinter Moultrie, and bring his remains back to Magnolia Cemetery in Charleston, where a handsome monument would be erected. The commission failed to locate the burial ground, and it would be more than a half-century before another attempt would be made. For patriotic and family reasons, in 1908 the Right Reverend William Alexander Guerry, bishop of South Carolina and Moultrie descendant, sought to discover the resting place of his ancestor. Acting on anecdotal evidence that General Moultrie had been buried at his request in a grave beside his son at Windsor Hill, Guerry located the old family graveyard behind the house to the right and down a hill. His search party found a white stone, which proved to be the headstone of the grave of William Moultrie Jr. When they dug around William Jr.'s grave, to the left they discovered the outline of a grave that they believed to belong to the general. The bishop subsequently recommended that a monument be placed in Windsor Hill, but this went unheeded.[3]

Another suggestion made in 1921 to place a stone over Moultrie's remains and a monument at White Point Gardens in Charleston also failed to gain traction. Nothing was done until 1955, when the bishop's son, the Reverend Canon Edward Brailsford Guerry, saw to the installation of a veteran's marker embossed with the emblem of the Society of the Cincinnati at the remote gravesite presumed to be Moultrie's. This was done quietly and without ceremony. In 1975 Reverend Guerry was shocked to find that the government marker was missing. A deer hunter subsequently stumbled upon the marker in the woods not far from the graveyard, moved there by vandals. With a sense of urgency arising from the vandalism, Guerry arranged for an archaeological examination of the Windsor Hill burial site.[4]

The archaeological excavation was coordinated through the Institute of Archaeology and Anthropology at the University of South Carolina. The project director, archaeologist Dr. Stanley A. South, began work at the site on March 14, 1977. South discovered eleven graves in the family cemetery, all buried between three-and-a-half and five feet deep. William Moultrie's grave was identified on June 28, 1977, the 201st anniversary of his victory at Fort Sullivan. His six-and-a-half-foot-long coffin was found a little more than four feet deep and to the left of his son. Excavation of the poorly preserved fragments revealed that Moultrie's coffin was ornate, decorated with three embossed metal plates on the lid and embellished with rows of brass tacks that circumscribed the lid, connected the plates, and formed diamond motifs on the top and sides. Six metal handles backed with thin, embossed escutcheon plates were found, three handles per side.[5]

The archaeologists found nothing of a military nature with the general's scant remains, not even a button. The rumor that Moultrie had been buried with his sword was just that—a rumor. The bone fragments were later examined by noted forensic anthropologist Dr. Ted A. Rathbun, who concluded that they were consistent with the skeleton of a seventy-five-year-old white male of Moultrie's height. Gov. James B. Edwards, an oral surgeon by training, examined the teeth and concurred.[6]

On Carolina Day, June 28, 1978, the yearly commemoration of the 1776 American victory of the Battle of Sullivan's Island, the remains of General Moultrie were recommitted at Fort Moultrie, laid to rest under an impressive stone tablet. During the ceremony a detachment of the reconstituted Second Regiment,

General Moultrie's grave at Fort Moultrie. Author's collection.

South Carolina Continental Establishment marched the slow march, arms reversed, flags waving while a band dressed in eighteenth-century uniforms played the "Dead March" from Handel's oratorio *Saul*.[7]

Still, there had yet to be placed anywhere a suitable monument honoring the hero of the palmetto fort. The idea for a monument in Charleston dated back to 1929. As the two hundredth anniversary of Moultrie's birth drew near, the St. Andrew's Society, the South Carolina Society, the Society of the Cincinnati, and a number of other organizations formed the Moultrie Memorial Association. The phrase "Where to hide myself from myself," reminiscent of General Moultrie's reply to Lord Charles Greville Montague's attempt to incite him to treason, was suggested as a fitting inscription for a monument. Before proposals for a Moultrie monument could be requested, the McNeill Marble Company of Marietta, Georgia, submitted a preliminary sketch for a large statue of Moultrie to look over the harbor from Castle Pinckney. As in the past, nothing happened.[8]

Aside from a marker erected in 1985 at the entrance of a residential subdivision on the site of Windsor Hill plantation, no plans were carried forward to recognize Moultrie until 1999, when members of the Brailsford family of Mt.

(a and b) The statue of William Moultrie erected at White Point Gardens in 2007. Photographs by Kim Bragg.

Pleasant, South Carolina, descendants of Moultrie through the general's grand-daughter, Charlotte, began discussing among themselves the idea of a monument somewhere in Charleston. In 2001 the Society of Colonial Wars in the State of South Carolina and the Society of the Cincinnati of the State of South Carolina made the undertaking their own when they formed the Major General William Moultrie Statue Committee.[9]

The committee, led by chairman Francis D. Rogers Jr., aided by vice chairman and Moultrie descendant George L. Brailsford and treasurer Myron C. Harrington, revealed plans to place a bronze statue of Moultrie at the eastern edge of White Point Gardens on the Battery at Charleston. The entire project was anticipated to cost nearly a quarter of a million dollars. Former South Carolina governor and president emeritus of the Medical University of South Carolina James B. Edwards also took a leading role in raising money for the statue. "All of the original states of the union except South Carolina have recognized their Revolutionary War heroes in this manner, and for good reasons," said Edwards, who acknowledged the importance of history to the state's tourism industry: "The Palmetto State is long overdue in getting this job done and we will not fail this time."[10]

John Ney Michel was commissioned to create the bronze sculpture of Moultrie. The retired College of Charleston art professor had sculpted the bronze statue of George Washington that was unveiled in Washington Park at Meeting and Broad Streets in Charleston in 1999. The artist based his work on a steel engraving of Moultrie and depicted the forty-five-year-old colonel reflecting on his military experience and leadership before the Battle of Fort Sullivan. Michel's Moultrie statue would look seaward from the Battery, hat held in his right hand and his sword sheathed in its scabbard at his left side. The eight-foot-tall figure was stood upon a seven-foot-tall pedestal designed by Charleston architect Christopher C. Liberatos.[11]

On Carolina Day, Thursday, June 28, 2007, the statue of William Moultrie was unveiled under the shade of the Battery's live oak trees amid a sea of well-dressed ladies and gentlemen in seersucker suits. He had at last received overdue tribute. But more than that, Moultrie's monument at White Point Gardens serves as a reminder of our nation's tradition and heritage of self-sacrifice. "Like the men who signed the Declaration of Independence," observed Charleston mayor Joseph P. Riley Jr. in his address at the monument dedication, "Moultrie had risked his life, his fortune, and his sacred honor in the Patriot cause."[12]

Notes

Preface

1. Griswold, Simms, and Ingraham, *Washington and the Generals of the American Revolution,* 2:32.

2. Appendix following page 457, Thomas, "William Moultrie," 40–41; Halévy, *Péguy et les Cahiers de la Quinzaine,* 31 (quoted in Samuel Eliot Morison, *John Paul Jones,* xii).

3. Hollinshead, *Discourse,* 14–15.

Prologue

1. Edgar, *South Carolina,* 161–62, 164, 167, 171–74, 181.

2. Ibid., 156, 164–66, 174–76, 181–83, 202.

Chapter 1: The Second Son

1. Moultrie, "Moultries, Part II," 247, 247n4, 257; Salley, *Register of St. Philip's Parish,* 69, 117; Thomas, "William Moultrie," 13.

2. Thomas, "William Moultrie," 1–12; Moultrie, "Moultries, Part I," 229–46.

3. Thomas, "William Moultrie," 15–16; Heitzler, *Goose Creek,* 126, 169; Simons and Simons, "William Burrows House," 175–76; Edgar and Bailey, *Biographical Directory II,* 483; McCrady, *Royal Government,* 432; Packard, *History of Medicine in the United States,* 61 (quoted); Townsend, *John Moultrie,* 100.

4. Edgar and Bailey, *Biographical Directory II,* 483.

5. Townsend, *John Moultrie,* 99; Moultrie, "Moultries, Part II," 247, 247n2; Thomas, "William Moultrie," 13; Salley, *Marriage Notices in the South-Carolina Gazette,* 13 (quoted). John Moultrie and Lucretia Cooper married on April 22, 1728. He married Elizabeth Mathewes on June 29, 1748.

6. Thomas, "William Moultrie," 16–17; Townsend, *John Moultrie,* 99–107; Moultrie, "Moultries, Part II," 248–49; Keith Krawczynski, "Moultrie, John, Jr.," *American National Biography* (hereinafter *ANB*), 16:30–31. The University of Edinburgh in Scotland was considered the world's foremost medical school. The title of Dr. Moultrie's thesis is "Dissertatio Medica Inauguralis de Febre Maligna Biliosa Americae."

7. Thomas, "William Moultrie," 17; Townsend, *John Moultrie,* 107–8; Moultrie, "Moultries, Part II," 248–49; Krawczynski, "Moultrie, John, Jr.," *ANB* 16:30–31.

8. Thomas, "William Moultrie," 22; Moultrie, "Moultries, Part II," 259–60.

9. Thomas, "William Moultrie," 23–24; Moultrie, "Moultries, Part II," 260; DeSaussure, "Remarks," 2; John Moultrie to Alexander Moultrie, July 8, 1780, Gubbins, M.C.B, Transcripts

and abstracts of Moultrie family papers, 1746–1965, Letters (43/36), South Carolina Historical Society, Charleston, S.C. (hereinafter SCHS); Hemphill and Wates, *Extracts,* 71–72n2.

10. Thomas, "William Moultrie," 30–32.

11. Ibid., 30–35.

12. Edgar and Bailey, *Biographical Directory II,* 487; McCrady, *Education in South Carolina,* 14.

13. Salley, *Register of St. Philip's Parish,* 115, 193; Green and Green, *Pioneer Mothers of America,* 2:195–96; Moultrie, "Moultries, Part II," 259.

14. Ravenel, *Records,* 133; Salley, *Register of St. Philip's Parish,* 115, 158, 193, 250; Hirsch, *Huguenots of Colonial South Carolina,* 25, 96–98, 237–38. According to Ravenel, Damaris Elizabeth de St. Julien was born September 5, 1724.

15. Indenture between Benjamin de St. Julien and William Moultrie, August 18, 1752, Moultrie Papers, oversized items, South Caroliniana Library, University of South Carolina, Columbia (hereinafter SCL) (quoted); "Former Home of Moultrie Doomed in Plans for Canal," *Charleston News and Courier,* August 25, 1935; Thomas, "William Moultrie," 72–73; DeSaussure, "Remarks," 4. See also Langley, *South Carolina Deed Abstracts,* 2:274.

16. Ravenel, *Records,* 118; Bostick, *Sunken Plantations,* 69–72; Langley, *South Carolina Deed Abstracts,* 3:35. North Hampton is now submerged under the waters of Lake Moultrie.

17. McCrady, *Proprietary Government,* 349–50; McCrady, *Royal Government,* 265–70.

18. McCrady, *Royal Government,* 72–73, 77–80, 87.

19. Manigault, "Extracts from the Journal," 12–13n28½; McCrady, *Royal Government,* 521–23; South Carolina Jockey Club, *History of the Turf,* pt. 3:40; "Starling," *South Carolina and American General Gazette* (Charleston), February 20–27, 1767; "Old Starling," *South Carolina and American General Gazette,* April 24–May 1, 1771; Sparks, "Gentleman's Sport," 17.

20. McCrady, *Royal Government,* 523; South Carolina Jockey Club, *History of the Turf,* pt. 4:5, 13, 14, 16; pt. 7:167, 168; "Jockey Club," *Charleston City Gazette,* December 25, 1795; Rosen, *Short History of Charleston,* 33.

21. Moultrie, *Memoirs,* 2:355–56.

22. Ford, *Deliver Us from Evil,* 8, 10, 147–48.

23. Moultrie's remarks on slavery are found in an undated manuscript, possibly a part of a letter, in box 2, folder 48, Moultrie Papers, SCL. See also Chaplin, "Slavery and the Principle of Humanity," 299; Ford, *Deliver Us from Evil,* 148.

Chapter 2: A Military Apprenticeship

1. Smith, *South Carolina as a Royal Province,* 73–92; Whitney, *Government of the Colony of South Carolina,* 38–45; Edgar, *South Carolina,* 114–19.

2. Smith, *South Carolina as a Royal Province,* 95–104; Whitney, *Government of the Colony of South Carolina,* 47–55; Edgar, *South Carolina,* 119–23.

3. Edgar and Bailey, *Biographical Directory II,* 485–86, and Edgar, *South Carolina,* 120.

4. Lipscomb and Olsberg, *Journal of the Commons House of Assembly* (hereinafter *JCHA*) *November 14, 1751–October 7, 1752,* 127, 158. Thomas Glen was Governor Glen's brother.

5. Lipscomb, *JCHA November 12, 1754–September 23, 1755,* xi–xxxv.

6. Ibid.

7. Salley, *JCHA January 8, 1765–August 9, 1765,* 21, 24, 61, 95–96, 102, 112, 132; Lipscomb, *JCHA November 21, 1752–September 6, 1754,* 25, 27, 87, 215, 308, 369.

8. Dalcho, *Historical Account,* 270; Zahniser, *Charles Cotesworth Pinckney,* 30; Lipscomb, *JCHA November 20, 1755–July 6, 1757,* 76, 102–3.

9. Courtenay, *Correspondence of Lord Montague*, 1–19.

10. Smith, *South Carolina as a Royal Province*,171–82; Edgar and Bailey, *Biographical Directory II*, 486; Thomas, "William Moultrie," 89; "The Staff-Officers Appointed for This Expedition Are," *South Carolina Gazette* (Charleston), October 27–November 1, 1759.

11. McCrady, *Royal Government*, 330–31; Ramsay, *Ramsay's History*, 1:94–95.

12. Ramsay, *Ramsay's History*, 1:95–98; McCrady, *Royal Government*, 331, 335–36; Hatley, *Dividing Paths*, 114–15; Thomas, "William Moultrie," 89; "It Was on Friday the 26th Ult.," *South Carolina Gazette*, November 1–3, 1759.

13. Ramsay, *Ramsay's History*, 1: 96–98; Edgar, *South Carolina*, 206; McCrady, *Royal Government*, 336, 339, 343.

14. Ramsay, *Ramsay's History*, 1:98–100; McDonough, *Christopher Gadsden and Henry Laurens*, 36; Nelson, *General James Grant*, 25–26. Some sources maintain that the request for assistance to Amherst came not from Lyttelton but from the Commons House of Assembly. Edgar, *South Carolina*, 206–7.

15. Ramsay, *Ramsay's History*, 1:100–101; Nelson, *General James Grant*, 26–27; "The Gentlemen Volunteers," *South Carolina Gazette*, November 3–10, 1759. The Cherokee Lower Towns closest in proximity to South Carolina's white backcountry settlements occupied the headwaters of the Savannah River in northwestern South Carolina and northeast Georgia. The Middle and Valley Towns were located in present-day western North Carolina. The Overhill Towns were found in what is now eastern Tennessee. The Lower Town of Keowee was a short distance north of present-day Clemson. Bryan Forrest McKown, "Fort Prince George and the Cherokee-South Carolina Frontier, 1753–1768." M.A. thesis, Clemson University, Clemson, S.C., 1988, 1–2, 9.

16. Ramsay, *Ramsay's History*, 1:101–2; Hatley, *Dividing Paths*, 130–32; Nelson, *General James Grant*, 27–28.

17. Ramsay, *Ramsay's History*, 1:105; Hatley, *Dividing Paths*, 133; Laws, "Campaign in Carolina," 229.

18. James Grant to Jeffery Amherst, January 17, 1761, in Mays, *Amherst Papers*, 174–80; Nelson, *General James Grant*, 30–31; Hatley, *Dividing Paths*, 131; McDonough, *Christopher Gadsden and Henry Laurens*, 37–38.

19. Cooper, *Statutes at Large*, 4:144–48; Salley, "Officers of the South Carolina Regiment," 202–6; Moultrie, "Moultries, Part II," 257; Simms, *Life of Francis Marion*, 46, 48; Nelson, *General James Grant*, 33.

20. McMaster, *Soldiers and Uniforms*, 43–45, 72–73; Jones and McMaster, "South Carolina Provincial Regiment," 119; O'Kelley, *Unwaried Patience and Fortitude*, 607n70. The original source of McMaster's information on page 45 of *Soldiers and Uniforms* was the *South Carolina Gazette*, September 20–27, 1760. Middleton's appointment to the rank of colonel of the Provincial Regiment is dated September 16, 1760. "In the upper left hand corner of the recorded copy of the commission (the original of which was given to Col. Middleton, of course) a rough sketch of Gov. Bull's arms is given as the seal used on the commission. The arms there depicted are the same as those shown on the Bull monument at Ashley Hall, with the same motto: *Ducit Armor Patrice*. In the right upper corner of the 'scutcheon is the crescent indicating a younger son." Salley, "Officers of the South Carolina Regiment," 202n1.

21. Nelson, *General James Grant*, 30, 32; Krawczynski, "Moultrie, John, Jr.," *ANB*, 16:31; Grant to Amherst, January 17, 1761, and James Grant to Jeffery Amherst, March 30, 1761, in Mays, *Amherst Papers*, 176, 222.

22. John Moultrie to Eleanor Austin, March 28, 1761, SCHS Letters (43/36).

23. Record of general court-martial, April 6, 1761, in Mays, *Amherst Papers*, 234–38.

24. Grant, "Journal of Lieutenant-Colonel James Grant," 26–28; Nelson, *General James Grant*, 33–35; Ramsay, *Ramsay's History*, 1:106; Withrow, "Cherokee Field School," 9–12; "This day a light infantry company was form'd [May 31]," *South Carolina Gazette*, June 13–20, 1761.

25. Nelson, *General James Grant*, 35; Ramsay, *Ramsay's History*, 1:106; Withrow, "Cherokee Field School," 12–14; "A Letter Signed Philolethes" [March 2, 1763], in *Papers of Henry Laurens* 3:308–10; Grant, "Journal of Lieutenant-Colonel James Grant," 27–29 (quoted).

26. Grant, "Journal of Lieutenant-Colonel James Grant," 29–36; Ramsay, *Ramsay's History*, 1:106–7; Nelson, *General James Grant*, 35–36; John Moultrie to Eleanor Austin, July 10, 1761, SCHS Letters (43/36).

27. Ramsay, *Ramsay's History*, 1:107–8; "Preliminary Negotiations with the Cherokees, Shem Town, Ashley Ferry, September 10–22, 1761," in *Papers of Henry Laurens*, 3:83, 83n9.

28. Ramsay, *Ramsay's History*, 107–8; Nelson, *General James Grant*, 37.

29. Simms, *Life of Francis Marion*, 46; Griswold, Simms, and Ingraham, *Washington and the Generals*, 2:33–34; Moultrie, "Moultries, Part II," 257; Edgar and Bailey, *Biographical Directory II*, 487–88.

Chapter 3: A Shadow Government

1. Cooper, *Statutes at Large*, 4:53–73, 113–17.

2. McCrady, *Royal Government*, 553–54.

3. Drayton, *Memoirs*, 1: 36–37, 41–42; Edgar and Bailey, *Biographical Directory II*, 487–88.

4. The quotation is excerpted from the Declaratory Act of March 18, 1767; McCrady, *Royal Government*, 586–90.

5. McCrady, *Royal Government*, 596–611.

6. Ibid., 609–14, 609–10n1.

7. Ibid., 614, 617–20.

8. Announcement of the formation of a General Association, *South Carolina Gazette*, July 27, 1769; McCrady, *Royal Government*, 650–52, 651n1.

9. McCrady, *Royal Government*, 654–58, 668–76, 679–81; McDonough, *Christopher Gadsden and Henry Laurens*, 103–8; Edgar, *South Carolina*, 219.

10. Edgar, *South Carolina*, 218–19.

11. Davis, "Journal of William Moultrie," 549–50; Temple, "Troublesome Boundaries," 12–14.

12. Davis, "Journal of William Moultrie," 549–50; Temple, "Troublesome Boundaries," 14–15.

13. Zahniser, *Charles Cotesworth Pinckney*, 29–30.

14. Davis, "Journal of William Moultrie," 550–51.

15. Ibid., 551–52.

16. Ibid., 552.

17. Ibid., 552–54. The mileage of a modern route from Charleston to Kings Mountain is approximately 220 miles.

18. Davis, "Journal of William Moultrie," 555, 555n26; Temple, "Troublesome Boundaries," 16; Edgar and Bailey, *Biographical Directory II*, 487; Plats for William Moultrie for acreage in Craven County, S.C., dated 1772–73, South Carolina Surveyor General's Office, Colonial Plat Books (Copy Series), 1731–75, Series 213184, vols. 18 and 21, South Carolina Department of Archives and History, Columbia (hereinafter SCDAH); Land grants for William Moultrie

from the State of North Carolina issued March 14, 1775, grants 1243–1253 located in files no. 1018–1028, Land Warrants, Plats of Survey, and Related Records, Tryon County, North Carolina State Archives, Raleigh.

Chapter 4: A Martial Spirit

1. Zahniser, *Charles Cotesworth Pinckney,* 32–34; Edgar, *South Carolina,* 220.

2. Moultrie, *Memoirs,* 1:9–10; McCrady, *Royal Government,* 733–34.

3. McCrady, *Royal Government,* 733–43, 745–46.

4. McCrady, *Royal Government,* 741–42; Edgar, *South Carolina,* 222; Edgar and Bailey, *Biographical Directory II,* 485.

5. Moultrie, *Memoirs,* 1:12–13.

6. Ibid. (quoted); Hemphill and Wates, *Extracts,* 38, 49, 73, 90, 122, 206; McCrady, *Revolution 1775,* 11n3.

7. Moultrie, *Memoirs,* 1:18–55.

8. Ibid., 1:55, 57–58 (quoted).

9. Zahniser, *Charles Cotesworth Pinckney,* 34.

10. Moultrie, *Memoirs,* 1:62–64.

11. Ibid., 1:64; McCrady, *Royal Government,* 792–93; McCrady, *Revolution 1775,* 10–15, 14n1; Hemphill and Wates, *Extracts,* 39.

12. Hemphill and Wates, *Extracts,* 45–48; Thomas, "William Moultrie," 95–96; Heitman, *Historical Register,* 406; Moultrie, *Memoirs,* 1:64–66, 74–75; SCHS, "Journal of the Second Council of Safety," 271.

13. "Regimental Orders by Col. [William] Moultrie (n.d.)," in Gibbes, *Documentary History,* 1:104 (quoted); Lefferts, *Uniforms,* 58; Drayton, *Memoirs,* 2:36; Erd and McMaster, "First and Second South Carolina Regiments," 70–72. William Henry Drayton's remembrance was that the crescent was engraved only with "Liberty."

14. Hemphill and Wates, *Extracts,* 63; Moultrie, *Memoirs,* 1:66–67, 74–75; Certificate of rank of colonel of the Second Regiment of Foot in the provincial service, William Moultrie Papers, 1775–81, Miscellaneous Manuscripts Collection (MSS790), Manuscript Division, Library of Congress (hereinafter LOC) (quoted).

15. Moultrie, *Memoirs,* 1:75–76, 75n80. According to a return submitted by Moultrie on July 17, 1775, Gadsden's regiment numbered 263; Moultrie's numbered 207. SCHS, "Journal of the Council of Safety," 47.

16. William Moultrie to Christopher Gadsden, July 28, 1775, in Gibbes, *Documentary History,* 1:124.

17. Godbold and Woody, *Christopher Gadsden,* 156–57; Fraser, "Reflections of 'Democracy,'" 11–20.

18. Moultrie, *Memoirs,* 1:84–85.

19. Ibid., 1:91–92; Henry Laurens to John Laurens, August 20, 1775, *Papers of Henry Laurens,* 10:322n5; general orders, September 17, 1775, in O'Kelley, *Unwaried Patience and Fortitude,* 15–16.

Chapter 5: The Dawn of Revolution

1. Hemphill and Wates, *Extracts,* 65; McCrady, *Revolution 1775,* 6–8.

2. Hemphill and Wates, *Extracts,* 65; McCrady, *Revolution 1775,* 6–8, 56.

3. McCrady, *Revolution 1775,* 2, 6–10, 53–62, 66; Edgar, *South Carolina,* 224–25.

4. Lipscomb, *Carolina Lowcountry*, 11, 16; Moultrie, *Memoirs*, 1:84.

5. Moultrie, *Memoirs*, 1:86–87; Lipscomb, *Carolina Lowcountry*, 15; Kaufmann and Kaufmann, *Fortress America*, 49, 99; Mustard, "On the Building of Fort Johnson," 129–35.

6. Moultrie, *Memoirs*, 1:88; Lipscomb, *Carolina Lowcountry*, 12.

7. Moultrie, *Memoirs*, 1:86, 88; Lipscomb, *Carolina Lowcountry*, 12.

8. McCrady, *Revolution 1775*, 68; Edgar, *South Carolina*, 226.

9. Lipscomb, *Carolina Lowcountry*, 12; Moultrie, *Memoirs*, 1:83, 83n, 88–92; Henry Laurens to Isaac Motte, September 12, 1775, in Salley, "Papers of the First Council of Safety," 280–81; orders, October 6, 1775, in O'Kelley, *Unwaried Patience and Fortitude*, 20.

10. Moultrie, *Memoirs*, 1:90–91. See also Drayton, *Memoirs*, 2:52; Wates, *Flag Worthy of Your State*, 2, 8–11, 16–19, 22; Salley, "Officers of the South Carolina Regiment," 202–3; Fischer, *Liberty and Freedom*, 71–72.

11. Moultrie, *Memoirs*, 1:94, 145. Tabby, a common southeast coastal building material, was composed of a mixture of lime, oyster shells, sand, and water.

12. Thomas Ferguson to Christopher Gadsden, October 3, 1775, in Gibbes, *Documentary History*, 1:98.

13. Ibid., 1:101; Hemphill and Wates, *Extracts*, 112.

14. SCHS, "Journal of the Second Council of Safety," 44; Moultrie, *Memoirs*, 1:94–95; Hemphill and Wates, *Extracts*, 143, 159, 160.

15. Moultrie, *Memoirs*, 1:95–96.

16. Ibid., 1:96; DeSaussure, "Remarks," 6–7.

17. Hemphill and Wates, *Extracts*, 92; Moultrie, *Memoirs*, 1:92–93, 93n, 108; SCHS, "Journal of the Second Council of Safety," 145, 149.

18. Hemphill and Wates, *Extracts*, 111, 121–24; Drayton, *Memoirs*, 2:71.

19. Drayton, *Memoirs*, 2:71–74; Moultrie, *Memoirs*, 1:107.

20. Moultrie, *Memoirs*, 1:110–11 (quoted); Hemphill and Wates, *Extracts*, 122; Drayton, *Memoirs*, 2:161–62, 162n*.

21. "Deaths," *South Carolina and American General Gazette*, November 17–24, 1775.

22. SCHS, "Journal of the Second Council of Safety," 88, 94. Sarah Izard was the daughter of Ralph Izard, a Patriot diplomat and politician.

23. Drayton, *Memoirs*, 2:163.

24. Moultrie, *Memoirs*, 1:113–16; SCHS, "Journal of the Second Council of Safety," 64–65, 73.

25. Moultrie, *Memoirs*, 1:115; Thomas Pinckney to Harriott Pinckney Horry, December 24, 1775, in Cross, "Letters of Thomas Pinckney," 24–25.

26. Moultrie, *Memoirs*, 1:114–16 (quoted); Pinckney to Horry, December 24, 1775, in Cross, "Letters of Thomas Pinckney," 25.

Chapter 6: Open Rebellion

1. McCrady, *Revolution 1775*, 135–36.

2. Moultrie, *Memoirs*, 1:122n; McCrady, *Revolution 1775*, 135–36.

3. Drayton, *Memoirs*, 2:164; SCHS, "Journal of the Second Council of Safety," 151, 156–57; Lipscomb, *Carolina Lowcountry*, 20.

4. SCHS, "Journal of the Second Council of Safety," 157, 167; Moultrie, *Memoirs*, 1:121–22, 122n; Bearss, *First Two Fort Moultries*, 4.

5. Moultrie, *Memoirs*, 1:116; SCHS, "Journal of the Second Council of Safety," 159, 168; Drayton, *Memoirs*, 2:164.

6. SCHS, "Journal of the Second Council of Safety," 168–71; Drayton, *Memoirs,* 2:164–65; Henry Laurens to John Laurens, January 16, 1776, in Salley, "Letters from Hon. Henry Laurens," 139–40; Moultrie, *Memoirs,* 1:116–17.

7. SCHS, "Journal of the Second Council of Safety," 168; Laurens to Laurens, January 16, 1776, in Salley, "Letters from Hon. Henry Laurens," 140 (first quote); Moultrie, *Memoirs,* 1:121–22, 139 (second quote). The *Tamar* and *Cherokee* were later found to be anchored off Cockspur Island near Savannah. SCHS, "Journal of the Second Council of Safety," 217, 221.

8. SCHS, "Journal of the Second Council of Safety," 185; Moultrie, *Memoirs,* 1:117–20 (quoted).

9. SCHS, "Journal of the Second Council of Safety," 175–185; Buchanan, *Road to Guilford Courthouse,* 8.

10. SCHS, "Journal of the Second Council of Safety," 192, 202–4, 231–32.

11. Ibid., 254; Hemphill and Wates, *Extracts,* 182–83; Drayton, *Memoirs,* 2:171–72; Continental Congress, *Journals of the Continental Congress* (hereinafter *JCC*), 4:15–16 (quoted).

12. Hemphill and Wates, *Extracts,* 203, 212–13, 217; Drayton, *Memoirs,* 2:174–75.

13. SCHS, "Journal of the Second Council of Safety," 176, 205, 225–26 (quoted); Wates, *Flag Worthy of Your State,* 1–2, 22; Drayton, *Memoirs,* 2:290. A more elaborate system of signals was devised by Gadsden and implemented in March 1776. Godbold and Woody, *Christopher Gadsden,* 158, 278n24; general orders, March 9, 1776, in Elliott, "Diary of Captain Barnard Elliott," 194–95.

14. Hemphill and Wates, *Extracts,* 86, 173–75; Salley, *Journal of the General Assembly,* , 1:42; Moultrie, *Memoirs,* 1:122–23.

15. McCrady, *Revolution 1775,* 103–9; Hemphill and Wates, *Extracts,* 181–82.

16. McCrady, *Revolution 1775,* 111–13; Moultrie, *Memoirs,* 1:125–29; Hemphill and Wates, *Extracts,* 255–67.

17. McCrady, *Revolution 1775,* 114–15; Hemphill and Wates, *Extracts,* 241–42, 263, 265.

18. Moultrie, *Memoirs,* 1:138; Hemphill and Wates, *Extracts,* 266; Edgar and Bailey, *Biographical Directory II,* 485–86.

19. SCHS, "Journal of the Second Council of Safety," 259; Moultrie, *Memoirs,* 1:123.

20. Moultrie, *Memoirs,* 1:123–24.

21. Hemphill and Wates, *Extracts,* 206.

Chapter 7: "I never was uneasy"

1. Robson, "Expedition to the Southern Colonies," 538–41; Clinton, *American Rebellion,* 23–24.

2. Clinton, *American Rebellion,* 25–28; Gordon, *South Carolina and the American Revolution,* 36–37; Robson, "Expedition to the Southern Colonies," 540–41, 551–55. Accounts of number of troops that Cornwallis brought to America from Cork in 1776 vary between two thousand and three thousand.

3. Clinton, *American Rebellion,* 28–29, 29n22; Robson, "Expedition to the Southern Colonies," 554–55.

4. *JCC,* 4:181; Moultrie, *Memoirs,* 1:140; Drayton, *Memoirs,* 2:278–79, 281–82. The total troop strength for Charlestown's defense given by Drayton is 6,522. The Eighth Virginia Regiment commanded by Col. John Peter Gabriel Muhlenberg, arrived in Charlestown on June 23, 1776.

5. Moultrie, *Memoirs,* 1:140.

6. Ibid., 1:139. The Sampit River originates in the swamps of western Georgetown County and flows eastward, merging into Winyah Bay at Georgetown.

7. Ibid., 1:139–40 (quoted); Drayton, *Memoirs*, 2:279.

8. Moultrie, *Memoirs*, 1:146–47.

9. Ibid., 1:141–42; *Fort Moultrie Centennial*, 1:9; Charles Cotesworth Pinckney to Eliza Lucas Pinckney, June 15, 1776, in Gibbes, *Documentary History*, 2:4.

10. Bearss, *Battle of Sullivan's Island*, 34 (quoted), 34n17; Moultrie, *Memoirs*, 1:141; Lipscomb, *Carolina Lowcountry*, 23.

11. Moultrie, *Memoirs*, 1:140–41 (quoted); McCrady, *Revolution 1775*, 139. Removal of the presses suspended the printing of the gazettes from June 1 until August 1, 1776.

12. Moultrie, *Memoirs*, 1:140–41; Charles Cotesworth Pinckney to Eliza Lucas Pinckney, June 15, 1776, in Gibbes, *Documentary History*, 2:4 (quoted).

13. Charles Lee to John Rutledge, June 22, 1776, in Lee and Bunbury, *Lee Papers*, 2:80–81; *Fort Moultrie Centennial*, 1:10; Moultrie, *Memoirs*, 1:141.

14. Drayton, *Memoirs*, 2:283.

15. Ibid., 2:283–84; Charles Lee's general orders for June 19, 1776, and Charles Lee to Christopher Gadsden, June 19, 1776, in Lee and Bunbury, *Lee Papers*, 2:73–75; Charles Lee to George Washington, July 1, 1776, in *Papers of George Washington: Revolutionary War Series*, 5:169; Alden, *General Charles Lee*, 122–24; and Haw, *John and Edward Rutledge*, 87 (quoted).

16. *Fort Moultrie Centennial*, 1:11.

17. Moultrie, *Memoirs*, 1:141–42, 150, 152–54; William Moultrie to Charles Lee, "1/2 past 2 o'clock," June 11, 1776, in "Original Letters from Genl. Francis Marion and Genl. William Moultrie," *Year Book—1898, City of Charleston*, 383.

18. Moultrie, *Memoirs*, 1:142, 165–67.

19. Ibid., 1:142 (quoted), 163–65.

20. Clinton, *American Rebellion*, 30; Moultrie, *Memoirs*, 1:147–48; Bearss, *Battle of Sullivan's Island*, 39n24.

21. Moultrie, *Memoirs*, 1:148 (quoted); Bearss, *Battle of Sullivan's Island*, 39–40.

22. Moultrie, *Memoirs*, 1:149; Peter Parker to Philip Stephens, July 9, 1776, in Morgan, *Naval Documents*, 5:998 (quoted); Drayton, *Memoirs*, 2:286–88.

23. Moultrie, *Memoirs*, 1:149–50; Clinton, *American Rebellion*, 30; Bearss, *Battle of Sullivan's Island*, 40; Wilson, *Southern Strategy*, 46.

24. Moultrie, *Memoirs*, 1:150–51.

25. Ibid., 1:151–53; Bearss, *Battle of Sullivan's Island*, 41–42.

26. Parker to Stephens, July 9, 1776, in Morgan, *Naval Documents*, 5:998; Moultrie, *Memoirs*, 1:153–54; Moultrie to Lee, "1/2 past 2 o'clock," June 11, 1776, in "Original Letters," 383.

Chapter 8: The Eve of Destruction

1. Moultrie, *Memoirs*, 1:124, 157–58; Simms, *Life of Francis Marion*, 7–8, 70 (quoted); South, *Palmetto Parapets*, 98–99; Muller, *Treatise*, 205–10; *Fort Sullivan afterwards called Fort Moultrie in the unfinished State it was on the 28th June 1776*, Map 79.1.417, Robert Charles Lawrence Fergusson Collection, Society of the Cincinnati, Washington, D.C.; South, *Palmetto Parapets*, 59, 98–99, and fig. 1. Ferdinand De Brahm was the nephew of famous geographer and engineer William Gerard De Brahm.

2. Lipscomb, *Carolina Lowcountry*, 22–23; McCrady, *Revolution 1775*, 141n2; and SCHS, "Journal of the Second Council of Safety," 157.

3. Drayton, *Memoirs*, 2:290; South, *Palmetto Parapets*, 59–61, and fig. 1.

4. Drayton, *Memoirs*, 2:290; Map 79.1.417, Society of the Cincinnati; South, *Palmetto Parapets*, 59–61, fig. 1.

5. South, *Palmetto Parapets*, 39, 51–53, 92.

6. Ibid., 100–101, 111, 129; Charles Lee to William Moultrie, June 24, 1776, and Charles Lee's general orders for June 24, 1776, in Lee and Bunbury, *Lee Papers*, 2:81–82.

7. Drayton, *Memoirs*, 2:282, 291–93; Charles Lee, general orders, June 19, 1776, Lee and Langworthy, *Life and Memoirs of the Late Major General Lee*, 309–10 (quoted).

8. Drayton, *Memoirs*, 2:282, 288; Bearss, *First Two Fort Moultries*, 6; Moultrie, *Memoirs*, 1:144, 159–60.

9. Drayton, *Memoirs*, 2:290–91; Map 79.1.417, Society of the Cincinnati; South, *Palmetto Parapets*, fig. 1; Kloss and Skvarla, *United States Senate Catalogue of Fine Art*, 437.

10. Drayton, *Memoirs*, 2: 290–91; Map 79.1.417, Society of the Cincinnati; Kloss and Skvarla, *United States Senate Catalogue of Fine Art*, 437. Drayton's punctuation makes it difficult to determine with certainty whether or not the word *Liberty* was found on the crescent of the flag at the fort on Sullivan's Island or if it was set on the blue field. David Hackett Fischer makes an unconvincing argument for the word being set in the blue field. Fischer, *Liberty and Freedom*, 756n129. British artist Nicholas Pocock depicted the crescent flag without *Liberty* in his 1783 painting *A View of the Attack made by the British Fleet under the Command of Sir Peter*. In John Blake White's *The Battle of Fort Moultrie*, executed in 1826, the flag flying from the southeast bastion of the palmetto fort on Sullivan's Island during the battle of June 28, 1776, appears to have *Liberty* inscribed in the crescent. See also Lipscomb, *Carolina Lowcountry*, 51n58.

11. South, *Palmetto Parapets*, 99–100; Moultrie, *Memoirs*, 1:143 (quoted), 176.

12. Moultrie, *Memoirs*, 1:143–44.

13. Drayton, *Memoirs*, 2:290–91; Lipscomb, *Carolina Lowcountry*, 23, 49n42.

14. Moultrie to Lee, "12 o'clock," June 11, 1776, in "Original Letters from Genl. Francis Marion and Genl. William Moultrie," *Year Book—1898, City of Charleston*, 384.

15. Orders, June 16, 1776, in O'Kelley, *Unwaried Patience and Fortitude*, 73, 626n298; Drayton, *Memoirs*, 2:284–85; Charles Lee, general orders, June 24, 1776, in Lee and Langworthy, *Life and Memoirs of the Late Major General Lee*, 310.

16. Moultrie, *Memoirs*, 1:159; Drayton, *Memoirs*, 2:289; Clinton, *American Rebellion*, 32; Johnson, *Traditions and Reminiscences*, 91.

17. Moultrie, *Memoirs*, 1:142–3; Clinton, *American Rebellion*, 32.

18. Moultrie, *Memoirs*, 1:142–43 (quoted). Drayton also estimated Clinton's numbers at three thousand. Interestingly Clinton wrote to Lord George Germain, secretary of state for the American Department, that Thomson's position was defended by three or four thousand men. Drayton, *Memoirs*, 2:288–89; Clinton, *Narrative*, 13.

19. Drayton, *Memoirs*, 2:290; Moultrie to Lee, "12 o'clock," 384; Bearss, *Battle of Sullivan's Island*, 57–58, 60.

20. Moultrie, *Memoirs*, 1:154–55; Moultrie to Lee, "1/2 past 8 o'clock" and "12 o'clock," 383–84 (quoted). Lee requested an additional hundred men for Haddrell's Point on June 13.

21. Moultrie, *Memoirs*, 1:154–56; Drayton, *Memoirs*, 2:282–84 (quoted); Ravenel, *Charleston*, 242.

22. Moultrie, *Memoirs*, 1:156–58.

23. Charles Lee to John Rutledge, June 25, 1776, in Lee and Bunbury, *Lee Papers*, 2:83; Moultrie, *Memoirs*, 1:164–65 (quoted). Baron Massenbourg was likely Lt. Felix Lewis Massenbach (also found spelled Massenborough and Massenbaugh) from Germany. O'Kelley, *Unwaried Patience and Fortitude*, 627n307.

24. Bearss, *Battle of Sullivan's Island*, 52; Charles Lee to William Thomson, June 22, 1776; in Lee and Bunbury, *Lee Papers*, 2:76; Moultrie, *Memoirs*, 1:158–59, 161–63.

25. Moultrie, *Memoirs*, 1:157, 163, 165 (quoted).

26. Ibid., 1:165–67.

27. Ibid., 1:183; Drayton, *Memoirs*, 2:291, 318; McCrady, *Revolution 1775*, 143. McCrady's numbers are a repetition of those given by Drayton with the addition of the thirty-six men who were sick and unfit for duty.

28. Moultrie, *Memoirs*, 1:144.

29. Ibid., 1:144, 159–62 (quoted); *Fort Moultrie Centennial*, 1:11.

30. Moultrie, *Memoirs*, 1:161–62.

31. Ibid., 1:158–61; McCrady, *Revolution 1775*, 147–48.

Chapter 9: Never Did Men Fight More Bravely

1. Moultrie, *Memoirs*, 1:174; Savage, *River of the Carolinas*, 161–62.

2. Moultrie, *Memoirs*, 1:166–67.

3. Ibid., 1:174; Savage, *River of the Carolinas*, 161–62.

4. Moultrie, *Memoirs*, 1:174; Savage, *River of the Carolinas*, 169; general orders, March 9, 1776, in Elliott, "Diary of Captain Barnard Elliott," 194–95; Fischer, *Liberty and Freedom*, 73.

5. Parker to Stephens, July 9, 1776, in Morgan, *Naval Documents*, 5:998.

6. Clinton, *American Rebellion*, 29–30; Robson, "Expedition to the Southern Colonies," 555; Farrow, *Dictionary of Military Terms*, 147.

7. Parker to Stephens, July 9, 1776, in Morgan, *Naval Documents*, 5:998; Clinton, *American Rebellion*, 29–31; Wilson, *Southern Strategy*, 58; McCrady, *Revolution 1775*, 145,149, 153; Robson, "Expedition to the Southern Colonies," 558–59.

8. Clinton, *American Rebellion*, 31–32 (quoted); Peter Parker to Henry Clinton, June 25, 1776, in Morgan, *Naval Documents*, 5:745; Moultrie, *Memoirs*, 1:143.

9. Clinton, *American Rebellion*, 32–34; Peter Parker to Henry Clinton, June 25, 1776, in Morgan, *Naval Documents*, 5:745.

10. Parker to Stephens, July 9, 1776, in Morgan, *Naval Documents*, 5:999; Clark, Stevens, Alden, and Krafft, *Short History of the United States Navy*, 184n7.

11. Parker to Stephens, July 9, 1776, in Morgan, *Naval Documents*, 5:999; Bearss, *Battle of Sullivan's Island*, 75n3, 76, 76n4; McCrady, *Revolution 1775*, 149–50n3. The reported distance that the British men-of-war anchored off Sullivan's Island differs from source to source, varying between 350 and 800 yards depending on the position of the observer. Charles Cotesworth Pinckney to Eliza Lucas Pinckney, June 29, 1776, in Gibbes, *Documentary History*, 2:8; Richard Hutson to Thomas Hutson, June 30, 1776, in SCHS, *Divers Accounts of the Battle of Sullivan's Island*, 6; Moultrie, *Memoirs*, 1:180; Barnard Elliott to Susannah Elliott, June 29, 1776, in Gibbes, *Documentary History*, 2:6; Clinton, *American Rebellion*, 35; Charles Lee to George Washington, July 1, 1776, in *Papers of George Washington: Revolutionary War Series*, 5:168.

12. Moultrie, *Memoirs*, 1:166–67; Alden, *General Charles Lee*, 125; McCrady, *Revolution 1775*, 147–48.

13. Parker to Stephens, July 9, 1776, in Morgan, *Naval Documents*, 5:999; Moultrie, *Memoirs*, 1:174; "Extracts from Major Elliott's Orderly Book," June 28, 1776, in Gibbes, *Documentary History*, 2:3.

14. *Fort Moultrie Centennial*, 1:17.

15. Ibid.

16. Drayton, *Memoirs*, 2:296–99.

17. Ibid., 2:297–99; "Account of the Attack on Fort Moultrie," August 2, 1776, in Gibbes, *Documentary History,* 2:17.

18. Moultrie, *Memoirs,* 1:175–76 (quoted); Drayton, *Memoirs,* 2:298–99; "Account," August 2, 1776, in Gibbes, *Documentary History,* 2:17; Hutson to Hutson, June 30, 1776, in SCHS, *Divers Accounts of the Battle of Sullivan's Island,* 6.

19. McCrady, *Revolution 1775,* 154–55; Parker to Stephens, July 9, 1776, in Morgan, *Naval Documents,* 5:999.

20. Moultrie, *Memoirs,* 1:171; Parker to Stephens, July 9, 1776, in Morgan, *Naval Documents,* 5:999; Lipscomb, *Carolina Lowcountry,* 26.

21. Moultrie, *Memoirs,* 1:175 (quoted); Charles Cotesworth Pinckney to Eliza Lucas Pinckney, June 29, 1776, in Gibbes, *Documentary History,* 2:7–8; Drayton, *Memoirs,* 2:295; Lipscomb, *Carolina Lowcountry,* 27–28.

22. Moultrie, *Memoirs,* 1:174–78; Drayton, *Memoirs,* 2:296–97; "Battle of Fort Moultrie," June 28, 1776, and "Narrative of Thomas Bennett," June 28, 1776, in Gibbes, *Documentary History,* 2:10–11.

23. Moultrie, *Memoirs,* 1:166, 174–77; Drayton, *Memoirs,* 2:299–300; "Battle," June 28, 1776, and "Narrative," June 28, 1776, in Gibbes, *Documentary History,* 2:10–11; "This Was Indeed a Glorious Day," in SCHS, *Divers Accounts of the Battle of Sullivan's Island,* 16 (quoted).

24. Moultrie, *Memoirs,* 1:177–78.

25. Ibid., 1:167, 177–78; Drayton, *Memoirs,* 2:296, 300n‡; Simms, *Life of Francis Marion,* 73; Charles Cotesworth Pinckney to Eliza Lucas Pinckney, June 29, 1776, in Gibbes, *Documentary History,* 2:8; Lipscomb, *Carolina Lowcountry,* 32, 39.

26. Moultrie, *Memoirs,* 1:167 (first quote), 176–77 (second quote); Haw, *John and Edward Rutledge,* 88.

27. Drayton, *Memoirs,* 2:296–97; Moultrie, *Memoirs,* 1:181; William Bull to John Julius Pringle, August 13, 1776, in SCHS, *Divers Accounts of the Battle of Sullivan's Island,* 21; "Account," August 2, 1776, in Gibbes, *Documentary History,* 2:17.

28. Moultrie, *Memoirs,* 1:176n178–79 (quoted).

29. Ibid., 1:176; Parker to Stephens, July 9, 1776, in Morgan, *Naval Documents,* 5:999.

30. Moultrie, *Memoirs,* 1:176 (quoted), 176n; Lee to Washington, July 1, 1776, in *Papers of George Washington: Revolutionary War Series,* 5:169; Hutson to Hutson, June 30, 1776, in SCHS, *Divers Accounts of the Battle of Sullivan's Island,* 6.

Chapter 10: America's First Absolute Victory

1. McCrady, *Revolution 1775,* 152; "John Wells' Account of the British Attack on Charleston," June 28, 1776, in Morgan, *Naval Documents,* 5:805; Clinton, *American Rebellion,* 34.

2. Clinton, *American Rebellion,* 34–35; Henry Clinton to George Germaine, July 8, 1776, in Morgan, *Naval Documents,* 5:984; Bearss, *Battle of Sullivan's Island,* 88–89.

3. Clinton to Germaine, July 8, 1776, in Morgan, *Naval Documents,* 5:984–85; McCrady, *Revolution 1775,* 152–53; Bearss, *Battle of Sullivan's Island,* 89–91.

4. Moultrie, *Memoirs,* 1:179 (first quote); Barnard Elliott to Susannah Elliott, June 29, 1776, in Gibbes, *Documentary History,* 2:6 (second quote).

5. Moultrie, *Memoirs* 1:179–80 (quoted). See also Jones, *Sergeant William Jasper,* 19–20.

6. Moultrie, *Memoirs* 1:180; McCrady, *Revolution 1775,* 159.

7. Moultrie, *Memoirs,* 1:177n; Drayton, *Memoirs,* 2:302, 318, 326, 326nddd; "Account," August 2, 1776, in Gibbes, *Documentary History,* 2:17. A number of sources give the number of wounded Americans as twenty-three.

8. Heinl, *Dictionary of Military and Naval Quotations,* 122 (quoted); Parker to Stephens, July 9, 1776, in Morgan, *Naval Documents,* 5:1001; McCrady, *Revolution 1775,* 155–56.

9. Parker to Stephens, July 9, 1776, in Morgan, *Naval Documents,* 5:1001; McCrady, *Revolution 1775,* 155–56.

10. Moultrie, *Memoirs,* 1:180; McCrady, *Revolution 1775,* 159–60; SCHS, "Journal of the Second Council of Safety," 90.

11. Moultrie, *Memoirs,* 1:180 (quoted); McCrady, *Revolution 1775,* 160; "Account," August 2, 1776, in Gibbes, *Documentary History,* 2:17; "The Bell," Moncrief, William, Biographical and genealogical research, Genealogy (30–4 Moncrief), SCHS.

12. Orders, June 29, 1776, in O'Kelley, *Unwaried Patience and Fortitude,* 81 (quoted); "Anecdote of General Moultrie," *Maryland Journal and Baltimore Advertiser,* February 9, 1779.

13. Moultrie, *Memoirs,* 1:168–70.

14. Ibid.; entry for July 1, 1776, Orderly books of William Moultrie, June 20, 1775–December 15, 1780, MssHM 681, Huntington Library, fol. 32r; Richardson, *Standards and Colors of the American Revolution,* 132–34. The blue flag was captured at Savannah on October 9, 1779. The red flag was taken at the surrender of Charleston on May 12, 1780, and subsequently disappeared. For an exquisitely detailed description of the blue flag, see Richardson, *Standards and Colors of the American Revolution,* 132–34.

15. Moultrie, *Memoirs,* 1:182 (quoted); entry for July, 1, 1776, Orderly books of William Moultrie, Huntington Library, fols. 19r, 32r.

16. Moultrie, *Memoirs,* 1:170–71; "Narrative by Thomas Bennet," July 1, 1776, in Morgan, *Naval Documents,* 5:860–62; Clinton, *American Rebellion,* 35.

17. Moultrie, *Memoirs,* 1:171; "Narrative by Thomas Bennet," 5:861.

18. Moultrie, *Memoirs,* 1:171–72.

19. Ibid., 1:181; Haw, *John and Edward Rutledge,* 88.

20. Moultrie, *Memoirs,* 1:172–73.

21. Bearss, *Battle of Sullivan's Island,* 102–7; Clinton, *American Rebellion,* 37; Alexander Campbell to William Campbell July 21, 1776, in Morgan, *Naval Documents,* 5:1172–75.

22. *JCC,* 5:491–502; and McCrady, *Revolution 1775,* 170–79; Moultrie, *Memoirs,* 1:183. See also Lipscomb, *Carolina Lowcountry,* 40.

23. John Buchanan, letter to C. L. Bragg, January 31, 2009 ("the right man at the right place at the right time").

24. Moultrie, *Memoirs,* 1:144 (first quote); Lee to Washington, July 1, 1776, in *Papers of George Washington: Revolutionary War Series,* 5:168–70 (second quote).

25. *JCC,* 5:593; Charles Lee to John Hancock, July 2, 1776, in Lee and Bunbury, *Lee Papers,* 2:107–10; John Hancock to William Moultrie, July 22, 1776, in Continental Congress, Papers of the Continental Congress (hereinafter PCC), National Archives (hereinafter NA) microfilm series M247, roll 177 (vol. 2): 533 (quoted), 539. See also Continental Congress, 1776, Letter (published transcription) from the Continental Congress to Colonel William Moultrie, Rare Book and Special Collections Division, LOC.

26. Henry Laurens to Johann Rodolph Von Valltravers, May 22, 1775, in *Papers of Henry Laurens,* 10:133–34, 133–34n4; Henry Laurens to John Laurens, August 14, 1776, in *Papers of Henry Laurens,* 11:227 (quoted), 227n6.

27. Garden, *Anecdotes of the Revolutionary War in America,* 7–10; McCrady, *Revolution 1775,* 160–61.

28. Godbold and Woody, *Christopher Gadsden,* 160–61.

Chapter 11: South Carolina's Senior Brigadier

1. Moultrie, *Memoirs*, 1:184; Drayton, *Memoirs*, 2:333–35; Jonathan Bryan, John Houstoun, and Lachlan McIntosh, "Conference with the Georgia Deputies," enclosed with Lee to Hancock, July 2, 1776, and Lachlan McIntosh to Charles Lee, July 7, 1776, in Lee and Bunbury, *Lee Papers*, 2:114–17, 125; Bennett and Lennon, *Quest for Glory*, 46–47.

2. Moultrie, *Memoirs*, 1:184–85; Robert Howe to Charles Lee, August 10, 1776, in Lee and Bunbury, *Lee Papers*, 2:207–8; Bennett and Lennon, *Quest for Glory*, 47.

3. Moultrie, *Memoirs*, 1:185–86.

4. Ibid., 1:186; Bennett and Lennon, *Quest for Glory*, 49.

5. Moultrie, *Memoirs*, 1:187; *JCC*, 3:325; 4:235. See also Salley, *Journal of the General Assembly*, 2:23–24.

6. *JCC*, 5:461–62; Hemphill and Wates, *Extracts*, 202–6.

7. Moultrie, *Memoirs*, 1:187; *JCC*, 5:762; Drayton, *Memoirs*, 2:337, 383–84; entry for October 28, 1776, Orderly books of William Moultrie, June 20, 1775–December 15, 1780, MssHM 681, Huntington Library; Orders, October 28, 1776, in O'Kelley, *Unwaried Patience and Fortitude*, 114 (quoted).

8. Bennett and Lennon, *Quest for Glory*, 1–34, 49–50.

9. Ibid., 50–51, 63; Robert Howe to John Rutledge, October 6, 1776, in Gibbes, *Documentary History*, 2:36–42; Bennett and Lennon, *Quest for Glory*, 50, 63; Cooper, *Statutes at Large*, 4:379–81.

10. Mack, *Life of Gilbert Motier De Lafayette*, 33.

11. Ibid, 31, 32.

12. "Charlestown (S.C.), June 30," *Williamsburg Virginia Gazette*, August 15, 1777; "Charlestown [S. Carolina] July 7," *Philadelphia Pennsylvania Packet, or the General Advertiser*, July 29, 1777; "Palmetto Society," *Gazette of the State of South Carolina* (Charleston, S.C.), June 23, 1777; Purcell, *Sealed with Blood*, 45–46; Bennett and Lennon, *Quest for Glory*, 64; Orders, June 27, 1777, O'Kelley, in *Unwaried Patience and Fortitude*, 207; "Orders by General [Robert] Howe, Parole Moultrie," June 27, 1777, in Gibbes, *Documentary History*, 2:60–62.

13. Orders, July 7, 1777, in O'Kelley, *Unwaried Patience and Fortitude*, 210–211, 590, 593.

14. Orders, July 15, 1777, in O'Kelley, *Unwaried Patience and Fortitude*, 213, 602n8.

15. Moultrie, *Memoirs*, 1:192–94. The council of war consisted of Moultrie as president, Col. Isaac Huger, Col. Isaac Motte, Col. Owen Roberts, Col. Charles Cotesworth Pinckney, Col. Thomas Sumter, Lt. Col. Francis Marion, and Maj. Peter Horry.

16. Ibid., 194–96.

17. Ibid., 196–98.

18. Ibid., 199.

19. Moultrie, *Memoirs* 1: 199–200; McDonough, *Christopher Gadsden and Henry Laurens*, 237–38; Watson and Watson, *Men and Times of the Revolution*, 44–45.

20. Ibid., 1:201.

21. Ibid., 1:198–99; O'Kelley, *Unwaried Patience and Fortitude*, 280–81; Moultrie, *Memoirs*, 2:371–72 (quoted); Waldo, Adams, and Jefferson, *Biographical Sketches of Distinguished American Naval Heroes*, 68–70.

22. Moultrie, *Memoirs*, 1:198–99; Waldo, Adams, and Jefferson, *Biographical Sketches of Distinguished American Naval Heroes*, 68–70.

23. William Moultrie, receipt dated February 11, 1778, "for his share of a new [ ] building at Beaufort," Moultrie Papers, box 1, folder 8, SCL; Salley, *Journal of the Commissioners of the*

Navy of South Carolina, 113–42, 151; Coggins, *Ships and Seamen of the American Revolution,* 103; Biddle and Biddle, *Autobiography of Charles Biddle,* 107–9.

Chapter 12: Crisis in Georgia

1. Hemphill and Wates, *Extracts,* 181–82; Edgar and Bailey, *Biographical Directory II,* 488; McCrady, *Revolution 1775,* 235; Edgar, *South Carolina,* 230.

2. Edgar, *South Carolina,* 230.

3. Haw, *John and Edward Rutledge,* 107–9.

4. Robert Howe to John Hancock, November 3, 1777, PCC, NA microfilm series M247, roll 178 (item no. 160): 400–402.

5. Moultrie, *Memoirs,* 1:203–4, 203n; 2:363–64.

6. Moultrie, *Memoirs,* 1:205.

7. Ibid., 1:368–69.

8. Ibid., 1:369–70. See also Robert Howe to Rawlins Lowndes, April 14, 1778, PCC, NA microfilm series M247, roll 86 (item no. 72): 449–50.

9. Moultrie, *Memoirs,* 2:369–71.

10. Ibid., 2:371.

11. Ibid., 2:365–67, 371.

12. Ibid., 2:365–67, 371–72; William Moultrie to Henry Laurens, April 20, 1778, PCC, NA microfilm series M247, roll 177 (vol. 2): 453–57; Bennett and Lennon, *Quest for Glory,* 55; *JCC,* 10:139–40.

13. Moultrie, *Memoirs,* 2:365–67, 383; Bennett and Lennon, *Quest for Glory,* 55; *JCC,* 10:139–40; Moultrie to Laurens, April 20, 1778, PCC; Rawlins Lowndes to Henry Laurens, April 18, 1778, PCC, NA microfilm series M247, roll 86 (item no. 72): 456–59; Rawlins Lowndes to Henry Laurens, April 18, 1778, in *Papers of Henry Laurens,* 13:140–45; *JCC,* 11:551–53; Moultrie, *Memoirs,* 1:217 (quoted).

14. Moultrie, *Memoirs,* 2:373–75; Bennett and Lennon, *Quest for Glory,* 72.

15. Moultrie, *Memoirs,* 2:373, 376–80.

16. Bennett and Lennon, *Quest for Glory,* 73, 80; Moultrie, *Memoirs,* 1: 217–18.

17. Bennett and Lennon, *Quest for Glory,* 73–75; Moultrie, *Memoirs,* 2:381–82.

18. Moultrie, *Memoirs,* 1:213 (quoted), 218–19.

19. Ibid., 1:220–22.

20. Ibid., 1:224–25.

21. Ibid., 1:226–27.

22. Ibid., 1:227–36; McCrady, *Revolution 1775,* 322; Bennett and Lennon, *Quest for Glory,* 75, 76, 78–84.

23. Moultrie, *Memoirs,* 1:238–39.

24. Ibid., 1:239–40

Chapter 13: An Army Mostly Composed of Militia

1. Moultrie, *Memoirs,* 1:240–41.

2. Ibid., 1:241–42.

3. McCrady, *Revolution 1775,* 253–65; Henry Laurens to Horatio Gates, June 17, 1778, *Papers of Henry Laurens,* 13:473 (quoted).

4. Bennett and Lennon, *Quest for Glory,* 85–87.

5. *JCC,* 12:949–50.

6. Ibid., 12:951.

7. Mattern, *Benjamin Lincoln*, 56–60.

8. Henry Clinton to Archibald Campbell, November 8, 1778, in Campbell and Campbell, *Journal of an Expedition*, 4; Bennett and Lennon, *Quest for Glory*, 88–89; Moultrie, *Memoirs*, 1:249–51.

9. Bennett and Lennon, *Quest for Glory*, 85–87; Wilson, *Southern Strategy*, 71–72. Credit for use of the term *lame duck* belongs to David K. Wilson.

10. Moultrie, *Memoirs*, 1:243–47; Bennett and Lennon, *Quest for Glory*, 89–90; Wilson, *Southern Strategy*, 71–72.

11. Moultrie, *Memoirs*, 1:255–56; Mattern, *Benjamin Lincoln*, 60–61.

12. Moultrie, *Memoirs*, 1:247–49, 252–55; Bennett and Lennon, *Quest for Glory*, 90–95; Mattern, *Benjamin Lincoln*, 60–61. See also entry for December 29, 1778, Grimké, "Order Book," *South Carolina Historical and Genealogical Magazine* (hereinafter *SCHGM*) 14, no. 1 (1913): 54–56.

13. Bennett and Lennon, *Quest for Glory*, 96–99; Moultrie, *Memoirs*, 1:254. See also Savas and Dameron, *Guide to the Battles of the American Revolution*, 188–94.

14. Moultrie, *Memoirs*, 1:253–54 (quoted); Bennett and Lennon, *Quest for Glory*, 98–99. Howe organized the South Carolina Continentals into two brigades on August 26, 1778. Moultrie's brigade consisted of the First, Second, and Sixth Regiments. Col. Isaac Huger's brigade consisted of the Third and Fifth Regiments. Entry for August 26, 1778, Grimké, "Order Book," *SCHGM* 13, no. 1 (1912): 44.

15. Moultrie, *Memoirs*, 1:256–57.

16. Ibid.

17. Ibid., 1:256, 265, 270; Rowland, Moore, and Rogers, *History of Beaufort County*, 215; Wilson, *Southern Strategy*, 83, 113–14.

18. Moultrie, *Memoirs*, 1:258, 271n; Williams, *Founding Family*, 123–25, 127; Edgar and Bailey, *Biographical Directory II*, 522–24.

19. Moultrie, *Memoirs*, 1:258–59.

20. Ibid., 1:260–61.

21. Ibid., 1:261–63, 269–70.

22. Ibid., 1:266–69.

23. Ibid., 1:271–72.

24. Ibid., 1:272. Moultrie refers to Richardson as a colonel, but President Lowndes appointed him to the rank of brigadier general on March 25, 1778. See also McCord, *Statutes at Large*, 9:666–82.

25. Moultrie, *Memoirs*, 1:272–73; *JCC*, 5:805.

26. Moultrie, *Memoirs*, 1:275–76.

27. Ibid., 1:282.

28. Ibid., 1:286–87.

29. Ibid., 1:273; *JCC*, 12:950.

30. Moultrie, *Memoirs*, 1:273–75.

31. Ibid., 1:279, 285–86, 298–301, 313–16.

32. Ibid., 1:269–70, 274, 313–16.

33. Ibid., 1:299–300.

34. Ibid.

35. Ibid., 1:311–12.

36. Charles Pinckney to Frances Brewton Pinckney, February 24, 1779, in Gibbes, *Documentary History*, 2:106.

37. Ibid., 2:103–5; Cooper, *Statutes at Large*, 4:470–72; Haw, "Broken Compact," 36–39.

Chapter 14: Port Royal to Briar Creek

1. Archibald Campbell to George Germaine, January 19, 1779, in Campbell and Campbell, *Journal of an Expedition*, 43–44 (quoted); Wilson, *Southern Strategy*, 83–85.

2. Entries for February 11–14, 1779, in Campbell and Campbell, *Journal of an Expedition*, 62–64; Wilson, *Southern Strategy*, 85–91, 102.

3. Mattern, *Benjamin Lincoln*, 65–66; Moultrie, *Memoirs*, 1:307; Benjamin Lincoln to Samuel Elbert, January 31, and February 4, 1779, Benjamin Lincoln to Rawlins Lowndes, February 4, 1779, and Benjamin Lincoln to President of Congress [John Jay], February 4, 1779, in Lincoln, *Benjamin Lincoln Papers*, reel 3, items 83, 91, 94, and 100; Charles Pinckney to Frances Brewton Pinckney, February 24, 1779, in Gibbes, *Documentary History*, 2:106–7. Moultrie's upriver march is not well documented. It is mentioned in a letter from Charles Pinckney to his mother, but Moultrie does not mention it in his *Memoirs*.

4. Moultrie, *Memoirs*, 1:288–89; Lee and Lee, *Memoirs of the War*, 123; McCrady, *Revolution 1776*, 340; Rowland, Moore, and Rogers, *History of Beaufort County*, 216.

5. Rowland, Moore, and Rogers, *History of Beaufort County*, 215–16; Lincoln to Lowndes, February 4, 1779, in Lincoln, *Benjamin Lincoln Papers*, reel 3, item 94.

6. Lincoln to Lowndes, February 4, 1779; Moultrie, *Memoirs*, 1:290; "Extract of a Letter, dated Camp, at Port-Royal Ferry, February 9th," *South Carolina and American General Gazette*, February 11, 1779; Rowland, Moore, and Rogers, *History of Beaufort County*, 217; McCrady, *Revolution 1775*, 339–40.

7. "Extract of a Letter" (quoted); Moultrie, *Memoirs*, 1:291, 295–96; Rowland, Moore, and Rogers, *History of Beaufort County*, 216–17.

8. Rowland, Moore, and Rogers, *History of Beaufort County*, 189, 219; "Extract of a Letter"; Butler, *Letters of Pierce Butler*, xix.

9. "Extract of a Letter"; Rowland, Moore, and Rogers, *History of Beaufort County*, 217.

10. Moultrie, *Memoirs*, 1:291–92, 291n, 305, 354; "Extract of a Letter"; Rowland, Moore, and Rogers, *History of Beaufort County*, 215–17.

11. Rowland, Moore, and Rogers, *History of Beaufort County*, 217; "Extract of a Letter."

12. Moultrie, *Memoirs*, 1:291–92; "Extract of a Letter."

13. Moultrie, *Memoirs*, 1:292, 294; "Extract of a Letter."

14. Moultrie, *Memoirs*, 1:292, 294; "Extract of a Letter."

15. "Extract of a Letter."

16. Moultrie, *Memoirs*, 1:292–93 (quoted); Rowland, Moore, and Rogers, *History of Beaufort County*, 218.

17. Moultrie, *Memoirs*, 1:293; Rowland, Moore, and Rogers, *History of Beaufort County*, 218–19.

18. Moultrie, *Memoirs*, 1:293, 313; Rowland, Moore, and Rogers, *History of Beaufort County*, 218.

19. Moultrie, *Memoirs*, 1:294–97; Rowland, Moore, and Rogers, *History of Beaufort County*, 218; McCrady, *Revolution 1775*, 340, 340n2.

20. Moultrie, *Memoirs*, 1:294, 303, 305–6.

21. "Extract of a Letter" (first quote); Moultrie, *Memoirs*, 1:305 (second quote).

22. Ibid., 306, 308–9, 312.

23. Moultrie, *Memoirs,* 1:306–7.

24. Ibid., 1:310–11.

25. Ibid., 1:319–22, 326; Campbell to Germaine, January 19, 1779, in Campbell and Campbell, *Journal of an Expedition,* 41; McCrady, *Revolution 1775,* 343–44. Moultrie estimated the strength of the American army as follows: Lincoln had between three thousand and four thousand men at Purrysburg; Maj. Gen. John Ashe had twenty-three hundred men at Briar Creek on the Georgia side of the Savannah River; and Brig. Gen. Griffith Rutherford led seven hundred or eight hundred men at Black Swamp, east of the Savannah in South Carolina. The approximately twelve hundred militia in the vicinity of Augusta were commanded by Gen. Andrew Williamson. McCrady adjusted Ashe's numbers down to one thousand, which included Col. Samuel Elbert's remnant of one hundred Georgia Continentals and North Carolina militia.

26. Moultrie, *Memoirs,* 1:320–21.

27. Ibid., 1:313–14, 322–26, 379n; Wilson, *Southern Strategy,* 91.

28. Moultrie, *Memoirs,* 1:322–26; Wilson, *Southern Strategy,* 92–96; Heidler, "American Defeat at Briar Creek"; Rankin, *North Carolina Continentals,* 193–96.

29. Moultrie, *Memoirs,* 1:269–70, 281, 321, 325, 376–77.

30. Ibid., 1:326, 337–53.

31. Ibid., 1:326–27.

32. Jones, *Art of War in the Western World,* 65–70; Moultrie, *Memoirs,* 1:365 (quoted).

Chapter 15: "Let us Burgoyne them"

1. Moultrie, *Memoirs,* 1:359–60, 364, 384–85; Wilson, *Southern Strategy,* 101, 300n5; Mattern, *Benjamin Lincoln,* 69. On November 16, 1776, a cannon salute fired at St. Eustatius was the first international acknowledgement of the independence of the United States. See also Jameson, "St. Eustatius in the American Revolution," 683–708.

2. Moultrie, *Memoirs,* 1:319–20, 359–60.

3. Ibid., 1:367–74.

4. Ibid.

5. Ibid., 1:361–63, 366 (quoted), 374, 417. Pinckney's letter was dated March 22, 1779. Lt. Gov. Thomas Bee reiterated to Moultrie on May 2 that reinforcements would have to come from Orangeburgh, not Charlestown.

6. Ibid., 1:374–75; Wilson, *Southern Strategy,* 101; Rankin, *North Carolina Continentals,* 198; Mattern, *Benjamin Lincoln,* 69.

7. Moultrie, *Memoirs,* 1:377–78, 377n, 380; Wilson, *Southern Strategy,* 102.

8. Wilson, *Southern Strategy,* 101–2.

9. Moultrie, *Memoirs,* 1:379–81.

10. Ibid., 1:384–85, 415, 417; McCrady, *Revolution 1775,* 351.

11. Moultrie, *Memoirs,* 1:380, 380n, 383–84. McCrady's source (Stedman, *History of the Origin, Progress, and Termination of the American War,* 2:110) is remarkably consistent with the documentation in Moultrie's *Memoirs.*

12. Moultrie, *Memoirs,* 1:386, 401; Wilson, *Southern Strategy,* 103.

13. Moultrie, *Memoirs,* 1:386–89.

14. Ibid., 1:390–391 (quoted), 391n.

15. Ibid., 1:391.

16. Ibid., 1:392–93, 401–2. Wilson points out in *Southern Strategy* (300 n11) that according to Moultrie's account written decades after the fact (*Memoirs,* 1:402), the dry streambeds and

low rivers did not present much of an obstacle to the British. Prévost, however, complained in a contemporaneous letter to Henry Clinton that the Savannah River was swollen with rain.

17. Moultrie, *Memoirs*, 1:391, 393, 420–21; Ramsay, *History of the American Revolution*, 2:154; Wilson, *Southern Strategy*, 104. Thomas Bee reported to Moultrie on May 2 that the British fleet was bound for Jamaica rather than Beaufort or Charleston.

18. Moultrie, *Memoirs*, 1:393–94, 400–401.

19. Ibid., 1:396–97, 412.

20. Ibid., 1:418–22.

21. Ibid., 1:395–96 (quoted), 398.

22. Ibid., 1:398–400.

23. Ibid., 1:393–95, 397–98, 406, 416.

24. Ibid., 1:395, 397–98 (quoted), 417, 420.

25. Ibid., 1:398–99.

26. Ibid., 1:402; Massey, *John Laurens,* passim.

27. Moultrie, *Memoirs*, 1:402–3.

28. Ibid., 1:403, 407; Rowland, Moore, and Rogers, *History of Beaufort County*, 221; Wilson, *Southern Strategy*, 104–5.

29. Moultrie, *Memoirs*, 1:403–4.

30. Ibid., 1:403.

31. Ibid., 1:404.

32. Ibid., 1:265, 404–10, 432. Senf held the rank of captain in the Continental engineers and lieutenant colonel in the South Carolina militia. Moultrie described him as an extraordinary field engineer. See also entry for November 29, 1778, Grimké, "Order Book," *SCHGM* 13–4: 208; Edwards, *Journals of the Privy Council, 1783–1789* (hereinafter *JPC*), 182.

33. Moultrie, *Memoirs*, 1: 407–10 (quoted); Wilson, *Southern Strategy*, 105.

34. Moultrie, *Memoirs*, 1: 403–8; Wilson, *Southern Strategy*, 105–6; Rowland, Moore, and Rogers, *History of Beaufort County*, 221–22.

35. Moultrie, *Memoirs*, 1:408–10.

36. Ibid., 1:409.

37. Ibid., 1:407 (quoted); Mattern, *Benjamin Lincoln*, 70.

Chapter 16: *"We will fight it out"*

1. Moultrie, *Memoirs*, 1:410–13 (quoted); Ripley, *Battleground*, 33.

2. Moultrie, *Memoirs*, 1:411–12; McCrady, *Revolution 1775*, 355–56.

3. McCrady, *Revolution 1775*, 356; Wilson, *Southern Strategy*, 106.

4. McCrady, *Revolution 1775*, 356–57.

5. Ibid; Moultrie, *Memoirs*, 1:411–12, 427n. See also the indented certificate issued by South Carolina to William Moultrie on February 3, 1786, *Accounts Audited,* SCDAH, roll 109, file 5387.

6. McCrady, *Revolution 1775*, 356–57; Moultrie, *Memoirs* 1:413–14.

7. Moultrie, *Memoirs*, 1:411, 432; Borick, *Gallant Defense*, 41–42.

8. Moultrie, *Memoirs*, 1:413–14.

9. Ibid., 1:414 (quoted), 414n.

10. Paul David Nelson, "Pulaski, Casimir," in *ANB*, 17: 926–27; Spencer, "Pulaski's Legion," Browne, William Hand, and Louis Henry Dielman. Maryland Historical Magazine. Baltimore: Maryland Historical Society, 1906.214–26; Moultrie, *Memoirs*, 1:413–14; Wilson, *Southern Strategy*, 107–8.

11. Nelson, "Pulaski, Casimir"; Spencer, "Pulaski's Legion," Browne, William Hand, and Louis Henry Dielman. Maryland Historical Magazine. Baltimore: Maryland Historical Society, 1906.214–26; *JCC,* 10:291; Moultrie, *Memoirs,* 1:413–14, 423; Wilson, *Southern Strategy,* 108.

12. Wilson, *Southern Strategy,* 107–8, 114–15.

13. Ibid., 108; Moultrie, *Memoirs,* 1:423–424.

14. Moultrie, *Memoirs,* 1:412–13, 424.

15. Ibid., 1:424 (quoted); Journal of James Fergus, May 11, 1783, in Dann, *Revolution Remembered,* 177, 183.

16. Moultrie, *Memoirs,* 1:424–26.

17. McCrady, *Revolution 1775,* 360.

18. Moultrie, *Memoirs,* 1: 424–27.

19. Ibid., 1:426–27 (quoted), 426n.

20. Ibid., 1:427–28 (quoted); Wilson, *Southern Strategy,* 109–10.

21. Moultrie, *Memoirs,* 1:428–31, 440; Henry Laurens to Jonathan Trumbull Sr., July 8, 1779, in *Papers of Henry Laurens,* 15:130–31, 130–31nn5–7; Wilson, *Southern Strategy,* 110. In his memoirs Moultrie broke down the numbers on which he based his troop strength estimates, but McCrady points out the errors in his calculations. In contrast Rutledge better approximated American numbers than did Moultrie. McCrady, *Revolution 1775,* 363–65, 365n1. The Privy Council consisted of Lt. Gov. Thomas Boone, Charles Cotesworth Pinckney, Christopher Gadsden, Roger Smith, Thomas Ferguson, John Edwards, John Neufville, Isaac Motte, and John Parker. McCrady, *Revolution 1775,* 362.

22. Moultrie, *Memoirs,* 1:429–32; McCrady, *Revolution 1775,* 364–65; Wilson, *Southern Strategy,* 110.

23. Moultrie, *Memoirs,* 1:431.

24. Ibid., 1:432–33; Wilson, *Southern Strategy,* 110; McCrady, *Revolution 1775,* 373; Haw, "Broken Compact," 48–50, 50n59; Godbold and Woody, *Christopher Gadsden,* 194. John Rutledge maintained after the war that the negotiations were meant to delay a British attack and allow Lincoln time to return to Charleston. See McCrady, *Revolution 1775,* 370–71.

25. Moultrie, *Memoirs,* 1:432–33; McCrady, *Revolution 1775,* 366–74; Godbold and Woody, *Christopher Gadsden,* 194. See also Wilson, *Southern Strategy,* 111; and Borick, *Gallant Defense,* 255–56n30. William Gilmore Simms argued that the negotiations were a ruse meant to gain time and that in his memoirs Moultrie mistakenly spread the "miserable misconception" that neutrality was seriously considered. According to Simms, Rutledge and his council did not let Moultrie, his soldiers, or the townspeople in on the secret that the neutrality proposal was a sham. William Gilmore Simms to Lorenzo Sabine, October 12, 1856, Lorenzo Sabine Papers, box 2, folder 19, New Hampshire Historical Society; Simms, *History of South Carolina,* 233.

26. Moultrie, *Memoirs,* 1:433; Godbold and Woody, *Christopher Gadsden,* 194.

27. John Laurens, "Account of the operations in South Carolina, respecting Capitulation, May 1779," Henry Laurens Papers, 1747–1860, Manuscripts (37/45B oversize), SCHS, fol. 2 (quoted); McCrady, *Revolution 1775,* 371–72. See also Haw, "Broken Compact," 30–53.

28. *JCC,* 13:385–88 (quoted); Haw, *John and Edward Rutledge,* 121–22; Massey, *John Laurens,* 136–37, 139. In July the legislature reacted to the recommendation of arming slaves with horror and disgust.

29. Moultrie, *Memoirs,* 1:433–34 (quoted). According to McCrady, General Prévost refused to negotiate with the Americans, leading Governor Rutledge and the Privy Council to consider capitulation in exchange for neutrality. McCrady, *Revolution 1775,* 366–70.

30. Moultrie, *Memoirs,* 1:434.

31. Laurens, "Account of the operations," fol. 2.
32. Moultrie, *Memoirs*, 1:434–35.

Chapter 17: Lost Opportunity at Stono Ferry

1. Moultrie, *Memoirs*, 1:435–36, 438–40.
2. Ibid., 1:436–37.
3. Ibid., 1:442–44, 450–51.
4. Wilson, *Southern Strategy*, 116.
5. Moultrie, *Memoirs*, 1:441, 443–44.
6. Ibid., 1:444–46, 445n.
7. Ibid., 1:446–49.
8. Ibid., 1:451–55; Wilson, *Southern Strategy*, 118, 121.
9. Moultrie, *Memoirs*, 1:455n†, 460–67 (quoted).
10. Ibid., 1:450, 454–60, 455n*, 462–63, 467–70.
11. Ibid., 1:468.
12. Mattern, *Benjamin Lincoln*, 72–73, 75; *JCC*, 13:464–66.
13. *JCC*, 14:585–86 (first quote); Moultrie, *Memoirs*, 1:470–71 (second quote).
14. Moultrie, *Memoirs*, 1:471–72, 475–78 (first quote); William Moultrie to Benjamin Lincoln, June 8, 1779, quoted in Mattern, *Benjamin Lincoln*, 73 (original in the Thomas Addis Emmet Collection, MssCol 927, New York Public Library [second quote]).
15. Mattern, *Benjamin Lincoln*, 72–73; Wilson, *Southern Strategy*, 121; Henry Laurens to Benjamin Lincoln, August 13, 1779, *Papers of Henry Laurens*, 15:151, 151n7.
16. Moultrie, *Memoirs*, 1:476–77.
17. Ibid., 1:479–80. Wilson, *Southern Strategy*, 271–72.
18. Moultrie, *Memoirs*, 1:488–89 (quoted); Wilson, *Southern Strategy*, 270; William Moultrie to Benjamin Lincoln, June 20 [4:30 P.M.], 1779, in Lincoln, *Benjamin Lincoln Papers*, reel 4.
19. Moultrie to Lincoln, June 19, 1779 [8:00 P.M.], in Lincoln, *Benjamin Lincoln Papers*, reel 4 (quoted); Moultrie, *Memoirs*, 1:488.
20. Moultrie, *Memoirs*, 1:473–74; Wilson, *Southern Strategy*, 269–70; Moultrie to Lincoln, June 20 [6:00 A.M.], 1779, in Lincoln, *Benjamin Lincoln Papers*, reel 4.
21. Moultrie, *Memoirs*, 1:489–90; Wilson, *Southern Strategy*, 269–70; Moultrie to Lincoln, June 20 [4:30 P.M.], 1779, in Lincoln, *Benjamin Lincoln Papers*, reel 4 (quoted).
22. Moultrie, *Memoirs*, 1:491, 495–98; Wilson, *Southern Strategy*, 123–26, 13–31.
23. Moultrie, *Memoirs*, 1:492–93; Wilson, *Southern Strategy*, 126–29.
24. Moultrie, *Memoirs*, 1:491–92 (quoted), 498. See also Snowden and Cutler, *History of South Carolina*, 1:367–68.
25. McCrady, *Revolution 1775*, 384, 386, 389–90; Wilson, *Southern Strategy*, 269–70.
26. Gardner, "Life of General William Moultrie," 15; Johnson, *Traditions and Reminiscences*, 224–25.
27. Johnson, *Traditions and Reminiscences*, 224–25. Very little can be found about Robert Dewar, and so his credibility cannot be ascertained.
28. Moultrie to Lincoln, June 19, 1779 [8:00 P.M.], in Lincoln, *Benjamin Lincoln Papers*, reel 4; Moultrie to Lincoln, June 20 [6:00 A.M.], 1779, in Lincoln, *Benjamin Lincoln Papers*, reel 4.

Chapter 18: "We were sure of success"

1. Moultrie, *Memoirs*, 1:494; Rowland, Moore, and Rogers, *History of Beaufort County*, 223–24.

2. Moultrie, *Memoirs*, 1:499–501, 499n.

3. Ibid., 1:501–2.

4. Ibid., 1:503–4, 504n.

5. Ibid., 2:3.

6. Ibid.

7. Ibid., 1:505 (quoted), 505n; 2:4–6.

8. Ibid., 1:495 (quoted); 2:5–6.

9. Ibid., 2:7–8.

10. Ibid., 2:7, 15.

11. Ibid., 2:11 (first quote), 15–16 (second quote).

12. Ibid., 2:8, 10, 17, 18, 21; Rowland, Moore, and Rogers, *History of Beaufort County*, 224.

13. Moultrie, *Memoirs*, 2:10, 15, 22, 24.

14. Ibid., 2:18, 23–24, 26 (quoted).

15. Ibid., 2:24n (quoted), 26.

16. Ibid., 2:21, 23–27; Benjamin Lincoln to Henry Laurens, July 20, 1779, in *Papers of Henry Laurens*, 15:145.

17. Moultrie, *Memoirs*, 2:21 (quoted), 23, 25.

18. Ibid., 2:22, 26, 28–29 (quoted).

19. McCrady, *Revolution 1775*, 400–402; Cooper, *Statutes at Large*, 4:465–68, 502–4; William Moultrie to Francis Marion, November 13, 1779, in Gibbes, *Documentary History*, [1853], 2–3.

20. Kennedy, *Muskets, Cannon Balls and Bombs*, 39–40; Wilson, *Southern Strategy*, 133–35.

21. Moultrie *Memoirs*, 2:33–34.

22. Ibid., 2:34–35.

23. Ibid., 2:39–40; Hough, *Siege of Savannah*, 89–90; Wilson, *Southern Strategy*, 36 (map).

24. Moultrie, *Memoirs*, 2:40; Prévost to Germaine, November 1, 1779, in Kennedy, *Muskets, Cannon Balls and Bombs*, 100–102; Wilson, *Southern Strategy*, 162–73.

25. Moultrie, *Memoirs*, 2:40–41; Wilson, *Southern Strategy*, 160, 167–68, 279; Garden, *Anecdotes of the Revolutionary War in America*, 13; Richardson, *Standards and Colors of the American Revolution*, 132; O'Kelley, *Unwaried Patience and Fortitude*, 618–619n216; Lawrence, *Storm over Savannah*, 108–9.

26. Moultrie, Memoirs, 2:40–41; Wilson, *Southern Strategy*, 168–71, 181–82.

27. Moultrie, Memoirs, 2:42.

28. Ibid., 2:43 (quoted); "Journal of the Siege of Savannah, with some observations by M. le comte d'Estaing," in Kennedy, *Muskets, Cannon Balls and Bombs*, 68.

Chapter 19: "I think they cannot pass this way"

1. Salley, *Marriage Notices in the South-Carolina and American General Gazette*, 33; Smith and Salley, *Register of St. Philip's Parish, 1754–1810*, 237.

2. Smith and Smith, *Dwelling Houses of Charleston*, 48.

3. Moultrie, *Memoirs*, 1:63.

4. Ibid., 1:47, 285n (first quote), 362, 362n (second quote); 2:35n; McCrady, *Revolution 1775*, 223–28. McCrady reproduced a table created by David Ramsay that illustrated the progressive depreciation of currency from 1777 to 1780.

5. Moultrie, *Memoirs*, 2:23 (first quote); 1:288–89 (second quote); Cooper, *Statutes at Large*, 4:485–86; South Carolina to William Moultrie, receipt no. 507 for loan of nine thousand pounds dated December 18, 1779, *Accounts Audited*, SCDAH, roll 109, file 5387; South

Carolina to William Moultrie, receipt no. 508 for loan of nine thousand pounds dated December 18, 1779, document in private hands after being sold at auction on December 10, 2008, by Bloomsbury Auctions of New York.

6. Clinton, *American Rebellion*, 151; McCrady, Revolution 1775, 425; Lumpkin, *From Savannah to Yorktown*, 41–42.

7. Wilson, *Southern Strategy*, 193–95. See also Haw, "Broken Compact," 30–53.

8. Clinton, *American Rebellion*, 151, 153–54, 158–59; Uhlendorf, *Siege of Charleston*, 21, 23; Moultrie, Memoirs, 2:44; Symonds and Clipson, *Naval Institute Historical Atlas*, 16; Wilson, *Southern Strategy*, 198–99, 205, 239–41.

9. Mattern, *Benjamin Lincoln*, 88–91; Laurens to Lincoln, August 13, 1779, in *Papers of Henry Laurens*, 15:151; Wilson, *Southern Strategy*, 193, 195–96, 275–76.

10. Wilson, *Southern Strategy*, 196, 208.

11. McCrady, *Revolution 1775*, 432–33.

12. Mattern, *Benjamin Lincoln*, 93–95, 98; McCrady, *Revolution 1775*, 442–44; Wilson, *Southern Strategy*, 193.

13. Bernard Beekman's notes, February 12, 1780, in McIntosh, *Lachlan McIntosh Papers*, 112; Mattern, *Benjamin Lincoln*, 93–95, 98; Wilson, *Southern Strategy*, 200–201.

14. Clinton, *American Rebellion*, 160–61; Moultrie, Memoirs, 2:44.

15. Clinton, *American Rebellion*, 161–63; Uhlendorf, *Siege of Charleston*, 25, 27; Moultrie, Memoirs, 2:45; Borick, *Gallant Defense*, 50–52, 63–65.

16. Moultrie, Memoirs, 2:45–46, 50.

17. Ibid., 2:47, 50; Wilson, *Southern Strategy*, 201.

18. Moultrie, *Memoirs*, 2:43–44, 47 (quoted), 52n.

19. Ibid., 2:55–56.

20. Clinton, *American Rebellion*, 162; Moultrie, *Memoirs* 2:47–48 (quoted).

21. Moultrie, *Memoirs*, 2:48.

22. Ibid., 2:50–55; Wilson, *Southern Strategy*, 203.

23. Moultrie, *Memoirs*, 2:56–57; Borick, *Gallant Defense*, 64.

24. Moultrie, *Memoirs*, 2:57; Francis Marion to Isaac Harleston, February 27 and March 8, 1780, in "Letters of General Francis Marion," *Year Book—1895, City of Charleston*, 327, 329; Buchan, *Domestic Medicine*, 38–42; Heitman, *Historical Register*, 538.

Chapter 20: "Had Moultrie been in command"

1. Wheeler, *Text-Book of Military Engineering*, 1–21; Mercur, *Attack of Fortified Places*, 12.

2. Moultrie, *Memoirs*, 2:58; Murdoch, "French Account of the Siege of Charleston," 143; McCrady, *Revolution 1775*, 446.

3. Clinton, *American Rebellion*, 162–63; Uhlendorf, *Siege of Charleston*, 35; Moultrie, *Memoirs*, 2:61–65, 62n; Borick, *Gallant Defense*, 103–5; Wilson, *Southern Strategy*, 206–7.

4. McCrady, *Revolution 1775*, 435; Wilson, *Southern Strategy*, 195, 238–41.

5. McCrady, *Revolution 1775*, 451–52; Borick, *Gallant Defense*, 42.

6. Uhlendorf, *Siege of Charleston*, 95; Borick, *Gallant Defense*, 42–43; Moultrie, *Memoirs*, 2:106; McIntosh journal, April 13, 1780, in McIntosh, *Lachlan McIntosh Papers*, 100–101; Clinton, *American Rebellion*, 163–64 (quoted).

7. Lumpkin, *From Savannah to Yorktown*, 46; Uhlendorf, *Siege of Charleston*, 39, 93, 95, 227–29; Murdoch, "French Account of the Siege of Charleston," 144; Gidick, *By No Means Contemptible*, 17; Borick, *Gallant Defense*, 115–17.

8. Lumpkin, *From Savannah to Yorktown,* 46; Uhlendorf, *Siege of Charleston,* 39, 91; Gidick, *By No Means Contemptible,* 8–9; Murdoch, "French Account of the Siege of Charleston," 150; Borick, *Gallant Defense,* 42, 115, 117.

9. Lincoln, *Original Papers,* 26.

10. Ibid., 27–32; Moultrie, *Memoirs,* 2:60. See also Wilson, *Southern Strategy,* 207–13; Borick, *Gallant Defense,* 73–85.

11. Lincoln, *Original Papers,* 30–31; Moultrie, *Memoirs,* 2:59–60; Wilson, *Southern Strategy,* 208; Borick, *Gallant Defense,* 80.

12. Moultrie, *Memoirs,* 2:58–59, 59n†. See also Murdoch, "French Account of the Siege of Charleston," 143; Henry Laurens to Samuel Huntington, December 20, 1779, in *Papers of Henry Laurens,* 15:218n2; Coggins, *Ships and Seamen of the American Revolution,* 102–3. The American naval force consisted of Continental frigates *Boston, Providence,* and *Queen of France* and the sloop *Ranger;* French frigates *La Bricole, La Truite,* and *L'Aventure;* and the South Carolina brigs *General Lincoln* and *Notre Dame.*

13. Moultrie, *Memoirs,* 2:59; Wilson, *Southern Strategy,* 210–11.

14. Lincoln, *Original Papers,* 32–33; Moultrie, *Memoirs,* 2:58–60; Benjamin Lincoln to Samuel Huntington, March 24, 1780, PCC, NA microfilm series M247, roll 177 (vol. 2): 347–50.

15. Moultrie, *Memoirs,* 2:61; Murdoch, "French Account of the Siege of Charleston," 143; Borick, *Gallant Defense,* 131–32; McCrady, *Revolution 1775,* 440–41 (quoted).

16. Moultrie, *Memoirs,* 2:60, 65–66, 106–7; Borick, *Gallant Defense,* 118–19; William Moultrie to Samuel Tucker, March 25, 1780, Samuel Tucker Papers, 1777–1781, Papers and Collection of Peter Force, 1170–1961, MSS63511, series 7E: item 145, microfilm 19,061 (reel 54), frame 464, Manuscript Division, LOC. According to a British return submitted after the capitulation, 311 pieces of ordinance were captured at Charlestown along with 80 or 90 pieces taken at Fort Moultrie, Lempriere's Point, Mount Pleasant, and the armed vessels in the harbor. Hough, *Siege of Charleston,* 116–19, 166.

17. Moultrie, *Memoirs,* 2:62 (quoted), 66; John Habersham's journal, April 2, 1780, in McIntosh, *Lachlan McIntosh Papers,* 113; Clinton, *American Rebellion,* 163; Uhlendorf, *Siege of Charleston,* 235.

18. Uhlendorf, *Siege of Charleston,* 39–41, 231–35; Borick, *Gallant Defense,* 123–27, 139–40,142, 164–65; Wilson, *Southern Strategy,* 215–17; Ravenel, *Charleston,* 337; Lachlan McIntosh's journal, April 13, 1780, in McIntosh, *Lachlan McIntosh Papers,* 100.

19. Garden, *Anecdotes of the Revolutionary War in America,* 11 (quoted). The same story is recounted in Ravenel, *Charleston,* 271.

20. Lincoln, *Original Papers,* 9–10; Moultrie, *Memoirs,* 2:61, 63, 67–68; Uhlendorf, *Siege of Charleston,* 51–53, 51n2, 241–43; Wilson, *Southern Strategy,* 211–12, 311–12n43.

21. Moultrie, *Memoirs,* 2:68–70; Borick, *Gallant Defense,* 136–37 (quoted), 284n43; McIntosh journal, April 10, 1780, in McIntosh, *Lachlan McIntosh Papers,* 99; Mattern, *Benjamin Lincoln,* 99–100.

22. Borick, *Gallant Defense,* 182–83, 189.

23. Ibid., 145, 182–83. Moultrie refers to Lempriere's Point as Hobcaw Point in his memoirs.

24. Moultrie, *Memoirs,* 2:105; Mattern, *Benjamin Lincoln,* 100; McCrady, *Revolution 1775,* 465.

25. Moultrie, *Memoirs,* 2:105–6.

26. Borick, *Gallant Defense,* 54; Simms, *Life of Francis Marion,* 96–97.

27. Moultrie, *Memoirs,* 2:222.

28. Henry Laurens to the South Carolina delegates in Congress, May 14, 1780, in *Papers of Henry Laurens*, 15:295.

29. McIntosh journal, April 13, 1780, in McIntosh, *Lachlan McIntosh Papers*, 100–101.

30. Ibid.

31. Moultrie, *Memoirs*, 2:70; Uhlendorf, *Siege of Charleston*, 59.

32. Moultrie, *Memoirs*, 2:64, 70–71; Garden, *Anecdotes of the Revolutionary War in America*, 94; Uhlendorf, *Siege of Charleston*, 59, 249. See also Gidick, *By No Means Contemptible*, 32, 34.

33. Moultrie, *Memoirs*, 2:72, 72n*, 82, 84.

34. Ibid., 2:72n*.

Chapter 21: "It was our last great effort"

1. McIntosh journal, April 19, 1780, in McIntosh, *Lachlan McIntosh Papers*, 103; Moultrie, *Memoirs*, 2:77–78; Uhlendorf, *Siege of Charleston*, 63–65; Wilson, *Southern Strategy*, 225–26. According to the McIntosh journal, the council met over April 19–20. An account of the council of war dated April 20 and 21, 1780, is found in PCC, NA microfilm series M247, roll 177 (vol. 2): 391–92. Lincoln included this account in a letter to General Washington dated July 17, 1780, published in Lincoln, *Original Papers*, 14–26.

2. McIntosh journal, April 19, 1780, in McIntosh, *Lachlan McIntosh Papers*, 103–4; Clinton, *American Rebellion*, 167; Wilson, *Southern Strategy*, 226. Transports carrying Clinton's reinforcements arrived offshore on April 18.

3. McIntosh journal, April 18, 1780, in McIntosh, *Lachlan McIntosh Papers*, 104; McCrady, *Revolution 1775*, 474–75.

4. McIntosh journal, April 18, 1780, in McIntosh, *Lachlan McIntosh Papers*, 104.

5. Ibid.

6. Ibid., 104–5.

7. Ibid., 105; Lincoln, *Original Papers*, 19–20 (quoted).

8. McIntosh journal, April 20, 1780, in McIntosh, *Lachlan McIntosh Papers*, 105.

9. John Lewis Gervais to Henry Laurens, April 28, 1780, in *Papers of Henry Laurens*, 15:284, 284n8; McIntosh journal, April 20, 1780, in McIntosh, *Lachlan McIntosh Papers*, 105.

10. McIntosh journal, April 18, 1780, in McIntosh, *Lachlan McIntosh Papers*, 105; Borick, *Gallant Defense*, 170–71.

11. Entry for December 27, 1778, Grimké, "Order Book," *SCHGM* 14–1: 50; McIntosh journal, April 21, 1780, in McIntosh, *Lachlan McIntosh Papers*, 106; Moultrie, *Memoirs*, 2:73–77; Borick, *Gallant Defense*, 171–72.

12. McIntosh journal, April 20, 1780, and Subaltern's journal, April 21, 1780, in McIntosh, *Lachlan McIntosh Papers*, 106, 116; Borick, *Gallant Defense*, 172–73.

13. Uhlendorf, *Siege of Charleston*, 61–71, 255–73; Clinton, *American Rebellion*, 169–70; Moultrie, *Memoirs*, 2:78; Wilson, *Southern Strategy*, 217, 220; Borick, *Gallant Defense*, 176, 197.

14. Moultrie, *Memoirs*, 2:85n†.

15. Ibid., 2:78–79; entry for April 24, 1784, Journal accompanying John F. Grimké, "Orderly book (1778 Aug. 24–1780 May 10)," Mss 34/0201, SCHS; entry for April 23, 1780, John F. Grimké, "Orderly book (1778 Aug. 24–1780 May 10)," Mss 34/0201, SCHS; McIntosh journal, April 24, 1780, in McIntosh, *Lachlan McIntosh Papers*, 107; Borick, *Gallant Defense*, 177–78; Uhlendorf, *Siege of Charleston*, 265; Smith and Salley, *Register of St. Philip's Parish: 1754–1810*, 336.

16. Moultrie, *Memoirs*, 2:79 (quoted); Francis Marion to Isaac Harleston, January 26, 1780, in "Letters of General Francis Marion," *Year Book—1895, City of Charleston*, 326; Moultrie, *Memoirs*, 2:64; Borick, *Gallant Defense*, 177.

17. Extracts of a letter from John Moultrie to Alexander Moultrie, July 8, 1780, Gubbins, M.C.B, Transcripts and abstracts of Moultrie family papers, 1746–1965, SCHS Letters (43/36).

18. Ibid. (quoted); Moultrie, *Memoirs,* 1:185.

19. Moultrie, *Memoirs,* 2:80 (quoted), 80n; McIntosh journal, April 26 and 30, 1780, in McIntosh, *Lachlan McIntosh Papers,* 108–9, 110–11; Lincoln, *Original Papers,* 20–21; Wilson, *Southern Strategy,* 229, 314n106; Borick, *Gallant Defense,* 180–81.

20. Moultrie, *Memoirs,* 2:84 (first quote); and Uhlendorf, Siege of Charleston, 75–83 (second quote).

21. Moultrie, *Memoirs,* 2:71, 83n (quoted).

22. Ibid., 2:83n (quoted).

23. Ibid., 2:85, 85n*.

24. Ibid.

25. Borick, *Gallant Defense,* 159; Moultrie, *Memoirs,* 2:72n† (quoted).

26. Borick, *Gallant Defense,* 148–50, 188–89; Moultrie, *Memoirs,* 2:64 (quoted); McIntosh journal, April 24–27, 1780, and Subaltern's journal, April 24, 1780, in McIntosh, *Lachlan McIntosh Papers,* 107–9, 118.

27. Moultrie, *Memoirs,* 2:60–61 (quoted), 79; Subaltern's journal, April 24, 1780, in McIntosh, *Lachlan McIntosh Papers,* 118.

28. Moultrie, *Memoirs,* 2:84–85; Clinton, *American Rebellion,* 169; Uhlendorf, *Siege of Charleston,* 283, 285; Tarleton, *History of the Campaigns of 1780 and 1781,* 55–57; John Lewis Gervais to Henry Laurens, May 13, 1780, in *Papers of Henry Laurens,* 15:289, 289n1; Murdoch, "French Account of the Siege of Charleston," 152, 152n53; Hough, *Siege of Charleston,* 166–69 (quoted).

29. Moultrie, *Memoirs,* 2:84–85, 84n†, 106–7; McCrady, *Revolution 1775,* 492; Hough, *Siege of Charleston,* 166; Tarleton, *History of the Campaigns of 1780 and 1781,* 57–58; Wilson, *Southern Strategy,* 230–31. Moultrie stated in his memoirs that a British flag flew over Fort Moultrie on May 6, 1780.

30. Moultrie, *Memoirs,* 2:84, 85–87; Borick, *Gallant Defense,* 209; Lincoln, *Original Papers,* 11–13.

31. Moultrie, *Memoirs,* 2:87–92 (quoted); Subaltern's journal, May 10, 1780, in McIntosh, *Lachlan McIntosh Papers,* 120; Borick, *Gallant Defense,* 213.

32. Moultrie, *Memoirs,* 2:92–96; Gervais to Laurens, May 13, 1780, in *Papers of Henry Laurens,* 15:290.

33. Moultrie, *Memoirs,* 2:96 (quoted), 96n.

34. Ibid., 2:96–97 (quoted); Uhlendorf, *Siege of Charleston,* 85.

35. Lincoln, *Original Papers,* 56–70; Borick, *Gallant Defense,* 216–18.

36. Moultrie, *Memoirs,* 2:99–103.

37. Ibid., 2:106–7, 114, 117; Wilson, *Southern Strategy,* 241; McCrady, *Revolution 1775,* 506–11, 507–10n4; Borick, *Gallant Defense,* 222.

Chapter 22: Prisoner of War

1. Moultrie, *Memoirs* 2:101n, 108; Wilson, *Southern Strategy,* 234; Borick, *Gallant Defense,* 219; Burgoyne, *Enemy Views,* 389 (quoted).

2. Moultrie, *Memoirs,* 2:108 (quoted), 114.

3. Ibid., 2:109 (quoted); Uhlendorf, *Siege of Charleston,* 89; Pancake, *This Destructive War,* 66, 252–53n18.

4. Moultrie, *Memoirs,* 2:110–11 (quoted); Godbold and Woody, *Christopher Gadsden,* 201.

5. Moultrie, *Memoirs,* 2:108, 115–16, 122–23 (quoted), 147n; Ervin, *South Carolinians in the Revolution,* 56; Borick, *Relieve Us of This Burthen,* 47, 51.

6. Moultrie, *Memoirs,* 2:115–16; Borick, *Relieve Us of This Burthen,* 47–48, 52 (map), 142n4; Cooper, *Statutes at Large,* 4:379–81.

7. Moultrie, *Memoirs,* 2:115–16, 115n; Ravenel, *Charleston,* 279–81 (quoted); Nisbet Balfour to Charles Cornwallis, September 27, 1781, in Cornwallis, *Cornwallis Papers,* 2:111.

8. Ravenel, *Charleston,* 279–81; Zahniser, *Charles Cotesworth Pinckney,* 64–66.

9. Moultrie, *Memoirs,* 2:112–13, 115–16, 118; Borick, *Relieve Us of This Burthen,* 48, 142n6.

10. Moultrie, *Memoirs,* 2:115, 129–130.

11. Ibid., 2:117; entry for November 20, 1778, Grimké, "Order Book," *SCHGM* 13–3: 153; *JCC,* 28:71–72; George Turner to President of Congress, October 7, 1780, PCC, NA microfilm series M247, roll 103 (vol. 22): 429–31; George Turner, memorial to the Continental Congress, May 19, 1780, PCC, NA microfilm series M247, roll 52 (vol. 10): 157–58.

12. George Turner memorial.

13. Moultrie, *Memoirs,* 2:117–18, 124–26, 129–30; George Turner memorial; *JCC,* 28:71–72; *JCC,* 22:290; Diary, March 21, 1782, *Papers of Robert Morris,* 4:428–29, 429–30n4; George Turner to President of Congress, October 7, 1780, PCC, NA microfilm series M247, roll 103 (vol. 22): 429–31; George Turner to Thomas McKean, August 23, 1781, PCC, NA microfilm series M247, roll 103 (vol. 22): 473–76; Samuel Huntington to Horatio Gates, August 17, 1780, PCC, NA microfilm series M247, roll 24 (item no. 15): 76; Samuel Huntington to William Moultrie, August 14, 1780, PCC, NA microfilm series M247, roll 24 (item no. 15): 77.

14. Borick, *Relieve Us of This Burthen,* 61–64; "Court of Inquiry," December 19, 1780, PCC, NA microfilm series M247, roll 103 (vol. 22): 485.

15. Moultrie, *Memoirs,* 2:384–86; McCrady, *Revolution 1775,* 552–60.

16. Moultrie, *Memoirs,* 2:119–20.

17. Ibid., 2:120–21, 123–24 (quoted).

18. Ibid., 2:126–27 (quoted), 211, 300.

19. Ibid., 2:130–31.

20. Ibid.

21. Ibid., 2:132–35 (quoted); Taliaferro, *Revolutionary War Diary and Order Book,* entries for July 6–9, 1780.

22. Davis, "Lord Montagu's Mission," 95; Borick, *Relieve Us of This Burthen,* 54; Moultrie, *Memoirs,* 2:99–103.

23. Moultrie, *Memoirs,* 2:142–45; Ranlet, "In the Hands of the British," 744 (quoted).

24. Moultrie, *Memoirs,* 2:252, 300.

25. Ibid., 138–39; McCrady, *Revolution 1775,* 716–21; Lists of inhabitants of Charlestown transported to St. Augustine, East Florida, in September and November 1780, Collection re South Carolina, 1780–1782, Papers and Collection of Peter Force, MSS63511, series 7E: item 129, microfilm 19,061 (reel 42), frames 400–02, Manuscript Division, LOC.

26. Moultrie, *Memoirs,* 2:138–42 (quoted), 194–95; Davis, "Lord Montagu's Mission," 95. Balfour termed Moultrie's objections over the transportation of prisoners as "high and violent." Nisbet Balfour to Charles Cornwallis, September 5, September 27, and October 22, 1781, in Cornwallis, *Cornwallis Papers,* 2:78, 130.

27. Moultrie, *Memoirs,* 2:151, 155–60, 159n†, 193–95; Davis, "Lord Montagu's Mission," 94–96; Borick, *Relieve Us of This Burthen,* 30, 32, 72, 76.

28. McCrady, *Revolution 1780,* 349–50; Borick, *Relieve Us of This Burthen,* 58–59.

29. Moultrie, *Memoirs*, 2:140–41, 164–66, 193–95; William Moultrie to John Mathews, March 21, 1781, PCC, NA microfilm series M247, roll 177 (vol. 2): 489 (quoted); William Moultrie to Samuel Huntington, April 3, 1781, PCC, NA microfilm series M247, roll 177 (vol. 2): 497.

30. *JCC*, 20:620–23.

31. Moultrie, *Memoirs*, 2:148–49, 152–53.

32. Ibid., 2:154–55 (quoted), 157–58.

33. Ibid., 2:160.

34. Nadelhaft, *Disorders of War*, 64; Davis, "Lord Montagu's Mission," 89–109.

35. Charles Montague to William Moultrie, February 9, 1781, in *Correspondence of Lord Montague with General Moultrie*, 7–8.

36. Charles Montague to William Moultrie, March 11, 1781, in Courtenay, *Correspondence of Lord Montague with General Moultrie*, 9–10.

37. Ibid., 10–11.

38. William Moultrie to Charles Montague, March 12, 1781, in Courtenay, *Correspondence of Lord Montague with General Moultrie*, 13–15.

39. Ibid., 16.

40. Ibid., 18–19 (quoted); Moultrie, *Memoirs*, 2:170.

41. Moultrie, *Memoirs*, 2:149–50.

42. Thomas, "William Moultrie," 401.

Chapter 23: Exchange and Repatriation

1. Moultrie, *Memoirs*, 2:256 (quoted), 258, 258n.

2. Nathanael Greene to William Moultrie, December 18, 1780, in Greene, *Papers of General Nathanael Greene*, 6:597; William Moultrie to Nathanael Greene, January 1, 1781, in Greene, *Papers of General Nathanael Greene*, 7:37 (quoted).

3. Moultrie to Greene, January 1, 1781, in Greene, *Papers of General Nathanael Greene*, 7:37; Moultrie, *Memoirs*, 2:162–63; William Moultrie to Samuel Huntington, March 19, 1781, PCC, NA microfilm series M247, roll 177 (vol. 2): 481; *JCC*, 20:468.

4. Moultrie, *Memoirs*, 2:172–93, 200–201.

5. Ibid.

6. Ibid., 2:152–53; Moultrie to Greene, January 1, 1781, and William Moultrie to Nathanael Greene, January 30, 1781, in Greene, *Papers of General Nathanael Greene*, 7:37, 222–23.

7. Moultrie, *Memoirs*, 2:162 (quoted), 174.

8. Ibid., 2:171–72, 193–94 (quoted).

9. Ibid., 2:173–74, 194–95, 194n.

10. Ibid., 2:174 (first quote), 223n; William Moultrie to Francis Marion, April 16, 1781, in Gibbes, *Documentary History* [1853], 52 (second quote). See also William Harden to Nathanael Greene, November 7, 1781, in Greene, *Papers of General Nathanael Greene*, 9:543–44, 544n4.

11. Moultrie, *Memoirs*, 2:171–74, 193–200; Nisbet Balfour to William Moultrie, April 2, 1781, PCC, NA microfilm series M247, roll 177 (vol. 2): 505; Knight, "Prisoner Exchange and Parole," 210.

12. Entry for December 31, 1781, in Smith, "Josiah Smith's Diary," 78; Zahniser, *Charles Cotesworth Pinckney*, 66; McCrady, *Revolution 1780*, 375–79.

13. Knight, "Prisoner Exchange and Parole," 210; Moultrie, *Memoirs*, 2:200, 353–44; William Moultrie to [Thomas McKean], July 19, 1781, Washington Irving Collection, Stanford University; Thomas, "William Moultrie," 24. Moultrie intended to leave for Philadelphia on

June 15. William Moultrie to Major [Isaac] Harleston, June 8, 1781, SCHS Letters (43/0911). On page 200 of the second volume of *Memoirs of the American Revolution,* he claims to have departed Charleston in June 1781; however on page 354 he presents a parole that he signed on July 8, 1781, in Charleston.

14. Knight, "Prisoner Exchange and Parole," 212.

15. Officers of the states of South Carolina and Georgia to William Moultrie, August 13, 1871, PCC, NA microfilm M247, roll 177 (vol. 2): 525–26.

16. William Moultrie to Thomas McKean, August 16, 1781, PCC, NA microfilm M247, roll 177 (vol. 2): 521–22; Knight, "Prisoner Exchange and Parole," 211–12; *JCC,* 21:881, 886, 976, 1026–27; Diary, October 2, 1781, in Morris, *Papers of Robert Morris,* 3:9.

17. Entry for the Pennsylvania ship *Columbia,* in Lincoln, *Naval Records of the American Revolution,* 254. The *Columbia* was not Moultrie's first maritime venture. In 1778 he invested in a new brig under construction at Beaufort. See Receipt, February 11, 1778, Moultrie Papers, box 1, folder 8, SCL.

18. "On Thursday the 30th of August," *Philadelphia Pennsylvania Packet,* September 1, 1781; Diary, August 30, 1781, in Morris, *Papers of Robert Morris,* 2:158.

19. George Washington to Comte de Rochambeau, January 14, 1782, in *Writings of George Washington,* 23:446; Moultrie, *Memoirs,* 2:200, 352–54; "An Exchange of an equivalent number of American Officers and Privates prisoners of war for Lieut. Gen'l. Burgoyne," PCC, NA microfilm series M247, roll 171 (vol. 10): 451; Knight, "Prisoner Exchange and Parole," 213.

20. Moultrie, *Memoirs,* 2:361 (quoted); Sellers, "Portraits and Miniatures by Charles Willson Peale," 149–50.

21. William Moultrie to John Hanson, February 21, 1782, PCC, NA microfilm series M247, roll 177 (vol. 2): 529–31 (quoted); Heitman, *Historical Register,* 9–10.

22. Moultrie to Hanson, February 21, 1782, PCC, NA microfilm M247, roll 177 (vol. 2): 521–22. See also William Moultrie and Lachlan McIntosh, "Letter intended for Congress from the Genls. Moultrie & McIntosh on the promotion of Knox & Duportail," [February 1782], in McIntosh, *Lachlan McIntosh Papers,* 48–50.

23. *JCC,* 22:105, 143–48.

24. Richard Parker to Nathanael Greene, May 12, 1779, in Greene, *Papers of General Nathanael Greene,* 4:16–17, 17n2; *JCC,* 22:349–50, 451–52; *JCC,* 23:650–51.

25. *JCC,* 22:349–50.

26. George Washington to James Clinton, August 8, 1782, in *Writings of George Washington,* 24:491.

27. William Moultrie to Charles Cotesworth Pinckney, March 3, 1782, Charles Cotesworth Pinckney Family Papers, LOC; Williams, *Founding Family,* 182–83; Nathanael Greene to Francis Marion, April 10, 1782, in Gibbes, *Documentary History,* 2:159.

28. Moultrie to Pinckney, March 3, 1782, Charles Cotesworth Pinckney Family Papers, LOC (first quote); William Moultrie to Hannah Moultrie, August 17, 1782, private collection, Charleston, S.C.; Moultrie, *Memoirs,* 2:354–55 (second quote), 355n.

29. Moultrie, *Memoirs,* 2:355.

30. Tarleton, *History of the Campaigns of 1780 and 1781,* 91 (first quote), 190–95; Moultrie, *Memoirs,* 2:356 (second quote).

31. "Ky!" is supposedly "an African interjection, showing a delighted astonishment, equivalent to 'is it possible?—can the good news be really true!'" Griswold, Simms, and Ingraham, *Washington and the Generals of the American Revolution,* 2:56. Moultrie, *Memoirs,* 2:355–56; William Moultrie to Hannah Moultrie, August 17, 1782, private collection, Charleston, S.C.

(quoted). Moultrie's letter to his wife refutes the notion that nostalgia clouded his twenty-year-old recollection of his homecoming. Olwell, *Masters, Slaves and Subjects*, 274–75, 275n11.

32. Moultrie, *Memoirs*, 2:298, 356; William Moultrie to Nathanael Greene, October 31, 1782, in Greene, *Papers of General Nathanael Greene*, 12:131.

33. William Moultrie to Hannah Moultrie, August 17, 1782, private collection, Charleston, S.C.; John Mathews to Alexander Leslie, August 17, 1782, in Historical Manuscripts Commission, *Report on the American Manuscripts*, 3:76.

34. William Moultrie to Hannah Moultrie, August 17, 1782, private collection, Charleston, S.C.; Moultrie, *Memoirs*, 2:356.

35. Moultrie to Nathanael Greene, October 31, 1782, in Greene, *Papers of General Nathanael Greene*, 12:131; Moultrie, *Memoirs*, 2:357–58; William Moultrie to Hannah Moultrie, November 29, 1782, copy in Moultrie Papers, box 1, folder 12, SCL.

36. William Moultrie to Hannah Moultrie, November 29, 1782, copy in Moultrie Papers, box 1, folder 12, SCL.

37. Moultrie, *Memoirs*, 2:359–60; McCrady, *Revolution 1780*, 730; Williams, *Founding Family*, 191; Simms, "Marion—The Carolina Partisan," 113–14 (quoted).

38. Moultrie, *Memoirs*, 2:359–60. Mordecai Gist was a brigadier general in the Maryland Line in the Continental Army.

39. Ibid.; *JCC*, 23:653–56.

Chapter 24: Restoring Civil Government

1. Moultrie, *Memoirs*, 2:301.

2. Ibid., 2:303.

3. John A. Hall, "Quieting the Storm: The Establishment of Order in Post-Revolutionary South Carolina," Ph.D. thesis, Oxford University, 1989, 739.

4. Coker, "Case of James Nassau Colleton," 106. For more about confiscation and amercement, see Cooper, *Statutes at Large*, 4:516–28; McCord, *Statutes at Large*, 6:629–35; Singer, *South Carolina in the Confederation*, 102–25.

5. Moultrie, *Memoirs*, 2:303–4, 325–26 (quoted).

6. Smith, "Baronies of South Carolina IV," 43, 51.

7. Edgar and Bailey, *Biographical Directory, Volume II*, 487–88; Thompson and Lumpkin, *Journals of the House of Representatives* (hereinafter *JHR*) *1783–1784*, ix–xii, 43, 130.

8. Thompson and Lumpkin, *JHR 1783–1784*, 341; Moultrie, *Memoirs*, 2:85.

9. Thompson and Lumpkin, *JHR 1783–1784*, 408; Moultrie, *Memoirs*, 2:325–26 (quoted).

10. Hall, "Quieting the Storm," 17–44, 55–84; Thompson and Lumpkin, *JHR 1783–1784*, 370; McCord, *Statutes at Large*, 7:97–101.

11. Thompson and Lumpkin, *JHR 1783–1784*, xii, 438, 453–54, 521, 621, 629.

12. Edgar and Bailey, *Biographical Directory, Volume II*, 487–88; Adams and Lumpkin, *JHR 1785–1786*, 76–88 (quoted).

13. Thompson and Lumpkin, *JHR 1783–1784*, xii, 287; Wallace, "Constitution of 1790," in Snowden and Cutler, *History of South Carolina*, 1:507 (quoted).

14. Adams and Lumpkin, *JHR 1785–1786*, vii–viii; Thompson and Lumpkin, *JHR 1783–1784*, 287.

15. Thompson and Lumpkin, *JHR 1783–1784*, 287, 288, 296, 300; Benjamin Guerard to Nathanael Greene, March 28, 1783, in Greene, *Papers of General Nathanael Greene*, 12:546n1, 546–47, 546–47n1.

16. McCord, *Statutes at Large*, 9:682–91; Adams and Lumpkin, *JHR 1785–1786*, 97 (quoted).

17. Adams and Lumpkin, *JHR 1785–1786*, 97, 133.

18. Ibid., 365–66 (quoted); Stevens and Allen, *JHR 1787–1788*, 38; McCord, *Statutes at Large*, 8:485–97.

19. Edgar, *South Carolina*, 245–46; Klein, *Unification of a Slave State*, 126–27; Singer, *South Carolina in the Confederation*, 118–19.

20. Edwards, *JPC*, 167.

21. Adams and Lumpkin, *JHR 1785–1786*, 313.

22. Ibid., 313–14.

23. Adams and Lumpkin, *JHR 1785–1786*, 315; Klein, *Unification of a Slave State*, 127–28; Edgar, *South Carolina*, 246–47; Cooper, *Statutes at Large*, 4:710–16.

24. Singer, *South Carolina in the Confederation*, 119; Cooper, *Statutes at Large*, 4:640–41; *JCC*, 26:26–27 (quoted).

25. William Moultrie to John Jay, June 21, 1786, PCC, NA microfilm series M247, roll 86 (item no. 72): 599–600.

26. Edgar, *South Carolina*, 247; Stevens and Allen, *JHR 1787–1788*, xii–xx; Cooper, *Statutes at Large*, 5:36–38; South Carolina General Assembly, Senate Journals (engrossed manuscripts) 1782–1877, Series 165208, Entry on February 18, 1788, Senate Journals, January 8, 1788–February 29, 1788, SCDAH, 163; Klein, *Unification of a Slave State*, 123–35.

27. Benjamin Hawkins and Andrew Pickens to William Moultrie, January 6, 1786, South Carolina General Assembly, Legislative Papers 1782–1866, Governors' Messages 1783–1870, Series 165009, message 378, SCDAH; Adams and Lumpkin, *JHR 1785–1786*, 386; Cooper, *Statutes at Large*, 4:590–93.

28. Adams and Lumpkin, *JHR 1785–1786*, 97.

29. Ibid., 511–12, 549, 589, 591; "A Proclamation," *Columbian Herald* (Charleston, S.C.), March 30, 1786.

30. Adams and Lumpkin, *JHR 1785–1786*, 428–29, 442; Kappler, *Indian Affairs, Laws and Treaties*, 2:11.

31. Adams and Lumpkin, *JHR 1785–1786*, 568–69; Edwards, *JPC*, 171–72 (quoted).

32. Edwards, *JPC*, 172.

33. Ibid., 172–75 (quoted); Adams and Lumpkin, *JHR 1785–1786*, 574–75.

34. Entry on February 28, 1787, Senate Journals, January 1, 1787–March 28, 1787, SCDAH, 117; "The following Members were elected for Saint John's Parish, Berkeley county," *Columbian Herald* (Charleston, S.C.), December 4, 1789; Stevens and Allen, *JHR 1787–1788*, 118–19.

35. Lockhart, "'Under the Wings of Columbia,'" 186–87.

36. Edgar, *South Carolina*, 248; Lockhart, "'Under the Wings of Columbia,'" 187–90; Klein, *Unification of a Slave State*, 143, 143n74. See also Cooper, *Statutes at Large*, 4:751–52, 5:102–3.

Chapter 25: South Carolina's Cincinnatus

1. Myers, *Liberty without Anarchy*, 1–5, 15–18.

2. Ibid., 18–19, 31, 198–99. See also Creighton, *History of Rome*, 23.

3. Moultrie, *Memoirs*, 1:305 (first quote); William Moultrie to Nathanael Greene, May 5, 1783, Moultrie Papers, SCL (second quote).

4. Rogers, "Society of the Cincinnati," 9; Proceedings of the Society of the Cincinnati of the State of South Carolina, August 29, 1783, General Society Archives, State Societies, Correspondence and Documents, Box XIII, Folder 6A [South Carolina], Society of the Cincinnati.

5. Proceedings of the Society of the Cincinnati of the State of South Carolina, August 29, September 13, and October 6, 1783, General Society Archives, Box XIII, Folder 6A, Society of the Cincinnati; "A Quarterly Meeting," *South Carolina Gazette,* September 23–27, 1783.

6. William Moultrie to Friedrich Wilhelm Augustin von Steuben, October 13, 1783, General Society Archives, Box XIII, Folder 6A, Society of the Cincinnati. See also Circular to the Senior Officer of the Cincinnati in Certain States, October 24, 1783, in *Writings of George Washington,* 27:207–8.

7. Myers, *Liberty without Anarchy,* 40, 48–50.

8. Ibid.; Meleney, *Public Life of Aedanus Burke,* 61; Hünemörder, *Society of the Cincinnati,* 86, 145.

9. Meleney, *Public Life of Aedanus Burke,* 85n19; Burke, *Considerations on the Society,* passim.

10. Myers, *Liberty without Anarchy,* 51–66, 70–74, 139; Moore, *Fabric of Liberty,* 57 (quoted).

11. George Washington to William Moultrie (circular letter), January 5, 1784, Mss 1280.1, Society of the Cincinnati; Rogers, "Society of the Cincinnati," 11; William Moultrie to George Washington, April 6, 1784, in *Papers of George Washington: Confederation Series,* 1:1, 269–70, 270–71nn1, 3; "Monday last being the Anniversary of the Society of the Cincinnati," *South Carolina Weekly Gazette* (Charleston), January 9, 1784; *JCC,* 27:646; Thompson and Lumpkin, *JHR 1783–1784,* 438, 453–54, 521, 621, 629; William Moultrie to George Washington, April 6, 1784, and Proceedings of the Society of the Cincinnati of the State of South Carolina, January 5 and April 5, 1784, General Society Archives, Box XIII, Folder 6B, Society of the Cincinnati; Society of the Cincinnati, *Proceedings of the General Society of the Cincinnati,* 10. See also William Moultrie, 1730–1805, State Society of the Cincinnati of Pennsylvania, Minutes, May 4–18, 1784, Mss Collection, BV Moultrie, New-York Historical Society.

12. Myers, *Liberty without Anarchy,* 31, 58, 64, 93, 115; Circular letter from George Washington to the Society of the Cincinnati, October 31, 1786, in *Papers of George Washington: Confederation Series,* 4:316–17.

13. William Moultrie to George Washington, February 23, 1787, in *Papers of George Washington: Confederation Series,* 5:48.

14. Ellis, *His Excellency,* 158–59; Myers, *Liberty without Anarchy,* 93–98, 198–99.

15. "Address of the Society of the Cincinnati of the State of South-Carolina, Voted November, 17, 1789, to George Washington, President of the United States," *New York Daily Gazette,* March 8, 1790.

16. "The President's Answer to the State Society of the Cincinnati in South Carolina," *New York Daily Gazette,* March 8, 1790.

17. Myers, *Liberty without Anarchy,* 16. Myers quotes Thomas Jefferson's "Memorandums on a tour from Paris to Amsterdam, Strasburg, and back to Paris, 3 March 1788 [to 23 April 1788]," entry for March 16, 1788, in Jefferson, *Papers of Thomas Jefferson,* 13:11.

18. Myers, *Liberty without Anarchy,* 19, 32–34, 262–63; Society of the Cincinnati, *Proceedings of the General Society of the Cincinnati,* 13–15.

19. Certificate of John McFarlane regarding eagles for the South Carolina Society, October 29, 1787, General Society Archives, Box XI (L'Enfant Correspondence), Folder 4M, Society of the Cincinnati; Resolutions of the South Carolina Society, signed by William Moultrie, November 5, 1787, General Society Archives, Box XI (L'Enfant Correspondence), Folder 4N, Society of the Cincinnati; "The subscriber informs those indebted to Mr. William Thompson," *South Carolina Gazette,* February 9–12, 1785; list of South Carolina members who

ordered eagles from Major Pierre L'Enfant, copied July 21, 1787, General Society Archives, Box XI (L'Enfant Correspondence), Folder 4J, Society of the Cincinnati.

20. Friedrich Wilhelm Augustin von Steuben to William Moultrie, July 28, 1786, in von Steuben, *Papers of General Friedrich Wilhelm von Steuben,* microform, roll 7, item 37–2.

21. William Moultrie to Friedrich Wilhelm Augustin von Steuben, October 17, 1786, James Dudley Morgan Collection of Digges-L'Enfant-Morgan Papers, LOC.

22. Ibid.

23. Society of the Cincinnati, *Proceedings of the General Society of the Cincinnati,* 24–25, 32–34.

24. William Moultrie to Pierre Charles L'Enfant, May 29, 1788, Digges-L'Enfant-Morgan Papers, LOC.

25. St. Andrew's Society of the City of Charleston, Charleston, S.C., *Rules of the St. Andrew's Society,* 26, 66, 115–16 (quoted), 125, 130. Sometime between 1788 and 1798, the name of the St. Andrew's Club was changed to St. Andrew's Society.

Chapter 26: Canals, Constitutions, and Commissioners

1. Kapsch, *Historic Canals and Waterways,* 8–14, 17–18, 21–23.

2. Ibid., 23–24; "Thursday last . . . ," *South Carolina Gazette* (Charleston), November 12, 1785 (quoted).

3. Kapsch, *Historic Canals and Waterways,* 23–24; Porcher, *History of the Santee Canal,* 3; "Extracts from the Minutes of the General Assembly of South-Carolina," *State Gazette of South Carolina* (Charleston), February 9, 1786; Adams and Lumpkin, *JHR 1785–1786,* 98 (quoted), 378–79.

4. McCord, *Statutes at Large,* 7:541–43; "At a meeting of the incorporated Company for opening inland navigation between the Santee and Cooper Rivers," *Charleston Evening Gazette,* March 25, 1786; "At a meeting of the Vice-President and Board of Directors," *State Gazette of South Carolina* (Charleston), April 19, 1787; Edgar, *South Carolina,* 282.

5. William Moultrie to George Washington, April 7, 1786, in *Papers of George Washington: Confederation Series,* 4:6–7 (quoted); Levine, "Letter from William Moultrie," 116–20.

6. George Washington to William Moultrie, May 25, 1786, in *Papers of George Washington: Confederation Series,* 4:73–75.

7. William Moultrie to George Washington, August 7, 1786, in *Papers of George Washington: Confederation Series,* 4:201–2, 202n1; Christian Senf to George Washington, February 24, 1790, in *Papers of George Washington: Presidential Series,* 5:173; Kapsch, *Historic Canals and Waterways,* 26–27; Moultrie, *Memoirs,* 1:265.

8. "Yesterday the stockholders of the Santee Canal Company held a meeting," *Charleston City Gazette,* July 2, 1793 (quoted); Webber, "Col. Senf's Account," part 2, 119; Porcher, *History of the Santee Canal,* 4–5; Kapsch, *Historic Canals and Waterways,* 27, 32–35, 42.

9. Webber, "Col. Senf's Account," part 2, 120; Kapsch, *Historic Canals and Waterways,* 41–42, 45–46, 49–52; Porcher, *History of the Santee Canal,* 7.

10. "At a meeting of the stockholders of the Santee Canal Company," *Charleston City Gazette,* January 22, 1794; Advertisements for Santee Canal lotteries, *Charleston City Gazette,* May 4, June 12, August 13, and November 6, 1795; "A committee of the directors of the Santee Canal Company," *Charleston City Gazette,* March 26, 1795 (quoted); "Santee Canal," *Charleston City Gazette,* July 10, 1797; "Shares in the Santee Canal," *Charleston City Gazette,* July 8, 1797.

11. Porcher, *History of the Santee Canal,* 4, 7–8, 47; Kapsch, *Historic Canals and Waterways,* 21–23, 26–27, 52–53; Webber, "Col. Senf's Account," part 1, 9; "Yesterday the Stockholders in

the Santee Canal Company held a meeting," *Charleston City Gazette*, March 1, 1797; Drayton, *View of South-Carolina*, 155.

12. Entry on February 23, 1787, South Carolina General Assembly, Senate Journals, January 1, 1787–March 28, 1787, Series 165208, SCDAH, 89–99; McCord, *Statutes at Large*, 7:545–47, 549–51, 558–59; Stevens and Allen, *JHR 1789–1790*, 136 (quoted), 136n7, 163, 191–92; Kapsch, *Historic Canals and Waterways*, 54, 63–65.

13. The quotation is attributed to a letter from William Moultrie to James Bowdoin that George Bancroft variably dates as October 18, 1785, September 20, 1785, and September 10, 1785. Bancroft, *History of the Formation of the Constitution*, 1:208, 458–59; Bancroft, *History of the United States of America*, 6:153.

14. Adams and Lumpkin, *JHR 1785–1786*, 365; Starr, *School for Politics*, 100–101.

15. Cooper, *Statutes at Large*, 4:596, 720; William Moultrie to Charles Thompson, March 29, 1786, PCC, NA microfilm series M247, roll 86 (item no. 72): 595 (quoted).

16. William Moultrie to Patrick Henry, June 27, 1786, Patrick Henry Papers, 1776–1818, MSS25767, LOC.

17. Stevens and Allen, *JHR 1787–1788*, vii, 14–15; "Message from His Excellency the Governor," *Charleston Morning Post and Daily Advertiser*, January 27, 1787.

18. Edgar, *South Carolina*, 250–51; Elliot, *Debates in the Several State Conventions*, 4:253–317.

19. Elliot, *Debates in the Several State Conventions*, 4:316–41 (quoted); Edgar, *South Carolina*, 251–52; Stevens and Allen, *JHR 1787–1788*, 558.

20. Edgar, *South Carolina*, 254–57; Hutson, Journal of the Constitutional Convention of South Carolina, 3, 7, 18.

21. "Died in Charleston . . . ," *Savannah Georgia Gazette*, December 31, 1789; William Moultrie to Hannah Moultrie, November 29, 1782, copy in Moultrie Papers, box 1, folder 12, SCL; "Col. R. John West Speaks on Gen. Moultrie's Life," *Charleston News and Courier*, October 6, 1929 (quoted).

22. Ramsay, *Ramsay's History of South Carolina*, 2:108.

23. Stevens and Allen, *JHR 1791*, xiv, 273, 273nn3–4; Cooper and McCord, *Statutes at Large*, 1:193.

24. Cooper, *Statutes at Large*, 5:171–75 (quoted); South Carolina General Assembly, *Acts of the General Assembly*, 66–72.

25. Stevens and Allen, *JHR 1791*, 395–99.

26. Ibid.; William Moultrie, John Lewis Gervais, and Arnoldus Vanderhorst, "General Account of Principal Indents Issued Since 22d March 1783," December 14, 1791, General Assembly and Other Miscellaneous Records, 1774–1910, Series 390008, Year: 1791, item 19, SCDAH.

27. Report of William Moultrie, Arnoldus Vanderhorst, and John Lewis Gervais, Commissioners to Settle the Public Accounts, November 22, 1792, South Carolina General Assembly, Legislative Papers 1782–1866, Governors' Messages 1783–1870, Series 165009, message 553 (quoted), SCDAH; Stevens, *JHR 1792–1794*, 49–50, 49–50n18, 542–43n2.

Chapter 27: *"The honor of being one of your family"*

1. Haynesworth, "Washington's 1791 Visit," 29.

2. Lipscomb, *South Carolina in 1791*, 1–2; Flexner, *George Washington and the New Nation*, 268–71, 286, 289–90; Moore, *Fabric of Liberty*, 89–90.

3. Editorial note, in *Papers of George Washington: Presidential Series*, 7:472–74; Washington, *Diaries of George Washington*, 6:96–98; George Washington to Thomas Jefferson, April

1, 1791, in *Papers of George Washington: Presidential Series,* 8:35–36 (quoted); Flexner, *George Washington and the New Nation,* 287, 289.

4. Henderson, *Washington's Southern Tour,* 145–46, 150–52; "The members of the Society of the Cincinnati . . . ," *Charleston City Gazette,* April 19, 1791 (quoted); "Charleston," *Charleston City Gazette,* May 2, 1791.

5. Washington, *Diaries,* 6:121–24; Salley, *President Washington's Tour,* 11, 14.

6. Charles Pinckney to George Washington, April 26, 1791, in *Papers of George Washington: Presidential Series,* 8:138–39 (quoted).

7. Williams, *Founding Family,* 292; Lipscomb, *South Carolina in 1791,* 16; Levine, "Letter from William Moultrie," 116–20.

8. Pinckney to Washington, April 26, 1791, in *Papers of George Washington: Presidential Series,* 8: 138–39; Washington, *Diaries,* 6:126.

9. *Charleston City Gazette,* May 14, 1791; Lipscomb, *South Carolina in 1791,* 21.

10. *Charleston City Gazette,* May 14, 1791; Washington, *Diaries,* 6:126–27; Lipscomb, *South Carolina in 1791,* 21.

11. *Charleston City Gazette,* May 14, 1791; Lipscomb, *South Carolina in 1791,* 23–24; "Exchange and Provost," *National Register of Historic Places Nomination Form,* December 17, 1969, on file at SCDAH.

12. *Charleston City Gazette,* May 14, 1791; Washington, *Diaries* 6:127–29; Henderson, *Washington's Southern Tour,* 159–61; Pinckney to Washington, April 26, 1791, in *Papers of George Washington: Presidential Series,* 8:138–39.

13. *Charleston City Gazette,* May 14, 1791.

14. Ibid.; Henderson, *Washington's Southern Tour,* 172–73; Lipscomb, *South Carolina in 1791,* 29–30.

15. *Charleston City Gazette,* May 14, 1791; Lipscomb, *South Carolina in 1791,* 29–30.

16. *Charleston City Gazette,* May 14, 1791; Washington, *Diaries,* 6:130 (quoted); Lipscomb, *South Carolina in 1791,* 30–31; Mattern, *Benjamin Lincoln,* 98.

17. *Charleston City Gazette,* May 14, 1791; Washington, *Diaries,* 6: 130; Lipscomb, *South Carolina in 1791,* 31–32.

18. *Charleston City Gazette,* May 14, 1791.

19. Ibid.

20. Ibid. (quoted); Washington, *Diaries,* 6:131.

21. *Charleston City Gazette,* May 14, 1791; Washington, *Diaries,* 6:131; Henderson, *Washington's Southern Tour,* 180; Lipscomb, *South Carolina in 1791,* 35.

22. *Charleston City Gazette,* May 14, 1791 (quoted); Washington, *Diaries,* 6:132–33.

23. Holmes, *Historic Sketch of the Parish Church of St. Michael,* 41.

24. *Charleston City Gazette,* May 14, 1791; "For Sale," *Charleston City Gazette,* March 30, 1790 (quoted); McElligott, *Charleston Residences,* 56.

25. Chernow, *Washington,* 122, 290–91; Adams, *Life and Writings of Jared Sparks,* 1:558; Lee, *Experiencing Mount Vernon,* 30; Ravenel, *Charleston,* 357 (quoted).

26. *Charleston City Gazette,* March 30, 1790; George Washington to William Blake, June 30, 1785, in *Papers of George Washington: Confederation Series,* 3:86–87; George Washington to William Washington, April 10, 1786, in *Papers of George Washington: Confederation Series,* 4:13; De Forest, *Gardens and Grounds at Mount Vernon,* 27, 64, 81, 107, 110.

27. George Washington to William Moultrie, November 8, 1791, William Moultrie to George Washington, December 29, 1791, and George Washington to Otho Holland Williams,

February 7, 1792, in *Papers of George Washington: Presidential Series*, 9:154–55, 346, 346n1, 551–52, 552n2; William Moultrie to George Washington, November 28, 1791, George Washington Papers, Series 4, General Correspondence, LOC; George Washington to William Moultrie, March 14, 1792 (quoted), and George Washington to William Moultrie, May 5, 1792, in *Papers of George Washington: Presidential Series*, 10:109, 355; De Forest, *Gardens and Grounds at Mount Vernon*, 107; Lipscomb, *South Carolina in 1791*, 43. Sweet shrub is also called Carolina allspice.

28. *Charleston City Gazette*, May 14, 1791; Washington, *Diaries*, 6:133–34 (quoted); Lipscomb, *South Carolina in 1791*, 45.

29. Washington, *Diaries*, 6:133–34. Augusta was Georgia's capital at the time.

30. Ibid. (quoted); Lipscomb, *South Carolina in 1791*, 45–46, 48–51.

31. Washington, *Diaries*, 6:135; Britt, "Society of the Cincinnati in the State of Georgia," 558.

32. George Washington to David Humphreys, July 20, 1791, in *Papers of George Washington: Presidential Series*, 8:358; William Moultrie to George Washington, July 10, 1791, George Washington Papers, Series 4, General Correspondence, LOC (quoted).

33. George Washington to William Moultrie, August 9, 1791, in *Papers of George Washington: Presidential Series*, 8:415 (quoted).

Chapter 28: Security Without and Within

1. "Memorandum on General Officers," March 9, 1792, in *Papers of George Washington: Presidential Series*, 10:74–78 (quoted), 79n8. General St. Clair resigned from the army following his defeat near the Wabash River by Indians on November 4, 1791.

2. Ibid., 74 (quoted), 78n1.

3. Stevens and Allen, *JHR 1791*, xv, 256–57, 257n1; Stevens, *JHR 1792–1794* , x, 74–75, 74n18. Moultrie defeated Colhoun by eleven votes. Vanderhorst received two votes.

4. Stevens, *JHR 1792–1794*, 88, 91 (quoted); "On Wednesday last, at noon, gen. Moultrie was proclaimed governor of this state," *Charleston City Gazette*, December 17, 1792.

5. Stevens, *JHR 1792–1794*, xvii–xix. Credit for the comparisons of Moultrie's two terms as governor belongs to Edgar and Bailey, *Biographical Directory II*, 486.

6. Stevens, *JHR 1792–1794*, 205–11, 218–20, 579–86.

7. Plats for acreage in Craven County, S.C., dated from 1772 to 1773, and other locations in South Carolina dated from 1770 to 1775, South Carolina Surveyor General's Office, Colonial Plat Books (Copy Series), 1731–1775, Series 213184, vols. 18 and 21, SCDAH; Land grants for William Moultrie in Craven County and other parts of South Carolina, dated 1771–1772 and 1775, South Carolina Secretary of State, Recorded Instruments, Colonial Land Grants (Copy Series), 1675–1788, Series 213019, vols. 23, 25, 26 and 28, SCDAH; Several plats for acreage in Ninety-Six District, S.C., dated 1784–1785, South Carolina Surveyor General's Office, State Plat Books (Charleston Series), 1784–1860, Series 213190, vols. 6, 9, and 13, SCDAH; Edgar and Bailey, *Biographical Directory II*, 487; Klein, *Unification of a Slave State*, 179; Land grants for William Moultrie from the State of North Carolina issued March 14, 1775, grants 1243–1253 located in files no. 1018–1028, Land Warrants, Plats of Survey, and Related Records, Tryon County, North Carolina State Archives, Raleigh.

8. Stevens, *JHR, 1792–1794*, xxiv, 275–76 (first quote), 287, 297, 335 (second quote), 470–71; Klein, *Unification of a Slave State*, 186–87; "In compliance with the second of the foregoing resolutions," *Columbian Herald* (Charleson, S.C.), February 3, 1794.

9. Cooper, *Statutes at Large,* 5:233–35 (quoted); Stevens, *JHR, 1792–1794,* xxiv; Entry for December 19, 1794, South Carolina General Assembly, Senate Journals, November 24, 1794-December 20, 1794, Series 165208, SCDAH, 577–78; Klein, *Unification of a Slave State,* 187–88.

10. Bounty land grant warrant no. 1538 for William Moultrie, U.S. War Department, Office of the Secretary. Revolutionary War Pension and Bounty Land Warrant Application Files. RG 15. NA microfilm series M804, roll 1784.

11. "At a meeting of the officers of the late American army," *Charleston City Gazette,* February 16, 1793.

12. Ibid.

13. Myers, *Liberty without Anarchy,* 181–85.

14. Stevens, *JHR, 1792–1794,* xiv, 182, 233, 285.

15. Henry Knox to Tobias Lear, February 6, 1793, William Moultrie to George Washington, February 15, 1793 (quoted), and George Washington to William Moultrie, March 15, 1793, in *Papers of George Washington: Presidential Series,* 12:102–3, 147–48, 321–22.

16. "An Express has arrived from General Pickens," *State Gazette of South Carolina,* May 8, 1793; William Moultrie to George Washington, July 11, 1793, Memorandum from Andrew Pickens, July 26, 1793, and George Washington to William Moultrie, August 28, 1793, in *Papers of George Washington: Presidential Series,* 13:213–14, 214nn1–2, 357–59, 359nn1–2, 570 (quoted); Henry Knox to William Moultrie, June 10, 1793, and September 5, 1793, *American State Papers, Indian Affairs, Vol. 1* [1789–1814], 366.

17. Stevens, *JHR, 1792–1794,* xiv, 275 (quoted), 334–35.

18. "We understand, that his excellency the governor has given orders to have this harbor put in a temporary state of defense," *Charleston City Gazette,* April 13, 1793; "Neutrality Proclamation," April 22, 1793 (second quote), and William Moultrie to George Washington, April 26, 1793, in *Papers of George Washington: Presidential Series,* 12:472–73, 484 (first quote).

19. "A Proclamation," *Charleston City Gazette,* June 17, 1793.

20. "A Proclamation," *Charleston City Gazette,* August 21, 1793 (quoted); Stevens, *JHR 1792–1794,* 279–80. Dr. James Moultrie was the son of William's older brother John Moultrie. Moultrie, "Moultries, Part II," 248, 251.

21. "A Proclamation," *Columbian Herald* (Charleston, S.C.), October 15, 1793.

22. Stevens, *JHR 1792–1794,* xiv, 485, 489, 521 (quoted); McCord, *Statutes at Large,* 8:485–502.

23. Stevens, *JHR 1792–1794,* 521, 566–67.

24. Ibid., 542, 547, 564–65.

25. Ibid., 547 (quoted), 564–65.

26. William Moultrie to the South Carolina Senate, November 28, 1794, South Carolina General Assembly, Legislative Papers 1782–1866, Governors' Messages 1783–1870, Series 165009, message 613, SCDAH.

27. Tinkler, *James Hamilton of South Carolina,* 25, 25n34; Holcomb, *South Carolina Deed Abstracts, 1783–1788,* books I-5 through Z-5, 462.

28. State Agricultural Society of South Carolina, *History of the State Agricultural Society of South Carolina,* 152–53.

29. Undated manuscript, Moultrie Papers, SCL, box 2, folder 48; "Lands for Sale," *Charleston City Gazette,* January 26, 1793.

30. Undated manuscript, Moultrie Papers, SCL, box 2, folder 48.

Chapter 29: The Governor and Citizen Genet

1. For a concise breakdown of the stages of the French Revolution, see Ammon, *Genet Mission,* viii n3; Alderson, *This Bright Era of Happy Revolutions,* 6–9.

2. Myers, *Liberty without Anarchy,* 162–67.

3. Ammon, *Genet Mission,* viii.

4. Alderson, *This Bright Era of Happy Revolutions,* 15.

5. Ibid., 38–42, 49–50; Edmond Charles Genet to Pierre-Henri-Hélène-Marie Lebrun-Tondu, April 16, 1793, in Turner, "Correspondence of the French Ministers," 212.

6. "Friday the 11th instant, being the day appointed by the consul of the French republic," *Charleston City Gazette,* January 15, 1793.

7. Ibid.

8. Ibid.

9. Ammon, *Genet Mission,* vii, 2–9, 17–31.

10. Ibid., 44; Alderson, *This Bright Era of Happy Revolutions,* 21–22, 203–4n7; Minnigerode, *Jefferson, Friend of France,* 190.

11. Turner, "Correspondence of the French Ministers," 211–13; Witt, *Jefferson and the American Democracy,* 417.

12. "We are instructed from a reliable authority," *Charleston City Gazette,* April 16, 1793 (first quote); "The articles which you have inserted in your paper of the 16th inst.," *Charleston City Gazette,* April 20, 1793 (second quote).

13. "For the Printers of the *City Gazette and Daily Advertiser,*" *Charleston City Gazette,* April 29, 1793; Edmond Charles Genet to Thomas Jefferson, May 27, 1793, *American State Papers, Foreign Relations,* 1:149–50; Hyneman, *First American Neutrality,* 35, 56; Alderson, *This Bright Era of Happy Revolutions,* 63–64; "Memorial from George Hammond," June 7, 1793, in Jefferson, *Papers of Thomas Jefferson,* 26:216–18.

14. William Moultrie to George Washington, April 21, 1793, in *Papers of George Washington: Presidential Series,* 12:463; Alderson, *This Bright Era of Happy Revolutions,* 22–23.

15. Alderson, *This Bright Era of Happy Revolutions,* 23; Ammon, *Genet Mission,* 32–55.

16. Genet to Jefferson, May 27, 1793, *American State Papers, Foreign Relations,* 1:149–50 (first quote); "Memorandum of Conversations with Edmond Charles Genet," July 26, 1793, in Jefferson, *Papers of Thomas Jefferson,* 26:571–73 (second quote).

17. Letter from "Amicus," *Charleston City Gazette,* January 21, 1794; letter from "Pro Aris et Focis," *Charleston City Gazette,* November 22, 1793 (quoted).

18. "Notes on the *Citoyen Genet* and Its Prizes," May 20, 1793, Henry Lee to Thomas Jefferson, June 28, 1793, and "Notes of Cabinet Meeting and Conversations with Edmond Charles Genet," July 5, 1793, in Jefferson, *Papers of Thomas Jefferson,* 26:71 (quoted), 391–92n, 438; "A Proclamation," *Charleston City Gazette,* August 21, 1793; editorial note accompanying Henry Knox to George Washington, May 24, 1793, in *Papers of George Washington: Presidential Series,* 12:623, 624n2; Josef de Jaudenes and Josef Ignacio de Viar to Thomas Jefferson, October 23, 1793, in Jefferson, *Papers of Thomas Jefferson,* 27:269n, 356; "A Proclamation," *Charleston City Gazette,* June 17, 1793.

19. Alderson, *This Bright Era of Happy Revolutions,* 24–31; Ammon, *Genet Mission,* 54–137.

20. "Copy of a Letter from Mr. William Moultrie, Governor of South Carolina, to Citizen Genet," *New York Daily Advertiser,* October 24, 1793.

21. Ibid.; Ammon, *Genet Mission,* 142–43; Alderson, *This Bright Era of Happy Revolutions,* 32.

22. Letter from "Americanus," *Columbian Herald* (Charleston, S.C.), November 9, 1793 (quoted). For the identity of Americanus, see Alderson, *This Bright Era of Happy Revolutions,* 210n37.

23. Ibid.

24. Letter from "A Carolinian," *Charleston City Gazette,* November 12, 1793 (first quote); letter from "Bob Short," *Columbian Herald* (Charleston, S.C.), November 14, 1793 (second quote).

25. Letter from "Bob Short"; "At a meeting of the Palmetto Society," *Charleston City Gazette,* June 30, 1794 (second quote).

26. Alderson, *This Bright Era of Happy Revolutions,* 41–43, 54–60, 185–88. Stephen Drayton had been involved with Alexander Moultrie in the South Carolina Yazoo Company.

27. "An Extra meeting of the Cincinnati," *State Gazette of South Carolina,* June 28, 1793; "American Independence," *Charleston City Gazette,* July 6, 1793.

28. Alderson, *This Bright Era of Happy Revolutions,* 33, 209–10n35. Alderson cites Mangourit to Genet, November 3, 1793, France, Archives des Affaires Étrangères, Correspondance politique, États-Unis, fol. 161v; "Copy of a letter from William Moultrie [to Edmond Charles Genet, February, 11, 1794]," *Easton (Md.) Republican Star, or Eastern Shore General Advertiser,* November 12, 1811 (quoted).

Chapter 30: "Brother love to the brave Republicans"

1. Stevens, *JHR 1792–1794,* xiv–xvi, 275, 275n1, 335; Alderson, *This Bright Era of Happy Revolutions,* 55; Gov. William Moultrie, "Information of Captain Paul," September 27, 1793 (quoted), message to the South Carolina Legislature, November 30, 1793, with enclosures, containing letters from Lt. Gov. James Wood of Virginia, and other correspondence concerning the discovery of a plot of a slave insurrection, South Carolina General Assembly, Legislative Papers 1782–1866, Governors' Messages 1783–1870, Series 165009, message 577, SCDAH. For parallels between St. Domingue and South Carolina, see Alderson, *This Bright Era of Happy Revolutions,* 14.

2. Secret Keeper letter (n.d.) and Thomas Newton Jr. to James Wood (n.d.), copies enclosed with James Wood to William Moultrie, August 14, 1793, Governors' Messages 1783–1870, Series 165009, message 577, SCDAH.

3. Peter Gram to Arnoldus Vanderhorst, August 16, 1793, Governors' Messages 1783–1870, Series 165009, message 577, SCDAH.

4. "A Black" to William Moultrie, received October 10, 1793, Governors' Messages 1783–1870, Series 165009, message 577, SCDAH (quoted); Stevens, *JHR 1792–1794,* 299.

5. Alderson, *This Bright Era of Happy Revolutions,* 95, 223n5.

6. Ibid., 98, 224n11; Stevens, *JHR 1792–1794,* xvi; "At a meeting of the Citizens in Charleston," *Charleston City Gazette,* October 9, 1793; "A Proclamation," *Columbian Herald* (Charleston, S.C.), October 17, 1793.

7. Alderson, *This Bright Era of Happy Revolutions,* 96–97, 223n7; "The citizen consul of the French republic," *Charleston City Gazette,* October 5, 1793; "A Proclamation," *Charleston City Gazette,* August 21, 1793.

8. Alderson, *This Bright Era of Happy Revolutions,* 49–50 (first quote), 97 (second quote), 223–24n8; Turner, "Correspondence of the French Ministers," 212. Alderson cites Mangourit to Genet, October 9, 1793, France, Archives des Affaires Étrangères, Correspondance politique, États-Unis, fol. 072v–073v.

9. Alderson, *This Bright Era of Happy Revolutions,* 97, 99, 101.

10. Ibid., 101.

11. Ibid., 99–100.

12. Ibid., 98, 99, 101, 225n16.

13. Ibid., 99, 102–7; Michel-Ange-Bernard Mangourit to Gaugain de Vitré, October 10, 1793, in Murdoch, "Correspondence of French Consuls," 15–16; Thomas Jefferson to William Moultrie, December 23, 1793, in Jefferson, *Papers of Thomas Jefferson,* 27:614 (quoted).

14. Turner, "Correspondence of the French Ministers," 211–13; Michel-Ange-Bernard Mangourit to Edmond Charles Genet, April 24, 1793, in Turner, "Mangourit Correspondence," 575; Alderson, *This Bright Era of Happy Revolutions,* 50, 215n28.

15. Michel-Ange-Bernard Mangourit to Edmond Charles Genet, April 28, 1793, in Turner, "Mangourit Correspondence," 579–80 (quoted). See also Alderson, *This Bright Era of Happy Revolutions,* 50.

16. Mangourit to Genet, April 28, 1793, in Turner, "Mangourit Correspondence," 579.

17. Ibid., 569–74, 599, 604–6; Alderson, *This Bright Era of Happy Revolutions,* 129–44. After the Revolutionary War, Tate became somewhat of an adventurer and soldier of fortune. Moultrie had provided Tate with a letter of introduction to George Washington in July 1789, advising Washington of Tate's plan to join the armies of the Turkish Empire to improve his military knowledge and also to help open the commerce of the Mediterranean to the United States. William Moultrie to George Washington, July 10, 1789, and William Tate to George Washington, August 3, 1789, in *Papers of George Washington: Presidential Series,* 3:170–71, 374–76, 376–77n.

18. Michel-Ange-Bernard Mangourit to François Louis Michel Chemin Deforgues, October 10, 1793, in Murdoch, "Correspondence of French Consuls (Continued)," 75–76.

19. William Moultrie to the Council of Safety of France, August 9, 1794, Moultrie Papers, SCL, box 1, folder 21.

20. Mangourit to Deforgues, October 10, 1793, in Murdoch, "Correspondence of French Consuls (Continued)," 75–76; Stevens, *JHR 1792–1794,* 287, 324, 328–29.

21. Stevens, *JHR 1792–1794,* xix–xx, 329–30. Pringle became South Carolina's attorney general after the 1792 resignation of Alexander Moultrie.

22. Ibid., 329.

23. Ibid.

24. Ibid., 337 (quoted), 427; "A Proclamation," *Charleston City Gazette,* December 23, 1793; William Moultrie to George Washington, December 7, 1793, and enclosed December 6, 1793, resolves of the South Carolina legislature, in *Papers of George Washington: Presidential Series,* 14: 482–86.

25. Turner, "Mangourit Correspondence," 604–5; Murdoch, "Citizen Mangourit," 532.

26. Alderson, *This Bright Era of Happy Revolutions,* 164–71, 241n12; "In the Name of the French Republic," *Charleston City Gazette,* March 28, 1794. Alderson cites Michel-Ange-Bernard de Mangourit, *Mémoire de Mangourit. Adresses des Municipalités, Sections, Société Républican de Charleston, et des Gouverneur et Citoyens de L'état de la Caroline Du Sud, à Mangourit, Consul de la République Française, Sur Sa Destitution* (Paris: de Guiffier, 1795).

27. Zahniser, *Charles Cotesworth Pinckney,* 119–35, 144–49.

28. "South Carolina Cincinnati," *Columbian Centinel* (Boston), September 19, 1798.

29. Ibid.

Chapter 31: The Lion in Winter

1. Thomas, "William Moultrie," 446; Moultrie, "Moultries, Part II," 259, 259n24; "Died, at his seat," *Charleston City Gazette,* December 19, 1796; Heitzler, *Goose Creek, South Carolina,* 191.

2. Newmyer, "Charles Stedman's *History of the American War,*" 924n1; William Moultrie to the South Carolina House of Representatives, November 10, 1803, Moultrie Papers, legal-sized items, folder 6, SCL.

3. Moultrie, *Memoirs,* 1:vii–viii.

4. "The hour to which we were obliged . . . ," *Charleston City Gazette,* May 15, 1802.

5. Aaron Burr to James Jackson, June 16, 1802, Manuscripts P, SCL.

6. Moultrie, *Memoirs,* 1:v; "In the brig, Charleston Packet," *Charleston City Gazette,* June 29, 1802; "General Moultrie arrived at New-York . . . ," *Charleston Carolina Gazette,* July 29, 1802 (quoted).

7. "Major General Moultrie has issued proposals . . . ," *Charleston City Gazette,* November 29, 1799 (quoted); "Proposals are issued at Charleston . . . ," *Massachusetts Spy, or Worcester Gazette,* May 7, 1800; "Just Received," *Charleston City Gazette,* May 18, 1803; William Moultrie to Edward Brailsford, September 2, 1802, Moultrie Papers, box 1, folder 27, SCL; "Gen. William Moultrie, with a number of other passengers . . . ," *Charleston City Gazette,* November 25, 1802; "This Day is Published," *New York Morning Chronicle,* April 11, 1803; "Those gentlemen who are in possession of Subscription Papers . . . ," *Charleston City Gazette,* March 15, 1803; "Just Received," *Charleston City Gazette,* May 18, 1803; "Moultrie's Memoirs," *Charleston City Gazette,* June 21, 1803.

8. Moultrie, *Memoirs,* 1:vii–viii (quoted); Moultrie, Orderly books of William Moultrie, June 20, 1775–December 15, 1780, MssHM 681, Huntington Library, San Marino, Cal. See also Lilla Mills Hawes's commentary on Moultrie's use of contemporaneous journals, in McIntosh, *Lachlan McIntosh Papers,* 129–30n62; and Journal accompanying John F. Grimké, "Orderly book (1778 Aug. 24–1780 May 10)," United States, Continental Army, Southern Department, Continental Army Southern Department Records, 1778–1790, Mss 34/0201, SCHS.

9. "Major General Moultrie has issued proposals . . . ," *Charleston City Gazette,* November 29, 1799; "Proposals are issued at Charleston . . . ," *Massachusetts Spy, or Worcester Gazette,* May 7, 1800; "Now in the Press," *New York Morning Chronicle,* November 3, 1802 (quoted).

10. Newton, "Three Patterns of Local History," 147–48.

11. Ibid., 147; Mattern, *Benjamin Lincoln,* 111–13; Lee, *Memoirs of the War in the Southern Department,* 157, 161.

12. William Moultrie to William Presstman, October 3, 1804, Moultrie Papers, box 1, folder 30, SCL.

13. Bennett, "Wooden House Where General Moultrie, Jailbound for Debt, Wrote His Memoirs, Is Being Stripped for Firewood," *Charleston News and Courier,* March 28, 1938. The source of John Bennett's anecdotal account of Moultrie's stint in debtor's prison is a typescript, "Reminiscences of William Harleston Huger, M.D. as taken down as he told them by Susan S. [Smythe] Bennett, c.1900," John Henry Bennett Papers, 1899–1991 (277.00), SCHS, box 7, fol. 1. If credible the story would have been passed intact through the family by John Huger (1744–1804) to his son Benjamin Huger (1793–1874), who related it to his son William Harleston Huger (1826–1906), who then recounted it to Susan Smythe Bennett about 1900.

14. Bennett, "Wooden House."

15. Julian V. Brandt III, "William Moultrie: Getting Down to Brass Tacks," *Charleston Mercury,* June 21, 2007 (*Palmetto Patriot* insert).

16. Wade H. Dorsey to C. L. Bragg, October 1, 2010; William Moultrie to Edward Brailsford, August 26, 1802, reproduced in Thomas, "William Moultrie," 447–48 (the original is in a private collection in Charleston); Hagy, *City Directories for Charleston, South Carolina*, 9, 15, 36, 45; "Appointments by the President," *Charleston Carolina Gazette*, July 29, 1802. Mrs. Hall was probably the widow Mary A. Hall who resided at 19 Magazine Street.

17. Robert E. Rector, "Thomas Bee and the Revolution in South Carolina, 1760–1790." Master of Arts thesis, University of South Carolina, 1971, 81–83; South Carolina to William Moultrie, receipt no. 507 for loan of nine thousand pounds dated December 18, 1779, *Accounts Audited*, SCDAH, roll 109, file 5387; South Carolina to William Moultrie, receipt no. 508 for loan of nine thousand pounds dated December 18, 1779, a document in private hands after being sold at auction on December 10, 2008, by Bloomsbury Auctions of New York; indented certificates to William Moultrie on February 28 and October 13, 1784, and February 3, 1786, *Accounts Audited*, SCDAH, roll 109, file 5387; Moultrie, *Memoirs*, 2:356. For more on the sequestration and seizure of estates belonging to "traitors," see John Cruden to Alexander Stewart, October 28, 1781, in Cornwallis, *Cornwallis Papers*, 5:269–70.

18. South Carolina Court of Common Pleas, Judgment Rolls, 1703–1790, Series 136002, box 130A, item 439A, SCDAH; Court of Common Pleas (Charleston County, S.C.), Judgment Rolls, 1791–1904, Series L10018, item 20A, SCDAH.

19. Langley, *South Carolina Deed Abstracts*, 4:251–52; Elizabeth Moultrie v. William Moultrie, 1786, South Carolina Court of Common Pleas, Judgment Rolls, 1703–1790, Series 136002, box 130A, item 439A, SCDAH; Protestant Episcopal Church of St. Philip's Parish v. William Moultrie, June 15, 1799, Court of Common Pleas (Charleston County, S.C.), Judgment Rolls, 1791–1904, Series L10018, item 515A, SCDAH (quoted).

20. William Moultrie to Pierce Butler, October 13, 1802, Moultrie Papers, legal-sized items, folder 6, SCL (quoted); Pierce Butler v. William Moultrie and William Ainslie Moultrie, September 16, 1805, Court of Common Pleas (Charleston County, S.C.), Judgment Rolls, 1791–1904, Series L10018, item 20A, SCDAH.

21. "Runaway," *Charleston City Gazette*, November 24, 1806; "For Sale," *Charleston City Gazette*, April 30, 1790; "For Private Sale," *Charleston City Gazette*, September 15, 1796; "For Sale at Public Auction," *Charleston City Gazette*, November 4, 1796; Mortgage, William Moultrie to the Commissioners of the Loan Office, May 5, 1786, series: S218157, volume 000A, 136; "For Sale," *Charleston City Gazette*, September 27, 1821; "Strayed," *South Carolina Gazette*, April 20 to April 22, 1784; "Sale of Land," *Columbian Herald* (Charleston, S.C.), March 13, 1795; "For Sale," *Charleston City Gazette*, January 21, 1792; "Lands for Sale," *Charleston City Gazette*, March 16, 1793; "Sheriff's Sales," *Charleston City Gazette*, March 16, 1798; "For Sale," *Charleston City Gazette*, July 29, 1801; Smith, "Baronies of South Carolina IV," 51.

22. "Died, yesterday morning," *Charleston Courier*, September 28, 1805; Roger and Peter Smith v. William Moultrie, Sheriff's sale of two slaves, on April 8, 1800, purchased by William A. Moultrie, Moultrie Papers, legal-sized items, folder 5, SCL; Robert Smith, loan to William and Hannah Moultrie, October 31, 1797, obligation assumed by William A. Moultrie on July 3, 1802, Moultrie Papers, legal-sized items, folder 4, SCL; Pierce Butler v. William Moultrie and William Ainslie Moultrie, September 16, 1805, Court of Common Pleas (Charleston County, S.C.), Judgment Rolls, 1791–1904, Series L10018, item 20A, SCDAH.

23. "'Secrets worth knowing' out at last," *Boston Gazette*, March 10, 1803; "Funeral Procession," *Charleston City Gazette*, January 16, 1800.

24. "The Legislature have appointed Gen. William Moultrie, State Treasurer in Charleston," *Charleston Courier*, December 14, 1803; Cooper, *Statutes at Large*, 5:349; "Notice,"

Charleston City Gazette, April 20, 1804; "We are informed," *Charleston Carolina Gazette,* June 22, 1804.

25. "Died, yesterday morning," *Charleston Courier,* September 28, 1805 (quoted); Hagy, *City Directories for Charleston,* 45; DeSaussure, "Remarks," 27–28; "Cincinnati" and announcement by the governor of South Carolina, *Charleston City Gazette,* September 30, 1805.

26. "Cincinnati" (quoted); "Notice," *Charleston City Gazette,* October 15, 1805.

27. Hollinshead, *Discourse,* 14–15.

28. Ibid., 17–21.

29. Alexander Garden eulogy of William Moultrie published in "Copy of a Letter from Major Thomas Pinckney, to Wm. A. Moultrie, esq., dated Charleston, November 13, 1805," *Charleston Carolina Gazette,* December 6, 1805.

Epilogue

1. Guerry, "Search for General Moultrie's Grave," 68, 71, 76–77 (quoted).

2. "At a Meeting of the Cincinnati of South-Carolina," *Charleston City Gazette,* December 27, 1826 (quoted); Guerry, "General Moultrie's Final Victory," 133; Guerry, "Search for General Moultrie's Grave," 64, 68.

3. Guerry, "Search for General Moultrie's Grave," 68–69, 72; DeSaussure, "Remarks," 27–28.

4. "The Tomb of Moultrie," newspaper clipping, source unknown, [May 11, 1921], Moultrie Papers, box 2, folder 45, SCL; Guerry, "Search for General Moultrie's Grave," 65–67; Guerry, "Moultrie's Gravestone Gone," *Charleston Post and Courier,* March 26, 1975; South, "General, the Major, and the Angel," 31–32.

5. South, "General, the Major, and the Angel," 32, 41–48.

6. Ibid., 48; Brandt, "William Moultrie," *Charleston Mercury,* June 21, 2007 (*Palmetto Patriot* insert).

7. Steedman, "General Moultrie's Reply," 46–51.

8. "To Discuss Plans Tonight for Monument to Moultrie," [*Charleston News and Courier*], September 30, 1929, copy in SCHS (30–4 Moultrie); St. Andrew's Society of Charleston, South Carolina, *Tribute to Major General William Moultrie,* copy at the Manuscripts Division, SCL; Thomas, "William Moultrie," vii; "Moultrie Monument Design Is Submitted to Association," unidentified newspaper clipping, copy in SCHS (30–4 Moultrie).

9. "Monument Dedicated," *Charleston News and Courier,* October 10, 1985; George L. Brailsford, conversation with the author, August 14, 2008; Daniel Conover and Jason Hardin, "Revolutionary War Statue Plans Announced," *Charleston Post and Courier,* June 29, 2001.

10. Conover and Hardin, "Revolutionary War Statue Plans Announced"; Burbage, "Moultrie Statue Is Wise Investment in Our Future," *Charleston Mercury Magazine* 2, no. 3 (2006): 6–8.

11. Waring, "John Michel, the Man to Create Moultrie," *Charleston Mercury Magazine* 2, no. 3 (2006): 11; Rob Young, "Revolutionary War Hero Statue Takes Long Enough, but Patriot Gets His Due," *Charleston Post and Courier,* June 24, 2007.

12. "Carolina Day," *Charleston Post and Courier,* June 26, 2007; David Slade, "Moultrie's statue unveiled amid pageantry, pomp," *Charleston Post and Courier,* June 29, 2007; Joseph P. Riley, Jr. "Address at the Dedication of the Moultrie Statue," *Charleston Mercury,* July 19, 2007.

Bibliography

Primary Sources

Records at the Library of Congress, Washington, D.C.

Collection re South Carolina, 1780–1782. Papers and Collection of Peter Force. MSS63511 (series 7E: item 129). Microfilm 19,061 (reel 42). Manuscript Division.

Continental Congress, 1776. Letter (published transcription) from the Continental Congress to Colonel William Moultrie. Rare Book and Special Collections Division.

Force, Peter, 1790–1868. Papers and Collection, 1170–1961. LCCN mm 80020990. Historical Working Papers (series 6, container 29). Manuscript Division.

Henry, Patrick, 1736–1799. Papers, 1776–1818. MSS25767. Library of Congress Manuscript Division.

Historic American Buildings Survey. Prints and Photographs Division.

Morgan, James Dudley, 1862–1919. Collection of Digges-L'Enfant-Morgan Papers, 1674–1923. Call no. MMC-3131. Manuscript Division.

Moultrie, William, 1730–1805. Papers, 1775–1781. Miscellaneous Manuscripts collection. MSS790. Manuscript Division.

Pinckney, Charles Cotesworth, 1746–1825. Family Papers, 1703–1947. Manuscript Division.

Society of the Cincinnati. Records, 1783–1850. Microfilm and photocopies of originals in the Archives and Library Collections of the Society of the Cincinnati at Anderson House, Washington, D.C. Reel 3 of six. Manuscript Division.

Tucker, Samuel. Papers, 1777–1781. Papers and Collection of Peter Force, 1170–1961 (Series 7E: entry 145). MSS43315. Microfilm 19,061 (reel 54). Manuscript Division.

Washington, George. Papers, 1592–1943. Series 4, General Correspondence.

Waterman, Thomas T. "A Survey of the Early Buildings in the Region of the Proposed Santee and Pinopolis Reservoirs in South Carolina." Typescript (1939). Historic American Buildings Survey. Prints and Photographs Division.

Records at the National Archives and Records Administration, Washington, D.C.

Continental Congress. Papers of the Continental Congress, 1774–1789. Record Group 360: Records of the Continental and Confederation Congresses and the Constitutional Convention, 1765–1821. Microfilm series M247, rolls 24, 86, 103, 141, 171, 177, 178, and 202.

U.S. War Department, Office of the Secretary. Revolutionary War Pension and Bounty Land Warrant Application Files. RG 15. Microfilm series M804, roll 1784.

Records at the South Carolina Department of Archives and History, Columbia, S.C.

Court of Common Pleas (Charleston County, S.C.). Judgment Rolls, 1791–1904. Series L10018.

South Carolina Court of Common Pleas. Judgment Rolls, 1703–1790. Series 136002. Microfilm.

South Carolina Department of Archives and History, Archives and Publications Division. *Accounts Audited of Claims Growing Out of the Revolution in South Carolina, 1775–1856* (Microcopy No. 8).

South Carolina General Assembly. General Assembly and Other Miscellaneous Records, 1774–1910. Series 390008.

South Carolina General Assembly. Legislative Papers 1782–1866. Governors' Messages 1783–1870. Series 165009. Microfilm.

South Carolina General Assembly. Senate Journals (engrossed manuscripts) 1782–1877. Series 165208. Microfilm.

South Carolina Secretary of State. Recorded Instruments. Colonial Land Grants (Copy Series), 1675–1788. Series 213019. Microfilm.

South Carolina Secretary of State. Recorded Instruments. Miscellaneous records (main series), 1732–1981. Series 213003. Microfilm.

South Carolina Surveyor General's Office. Colonial Plat Books (Copy Series), 1731–1775. Series 213184. Microfilm.

South Carolina Surveyor General's Office. State Plat Books (Charleston Series), 1784–1860. Series 213190. Microfilm.

Records at the South Carolina Historical Society, Charleston, S.C.

Bennett, John Henry. Papers, 1899–1991. Manuscripts (277.00).

Grimké, John F. Orderly book (1778 Aug. 24–1780 May 10), and "Journal of the siege of Charles Towne (1780 March 28–May 12)." United States, Continental Army, Southern Department, Continental Army Southern Department Records, 1778–1790. Mss 34/0201.

Gubbins, M. C. B. Transcripts and abstracts of Moultrie family papers, 1746–1965. Letters (43/36).

Laurens, John. "Account of the operations in South Carolina, respecting Capitulation, May 1779." Henry Laurens Papers, 1747–1860. Manuscripts (37/45B oversize).

Moncrief, William. Biographical and genealogical research. Genealogy (30–4 Moncrief).

Moultrie, William. Biographical and genealogical research. Genealogy (30–4 Moultrie).

Moultrie, William, 1730–1805. Letter: Stono, [S.C.], to Major General Lincoln, July 4, 1779. Letters (43/499).

Moultrie, William, 1730–1805. Note to Major [Isaac] Harleston, June 8, 1781. Letters (43/0911).

Moultrie, William, 1730–1805. William Moultrie correspondence, 1781. Letters (43/222).

Thomas, Robert Gibbes. "William Moultrie: Arms and the Man." Typescript (c. 1930). Microfiche.

Other Manuscripts and Original Documents

Brailsford, George L. Papers. Mount Pleasant, S.C.

Burr, Aaron. Letter to James Jackson, June 16, 1802. Manuscripts P. Manuscripts Division, South Caroliniana Library, University of South Carolina, Columbia.

Clinton, Henry. Letterbook of Clinton and [Commodore Sir Peter] Parker Correspondence, May 30, 1776–January 4, 1777. MSS L1996F104 [Bound]. Archives and Library Collections of the Society of the Cincinnati at Anderson House, Washington, D.C.

DeSaussure, Wilmot Gibbes. "Remarks on Offering the Regular Toast, on 22d February, 1885, to the South Carolina Cincinnati." N.p. [1885]. Archives and Library Collections of the Society of the Cincinnati at Anderson House, Washington, D.C.

Irving, Washington. Collection, 1683–1839. Call number Mo104/973.41.W31IRA F. Special Collections and University Archives, Cecil H. Green Library, Stanford University, Libraries, Stanford, Cal.

Moultrie, William. Orderly books of William Moultrie, June 20, 1775–December 15, 1780. MssHM 681. Manuscripts Department, Huntington Library, Art Collections, and Botanical Gardens, San Marino, Cal.

Moultrie, William. Papers, 1757–1963. Manuscripts Plb. Manuscripts Division, South Caroliniana Library, University of South Carolina, Columbia.

Moultrie, William, 1730–1805. State Society of the Cincinnati of Pennsylvania. Minutes, 1784, May 4–18. Mss Collection, BV Moultrie. New-York Historical Society, New York.

North Carolina, Office of Secretary of State. Secretary of State Record Group. Land Office: Land Warrants, Plats of Survey, and Related Records, Tryon County. North Carolina State Archives, Raleigh.

Sabine, Lorenzo. Papers. New Hampshire Historical Society, Concord.

Society of the Cincinnati. Archives and Library Collections of the Society of the Cincinnati at Anderson House, Washington, D.C.

Society of the Cincinnati. Papers, 1783–1861. Accession no. 24646. Library of Virginia, Richmond.

South Carolina State Society of Cincinnati. South-Carolina State Society of Cincinnati Records, 1908. Mss 0034-070. Special Collections, Marlene and Nathan Addlestone Library, College of Charleston, Charleston, S.C.

Published Primary Sources and Personal Accounts

Burgoyne, Bruce E., comp. and ed. *Enemy Views: The American Revolutionary War as Recorded by the Hessian Participants.* New York: Cambridge University Press, 1996.

Butler, Pierce. *The Letters of Pierce Butler, 1790–1794: Nation Building and Enterprise in the New American Republic.* Edited by Terry W. Lipscomb. Columbia: University of South Carolina Press, 2007.

Campbell, Archibald, and Colin Campbell. *Journal of an Expedition against the Rebels of Georgia in North America under the Orders of Archibald Campbell, Esquire, Lieut. Colol. of His Majesty's 71st Regimt., 1778.* Darien, Ga.: Ashantilly, 1981.

Cassius [Burke, Aedanus]. *Considerations on the Society or Order of Cincinnati.* Philadelphia: Robert Bell, 1783.

Clinton, Henry. *A Narrative of Sir Henry Clinton's Co-Operations with Sir Peter Parker, on the Attack of Sullivan's Island, in South Carolina, in the Year 1776.* [New York: Printed by James Rivington (?),] 1780.

———. *The American Rebellion: Sir Henry Clinton's Narrative of His Campaigns, 1775–1782, with an Appendix of Original Documents.* Edited by William B. Wilcox. New Haven: Yale University Press, 1954.

Continental Congress. *Journals of the Continental Congress, 1774–1789.* 34 vols. Edited by Worthington Chauncey Ford et al. Washington, D.C.: Government Printing Office, 1904–37.

Cooper, Thomas, and David James McCord, eds. *The Statutes at Large of South Carolina.* Vols. 1, 4, 5. Columbia: Johnston, 1836–39.

Cornwallis, Charles. *The Cornwallis Papers: The Campaigns of 1780 and 1781 in the Southern Theatre of the American Revolutionary War.* 6 vols. Edited by Ian Saberton. East Sussex, U.K.: Naval and Military Press, 2011.

Courtenay, William Ashmead, comp. *The Correspondence of Lord Montague with General Moultrie, 1781* [pamphlet]. New York: De Vinne, 1885. Pamphlets in American history. Revolutionary War, RW 390. Microfiche. Glen Rock, N.J.: Microfilming Corp. of America, 1978.

Cross, Jack L., ed. "Letters of Thomas Pinckney, 1775–1780." *South Carolina Historical Magazine* 58, no. 1 (1957): 19–33.

Dann, John C., ed. *The Revolution Remembered: Eyewitness Accounts of the War for Independence.* Chicago: University of Chicago Press, 1983.

Davis, Charles S., ed. "The Journal of William Moultrie While a Commissioner on the North and South Carolina Boundary Survey, 1772," *Journal of Southern History* 8 (1942): 549–55.

Drayton, John, *Memoirs of the American Revolution, from Its Commencement to the Year 1776, Inclusive; as Relating to the State of South-Carolina: and Occasionally Referring to the States of North-Carolina and Georgia.* 2 vols. 1821. Rpt., New York: Arno, 1969.

Edwards, Adele Stanton, ed. *Journals of the Privy Council, 1783–1789.* Columbia: University of South Carolina Press, 1971.

Elliot, Jonathan, comp. and ed. *The Debates in the Several State Conventions on the Adoption of the Federal Constitution, as Recommended by the General Convention at Philadelphia, 1787: Together with the Journal of the Federal Convention, Luther Martin's Letter, Yates's Minutes, Congressional Opinions, Virginia and Kentucky Resolutions of '98–'99, and Other Illustrations of the Constitution.* Vol. 4. Philadelphia: Lippincott, 1861.

Elliott, Barnard. "Diary of Captain Barnard Elliott." *Year Book—1889, City of Charleston, So. Ca.* (1889): 151–262.

Garden, Alexander. *Anecdotes of the American Revolution, Illustrative of the Talents and Virtues of the Heroes and Patriots, Who Acted the Most Conspicuous Parts Therein.* Charleston, S.C.: Miller, 1828.

———. *Anecdotes of the Revolutionary War in America: With Sketches of Character of Persons the Most Distinguished, in the Southern States, for Civil and Military Services.* Charleston, S.C.: Miller, 1822.

Gibbes, Robert Wilson., ed. *Documentary History of the American Revolution, 1764–1782.* 2 vols. New York: Appleton, 1855–57.

———, ed. *Documentary History of the American Revolution, 1781 and 1782.* Columbia: Banner Steam-Power Press, 1853.

Grant, James. "Journal of Lieutenant-Colonel James Grant, Commanding an Expedition against the Cherokee Indians, June–July, 1761." *Florida Historical Society Quarterly* 12, no. 1 (1933): 25–36.

Greene, Nathanael. *The Papers of General Nathanael Greene.* 13 vols. Edited by Richard K. Showman et al. Chapel Hill: University of North Carolina Press, 1976–2005.

Grimké, John F. "Order Book of John Faucheraud Grimké, August 1778 to May 1780." *South Carolina Historical and Genealogical Magazine* 13, no. 1 (1912): 42–55; 13, no. 3 (1912): 148–53; 13, no. 4 (1912): 205–12; 14, no. 1 (1913): 44–57.

Hagy, James W. *City Directories for Charleston, South Carolina: For the Years 1803, 1806, 1807, 1809, and 1813.* Baltimore: Clearfield, 1995.

Hemphill, William Edwin, and Wylma Anne Wates, eds. *Extracts from the Journals of the Provincial Congresses of South Carolina, 1775–1776.* Columbia: South Carolina Archives Department, 1960.

Historical Manuscripts Commission. *Report on the American Manuscripts in the Royal Institution of Great Britain.* Vol. 3 [1782–1783]. Heresford, U.K.: Anthony Brothers, 1907.

Holcomb, Brent H. *South Carolina Deed Abstracts, 1783–1788, Books I-5 through Z-5.* Columbia: S.C. Magazine of Ancestral Research, 1996.

Hollinshead, William. *A Discourse Commemorative of the Late Major-Gen. William Moultrie; Delivered in the Independent Church, on the Fifteenth of October, 1805, at the Request of the Society of the Cincinnati of South-Carolina, Before That Society and the American Revolution Society.* Charleston, S.C.: Peter Freneau, 1805.

Holmes, George S. *A Historic Sketch of the Parish Church of St. Michael, of Charles Town, in the Province of South Carolina.* Charleston, S.C.: Walker, Evans & Cogswell, 1887.

Hough, Franklin Benjamin. *The Siege of Charleston, by the British Fleet and Army under the Command of Admiral Arbuthnot and Sir Henry Clinton Which Terminated with the Surrender of That Place on the 12th of May, 1780.* Albany, N.Y.: Munsell, 1867.

———. *The Siege of Savannah: By the Combined American and French Forces, under the Command of Gen. Lincoln and the Count D'Estaing, in the Autumn of 1779.* Albany, N.Y.: Munsell, 1866.

Hutson, Francis M., ed. Journal of the Constitutional Convention of South Carolina. May 10–June 3, 1790. Columbia: State Commercial Printing Co., 1946.

Jefferson, Thomas. *The Papers of Thomas Jefferson.* 36 vols. Edited by Barbara B. Oberg et al. Princeton: Princeton University Press, 1950–2009.

Kappler, Charles Joseph, comp. and ed. *Indian Affairs, Laws and Treaties.* Vol. 2. Washington, D.C.: Government Printing Office, 1904.

Kennedy, Benjamin, ed. and trans., *Muskets, Cannon Balls and Bombs; Nine Narratives of the Siege of Savannah in 1779.* Savannah: Beehive, 1974.

Langley, Clara A., comp. *South Carolina Deed Abstracts, 1719–1772: Vol. II, 1740—1755, Books V–P-P.* Easley, S.C.: Southern Historical Press, 1984.

———, comp. *South Carolina Deed Abstracts, 1719–1772: Vol. III, 1755–1768, Books QQ–H-3.* Easley, S.C.: Southern Historical Press, 1983.

———, comp. *South Carolina Deed Abstracts, 1719–1772: Vol. IV, 1767–1773, Books I-3–E-4.* Easley, S.C.: Southern Historical Press, 1984.

Laurens, Henry. *The Papers of Henry Laurens.* 16 vols. Edited by David R. Chestnut et al. Columbia: University of South Carolina Press, 1968–2002.

Lee, Charles, and Edward Langworthy. *The Life and Memoirs of the Late Major General Lee, Second in Command to General Washington during the American Revolution, to Which Are Added His Political and Military Essays. Also, Letters to and from Many Distinguished Characters Both in Europe and America.* New York: Scott, 1813.

Lee, Charles, and Henry Edward Bunbury. *The Lee Papers, 1754–1811.* Vol. 2, *1776–1778.* New York: Printed for the Society, 1872.

Lee, Henry, and Robert E. Lee. *Memoirs of the War in the Southern Department of the United States.* 3rd ed. New York: University Publishing Co., 1869.

Lee, Jean B. *Experiencing Mount Vernon: Eyewitness Accounts: 1784–1865.* Charlottesville: University of Virginia Press, 2006.

Levine, Ida L. "A Letter from William Moultrie at Charleston to George Washington at Mount Vernon, April 7, 1786." South Carolina Historical Magazine 83, no. 2 (1982): 116–20.

Lincoln, Benjamin. *The Benjamin Lincoln Papers.* Edited by Frederick S. Allis and Wayne A. Frederick. Boston: Massachusetts Historical Society, 1967. Microfilm, reels 3 and 4.

———. *Original Papers Relating to the Siege of Charleston, 1780*. Charleston, S.C.: Walker, Evans & Cogswell, 1898.

Lincoln, Charles Henry. *Naval Records of the American Revolution, 1775–1788*. Washington, D.C.: Government Printing Office, 1906.

Lipscomb, Terry W., and R. Nicholas Olsberg, eds. *Journal of the Commons House of Assembly: November 14, 1751–October 7, 1752; November 21, 1752–September 6, 1754; November 12, 1754–September 23, 1755; and November 20, 1755–July 6, 1757*. Columbia: University of South Carolina Press, 1977–89.

Manigault, Ann. "Extracts from the Journal of Mrs. Ann Manigault, 1754–1781." Annotated by Mabel L. Webber. *South Carolina Historical and Genealogical Magazine* 21, no. 1 (1920): 10–23.

Marion, Francis, "Letters of General Francis Marion." *Year Book—1895, City of Charleston, So. Ca.* (1895): 326–32.

Marion, Francis, and William Moultrie, "Original Letters from Genl. Francis Marion and Genl. William Moultrie, 1781–1788." *Year Book—1898, City of Charleston, So. Ca.* (1898): 380–85.

Mays, Edith, ed. *Amherst Papers, 1756–1763: The Southern Sector: Dispatches from South Carolina, Virginia, and His Majesty's Superintendent of Indian Affairs*. Westminster, Md.: Heritage Books, 2006.

McCord, David J., ed. *The Statutes at Large of South Carolina*. Vols. 6–9. Columbia: Johnson, 1839–41.

McIntosh, Lachlan. *Lachlan McIntosh Papers in the University of Georgia Libraries*. Edited by Lilla Mills Hawes. Athens: University of Georgia Press, 1968.

Morgan, William James, ed. *Naval Documents of the American Revolution*. Vol. 5. Washington, D.C.: Naval History Division, Department of the Navy, and Government Printing Office, 1970.

Morris, Robert. *The Papers of Robert Morris, 1781–1784*. 8 vols. Edited by E. James Ferguson and John Catanzariti. Pittsburgh: University of Pittsburgh Press, 1973.

Moultrie, William. *Memoirs of the American Revolution So Far as It Related to the States of North and South-Carolina, and Georgia*. 2 vols. 1802. Rpt., New York: Arno, 1968. North Stratford, N.H.: Ayer, 2004.

Murdoch, Richard K. "Correspondence of French Consuls in Charleston, South Carolina, 1793–1797." *South Carolina Historical Magazine* 74, no. 1 (1973): 1–17.

———. "Correspondence of French Consuls in Charleston, South Carolina, 1793–1797 (Continued)." *South Carolina Historical Magazine* 74, no. 2 (1973): 73–79.

———. "A French Account of the Siege of Charleston, 1780." South Carolina Historical Magazine 67, no. 3 (1966): 138–54.

O'Kelley, Patrick, ed. *Unwaried Patience and Fortitude: Francis Marion's Orderly Book*. West Conshohocken, Penn.: Infinity, 2006.

St. Andrew's Society of the City of Charleston, Charleston, S.C. *Rules of the St. Andrew's Society, of the City of Charleston, South Carolina: Founded in the Year One Thousand Seven Hundred and Twenty-Nine. Incorporated in 1798*. Charleston: Walker, Evans & Cogswell, 1892.

Salley, Alexander S., Jr., ed. *Journal of the Commissioners of the Navy of South Carolina, October 9, 1776–March 1, 1779*. Columbia: State Co., 1912.

———, ed. *Journal of the Commons House of Assembly: January 8, 1765–August 9, 1765*. Columbia: Historical Commission of South Carolina, 1949.

————, ed. *Journal of the General Assembly of South Carolina, March 26, 1776–April 11, 1776, and September 17, 1776–October 20, 1776.* 2 vols. Columbia: Historical Commission of South Carolina, 1906–9.

————, ed. "Letters from Hon. Henry Laurens to His Son John, 1773–1776." *South Carolina Historical and Genealogical Magazine* 5, no. 3 (1904): 125–43.

————, ed. "Papers of the First Council of Safety of the Revolutionary Party in South Carolina, June–November, 1775 (Continued)." *South Carolina Historical and Genealogical Magazine* 1, no. 3 (1900): 183–205.

————, ed. *Register of St. Philip's Parish, Charles Town, South Carolina: 1720–1758.* Charleston, S.C.: Walker, Evans & Cogswell, 1904.

————, comp. and ed. *Marriage Notices in the South-Carolina and American General Gazette from May 30, 1766, to February 28, 1781, and in Its Successor the Royal Gazette (1781–1782).* Columbia: Printed for the Historical Commission of South Carolina by the State Co., 1914.

————, comp. and ed. *Marriage Notices in the South-Carolina Gazette and Its Successors (1732–1801).* 1902. Rpt., Baltimore: Genealogical Publishing, 1989.

Smith, D. E. Huger, and Alexander S. Salley, Jr., eds. *Register of St. Philip's Parish, Charles Town, South Carolina: 1754–1810.* Charleston, S.C.: South Carolina Society and Colonial Dames of America, 1927.

Smith, Josiah. "Josiah Smith's Diary, 1780–1781." Annotated by Mabel L. Webber. *South Carolina Historical and Genealogical Magazine* 34, no. 2 (1933): 67–84.

Society of the Cincinnati. *Proceedings of the General Society of the Cincinnati, 1784–1884.* Philadelphia: Review Printing House, 1887.

South Carolina General Assembly. *Acts of the General Assembly of the State of South Carolina, From February 1791, to December, 1904, Both Inclusive.* Columbia: D. & J. J. Faust, State Printers, 1808.

South Carolina Historical Society. *Divers Accounts of the Battle of Sullivan's Island in His Majesty's Province of South Carolina, the 28th June 1776.* Charleston: South Carolina Historical Society, 1976.

————. "Journal of the Council of Safety of the Province of South Carolina, 1775." *Collections of the South-Carolina Historical Society* 2 (1858): 22–74.

————. "Journal of the Second Council of Safety." *Collections of the South-Carolina Historical Society* 3 (1859): 35–271.

Taliaferro, Nicholas. *The Revolutionary War Diary and Order Book of Second Lieutenant Nicholas Taliaferro, Present at the Capture of Charleston, S.C., 1780.* Transcribed with introductory material by Betty Ann Smiddy. [West Chester, Ohio?: B. A. Smiddy, 1996].

Tarleton, Banastre. *A History of the Campaigns of 1780 and 1781, in the Southern Provinces of North America.* Dublin: Colles, Exshaw, White, H. Whitestone, Burton, Byrne, Moore, Jones & Dornin, 1787.

Thompson, Theodora J., Lark Emerson Adams, Rosa S. Lumpkin, Michael E. Stevens, and Christine M. Allen, eds. *Journals of the House of Representatives: 1783–1784, 1785–1786, 1787–1788, 1789–1790, 1791, and 1792–1794.* Columbia: University of South Carolina Press, 1977–79, 1981–88.

Turner, Frederick Jackson, ed. "Correspondence of the French Ministers to the United States, 1791–1797." *Annual Report of the American Historical Association for the Year 1903* Vol. 2 (1904).

————, ed. "The Mangourit Correspondence in Respect to Genet's Projected Attack upon the Floridas, 1793–94." Annual Report of the American Historical Association for the Year 1897 (1898): 569–679.

Uhlendorf, Bernhard A., trans. and ed. *The Siege of Charleston, with an Account of the Province of South Carolina: Diaries and Letters of Hessian Officers from the von Jungkenn Papers in the William L. Clements Library.* Ann Arbor: University of Michigan Press, 1938.

U.S. Congress. *American State Papers. Indian Affairs, Vol. 1* [1789–1814] and *Foreign Relations, Vol. 1* [1789–1797]. Edited by Walter Lowrie and Matthew St. Clair Clarke. Washington, D.C.: Gales & Seaton, 1832–33.

Von Steuben, Friedrich Wilhelm. *The Papers of General Friedrich Wilhelm von Steuben.* Edited by Edith von Zemenszky and Robert J. Schumann. Millwood, N.Y.: Kraus International Publications, 1982. Microform.

Washington, George. *The Diaries of George Washington.* Volume 6: *January 1790–December 1799.* Edited by Donald Jackson and Dorothy Twohig. Charlottesville: University Press of Virginia, 1979.

———. *The Papers of George Washington.* 56 vols. in 5 series. Edited by W. W. Abbott et al. Charlottesville: University Press of Virginia, 1983–2011.

———. *The Writings of George Washington from the Original Manuscript Sources 1745–1799.* 39 vols. Edited by John C. Fitzpatrick. Washington, D.C.: United States Government Printing Office, 1937.

Webber, Mabel L., ed. "Col. Senf's Account of the Santee Canal." Parts 1 and 2. *South Carolina Historical and Genealogical Magazine* 28, no. 1 (1927): 8–21; 28, no. 2 (1927): 112–31.

Newspapers

Boston Gazette, 1803.
Charleston Carolina Gazette, 1802–5.
Charleston City Gazette and Commercial Daily Advertiser, 1821–26.
Charleston City Gazette, or the Daily Advertiser, 1790–1806.
Charleston Courier, 1803–5.
Charleston Evening Gazette, 1786.
Charleston Mercury, 2007.
Charleston Morning Post and Daily Advertiser, 1787.
Charleston News and Courier, 1929–85.
Charleston Post and Courier, 1975–2007.
Columbian Herald, or the Independent Courier of North-America (Charleston, S.C.), 1786.
Columbian Herald: or the Southern Star (Charleston, S.C.), 1793–94.
Columbian Herald; the New Daily Advertiser (Charleston, S.C.), 1795.
Columbian Centinel (Boston), 1798.
Easton (Md.) Republican Star, or Eastern Shore General Advertiser, 1811.
Gazette of the State of South Carolina (Charleston, S.C.), 1777–79.
Maryland Journal and Baltimore Advertiser, 1779.
Massachusetts Spy, or Worcester Gazette, 1800.
New York Daily Advertiser, 1793.
New York Daily Gazette, 1790.
New York Morning Chronicle, 1802–3.
Philadelphia Pennsylvania Packet, or the General Advertiser, 1777–81.
Savannah Georgia Gazette, 1789.
South Carolina and American General Gazette (Charleston), 1767–79.
South Carolina Gazette (Charleston), 1759–69.
South Carolina Gazette and General Advertiser (Charleston), 1783–84.

South Carolina Gazette, and Public Advertiser (Charleston), 1785.
South Carolina Weekly Gazette (Charleston), 1784.
State Gazette of South Carolina (Charleston), 1786–93.
Williamsburg Virginia Gazette, 1777.

Secondary Sources

Books and Pamphlets

Adams, Herbert Baxter. *The Life and Writings of Jared Sparks: Comprising Selections from His Journals and Correspondence.* Vol. 1. Boston: Houghton, Mifflin, 1893.

Alden, John Richard. *General Charles Lee, Traitor or Patriot?* Baton Rouge: Louisiana State University Press, 1951.

Alderson, Robert J., Jr. *This Bright Era of Happy Revolutions: French Consul Michel-Ange-Bernard Mangourit and International Republicanism in Charleston, 1792–1794.* Columbia: University of South Carolina Press, 2008.

Ammon, Harry. *The Genet Mission.* New York: Norton, 1973.

Bancroft, George. *History of the Formation of the Constitution of the United States of America.* Vol. 1. New York: Appleton, 1882.

———. *History of the United States of America, from the Discovery of the Continent.* Vol. 6. New York: Appleton, 1888.

Barry, Richard. *Mr. Rutledge of South Carolina.* New York: Duell, Sloan & Pearce, 1942.

Bearss, Edwin C. *The Battle of Sullivan's Island and the Capture of Fort Moultrie; A Documented Narrative and Troop Movement Maps, Fort Sumter National Monument, South Carolina.* Washington, D.C.: Division of History, Office of Archeology and Historic Preservation, U.S. Dept. of the Interior, 1968.

———. *The First Two Fort Moultries: A Structural History.* Springfield, Va.: National Technical Information Service, 1968.

Bennett, Charles E., and Donald R. Lennon. *A Quest for Glory: Major General Robert Howe and the American Revolution.* Chapel Hill: University of North Carolina Press, 1991.

Biddle, Charles, and James S. Biddle. *Autobiography of Charles Biddle, Vice-President of the Supreme Executive Council of Pennsylvania, 1745–1821.* Philadelphia: Claxton, 1883.

Blachford, Michael. *Sailing Directions for the Coast and Harbours of North America, Comprehending the Entire Navigation from Nova Scotia to the Gulf of Florida.* London: Blachford, 1836.

Blunt, Edmund M. *The American Coast Pilot: Containing the Courses and Distances between the Principal Harbours, Capes, and Headlands, on the Coast of North and South America.* New York: Blunt, 1822.

Borick, Carl P. *A Gallant Defense: The Siege of Charleston, 1780.* Columbia: University of South Carolina Press, 2003.

———. *Relieve Us of This Burthen: American Prisoners of War in the Revolutionary South, 1780–1782.* Columbia: University of South Carolina Press, 2012.

Bostick, Douglas W. *Sunken Plantations: The Santee Cooper Project.* Charleston, S.C.: History Press, 2008.

Buchan, William. *Domestic Medicine: or, A Treatise on the Prevention and Cure of Diseases, by Regimen and Simple Medicines: With an Appendix, Containing a Dispensatory for the Use of Private Practitioners.* Halifax, [England]: Milner & Sowerby, 1859.

Buchanan, John. *The Road to Guilford Courthouse: The American Revolution in the Carolinas.* New York: Wiley, 1997.

Butler, Lewis. *The Annals of the King's Royal Rifle Corps.* Vol. 1, *The Royal Americans.* London: Smith, Elder, 1913.

Butler, Nicholas Michael. *Votaries of Apollo: The St. Cecilia Society and the Patronage of Concert Music in Charleston, South Carolina, 1766–1820.* Columbia: University of South Carolina Press, 2007.

Cashin, Edward J. *The King's Ranger: Thomas Brown and the American Revolution on the Southern Frontier.* New York: Fordham University Press, 1999.

Chernow, Ron. *Washington: A Life.* New York: Penguin, 2010.

Clark, George Ramsey, William Oliver Stevens, Carroll Storrs Alden, and Herman F. Krafft. *A Short History of the United States Navy.* Philadelphia: Lippincott, 1927.

Coggins, Jack B. *Ships and Seamen of the American Revolution.* Mineola, N.Y.: Dover, 2002.

Creighton, Mandell. *History of Rome.* New York: Appleton, 1890.

Dalcho, Frederick. *An Historical Account of the Protestant Episcopal Church in South Carolina, from the First Settlement of the Province to the War of the Revolution.* Charleston, S.C.: Thayer, 1820.

Davis, Derek. *Religion and the Continental Congress, 1774–1789: Contributions to Original Intent.* New York: Oxford University Press, 2000.

De Forest, Elizabeth Kellam. *The Gardens and Grounds at Mount Vernon: How George Washington Planned and Planted Them.* Mount Vernon, Va.: Mount Vernon Ladies' Association of the Union, 1982.

Drayton, John. *A View of South-Carolina, as Respects Her Natural and Civil Concerns.* Charleston, S.C.: Young, 1802.

Edgar, Walter. *South Carolina: A History.* Columbia: University of South Carolina Press, 1998.

Edgar, Walter, and N. Louise Bailey. *Biographical Directory of the South Carolina House of Representatives, Volume II: The Commons House of Assembly, 1692–1775.* Columbia: University of South Carolina Press, 1977.

Ellis, Joseph J. *His Excellency: George Washington.* New York: Random House, 2004.

Ervin, Sara Sullivan. *South Carolinians in the Revolution: With Service Records and Miscellaneous Data Also Abstract of Wills, Laurens County (Ninety-Six District) 1775–1855.* 1949. Rpt., Baltimore: Genealogical Publishing, 1965.

Farrow, Edward S. *A Dictionary of Military Terms.* New York: Crowell, 1918.

Fischer, David Hackett. *Liberty and Freedom: A Visual History of America's Founding Ideas.* New York: Oxford University Press, 2005.

Ford, Lacy K. *Deliver Us from Evil: The Slavery Question in the Old South.* Oxford: Oxford University Press, 2009.

Flexner, James Thomas. *George Washington and the New Nation, 1783–1793.* Boston: Little, Brown, 1969.

Flynn, Jean Martin. *The Militia in Antebellum South Carolina Society.* Spartanburg, S.C.: Reprint, 1991.

Fort Moultrie Centennial Being an Illustrated Account of the Doings at Fort Moultrie, Sullivan's Island, Charleston (S.C.) Harbor. Part 1. Charleston: Walker, Evans & Cogswell, 1876.

Garraty, John A., and Mark C. Carnes, eds. *American National Biography.* 24 vols. New York: Oxford University Press, 1999.

Gidick, Daniel L. *By No Means Contemptible: A Study of the American Defenses and the British Siege Works during the 1780 Siege of Charleston.* [Charleston, S.C.], 2004.

Godbold, E. Stanly, and Robert H. Woody. *Christopher Gadsden and the American Revolution.* Knoxville: University of Tennessee Press, 1982.

Gordon, John W. *South Carolina and the American Revolution: A Battlefield History.* Columbia: University of South Carolina Press, 2003.

Green, Henry Clinton, and Mary Wolcott Green. *The Pioneer Mothers of America: A Record of the More Notable Women of the Early Days of the Country, and Particularly of the Colonial and Revolutionary Periods.* Vol. 2. New York: Putnam, 1912.

Griswold, Rufus Wilmot, William Gilmore Simms, and E. D. Ingraham, eds., *Washington and the Generals of the American Revolution.* Vol. 2. Philadelphia: Carey & Hart, 1848.

Halévy, Daniel. *Péguy et les Cahiers de la Quinzaine.* Paris: Grasset, 1941.

Hamilton, John C. *History of the Republic of the United States of America, as Traced in the Writings of Alexander Hamilton and of His Contemporaries.* Vol. 3. New York: Appleton, 1859.

Hartley, Cecil B. *Heroes and Patriots of the South; Comprising Lives of General Francis Marion, General William Moultrie, General Andrew Pickens, and Governor John Rutledge. With Sketches of Other Distinguished Heroes and Patriots Who Served in the Revolutionary War in the Southern States.* Philadelphia: Evans, 1860.

Hatley, M. Thomas. *The Dividing Paths: Cherokees and South Carolinians through the Era of Revolution.* New York: Oxford University Press, 1993.

Haw, James. *John and Edward Rutledge of South Carolina.* Athens: University of Georgia Press, 1997.

Heinl, Robert Debs. *Dictionary of Military and Naval Quotations.* Annapolis: United States Naval Institute, 1981.

Heitman, Francis Bernard. *Historical Register of Officers of the Continental Army during the War of the Revolution, April 1775, to December, 1783.* Washington, D.C.: Rare Book Shop and Publishing, 1914.

Heitzler, Michael J. *Goose Creek, South Carolina: A Definitive History, 1670–1980. Vol. 1. Planters, Politicians, and Patriots.* Edited by Nancy Paul Kirchner. Charleston, S.C.: History Press, 2005.

Henderson, Archibald. *Washington's Southern Tour, 1791.* Boston: Houghton Mifflin, 1923.

Hennig, Helen Kohn. *Great South Carolinians: From Colonial Days to the Confederate War.* Chapel Hill: University of North Carolina Press, 1940.

Hirsch, Arthur Henry. *The Huguenots of Colonial South Carolina.* Durham, N.C.: Duke University Press, 1928.

Hünemörder, Markus. *The Society of the Cincinnati: Conspiracy and Distrust in Early America.* New York: Berghahn Books, 2006.

Hyneman, Charles S. *The First American Neutrality: A Study of the American Understanding of Neutral Obligations during the Years 1792 to 1815.* Urbana: University of Illinois, 1934.

Johnson, Joseph. *Traditions and Reminiscences, Chiefly of the American Revolution in the South: Including Biographical Sketches, Incidents, and Anecdotes, Few of Which Have Been Published, Particularly of Residents in the Upper Country.* Charleston, S.C.: Walker & James, 1851.

Jones, Archer. *The Art of War in the Western World.* Urbana: University of Illinois Press, 2001.

Jones, Charles C. *Sergeant William Jasper: An Address Delivered before the Georgia Historical Society in Savannah, Georgia, on the 3rd of January, 1876.* Savannah: Georgia Historical Society, 1876.

Julian, Paul Rowland. *Sorting out the Early Julian/Juliens: A History of the 18th and Early 19th Century Founding Families with the Surnames Julian, Julien, and St. Julien.* Baltimore: Gateway, 2004.

Kapsch, Robert J. *Historic Canals and Waterways of South Carolina.* Columbia: University of South Carolina Press, 2010.

Kaufmann, J. E., and H. W. Kaufmann. *Fortress America: The Forts That Defended America, 1600 to the Present.* Cambridge, Mass.: Da Capo, 2004.

Klein, Rachel N. *Unification of a Slave State: The Rise of the Planter Class in the South Carolina Backcountry, 1760–1808.* Chapel Hill: University of North Carolina Press, 1990.

Kloss, William, and Diane K. Skvarla. *United States Senate Catalogue of Fine Art* [Senate Document 107–11]. Edited by Jane R. McGoldrick. Washington, D.C.: Senate Commission on Art, 2002.

Lawrence, Alexander A. *Storm over Savannah: The Story of Count D'Estaing and the Siege of the Town in 1779.* Athens: University of Georgia Press, 1951.

Lefferts, Charles M. *Uniforms of the American, British, French, and German Armies in the War of the American Revolution, 1775–1783.* Edited by Alexander J. Wall. New York: New-York Historical Society, 1926.

Lipscomb, Terry W. *South Carolina in 1791: George Washington's Southern Tour.* Columbia: South Carolina Department of Archives and History, 1993.

———. *The Carolina Lowcountry, April 1775–June 1776 and the Battle of Fort Moultrie.* South Carolina Revolutionary War Battles, vol. 1. Columbia: South Carolina Department of Archives and History, 1994.

Lumpkin, Henry. *From Savannah to Yorktown: The American Revolution in the South.* Columbia: University of South Carolina Press, 1981.

Mack, Ebenezer. *The Life of Gilbert Motier De Lafayette . . . From Numerous and Authentick Sources.* Ithaca, N.Y.: Mack, Andrus & Woodward, 1841.

Magdol, Edward, and Jon L. Wakelyn, eds. *The Southern Common People: Studies in Nineteenth-Century Social History.* Contributions in American History, no. 86. Westport, Conn: Greenwood, 1980.

Massey, Gregory D. *John Laurens and the American Revolution.* Columbia: University of South Carolina Press, 2000.

Mattern, David B. *Benjamin Lincoln and the American Revolution.* Columbia: University of South Carolina Press, 1995.

McCowen, George Smith, Jr. *The British Occupation of Charleston, 1780–82.* Columbia: University of South Carolina Press, 1981.

McCrady, Edward. *Education in South Carolina Prior to and during the Revolution.* Charleston: South Carolina Historical Society, 1883.

———. *The History of South Carolina in the Revolution, 1775–1780.* New York: Macmillan, 1901.

———. *The History of South Carolina in the Revolution, 1780–1783.* New York: Macmillan, 1902.

———. *The History of South Carolina under the Proprietary Government, 1670–1719.* New York: MacMillan, 1897.

———. *The History of South Carolina under the Royal Government, 1719–1776.* New York: MacMillan, 1899.

McDonough, Daniel J. *Christopher Gadsden and Henry Laurens: The Parallel Lives of Two American Patriots.* Selinsgrove, Penn.: Susquehanna University Press, 2000.

McElligott, Carroll Ainsworth. *Charleston Residences, 1782–1794.* Westminster, Md.: Heritage Books, 1988.

McMaster, Fitzhugh. *Soldiers and Uniforms: South Carolina Military Affairs, 1670–1775.* Columbia: University of South Carolina Press, 1971.

Meleney, John C. *The Public Life of Aedanus Burke: Revolutionary Republican in Post-Revolutionary South Carolina.* Columbia: University of South Carolina Press, 1989.

Mercur, James. *Attack of Fortified Places. Including Siege-Works, Mining, and Demolitions. Prepared for the Use of the Cadets of the United States Military Academy.* New York: Wiley, 1894.

Minnigerode, Meade. *Jefferson, Friend of France, 1793: The Career of Edmond Charles Genet, Minister Plenipotentiary from the French Republic to the United States, as Revealed by His Private Papers, 1763–1834.* New York: Putnam, 1928.

Morison, Samuel Eliot. *John Paul Jones: A Sailor's Biography.* Boston: Little, Brown, 1959.

Moore, Alexander. *The Fabric of Liberty: A History of the Society of the Cincinnati of the State of South Carolina.* Charleston: Home House Press, 2012.

Muller, John. *A Treatise Containing the Elementary Part of Fortification, Regular and Irregular. 1746.* Rpt., Ottawa: Museum Restoration Service, 1968.

Myers, Minor, Jr. *Liberty without Anarchy: A History of the Society of the Cincinnati.* Charlottesville: University of Virginia Press, 2004.

Nadelhaft, Jerome J. *The Disorders of War: The Revolution in South Carolina.* Orono: University of Maine at Orono Press, 1981.

Nelson, Paul David, *General James Grant: Scottish Soldier and Royal Governor of East Florida.* Gainesville: University Press of Florida, 1993.

Olwell, Robert A. *Masters, Slaves and Subjects: The Culture of Power in the South Carolina Low Country, 1740–1790.* Ithaca, N.Y.: Cornell University Press, 1998.

Pancake, John S. *This Destructive War: The British Campaign in the Carolinas, 1780–1782.* Tuscaloosa: University of Alabama Press, 1985.

Packard, Francis Randolph. *The History of Medicine in the United States: A Collection of Facts and Documents Relating to the History of Medical Science in This Country, from the Earliest English Colonization to the Year 1800, with a Supplemental Chapter on the Discovery of Anaesthesia.* Philadelphia: Lippincott, 1901.

Porcher, Frederick A. *The History of the Santee Canal.* Charleston: South Carolina Historical Society, 1903.

Purcell, Sarah J. *Sealed with Blood: War, Sacrifice, and Memory in Revolutionary America.* Philadelphia: University of Pennsylvania Press, 2002.

Ramsay, David. *The History of the American Revolution.* Vol. 2. Trenton, N.J.: Wilson, 1811.

———. *The History of the Revolution in South Carolina: From a British Province to an Independent State.* Vol. 2. Trenton, N.J.: Collins, 1785.

———. *Ramsay's History of South Carolina: From Its First Settlement in 1670 to the Year 1808.* Vols. 1 and 2. 1809. Rpt., Newberry, S.C.: McDuffie, 1858.

Rankin, Hugh F. *The North Carolina Continentals.* Chapel Hill: University of North Carolina Press, 2005.

Ravenel, Harriott Horry. *Charleston, the Place and the People.* New York: Macmillan, 1925.

Ravenel, Henry Edmund. *Ravenel Records: A History and Genealogy of the Huguenot Family of Ravenel, of South Carolina; with Some Incidental Account of the Parish of St. Johns Berkeley, which was Their Principal Location.* Atlanta: Franklin: 1898.

Richardson, Edward W. *Standards and Colors of the American Revolution.* Philadelphia: University of Pennsylvania Press and the Pennsylvania Society of Sons of the Revolution and Its Color Guard, 1982.

Ripley, Warren. *Battleground, South Carolina in the Revolution.* Charleston, S.C.: News and Courier, 1983.

Rowland, Lawrence Sanders, Alexander Moore, and George C. Rogers. *The History of Beaufort County, South Carolina.* Columbia: University of South Carolina Press, 1996.

Rosen, Robert. *A Short History of Charleston.* Columbia: University of South Carolina Press, 1997.

Russell, David Lee. *The American Revolution in the Southern Colonies.* Jefferson, N.C.: McFarland, 2000.

———. *Victory on Sullivan's Island: The British Cape Fear/Charles Town Expedition of 1776.* Haverford, Penn.: Infinity, 2002.

St. Andrew's Society of Charleston, South Carolina. *Presented by the St. Andrew's Society on the Occasion of the Two Hundredth Anniversary, November Thirtieth, as a Tribute to Major General William Moultrie, Sixth President of the Society, 1787–1789, and in the Interest of the Proposed Monument.* Charleston, S.C., 1929. Copy at the Manuscripts Division, South Caroliniana Library, University of South Carolina, Columbia.

Salley, Alexander S., Jr. *President Washington's Tour through South Carolina in 1791.* Columbia, S.C.: Crowson-Stone, 1950.

Savage, Henry, Jr. *River of the Carolinas: The Santee.* New York: Rinehart, 1956.

Savas, Theodore P., and J. David Dameron. *A Guide to the Battles of the American Revolution.* New York: Savas Beatie, 2006.

Simms, William Gilmore. *The History of South Carolina from Its First European Discovery to Its Erection into a Republic; With a Supplementary Book, Bringing the Narrative Down to the Present Time.* New York: Redfield, 1860.

———. *The Life of Francis Marion.* Philadelphia: Evans, 1860.

Singer, Charles Gregg. *South Carolina in the Confederation.* 1941. Rpt., Philadelphia: Porcupine, 1976.

Smith, Alice R. Huger, and D. E. Huger Smith. *The Dwelling Houses of Charleston, South Carolina.* Philadelphia: Lippincott, 1917.

Smith, William Roy. *South Carolina as a Royal Province, 1719–1776.* New York: MacMillan, 1903.

Snowden, Yates, and Henry Gardner Cutler, eds. *History of South Carolina.* Vol. 1. Chicago: Lewis, 1920.

South Carolina Jockey Club. *History of the Turf in South Carolina.* Charleston, S.C.: Russell & Jones, 1857.

South, Stanley. *Palmetto Parapets: Exploratory Archaeology at Ft. Moultrie, South Carolina, 38CH50.* Anthropological Studies no. 1. Columbia: South Carolina Institute of Archaeology and Anthropology, 1974.

Starr, Rebecca. *A School for Politics: Commercial Lobbying and Political Culture in Early South Carolina.* Baltimore: Johns Hopkins University Press, 1998.

State Agricultural Society of South Carolina. *History of the State Agricultural Society of South Carolina from 1839 to 1845, Inclusive, of the State Agricultural Society of South Carolina from 1855 to 1861, Inclusive, of the State Agricultural and Mechanical Society of South Carolina from 1869 to 1916, Inclusive.* Columbia: Bryan, 1916.

Stedman, Charles. *The History of the Origin, Progress, and Termination of the American War.* Vol. 2. London: Printed for Charles Stedman, 1794.

Stevenson, Burton Egbert, comp. and ed. *Poems of American History.* Boston: Houghton Mifflin, 1908.

Symonds, Craig L., and William J. Clipson. *The Naval Institute Historical Atlas of the U.S. Navy.* Annapolis: Naval Institute Press, 2001.

Tinkler, Robert. *James Hamilton of South Carolina.* Baton Rouge: Louisiana State University Press, 2004.

Townsend, Eleanor Winthrop. *John Moultrie, Junior, M.D., 1729–1798.* New York: Hoeber, 1940.

Waldo, S. Putnam, John Adams, and Thomas Jefferson. *Biographical Sketches of Distinguished American Naval Heroes in the War of the Revolution, between the American Republic and the Kingdom of Great Britain; Comprising Sketches of Com. Nicholas Biddle, Com. John Paul Jones, Com. Edward Preble, and Com. Alexander Murray. With Incidental Allusions to Other Distinguished Characters.* Hartford, Conn.: Andrus, 1823.

Warren, Mary Bondurant, Robert S. Lowery, and Mary S. Warren. *South Carolina Newspapers: The South-Carolina Gazette, 1760.* Danielsville, Ga.: Heritage Papers, 1988.

Wates, Wylma A. *A Flag Worthy of Your State and People.* Columbia: South Carolina Department of Archives and History, 1996.

Watson, Elkanah, and Winslow C. Watson. *Men and Times of the Revolution; or, Memoirs of Elkanah Watson, Including Journals of Travels in Europe and America, from 1777 to 1842, with His Correspondence with Public Men and Reminiscences and Incidents of the Revolution.* New York: Dana, 1856.

Wheeler, Junius Brutus. *A Text-Book of Military Engineering: For the Use of the Cadets of the United States Military Academy, Parts II and III.* New York: Wiley, 1891.

Whitney, Edson Leone. *Government of the Colony of South Carolina.* Baltimore: Johns Hopkins Press, 1895.

Williams, Frances Leigh. *A Founding Family: The Pinckneys of South Carolina.* New York: Harcourt Brace Jovanovich, 1978.

Wilson, David K. *The Southern Strategy: Britain's Conquest of South Carolina and Georgia, 1775–1780.* Columbia: University of South Carolina Press, 2005.

Witt, Cornélis Henri de. *Jefferson and the American Democracy; An Historical Study.* Translated by R. S. H. Church. London: Longman, Green, Longman, Roberts & Green, 1862.

Zahniser, Marvin R. *Charles Cotesworth Pinckney: Founding Father.* Chapel Hill: University of North Carolina Press, 1967.

Articles from Journals, Magazines, and Periodicals

Azoy, Anastasio Carlos Mariano. "Palmetto Fort, Palmetto Flag." *American Heritage Magazine* 6, no. 6 (1955): 60–64, 99.

Britt, Albert Sidney, Jr. "The Society of the Cincinnati in the State of Georgia." *Georgia Historical Quarterly* 54, no. 4 (1970): 553–62.

Burbage, John. "Moultrie Statue Is Wise Investment in Our Future." *Charleston Mercury Magazine* 2, no. 3 (2006): 6–8.

Chaplin, Joyce E. "Slavery and the Principle of Humanity: A Modern Idea in the Early Lower South." *Journal of Social History* 24, no. 2 (1990): 299–315.

Coker, Kathy Roe. "The Case of James Nassau Colleton before the Commissioners of Forfeited Estates." *South Carolina Historical Magazine* 87, no. 2 (1986): 106–16.

Davis, Robert Scott, Jr. "Lord Montagu's Mission to South Carolina in 1781: American POWs for the King's Service in Jamaica." *South Carolina Historical Magazine* 84, no. 2 (1983): 89–109.

Erd, Darby, and Fitzhugh McMaster. "The First and Second South Carolina Regiments 1775–1780." *Military Collector and Historian* 29, no. 2 (1977): 70–73.

Franklin, W. Neil. Review of *Mr. Rutledge of South Carolina,* by Richard Barry. *Journal of Southern History* 9, no. 2 (1943): 263–64.

Gardner, Warren. "The Life of General William Moultrie." *Carologue* 17, no. 3 (2001): 10–17.

Guerry, Edward B. "General Moultrie's Final Victory." *Transactions of the Huguenot Society of South Carolina* 91 (1974): 131–34.

Guerry, William Alexander. "The Search for General Moultrie's Grave." *Transactions of the Huguenot Society of South Carolina* 79 (1974): 64–77.

Haynesworth, James Lafayette. "Washington's 1791 Visit to South Carolina." *Cincinnati Fourteen,* May 1983 (Bicentennial Issue), 29–31.

Haw, James. "A Broken Compact: Insecurity, Union, and the Proposed Surrender of Charleston, 1779." South Carolina Historical Magazine 96, no. 1 (1995): 30–53.

Heidler, David S. "The American Defeat at Briar Creek, 3 March 1779." *Georgia Historical Quarterly* 66, no. 3 (1982): 317–31.

Jameson, John Franklin. "St. Eustatius in the American Revolution." *American Historical Review* 3 (1903): 683–708.

Jones, Tom, and Fitzhugh McMaster. "South Carolina Provincial Regiment (Middleton's), 1760–1761." *Military Collector and Historian* 36, no. 3 (1984): 118–19.

Knight, Betsy. "Prisoner Exchange and Parole in the American Revolution." *William and Mary Quarterly.* 3rd ser., 48, no. 2 (1991): 201–22.

Laws, M. E. S. "The Campaign in Carolina, 1760–1761." *Royal United Service Institution Journal* 104, no. 3 (1959): 226–30.

Lockhart, Matthew A. "'Under the Wings of Columbia': John Lewis Gervais as Architect of South Carolina's 1786 Capital Relocation Legislation." *South Carolina Historical Magazine* 104, no. 3 (2003): 176–97.

Moultrie, Gerard. "The Moultries, Part I." *South Carolina Historical Magazine* 5, no. 4 (1904): 229–46.

Moultrie, James. "The Moultries, Part II: The Moultries of South Carolina," annotated by Alexander S. Salley Jr. *South Carolina Historical and Genealogical Magazine* 5, no. 4 (1904): 247–60.

Murdoch, Richard K. "Citizen Mangourit and the Projected Attack on East Florida in 1794." *Journal of Southern History* 14, no. 4 (1948): 522–40.

Mustard, Harry S. "On the Building of Fort Johnson." *South Carolina Historical Magazine* 64, no. 3 (1963): 129–35.

Newmyer, R. Kent. "Charles Stedman's *History of the American War.*" American Historical Review 63, no. 4 (1958): 924–34.

Newton, Craig A. "Three Patterns of Local History: South Carolina Historians, 1779–1830." *South Carolina Historical Magazine* 65, no. 3 (1964): 145–57.

Ranlet, Philip, "In the Hands of the British: The Treatment of American POWs during the War of Independence." *Historian* 62, no. 4 (2000): 731–58.

Robson, Eric. "The Expedition to the Southern Colonies, 1775–1776." English Historical Review 66, no. 261 (1951): 535–60.

Rogers, George C., Jr. "The Society of the Cincinnati of the State of South Carolina: 1783–1845." *Cincinnati Fourteen* 23, no. 2 (1987): 9–16.

Salley, Alexander S., Jr., "Col. Moses Thomson and Some of His Descendants." *South Carolina Historical and Genealogical Magazine* 3, no. 2 (1902): 98–108.

———, ed. "Officers of the South Carolina Regiment in the Cherokee War, 1760–61." *South Carolina Historical and Genealogical Magazine* 3, no. 4 (1902): 202–6.

Sellers, Charles Coleman. "Portraits and Miniatures by Charles Willson Peale." *Transactions of the American Philosophical Society* n.s. 42, no. 1 (1952): 1–369.

Simons Harriet P., and Albert Simons. "The William Burrows House of Charleston." *Winterthur Portfolio* 3, no. 1 (1967): 172–203.

Simms, William Gilmore. "Marion—The Carolina Partisan." *Russell's Magazine* 4, no. 2 (1858): 1–16.

Smith, Henry A. M. "The Baronies of South Carolina IV: Wadboo Barony." *South Carolina Historical and Genealogical Magazine* 12, no. 2 (1911): 43–52.

———. "The Baronies of South Carolina XIV: Ashepoo Barony." *South Carolina Historical and Genealogical Magazine* 15, no. 2 (1914): 63–72.

South Carolina Historical Society. "The Society." *South Carolina Historical and Genealogical Magazine* 50 (1949): 225.

South, Stanley A. "The General, the Major, and the Angel: The Discovery of General William Moultrie's Grave." *Transactions of the Huguenot Society of South Carolina* 82, no. 1 (1977): 31–49.

Sparks, Randy J. "Gentleman's Sport: Horse Racing in Antebellum Charleston." *South Carolina Historical Magazine* 93, no. 1 (1992): 15–30.

Spencer, Richard Henry. "Pulaski's Legion." *Browne, William Hand, and Louis Henry Dielman. Maryland Historical Magazine. Baltimore: Maryland Historical Society, 1906. Maryland Historical Magazine* 13, no. 3 (1918): 214–26.

Steedman, Marguerite Couturier. "Charlestown's Forgotten Tea Party." *Georgia Review* 21, no. 2 (1967): 244–59.

———. "General Moultrie's Reply." *Transactions of the Huguenot Society of South Carolina* 83 (1978): 46.

Stoesen, Alexander R. "The British Occupation of Charleston, 1780–1782." *South Carolina Historical Magazine* 63 (1962): 71–82.

Temple, Robert D. "Troublesome Boundaries: Royal Proclamations, Indian Treaties, Lawsuits, Political Deals, and Other Errors Defining Our Strange State Lines." *Carologue* 27, no. 1 (2011): 12–19.

Waring, Charles W., III. "John Michel, the Man to Create Moultrie." *Charleston Mercury Magazine* 2, no. 3 (2006): 11.

Withrow, Scott. "Cherokee Field School: Marion and the 1761 Grant Expedition." *American Revolution* 1, no. 1 (2009): 8–22.

Index

Page numbers in italic type indicate illustrations.

About the Author

C. L. BRAGG is the author of Distinction in Every Service: Brigadier General Marcellus A. Stovall, C.S.A. and coauthor of the critically acclaimed Never for Want of Powder: The Confederate Powder Works in Augusta, Georgia, also published by the University of South Carolina Press. Bragg's interest in William Moultrie was sparked while researching his family's South Carolina heritage and his personal connection to the Revolutionary War.